VOLUME SEVEN

ADVANCES IN TRANSPORT POLICY AND PLANNING

New Methods, Reflections and Application Domains in Transport Appraisal

VOLUME SEVEN

ADVANCES IN TRANSPORT POLICY AND PLANNING

New Methods, Reflections and Application Domains in Transport Appraisal

Edited by

NIEK MOUTER

Faculty of Technology, Policy and Management, Engineering Systems and Services Department, Transport and Logistics Group, Delft, The Netherlands

ELSEVIER

ACADEMIC PRESS

An imprint of Elsevier

Academic Press is an imprint of Elsevier
50 Hampshire Street, 5th Floor, Cambridge, MA 02139, United States
525 B Street, Suite 1650, San Diego, CA 92101, United States
The Boulevard, Langford Lane, Kidlington, Oxford OX5 1GB, United Kingdom
125 London Wall, London, EC2Y 5AS, United Kingdom

First edition 2021

Notices

Knowledge and best practice in this field are constantly changing. As new research and experience broaden our understanding, changes in research methods, professional practices, or medical treatment may become necessary.

Practitioners and researchers must always rely on their own experience and knowledge in evaluating and using any information, methods, compounds, or experiments described herein. In using such information or methods they should be mindful of their own safety and the safety of others, including parties for whom they have a professional responsibility.

To the fullest extent of the law, neither the Publisher nor the authors, contributors, or editors, assume any liability for any injury and/or damage to persons or property as a matter of products liability, negligence or otherwise, or from any use or operation of any methods, products, instructions, or ideas contained in the material herein.

ISBN: 978-0-323-85559-4
ISSN: 2543-0009

For information on all Academic Press publications
visit our website at https://www.elsevier.com/books-and-journals

Publisher: Zoe Kruze
Acquisitions Editor: Sam Mahfoudh
Developmental Editor: Shellie Bryant
Production Project Manager: James Selvam
Cover Designer: Alan Studholme

Typeset by SPi Global, India

Contents

Contributors

Paola Carolina Bueno
Former Member of the Transport Research Centre (TRANSyT), Universidad Politécnica de Madrid, Madrid, Spain

Matteo Jarre
Decisio BV, Amsterdam, The Netherlands

Zach J.L. Lee
Nanyang Technological University; TUMCREATE, Singapore, Singapore

Niek Mouter
Delft University of Technology; Faculty of Technology, Policy and Management, Engineering Systems and Services Department, Transport and Logistics Group, Delft, The Netherlands

Euston Quah
Nanyang Technological University; TUMCREATE, Singapore, Singapore

Vasco Reis
CERIS, Instituto Superior Técnico, Universidade de Lisboa, Lisboa, Portugal

Paolo Ruffino
Decisio BV, Amsterdam, The Netherlands

Ruth Shortall
TU Delft, Delft, The Netherlands

John Stanley
Institute of Transport and Logistics Studies, The University of Sydney Business School, Sydney, NSW, Australia

Tsiat Siong Tan
Singapore University of Social Sciences, Singapore, Singapore

Lóránt Tavasszy
Delft University of Technology, Delft, The Netherlands

Niels van Oort
Smart Public Transport Lab, Delft University of Technology, Delft, The Netherlands

Bert van Wee
Delft University of Technology, Delft, The Netherlands

José Manuel Vassallo
Transport Research Centre (TRANSyT), Universidad Politécnica de Madrid, Madrid, Spain

Menno Yap
Smart Public Transport Lab, Delft University of Technology, Delft, The Netherlands

Preface

Policy makers often want to be informed about the positive and negative impacts of a transport policy option before they take a decision. In general, they use standard appraisal methods such as cost-benefit analysis (CBA), multi-criteria analysis (MCA), or the environmental impact assessment (EIA) for this purpose. The previous book volume of this series (Mouter, 2020) aims to provide an up-to-date structured overview of the literature regarding these three appraisal methods in the context of transport policy and planning. However, the literature also offers various other methods that enable policy makers to judge whether the positive impacts of transport projects and policies can legitimate the negative impacts. The present book volume discusses three nonstandard appraisal methods in the context of the appraisal of transport projects and policies: The Sustainability Assessment, Deliberative Appraisal Methods, and methods which aim to directly infer people's preferences regarding (the impacts of) public policies such as willingness to allocate public budget (WTAPB) and Participatory Value Evaluation (PVE). Moreover, this book volume reviews the literature on the application of appraisal methods for the evaluation of cycling and walking projects, public transport projects, and freight projects. In addition, one of the chapters reviews the application of appraisal methods in developing countries. Finally, this volume includes a chapter which reflects on the role of equity in the evaluation of transport policies and a chapter which provides directions for further research.

I thought that composing this book volume was important because for most of the covered topics it holds true that reviews of the literature are missing. For instance, Shortall (2021) provides the first review of deliberative appraisal methods in transport. Her up-to-date structured overview of the literature regarding deliberative appraisal methods gives (graduation) students and PhD students the opportunity to get quickly up to speed with the state-of-the-art regarding these methods and get a grip on new developments, past developments, or knowledge gaps with regard to these appraisal methods. Moreover, this book is meant for teachers of courses who want to educate students in the state-of-the-art of nonstandard appraisal methods and the application of appraisal methods in different domains.

1. Overview of the book chapters

This book consists of 10 chapters. Before reviewing various nonstandard appraisals and discussing applications of appraisal methods in different transport domains, the first chapter (Mouter, 2021a) sets the stage by discussing the main characteristics of the three standard appraisal methods (CBA, MCA, and EIA). This chapter provides an outline of these methods and also addresses the main differences.

Chapter 2 (Vassallo and Bueno, 2021) addresses the sustainability assessment of transport policies, plans, and projects. Already for decades achieving sustainability has been an important goal of transport policy. This chapter reviews the main academic and practical achievements regarding sustainability appraisal of transport undertakings. Vassalo and Bueno, among others, analyze the aspects that the standard appraisal methods (CBA, MCA, and EIA) lack with regard to the assessment of sustainability. Subsequently, the chapter suggests a methodology, consisting of a set of steps, to appraise sustainability of transport projects. It finalizes with key reflections about future challenges to improve sustainability assessment.

Chapter 3 (Shortall, 2021) reviews the literature on deliberative appraisal methods. Deliberation is based on the premise that a diverse group of citizens, if given adequate information, resources, and time to deliberate on a given topic, can produce a rational, informed judgment. Participants must consider a policy question from multiple viewpoints, exchange perspectives, opinions, and understandings and think critically about all possible options. While the application of deliberative approaches in the transport domain is still in its early stages, this chapter provides an overview of the best-known deliberative approaches in use in transport policy-making today as well as introducing new developments in the physical and online spaces. The chapter also compares deliberative methods with other appraisal methods and potential advantages, disadvantages, and synergies are identified. Criticisms of deliberative methods are also outlined. Finally, some future research challenges are discussed.

CBA is the most widely applied appraisal method supporting government decision-making on transport projects. A CBA expresses the impacts of a government project in monetary metrics based on the number of euros affected individuals and parties are willing to pay from their private income. However, the private WTP valuation approach is contested in the literature. One central critique is that this approach fails to consider that private choices may not fully reflect citizens' preferences over public goods and means. In response to this critique, academics developed three types of preference elicitation methods: (1) collective willingness to pay, (2) willingness to allocate public budget, (3) Participatory Value Evaluation. Chapter 4 (Mouter, 2021b) elaborates on these preference elicitation methods. The chapter provides empirical examples of the application of these methods in the transport literature and pays attention to the fact that these three classes of preference elicitation methods give individuals the opportunity to express a broader range of preferences compared to private WTP-based valuation methods.

Chapter 5 (van Wee and Mouter, 2021) reviews and discusses the literature on how equity is operationalized for the purpose of evaluating the impacts of transport policies. The chapter discusses the concept of equity and presents the most common metrics to express inequalities of distributions. Subsequently, van Wee and Mouter point out the results of a review of the literature in the areas of accessibility, safety, and the environment. Finally, the chapter presents a research agenda and outlines some conclusions. It concludes, among others, that the equity of accessibility is the most evaluated topic studied and that the literature on ethical preferences of people, at least as far as related to the distribution of effects of candidate transport policy options, is in its infancy.

Chapters 6, 7, and 8 review the literature on the application of appraisal methods for the evaluation of public transport projects, cycling and walking projects, and freight projects. In chapter 6 (Van Oort and Yap, 2021) it is argued that standard transport appraisal methods such as CBA provide insights into the expected performance and benefits of public transport to some extent, but they often disregard many other (positive) effects. This is partly due to a limited focus, but also due to a lack of a framework and knowledge. In this chapter, van Oort and Yap present a framework, the 5E model, that supports the assessment of the broader benefits of public transport projects. The chapter also provides more detail about ways to quantify and monetize the improvements of service reliability, robustness and crowding relief.

Ruffino et al. (2021) provide a structured review of the methods and the practices of appraisal of walking and cycling policies and projects. They compare and discuss four methods: balance sheet calculations, cost–benefit analysis, cost-effectiveness analysis, and multicriteria analysis. They also provide examples of where these methods have been applied and discuss the strengths and weaknesses of these methods as well as their main limitations and knowledge gaps in their application to walking and cycling projects.

Ruffino et al. (2021) conclude that research is particularly needed into the quantification and valuation of specific effects of walking and cycling policies within CBA.

Tavasszy and Reis (2021) provide an overview of typical evaluation approaches used for freight transport policies and projects. They review the state-of-practice of freight transport appraisal practice and also introduce the main freight transport modeling approaches that support project appraisal. Tavasszy and Reis distinguish three types of freight projects and conclude that the appraisal techniques for these projects differ. They observe that CBA is the prevalent technique in global level projects and very common in national level projects. On the other hand, MCA dominates at the local level. Finally, the chapter identifies research challenges related to appraisal of freight transport projects and policies.

Quah et al. (2021) review the application of appraisal methods—particularly CBA—in developing countries. They conclude that conducting CBAs in developing countries is often fraught with complexities and may require a different treatment compared to the application of the method in developed countries. Examples of transportation projects are listed and the relevance of behavioral economics affecting CBA is also discussed, leading to an overview of the challenges in valuation techniques and an introduction to an alternative method of valuation involving paired-wise comparison.

Finally, Stanley (2021) analyses research priorities for transport appraisal. He analyses this topic through the lens of the policy cycle, with an emphasis on the initial stages of that cycle: identifying societal goals and associated needs for improving goal achievement, through transport initiatives. Stanley (2021) particularly highlights challenges for appraisal in the environmental and social goal areas and outlines the research implications of these challenges. The chapter also looks at transport and economic performance and notes some significant gaps in understanding of wider economic benefits.

References

Mouter, N., 2020. Standard appraisal methods. In: Advances in Transport Policy and Planning, vol. 6. Elsevier, Amsterdam.

Mouter, N., 2021a. Standard transport appraisal methods. Chapter 1. In: Mouter, N. (Ed.), New Methods, Reflections and Application Domains in Transport Appraisal. Series: Advances in Transport Policy and Planning, vol. 7. Elsevier, Amsterdam, pp. 1–7.

Mouter, N., 2021b. Willingness to allocate public budget and Participatory Value Evaluation. Chapter 4. In: Mouter, N. (Ed.), New Methods, Reflections and

Application Domains in Transport Appraisal. Series: Advances in Transport Policy and Planning, vol. 7. Elsevier, Amsterdam, pp. 83–102.

van Oort, N., Yap, M., 2021. Innovations in the appraisal of public transport projects. Chapter 6. In: Mouter, N. (Ed.), New Methods, Reflections and Application Domains in Transport Appraisal. Series: Advances in Transport Policy and Planning, vol. 7. Elsevier, Amsterdam, pp. 127–164.

Quah, E., Siong, T.T., Lee, Z.J.L, 2021. Cost-benefit analysis in developing countries. Chapter 9. In: Mouter, N. (Ed.), New Methods, Reflections and Application Domains in Transport Appraisal. Series: Advances in Transport Policy and Planning, vol. 7. Elsevier, Amsterdam, pp. 235–260.

Ruffino, P., Jarre, M., 2021. Appraisal of cycling and pedestrian projects. Chapter 7. In: Mouter, N. (Ed.), New Methods, Reflections and Application Domains in Transport Appraisal. Series: Advances in Transport Policy and Planning, vol. 7. Elsevier, Amsterdam, pp. 165–203.

Shortall, R., 2021. Deliberative appraisal methods. Chapter 3. In: Mouter, N. (Ed.), New Methods, Reflections and Application Domains in Transport Appraisal. Series: Advances in Transport Policy and Planning, vol. 7. Elsevier, Amsterdam, pp. 51–82.

Stanley, J., 2021. Research priorities in appraisal methodology. Chapter 10. In: Mouter, N. (Ed.), New Methods, Reflections and Application Domains in Transport Appraisal. Series: Advances in Transport Policy and Planning, vol. 7. Elsevier, Amsterdam, pp. 261–288.

Tavasszy, L., Reis, V., 2021. Appraisal of freight projects and policies. Chapter 8. In: Mouter, N. (Ed.), New Methods, Reflections and Application Domains in Transport Appraisal. Series: Advances in Transport Policy and Planning, vol. 7. Elsevier, Amsterdam, pp. 205–233.

van Wee, B., Mouter, N., 2021. Evaluating transport equity. Chapter 5. In: Mouter, N. (Ed.), New Methods, Reflections and Application Domains in Transport Appraisal. Series: Advances in Transport Policy and Planning, vol. 7. Elsevier, Amsterdam, pp. 103–126.

Vassallo, J.M., Bueno, P.C., 2021. Sustainability assessment of transport policies, plans and projects. Chapter 2. In: Mouter, N. (Ed.), New Methods, Reflections and Application Domains in Transport Appraisal. Series: Advances in Transport Policy and Planning, vol. 7. Elsevier, Amsterdam, pp. 9–50.

CHAPTER ONE

Standard transport appraisal methods

Niek Mouter*
Faculty of Technology, Policy and Management, Engineering Systems and Services Department, Transport and Logistics Group, Delft, The Netherlands
*Corresponding author: e-mail address: n.mouter@tudelft.nl

Contents

Abstract

Policy makers often want to receive structured information regarding the impacts of transport policy options before they take a decision. To provide such information governments often choose to use standard appraisal methods being Cost-Benefit Analysis (CBA), Multi-Criteria Analysis (MCA) or Environmental Impact Assessment (EIA). Before we introduce various non-standard appraisal methods in this book volume, this chapter sets the stage by discussing the main characteristics of these three standard appraisal methods. CBA measures a project's societal value by transferring the project's societal effects into monetary terms using the notion of the amount of money individuals are willing to pay from their private income. These monetary impacts are aggregated into a final indicator such as the net present value (NPV). If the NPV is positive the project is considered to be welfare enhancing. MCA identifies criteria against which to test transport policy options. Next, the different criteria are weighted or scored to arrive at a ranking of options. An EIA is an evaluation of the likely effects of a project that significantly affect the environment. The most important difference between CBA and MCA is that the former method is based on welfare economics which provides strict procedures for the criteria/impacts that are considered in the analysis and for the weighting of project impacts, while in an MCA there is more freedom with respect to the selection of evaluation criteria and procedures to determine the weights. The most important difference between CBA and MCA on the one hand and EIA on the other hand is that EIA puts emphasis on a specific set of effects being the environmental impacts of a project.

Keywords: Cost-benefit analysis, Multi-criteria analysis, Environmental impact assessment, Standard transport appraisal, Transport assessment

Advances in Transport Policy and Planning, Volume 7
ISSN 2543-0009
https://doi.org/10.1016/bs.atpp.2021.02.001

1. Introduction

Policy makers often want to receive structured information regarding the expected positive and negative effects of transport policy options before they take a decision. To provide such information governments often choose to use Cost-Benefit Analysis (CBA), Multi-Criteria Analysis (MCA) or Environmental Impact Assessment (EIA). These standard appraisal methods are described in excellent handbooks such as Boardman et al. (2018) concerning CBA and Dodgson et al. (2009) for MCA. The previous book volume of this series (Mouter, 2020) aims to provide an up-to-date structured overview of the literature regarding these three appraisal methods in the context of transport policy and planning. Koopmans and Mouter (2020) offer a literature review on CBA, Dean (2020) addresses new developments regarding MCA and Soria-Lara et al. (2020) reviews the literature regarding EIA. Before we introduce various non-standard appraisal methods in this book volume, this chapter will set the stage by discussing the main characteristics of these three standard appraisal methods.

2. Cost-benefit analysis

Particularly in western countries Cost-Benefit Analysis (CBA) is the most widely used appraisal method supporting government decision-making on transport projects (Mackie et al., 2014). A CBA measures the social desirability of a transport policy option in a systematic way based on welfare economics. Welfare economics is a branch of economics that surveys the social desirability of alternative economic outcomes (Boadway and Bruce, 1984). A CBA is built on the Kaldor-Hicks efficiency criterion (Boadway, 2006), which recommends projects where the sum of monetary gains outweigh the sum of monetary losses and winners can potentially compensate the losers. The conversion of positive and negative social impacts of government projects relies on the number of euros or dollars that individuals are willing to pay for these impacts from their private income (i.e., their willingness to pay). Monetary impacts are presented as present values using a discount rate which accounts for the notion that people prefer present impacts over future impacts (Mouter, 2018). Finally, present values are aggregated into a final indicator such as the benefit-cost ratio (BCR) or the net present value (NPV). If the NPV is positive or the BCR is higher than one the project is considered to be welfare enhancing as those who benefit can theoretically compensate those who suffer.

Welfare economics provides strict procedures for the objects that have standing in the CBA analysis, for the impacts that are considered in the analysis and for the way different impacts are valued. In principle, welfare economics adopts two principles when conducting a CBA being "individualism" and "non-paternalism." Individualism implies that the preferences of individual citizens form the basis of a CBA (Sen, 1979) and non-paternalism concerns that individuals are conceived to be the best judge of their own welfare. In combination these postulations imply that only the citizens who are affected by the policy are the objects who have standing in a CBA study and the preferences of these citizens are respected. In principle, preferences of experts, stakeholders and policy makers do not play any role in the analysis as these actors are only consulted to provide guidance for deriving the preferences of citizens regarding the impacts of the transport project. Welfare economics also equips CBA researchers with a clear frame of reference when selecting the impacts of transport policy options that should (not) be included in a CBA as only impacts that affect the welfare of individuals should be included. For instance, citizens' preferences for the way that the benefits and burdens of a transport policy options are distributed across society are not part of the total net benefits in a CBA (Mouter et al., 2017). Another consequence that is excluded from a CBA is public support for a transport policy option (Mouter, 2017).

Welfare economics also provides a clear direction for the weighting procedure that is adopted in CBA to value the impacts of a transport policy option. CBA measures a project's societal value by transferring the project's societal effects into monetary terms using the notion of the amount of money individuals are willing to pay from their private income. For a positive effect, the WTP is the maximum amount which a person is prepared to pay for it. For negative effects, the willingness-to-pay is negative (then coined as "willingness-to-accept"). For example, the most dominant empirical approach to derive the amount of money that individuals are willing to pay for reductions in travel time and accident risk relies on (hypothetical) route choice experiments in which travelers are asked to make a series of private choices between routes which differ in terms of travel time, accident risk and travel costs (e.g., Bahamonde-Birke et al., 2015; Batley et al., 2019; Börjesson and Eliasson, 2014; Hensher et al., 2009). Impacts of transport policy options on landscape, nature and noise pollution are evaluated through analyzing the private decisions of individuals in the real estate market (e.g., Allen et al., 2015; Seo et al., 2014).

3. Multi-criteria analysis

The multi-criteria analysis (MCA) typically starts with the identification of criteria against which to test transport policy options. Next, the different criteria are weighted or scored to arrive at a ranking of options. Dean (2020) points out that a distinction can be made between "sophisticated MCA methods" and "simple MCA methods." Sophisticated methods use advanced mathematical principles and procedures to weigh criteria and rank options. See, for instance, the Analytic Hierarchical Process (AHP) deployed by Saaty (1980) and the best-worst method (BWM) developed by Rezaei (2015). Simple MCA methods use relatively rough procedures to score options or even abstain from scoring and ranking the options. One example is the UK Appraisal Summary Table which does not aim to provide a final ranking of the options. Simplified MCA techniques are very popular, mainly due to practicality reasons (Dean, 2018). These simplified MCA techniques are also easier to apply than CBA as no specific training in economics is needed.

CBA and MCA are quite similar in several respects. Both appraisal methods aim to equip policy makers with information to assess the desirability of a transport policy option, both methods build their analyses on the outcomes of transportation model in which the impacts of an intervention scenario are compared with a do-nothing scenario. The most important difference between CBA and MCA is that welfare economics provides the theoretical framework underlying CBA, whilst MCAs are not built on this framework. This gives MCA analysts a relatively large degree of freedom when conducting the appraisal. Mouter et al. (2020) identify five inherent differences between the two methods: (1) a CBA investigates how the citizens and firms that are affected by a transport project experience the impacts of the project, whereas a MCA is based on the judgments of experts and/or stakeholders who might not experience any impacts of a transport project themselves; (2) a CBA only includes the impacts that affect the welfare of individuals, whereas MCA analysts have the full freedom to include every possible impact in their studies. For instance, a MCA analyst can decide to include distributional aspects and public support for a transport policy option as separate criteria which affect the final outcome of a

MCA; (3) The weighting procedure that is used in CBA to evaluate the impacts of a transport policy option is very clear in the sense that the only criterion that defines the weight that should be assigned to an impact concerns the amount of money individuals are willing to pay from their private income. The aggregation of impacts/criteria in a MCA can be partly based on translating impacts/criteria into monetary terms, but the aggregation is also based on at least one other weighting method (e.g., scoring or ranking); (4) CBA inherently accounts for the fact that social impacts of transport projects occur over a number of periods by discounting future impacts of the project, whereas the time dimension is rarely included in a MCA; (5) the final indicators of a CBA (e.g., the net present value or the benefit-cost ratio) communicate very clearly and are therefore easy to use in the media and the public/political debate. The interpretation of the outcome of a MCA is relatively unclear. One of the main advantages of MCA over CBA is that ensures a serious role for impacts that are difficult to quantify and monetize such as social inclusion, aesthetics, image and equity (Browne and Ryan, 2011).

4. Environmental impact assessment

An Environmental Impact Assessment (EIA) is a comprehensive evaluation of the likely effects of a project that significantly affect the environment. EIA provides decision makers with an indication of the likely environmental consequences of their selected policies (Jay et al., 2007). Since the 1970s EIA has become increasingly more important in transport policy and planning (Cornero, 2010). Due to the legal requirements for EIA implementation, there are now strict guidelines for the EIA process (Cornero, 2010). The usual information contained in an EIA report is: (a) a description of project alternatives and a baseline description of the environment where the project is located; (b) a prediction of potential effects of the project on the environment; (c) measures envisaged to avoid, prevent or reduce the effects on the environment. The most important differences between EIA on the one hand and CBA and MCA on the other hand is that the EIA puts emphasis on a specific set of effects (environmental effects). A second difference is that an EIA also includes recommendations regarding the mitigation and management of negative environmental impacts. The purpose of the other methods that were discussed is not to provide such recommendations.

5. Conclusion

The most important difference between CBA and MCA is that the former method is based on welfare economics which provides strict procedures for the criteria/impacts that are considered in the analysis and for the weighting of project impacts, whilst in an MCA there is more freedom with respect to the selection of evaluation criteria and procedures to determine the weights. The most important difference between CBA and MCA on the one hand and EIA on the other hand is that EIA puts emphasis on a specific set of effects being the environmental impacts of a project.

References

Allen, M.T., Austin, G.W., Swaleheen, M., 2015. Measuring highway impacts on house prices using spatial regression. J. Sustain. Real Estate 7 (1), 83–98.

Bahamonde-Birke, F.J., Kunert, U., Link, H., 2015. The value of a statistical life in a road safety context—a review of the current literature. Transp. Rev. 35 (4), 488–511.

Batley, R., Bates, J., Bliemer, M., Börjesson, M., Bourdon, J., Cabral, M.O., Chintakayala, P.K., Choudhury, C., Daly, A., Dekker, T., Drivyla, E., Fowker, T., Hess, S., Heywood, C., Johnson, D., Laird, J., Mackie, P., Parkin, J., Sanders, S., Sheldon, R., Wardman, M., Worsley, T., 2019. New appraisal values of travel time savings and reliability in Great Britain. Transportation 46 (3), 583–621.

Boadway, R., 2006. Principles of cost-benefit analysis. Public Policy Rev. 2 (1), 1–42.

Boadway, R., Bruce, M., 1984. Welfare Economics. Basil Blackwell, Oxford.

Boardman, A.E., Greenberg, D.H., Vining, A.R., Weimer, D.L., 2018. Cost-Benefit Analysis Concepts and Practice. Prentice Hall, New Jersey.

Börjesson, M., Eliasson, J., 2014. Experiences from the Swedish value of time study. Transp. Res. A Policy Pract. 59, 144–158.

Browne, D., Ryan, L., 2011. Comparative analysis of evaluation techniques for transport policies. Environ. Impact Assess. Rev. 31, 226–233.

Cornero, A., 2010. Improving the Implementation of Environmental Impact Assessment. Report, European Environmental Agency.

Dean, M., 2018. Assessing the Applicability of Participatory Multi-Criteria Analysis Methodologies to the Appraisal of Mega Transport Infrastructure. Ph.D. Dissertation, The Bartlett School of Planning, University College London, United Kingdom.

Dean, M., 2020. Multicriteria analysis. Chapter 6, In: Mouter, N. (Ed.), Standard Appraisal Methods. Advances in Transport Policy and Planning. vol. 6. Elsevier, Amsterdam.

Dodgson, J.S., Spackman, M., Pearman, A., Phillips, L.D., 2009. Multi-Criteria Analysis: A Manual. Department for Communities and Local Government, London.

Hensher, D.A., Rose, J.M., de Ortúzar, J.D., Rizzi, L.I., 2009. Estimating the willingness to pay and value of risk reduction for car occupants in the road environment. Transp. Res. A 43 (7), 692–707.

Jay, S., Jones, C., Slinn, P., Wood, C., 2007. Environmental impact assessment: retrospect and prospect. Environ. Impact Assess. Rev. 27 (4), 287–300.

Koopmans, C.C., Mouter, N., 2020. Cost-benefit analysis. Chapter 1, In: Mouter, N. (Ed.), Standard Appraisal Methods. Advances in Transport Policy and Planning. vol. 6. Elsevier, Amsterdam.

Mackie, P.J., Worsley, T., Eliasson, J., 2014. Transport appraisal revisited. Res. Transp. Econ. 47, 3–18.
Mouter, N., 2017. Dutch politicians' use of cost–benefit analysis. Transportation 44 (5), 1127–1145.
Mouter, N., 2018. A critical assessment of discounting policies for transport cost-benefit analysis in five European practices. Eur. J. Transp. Infrastruct. Res. 18 (4), 1–7.
Mouter, N., 2020. Standard Appraisal Methods. Advances in Transport Policy and Planning. vol. 6 Elsevier, Amsterdam.
Mouter, N., van Cranenburgh, S., van Wee, G.P., 2017. An empirical assessment of Dutch citizens' preferences for spatial equality in the context of a national transport investment plan. J. Transp. Geogr. 60, 217–230.
Mouter, N., Dean, M., Koopmans, C., Vassallo, J.M., 2020. Comparing cost-benefit analysis and multi-criteria analysis. Chapter 7, In: Mouter, N. (Ed.), Standard Appraisal Methods. Advances in Transport Policy and Planning. vol. 6. Elsevier, Amsterdam.
Rezaei, J., 2015. Best-worst multi-criteria decision-making method. Omega 53, 49–57.
Saaty, T.L., 1980. The Analytic Hierarchy Process. McGraw Hill.
Sen, A.K., 1979. Utilitarianism and Welfarism. J. Philos. 76 (9), 463–489.
Seo, K., Golub, A., Kuby, M., 2014. Combined impacts of highways and light rail transit on residential property values: a spatial hedonic price model for Phoenix, Arizona. J. Transp. Geogr. 41, 53–62.
Soria-Lara, J.A., Arce-Ruiz, R.M., Arranz-Lopez, A., Ariza-Alvarez, A., 2020. Environmental impact assessment for transport projects: a review of technical and process-related issues. Chapter 8, In: Mouter, N. (Ed.), Standard Appraisal Methods. Advances in Transport Policy and Planning. vol. 6. Elsevier, Amsterdam.

CHAPTER TWO

Sustainability assessment of transport policies, plans and projects

José Manuel Vassallo[a,*] and Paola Carolina Bueno[b]
[a]Transport Research Centre (TRANSyT), Universidad Politécnica de Madrid, Madrid, Spain
[b]Former Member of the Transport Research Centre (TRANSyT), Universidad Politécnica de Madrid, Madrid, Spain
*Corresponding author: e-mail address: josemanuel.vassallo@upm.es

Contents

Abstract

Ever since the term sustainability was firstly coined by the Brundtland Commission in 1987, this concept has become a key goal in assessing the impacts of transport policies, plans and projects. In the context of the book, this chapter conducts a review of the main academic and practical achievements conducted up to date regarding sustainability appraisal of transport undertakings. The chapter begins with an analysis of the key aspects embedded within the term "sustainability," as well as the evolution of the concept over time. It continues with a description of some of the methods specifically designed to assess sustainability—such as rating systems, models and

Advances in Transport Policy and Planning, Volume 7
ISSN 2543-0009
https://doi.org/10.1016/bs.atpp.2020.07.006

frameworks—from which it is concluded that they are rather incomplete. It continues with an analysis of the missing aspects that conventional appraisal methods—such as cost-benefit analysis, multi-criteria decision analysis or environmental impact assessment methods—lack to rightly address the requirements of sustainability assessment. After that, the chapter suggests a methodology, consisting of a set of steps, to appraise sustainability of transport projects. The chapter finalizes with key reflections about future challenges to improve sustainability assessment.

Keywords: Sustainability, Appraisal method, Rating systems, Transport policy, Infrastructure, Natural resources

1. The sustainability concept

1.1 Main principles of sustainability

The sustainability concept came up for the first time at the United Nations (UN) Conference on the Human Environment held in Stockholm in 1972. However, the most widely known definition of sustainable development was coined by the Brundtland Commission promoted by the UN, which defined sustainable development as the "development that meets the needs of the present without compromising the ability of future generations to meet their own needs" (World Commission on Environment and Development, 1987). According to Gudmundsson and Höjer (1996): "the concept evokes fundamental questions, such as how to define intergenerational equity, how to indicate quality of human life, how to maintain global life-support systems, how to value multifunctional natural resources, how to bring an end to global inequity, and how to design institutional frameworks for change, to name but a few prominent aspects."

The concept of sustainability became extremely popular after the Brundtland report was published. Only 2 years after its publication, Pezzey (1989) collected a list of definitions of sustainability coming from at least 27 separate sources. According to O'Riordan (1988) sustainability was intended to bridge the gap between "environmentalists" and "developers." On the basis of the discussion conducted by the first authors who intended to disentangle the concept of sustainable development, Jansson et al. (1994) concluded that it includes three main ideas: (1) the existence of a limit to economic development set by the capacity of the ecosystems and resources; (2) the need to reach a fair distribution of resources within and among generations; and (3) the need to achieve a socially efficient distribution of resources within the two restrictions previously mentioned in order to maximize global welfare.

The concept of sustainability has made a real contribution to the world insofar as it has strengthened the need of balancing human needs with the preservation of natural resources. However, according to Gilmour et al. (2011), its main problem is how to put it into effect or, in other words, how to operationalize the concept. Actually, it has been often criticized for the difficulty of predicting the needs, abilities and technological developments of future generations; and the problems to reach a global consensus among different priorities.

Daly and Cobb (1989) defined four operational principles of sustainability: "(1) The main principle is to limit the human scale (throughput) to a level which, if not optimal, is at least within carrying capacity and therefore sustainable... (2) Technological progress for sustainable development should be efficiency-increasing rather than throughput-increasing... (3) Renewable resources, in both their source and sink functions, should be exploited on a profit-maximizing sustained yield basis and in general not driven to extinction... (4) Nonrenewable resources should be exploited, but at a rate equal to the creation of renewable substitutes...."

The concept was further discussed in subsequent events and conferences, most of them promoted by the United Nations. According to Paul (2008), these conferences show a shift from a primary emphasis on environmental issues, through a growing impact on environmental, social and economic aspects. Nowadays, many definitions of sustainability are found in the literature, even though some of them are focused on specific aspects (see Gilmour et al., 2011; Parkin et al., 2003; Radermacher, 1999). However, irrespective of the existence of a universally accepted definition, there are two common features that are globally accepted. The first one is the right balance among economic, environmental and social aspects, which is usually acknowledged as the triple bottom line of sustainability. The second one is the intergenerational balance between current and future needs, taking special attention to avoid depleting natural resources. Over the years, the term sustainability has been incorporating additional goals such as ethical aspects, poverty reduction or transparent governance, which in a way or another may be embedded within the two aforementioned principles.

The feasibility of balancing the three sustainability pillars (economic, social and environmental) has been criticized by some authors (see Hirsch, 1999; Mieg, 2010) due to the difficulty of setting commonly agreed trade-offs among totally different aspects such as biodiversity, cultural values or profits. Actually, the complex interrelationships between human activities and the environment are rarely explored (Kates et al., 2001; Scholz, 2011; Schoolman et al., 2012).

It is also interesting to refer to the difference between what is usually known as strong and weak approaches to sustainability (Turner, 1993). According to Ramani et al. (2011): "a weak approach to sustainability is one in which trade-offs among various facets of sustainable development (i.e., the dimensions) are considered to be acceptable. In other words, the weak approach views human-made capital and natural resources as interchangeable, without consideration of the finite qualities of the ecosystem. In contrast, the strong approach views natural capital as the limiting factor."

Some authors have proposed specific paths of approaching sustainability such as the "natural step," the "ecological footprint," and the "sustainable resource usage." To ensure sustainability, the "natural step" requires that nature is not subjected to both a continuous increase of substances extracted from the earth's crust, concentrations of substances produced by society, or degradation by physical means; while at the same time human needs are met worldwide (Nattrass and Altomare, 1999). In other words, this approach intends to ensure quality of life without compromising the availability of natural resources. The "ecological footprint," see for instance Frey et al. (2000), evaluates the environmental impact of a specific action compared to the natural resources' restrictions and ecosystem functionality. The "sustainable resource usage," proposed by Graedel and Klee (2002), consists of determining a sustainable rate for the use of resources calculated as a function of the availability of virgin materials, accounting for recycling and stockpiles, among the world's population over a specific period of time.

Marshall and Toffel (2019) proposed a hierarchy with four levels showing the impact that certain actions may have on sustainability. Level 1 is made up of actions that, if continued at the expected rate, will endanger the survival of humans. Level 2 encompasses actions that may significantly reduce life expectancy or health. Level 3 includes actions that may cause the extinction of species or violating human rights. Finally, level 4 considers actions that reduce quality of life or are not compatible with other beliefs, or aesthetic preferences. The levels of actions are grouped in a pyramid, similar to the Maslow's one. The lower the level of the pyramid, the most critical the action will be to achieve sustainability.

1.2 The sustainable development goals of United Nations

In September 2015, the General Assembly of UN adopted the 2030 Agenda for Sustainable Development. The Agenda, that built on the principle of "leaving no one behind," envisions a holistic view to achieving sustainable development for all. At the heart of the Agenda there are 17 Sustainable

Development Goals (SDGs), aimed at urging all the countries, both developed and developing ones, to tackle the greatest problems of humanity. The goals are synergetic to each other. For instance, ending poverty must go hand-in-hand with the improvement of health and education, the reduction of inequality, and economic growth.

The SDGs were defined after years of work. In September 2000 at the UN Headquarters in New York, Member States unanimously adopted the Millennium Declaration that led to the elaboration of eight Millennium Development Goals (MDGs) to reduce extreme poverty by 2015. The Johannesburg Declaration on Sustainable Development reaffirmed the community's commitments to poverty eradication and the environment. In June 2012, at the United Nations Conference on Sustainable Development in Rio de Janeiro, Member States adopted the document "The Future We Want" that proposed to launch a process to develop a set of SDGs and to establish the UN High-level Political Forum on Sustainable Development. In 2013, the General Assembly set up an Open Working Group to develop a proposal on the SDGs. At the UN Sustainable Development Summit in September 2015, the General Assembly adopted the 2030 Agenda for Sustainable Development including the seventeen SDGs at its core. The UN sustainable development goals are summarized in Table 1. These goals are not directly addressed to sustainability assessment purposes. However, they can be used by planners and decision-makers as a checklist to identify indicators aimed at measuring sustainability from a global perspective using the methods that will be explained in Section 2.

2. Sustainability assessment of transport projects and policies

2.1 Sustainability assessment principles

Transport projects have several stages that have to be considered to rightly assess sustainability. Bueno et al. (2015a) state that "impacts to be considered for transport projects might be related to the construction (e.g., investment costs of the project, generally comprising land acquisition, design/legal/administration and construction costs); maintenance (e.g., air pollution costs covering short-term air quality effects caused by maintenance activities); operation of the facility (e.g., vehicle operating cost, including fixed costs, and operating costs); and the recycling/reuse stage (e.g., energy consumed by using fuel and electric power in the process of transporting and recycling)."

Table 1 Sustainable development goals set by United Nations.

	Sustainable development goals of UN
1	End poverty in all its forms everywhere
2	End hunger, achieve food security and improved nutrition and promote sustainable agriculture
3	Ensure healthy lives and promote well-being for all at all ages
4	Ensure inclusive and equitable quality education and promote lifelong learning opportunities for all
5	Achieve gender equality and empower all women and girls
6	Ensure availability and sustainable management of water and sanitation for all
7	Ensure access to affordable, reliable, sustainable and modern energy for all
8	Promote sustained, inclusive and sustainable economic growth, full and productive employment and decent work for all
9	Build resilient infrastructure, promote inclusive and sustainable industrialization and foster innovation
10	Reduce inequality within and among countries; (xi) Make cities and human settlements inclusive, safe, resilient and sustainable
11	Make cities and human settlements inclusive, safe, resilient and sustainable; (xii) ensure sustainable consumption and production patterns
12	Ensure sustainable consumption and production patterns
13	Take urgent action to combat climate change and its impacts
14	Conserve and sustainably use the oceans, seas and marine resources for sustainable development
15	Protect, restore and promote sustainable use of terrestrial ecosystems, sustainably manage forests, combat desertification, and halt and reverse land degradation and halt biodiversity loss
16	Promote peaceful and inclusive societies for sustainable development, provide access to justice for all and build effective, accountable and inclusive institutions at all levels
17	Strengthen the means of implementation and revitalize the global partnership for sustainable development

The construction or refurbishing of a transport project is a key stage for considering the basic principles of sustainability (Chaharbaghi and Willis, 1999; Parkin, 2000) since it will be crucial for defining the life cycle impacts of the project. In this phase, sustainability should comply with social awareness, environmental responsibility, and economic profitability (Shelbourn et al., 2006).

There is also a debate about whether sustainability should be part of the ex-post assessment of transport projects, or rather part of the decision-making process. Some authors such as Reid et al. (2012) acknowledge that it is good to consider sustainability at the planning stage since "the opportunities to incorporate sustainability vary and eventually diminish as a project moves through the project life cycle." In addition, Tsai and Chang (2012) pointed out that "great potential reductions in operations' sustainable impacts could be made if sustainability is considered early in planning and design."

Bueno et al. (2015a) claim that "the primary purpose of sustainability assessment should start with the appraisal and decision-making, because, at this point, decision-makers have great influence on the future sustainability performance of the project. In other words, implementing sustainability principles become more effective at the planning stage than as part of an ex-post evaluation. However, verifying the sustainability of an already existing project can be useful to 'recycle' best practices and procedures in future projects, due to the retrospective character it implies. Despite sustainability should be necessarily part of a primarily ex-ante assessment, it can also be used for other purposes."

There are several recommendations about crucial aspects to take into account in assessing sustainability. An international group of practitioners and researchers who met in Bellagio (Italy) in 1996, endorsed the following 10 principles of sustainability assessment: (i) guiding vision and goals, (ii) holistic perspective, (iii) essential elements, (iv) adequate scope, (v) practical focus, (vi) openness, (vii) effective communication, (viii) broad participation, (ix) ongoing assessment and (x) institutional capacity (Jesinghaus, 2014). Moreover, the OECD (2010), in its guidance on sustainability impact assessment points out the following principles: (i) consider the three pillars (economic, environmental and social), (ii) focus beyond numbers and metrics, (iii) involve stakeholders, (iv) demonstrate transparency and accountability, (v) match between level of detail and policy impact, and (vi) set clear lines of responsibility.

Bueno et al. (2015a) suggested two additional aspects to take into account when dealing with sustainability evaluation of transport projects and policies: (1) the "specific characteristics of the context," and (2) the "long term approach" of the analysis. The "specific characteristics of the context" where the project is located or the policy action is going to be implemented is essential to assess sustainability. For instance, emitting a certain air pollutant in a place where the concentration of this pollutant is at risk of compromising human health is much less sustainable than doing it in a place where the concentration of that pollutant is still low and not risky for society. The "long term approach" requires considering the whole life cycle from conception through construction, operation, maintenance, and the recycling/reuse stage. This later need has been also pointed out by some authors such as Munasinghe (2001) and Sijtsma (2006).

To help planners and decision-makers, Bueno et al. (2015a) point out five sine qua non requirements for the suitable appraisal of transport projects:

i. *Full approach*. This implies that no potential impact of the project affecting the triple bottom line (social, economic and environmental) at the present or in the future should be dismissed.

ii. *Life-cycle approach*. This means that the right sustainability assessments of transport projects should include the whole life cycle, and not just one of the stages. This point was addressed by the Brundtland Commission (World Commission on Environment and Development, 1987), and other academic authors (Gilmour et al., 2011; Munasinghe et al., 2001; Sijtsma, 2006; Stamford and Azapagic, 2011).

iii. *Rigorous trade-offs*. This means that despite the problems to balance the ecological, social, and economic perspectives within sustainability, it is still necessary to develop rigorous methods to set up the trade-offs across these attributes to facilitate the decision-making process. According to Browne and Ryan (2011): until now "decision-aiding techniques do not overcome the problems associated with incomparable quantities."

iv. *Adaptability to the context*. This implies considering the sensitivity of the criteria within its geographical and social context. Some authors such as Säynäjoki et al. (2011), Sev (2011), Veeravigrom et al. (2015) and Liang (2012) point out the fact that different location and time scales may lead to different priorities.

v. *Transparent approach*. This means that sustainability appraisal tools should not be black boxes nobody is able to understand. To that end, it is necessary to set up methods that are rational, transparent and unambiguous.

Few months after the writing of this chapter, the EU Technical Expert Group (TEG) on Sustainable Finance published the EU taxonomy to guide the transition to a low-carbon, resilient and resource-efficient economy (see European Commission, 2020). In this report, transport is recognized as an economic activity that makes a substantial contribution to climate change mitigation. Building on this conclusion, it agrees that transport activities should be rapidly decarbonized to demonstrate consistency with medium- and long-term climate goals.

2.2 Sustainability assessment methods

Although the concept of sustainability has gained increasing importance, its comprehensive appraisal is still at "the pilot phase." This is because currently, none of the existing methodologies and tools has been able to provide an internationally validated sustainability assessment covering the mentioned sine qua non requirements for the suitable appraisal of transport projects—see Bueno et al. (2015a).

In general, a number of tools and methodological frameworks are available for decision-makers—see Table 2. Some of these methods have been specifically developed to facilitate the ex-ante assessment of sustainability at the project level, while others are general policy evaluation tools which can be used for this purpose. Sustainability rating systems that grade and score projects based on their sustainability performance, frameworks and bespoke models can be classified within the first group of methods. On the other hand, the second category of methodologies to evaluate impacts of policy options include: (i) cost-benefit analysis (CBA); (ii) cost-effectiveness analysis (CEA);

Table 2 Methodologies and tools for the sustainability appraisal of transport projects.

Sustainability assessment methodologies	Project appraisal methods
Examples	*Examples*
Sustainability rating systems	Cost-benefit analysis, multi-criteria decision analysis
Frameworks, models and appraisal guidelines	Cost-effective analysis
Description	*Description*
Methods specifically designed to measure sustainability of transport projects	These commonly used techniques are commonly used in combination with other tools

and (iii) multi-criteria analysis (MCA). These traditional decision-making techniques were not initially intended to assess sustainability. However, they are currently evolving toward the appraisal of sustainable transport, while often being combined with other tools for a holistic sustainability assessment.

This section describes the tools and methods falling within the first category. The analysis to be performed includes sustainability self-evaluation tools focused on roads (e.g., Greenroads, GreenLITES) as well as rating systems for civil infrastructure in general such as CEEQUAL, Envision and LEED. Within this group, frameworks, models, checklists and appraisal guidelines for assessing the sustainability of infrastructure projects are also considered. An analysis of how other appraisal methods, such as CBA and MCA, consider sustainability will be undertaken in Section 3.

2.2.1 Sustainability rating systems

2.2.1.1 General overview

Sustainability rating systems are well established and increasingly popular tools to evaluate the sustainability of transport projects through score systems. According to the International Federation of Consulting Engineers (2012), rating and certification tools are "typically produced by reputable governmental or reputable non-governmental institutions offering schemes against which projects can be assessed and rated for their performance against sustainability." The report also highlights the following characteristics of these tools:

- *Guidelines provided.* They provide a complete guidance and best practices associated to the sustainability performance of projects, usually grouped into a series of categories devoted to specific sustainability areas.
- *Evidence collection.* The sustainability assessment of projects is based on evidence to prove the project performance. This should be collected throughout the evaluation process as information becomes available.
- *Credibility and recognition.* As they are produced by well-regarded institutions such as the Institution of Civil Engineers (ICE) or the US Department of Transport, rating systems are credible and recognized tools. In addition, the assessment is reviewed by trained experts of the awarding body.
- *Scoring.* A common score is available for each sustainability criterion within a certain category usually in the form of points or credits.
- *Performance levels.* The final score is used to assign the project a certain award level to be granted.

Hirsch (2012) pointed out that sustainability rating systems helps to promote engineering awareness into the transportation process and constitute a management tool for accountability and project comparison. Through a certification process, they also provide an international recognition for sustainable actions and may serve as tools for transportation decision-making processes.

There are several rating systems currently available for different sectors of the market (i.e., infrastructure, transport, roads, buildings, etc.). Some of the most remarkable examples include: (i) the Building Research Establishment Environment Assessment Method (BREEAM), one of the world's leading environment assessment method for buildings; (2) CEEQUAL, the sustainability Assessment and Awards for Civil Engineering, Infrastructure, Landscaping and the Public Realm for buildings, master planning and infrastructure; (3) LEED, leadership in Energy and Environmental Design created by the U.S. Green Building Council for evaluating buildings from the energy and sustainability perspective; and (4) ENVISION designed to evaluate the sustainability of infrastructure projects in general.

Most of the rating systems work in a similar way. A general description will be provided in this section, but will need to be treated with some caution given the particularities of each certification tool. In general, for a project to be initially considered by a rating system, it should meet a number of minimum pre-established requirements. If the project fails to meet those mandatory requirements the certification will not be awarded. After this initial filter, the project alternatives are now prepared for a more detailed sustainability assessment, usually structured as a series of questions grouped into different categories designed to encompass the full range of economic, environmental and social impacts. These categories differ from one rating system to another, as can be seen in Table 3 which presents a summary of eight of the most popular, influential and technically advanced rating tools available. This table was adapted from the study conducted by Bueno et al. (2015a).

Project alternatives can earn some points or credits corresponding to each category. The maximum amount of credits that can be obtained in each category work as weights representing the importance of each criterion over the others. Finally, the project may hold different certification levels depending on the total number of earned credits.

Apart from the different established categories, the difference however is the criteria weights assigned in each certification tool for a final sustainability assessment. As a result, "rating systems are not comparable enough due to

Table 3 Main characteristics of sustainability rating systems.

Area	Rating system	Main categories included and key features
Infrastructure	CEEQUAL (developed by the Institution of Civil Engineers)	• Nine categories: Project Strategy, Project Management, People and Communities, Land use and Landscape, Communities, Historic Environment, Ecology and Biodiversity, Water Environment, Physical Resources, Transport • Key feature: Applications outside the UK, with an adaptation of the weighting process
	ENVISION (developed by the Zofnass Program for Sustainable Infrastructure)	• Five categories included: Quality of Life, Leadership, Resource Allocation, Natural World, Climate and Risk • Key features: It includes a planning element in the analysis which aim to justify the selection of the project
	LEED (developed by US Green Building Council)	• Seven categories included: Sustainable Sites, Water Efficiency, Energy and Atmosphere, Materials and Resources, Indoor Environmental Quality, Innovation in Design, Regional Priority • Key features: All credits are equally weighted
Transport	GreenLITES (developed by the New York State Department of Transport)	• Five categories included: Sustainable Sites, Water Quality, Material Resources, Atmosphere, Innovation • Key features: It is part of a system which includes a collection of tools including spreadsheets, and other metrics to support the analysis
	GreenRoads (developed by University of Washington and CH2M HILL)	• Seven categories included: Project Requirements, Environment and Water, Access and Equity, Construction Activities, Materials and Resources, Pavement Technologies, Custom Credits • Key features: Focused on roadways with a particular view on material and design concerns. Specific attention is paid to pavements

	I-LAST (developed by: The Illinois Department of Transportation, the American Consulting Engineers Council and the Illinois Road and Transportation Builders Association)	• Eight categories included: Planning Design, Environmental Water Quality, Transportation, Lighting, Materials, Innovation • Key features: With a strong emphasis on environmental criteria, it encourages sustainable practices in highway construction
	INVEST (developed by: US Department of Transport Federal Highway Administration)	• Three categories included: Systems planning, Project Development, and Operations and Maintenance • Key features: used by the Federal Highway as a tool to encourage sustainable highway projects. However, as there is no third party evaluator, this system serves as unofficial recognition
	BE2ST-In Highways (developed by Recycled Materials Resource Center based at the College of Engineering at the University of Wisconsin)	• Nine categories included: Social Requirements Including Regulation and Local Ordinances, Greenhouse Gas Emission, Energy Use, Waste Reduction (in-situ/ex-situ), Water Consumption, Social Carbon • Key features: The main focus of this system is to quantify the sustainability impact of using recycled materials in pavements

their unique characteristics and focus. Each tool works as an independent performance metric, with a particular philosophy and different sustainability objectives" (Bueno et al., 2015a, p. 104).

2.2.1.2 Advantages and disadvantages of rating systems

According to Muench et al. (2012), rating systems are increasingly popular as "(i) they provide a common metric for the entire range of sustainable solutions, (ii) they measure sustainability and thus make it manageable, (iii) they allow for straightforward communication of sustainability goals, efforts and achievement, and (iv) they provide a reasonable context within which designers, contractors and material suppliers can be innovative in their solutions" (Muench et al., 2012, p. 4).

Rating and certification tools are well-known systems, as they are linked to credible and reputable organizations. They provide best practice guidance for integrating sustainability over the whole life cycle of a project, from planning through operation and maintenance. Rating systems set credible sustainability items against which projects can be assessed, including environmental, economic and social aspects together. In addition, they are simple to understand, and its implementation is straightforward. As Bueno et al. (2015a) recognized "considering the proliferation of rating systems throughout the civil engineering field in some markets, they have been successful tools with large-scale application and acceptance into the hands of practitioners."

However, rating systems also have a number of disadvantages. One of the key limitations is that most rating systems are focused on the environmental pillar while giving the social pillar the least importance (Awadh, 2017). On the other and, although they cover all project development phases (planning, design, construction, maintenance), in practice they are mostly focused on the construction stage. As mentioned in the literature—see Lee et al. (2011) and Bueno et al. (2015a)—rating systems are limited due to the lack of transparency and objectiveness in the assigning of weights to different criteria, which may lead to subjective and non-transparent biasing.

2.2.2 Frameworks, models and appraisal guidance

In addition, practitioners and policy makers sometimes use tailor made decision support tools, calculators and guidelines. According to the International Federation of Consulting Engineers (2012), these are "typically produced by engineering consultancies, engineering and construction firms that wish to ensure the sustainability of their own projects and to offer sustainability services to their clients." They are mostly based on the multi-criteria decision analysis and cover a range of sectors including infrastructure, transport, urban planning and buildings. Examples of such decision tools include: (i) MAESTRO—Arrival Departure Manager for the aviation sector; (ii) SPeAR® (Sustainable Project Appraisal Routine) a sustainability tool developed by Arup for comparing project alternatives from the sustainability viewpoint; and the SymbioCity Approach developed by SWECO to evaluate sustainable urban development.

As these methodologies with hands-on application are created to assist client projects, they are not usually available in the public domain. However, as the International Federation of Consulting Engineers (2012) acknowledges, they usually:

i. *Include a baseline assessment prior to the project development.* This step typically identifies the project context and the drivers for considering the investment. It also describes the expected outcomes and benefits the project will help to deliver.
ii. *Provide a set of sustainability criteria to consider during the assessment,* which sometimes includes assigning criteria weights. In some cases, all criteria are considered to have the same importance in order to avoid adding subjectivity to the assessment.
iii. *Assessing the sustainability of design options based on a specific point by point guidance provided.* As in the case of rating systems, this step also includes evidence gathering to inform the process.

This category of tools/methods also includes a number of appraisal guidelines developed by different governments. For example, in the UK, the Department for Transport uses the Transport Analysis Guidance (TAG) as a mandatory requirement for projects that need government approval. In Scotland, a similar appraisal guidance called "STAG" provides detailed guidance on the methodology and reporting structure to be used when completing a transport appraisal. Similar guidance (called "Werkwijzer MKBA bij MIRT-Verkenningen") has also been produced to evaluate major infrastructure plans funded by the Dutch Government.

As pointed out by Bueno et al. (2015a), appraisal guidance frameworks represent best practice providing expert advice for the appraisal of transport projects. They develop standardized and robust approaches to assess the impacts of transport interventions in a consistent manner. National approaches to transport project appraisal differ from one country to another and they are employed to evaluate sustainability to a different extent. However, most of them use conventional decision-making methods such as CBA or MCA and include both qualitative and quantitative approaches to express project impacts in monetary units or in other terms. A complete and detailed evaluation of this category of tools is beyond the scope of this work. For a comprehensive evaluation of different economic appraisal frameworks in the transport sector and its use in the decision-making process, the reader is referred to University of Leeds (2013) and Koopmans and Mouter (2020) for a discussion of the literature on MCA, the reader is referred to Dean (2020). Mouter et al., (2020) discuss differences between CBA and MCA.

From the sustainability viewpoint, these tools provide guidance on what constitutes economic, environmental and social criteria. Therefore, they have contributed to the literature by setting credible lists of sustainability criteria against which project options can be assessed according to their performance. Existing guidelines constitute best practice in transport project appraisal, and in addition they are made publicly available in all detail. This can inspire the development of other appraisal guidelines throughout the world.

However, as no weighting information is provided in such appraisal guidelines, they do not overcome the issue of "putting all the aspects together," either because they do not aggregate impacts of a different nature (e.g., appraisal guidance) or because they fail to derive criteria weighting in a precise way. As a result, the final selection of the best alternative may continue to be based on subjective judgments.

2.2.3 Do the available methods correctly appraise sustainability?

Bueno et al. (2015a) conducted a comparative study of sustainability assessment tools in the literature concluding that none of the described methodologies is able to satisfy all the sine qua non requirements for the suitable appraisal of transport projects previously explained in Section 2. The analysis revealed that there are a number of limitations associated to rating systems and other frameworks, models and appraisal guidelines for rightly appraising sustainability.

Rating systems and certification tools provide a theoretical good balance between social, economic and environmental aspects. However, in practice, they are mostly focused on environmental impacts related to construction processes and materials. In addition, making a comparison across different voluntary certification tools is not possible as each one establishes its own criteria and its own weighting process.

Other tools such as frameworks, models and guidelines have shown to effectively guide engineering consultants and analysts when appraising social, economic and environmental impacts of transportation projects. However, the guidance on social and distributional impacts is less developed than the guidance for economic/environmental dimension. Moreover, they do not provide a framework for evaluating all the aspects together. As a consequence of that, the selection of the preferred option may not always be objective.

3. To what extent can conventional appraisal methods assess sustainability?

For the purpose of this section, conventional appraisal methods are those often implemented by decision-makers to appraise transport projects, such as cost-benefit analysis (CBA), multi-criteria decision analysis (MCA), environmental impact assessment (EIA) and life cycle assessment (LCA). Although these techniques offer valuable support for assessing transport sustainability, none of them comply with all the requirements demanded by the concept of sustainability as it was defined in Section 2 of this chapter. CBA, for instance, has still serious problems in evaluating incommensurable goods, while MCA is often challenged for the subjectivity in setting the weights for trading off different criteria.

In this section, we conduct an evaluation of the main contributions and limitations of conventional transport appraisal tools to rightly assess sustainability. The analysis specifically focuses on cost-benefit analysis (CBA), multi-criteria decision analysis (MCA) and other techniques for assessing environmental and social impacts.

3.1 Cost-benefit analysis

CBA is the most popular technique to support decision-makers in appraising transport projects and policy measures. As discussed by Koopmans and Mouter (2020), its objective is to compare different alternatives with the do-nothing alternative with the aim of quantifying the social welfare increase or decrease as the summation of consumer and producer surpluses plus externalities during the life cycle of the project or policy measure to be examined. This approach requires to weigh present and future benefits by using a social discount rate. It also needs that all the benefits and costs are valued in monetary terms, which is not always possible, thereby representing one of the greatest limitations of this approach for rightly addressing sustainability. One of the greatest limitations of CBA, according to Iacono and Levinson (2015), is the difficulty to rightly estimate the costs and benefits of a certain alternative over its life cycle because factors on which they depend are highly dynamic.

CBA is not able to consider the triple bottom line according to the needs of sustainability assessment since the monetization process is questionable for these intangible items. Pricing "priceless goods," such as many environmental and social ones, is not possible according to CBA premises while these "priceless goods" are the cornerstone of sustainability. Furthermore, it usually does not conduct a full life cycle analysis as end of life aspects are rarely included within CBA (Jones et al., 2014).

As discussed by Koopmans and Mouter (2020), the inter-temporal aggregation is another big issue of CBA for rightly dealing with sustainability assessment since social discount rates do not necessarily make a sensible inter-temporal aggregation of the consumption of natural resources that may be depleted, or the consequences of large concentration of pollution or greenhouse gases in the atmosphere. Mouter (2018) shows how various authors criticize the use high discount rates as they may compromise intergenerational justice. To circumvent this issue, some authors (see Almansa and Calatrava, 2007) suggest using (lower) environmental discount rates that may correct the problems previously mentioned.

3.2 Multi-criteria decision analysis

Dean (2020) states that Multicriteria Analysis (MCA) is a technique which is a suitable decision-making methodology for "addressing complex problems featuring high uncertainty, conflicting objectives, different forms of data and information, multiple interests, and perspectives, and the accounting for complex and evolving biophysical and socio-economic systems" (Kowalski et al., 2009). According to Munda et al. (1998), MCA is not a single evaluation tool, but rather a big group of techniques with lower or greater levels of sophistication. An extensive review of these methods can be found in Huang et al. (2011), Kabir et al. (2013) and Wang et al. (2009). Through MCA, different criteria can be incorporated simultaneously, even those difficult to monetize or quantify (Thomopoulos et al., 2009). Therefore, the main advantage of this method over CBA is that it enables incorporating impacts that cannot be monetized (Gühnemann et al., 2012).

Given its flexibility and adaptability, some authors (Janic, 2003; Tudela et al., 2006; Walker, 2010) have suggested that MCA may be a useful tool on the basis of which setting the foundation of sustainability assessment.

To that end, it is necessary to identify the sustainability criteria, set the different alternatives to appraise, define the weights across those criteria in order to finally rank the different options available. According to Bueno et al. (2015a): "given the need to holistically capture economic, environmental, and social impacts to rightly evaluate sustainability, the multi-criteria scheme could be very effective since it accomplishes the goal of being multi-disciplinary. In addition, the MCA scheme should be used to account for a more comprehensive range of impacts, taking advantage of recent advances in the environmental and social assessment fields of research."

3.3 Techniques to assess environmental impacts

Some techniques have been also developed to assess the environmental impacts of transport projects. The literature points out several limitations with "environmental tools" since they have a "general objective of encouraging greater environmental responsibility within the construction industry, but not toward sustainability as a whole" (Treloar et al., 2004).

According to Sharma and Geerlings (2017), environmental impact assessment (EIA) "can be considered as yet another successful method of project appraisal which has a long history of application. However, the main role of EIA is to assess the environmental impacts of transport-sector policies, plans, and projects. As a tool for sustainability assessment, EIA is inadequate because, over and above its intrinsic technical limitations, it provides information about only one pillar of sustainability (environment)."

Life cycle assessment (LCA) is a method for assessing the environmental impacts of a product, activity, or process over the whole life cycle from "cradle to grave." This includes extraction of materials, manufacturing processes, transport distribution, use, service and maintenance, and end-of-life such as reuse, recycling, energy recovery, and final waste handling (Stripple and Erlandsson, 2004). Despite the fact that LCA can be used for any type of transport project, it has been mostly implemented in roads (Stripple, 2001).

LCA provides valuable insight for sustainability assessment since it quantifies the environmental efficiency on the basis of a life-cycle approach. As some authors acknowledge (Baker and Lepech, 2009; Keoleian and Spitzley, 2006), LCA has become a common tool for the evaluation of the environmental performance thereby producing useful input for sustainability assessment.

However, according to Reap et al. (2008) LCA still "suffers from problems that degrade accuracy and increase uncertainty of assessment results." These authors pointed out 15 major inaccuracies of the tool, such as subjective values using weightings, problems in monetization methods, difficulties with selecting impact categories, indicators and models, and spatial variation, among others.

When accounting for sustainability, according to Loiseau et al. (2012), LCA has some issues to improve its accuracy. On the one hand, this approach does not include all the sustainability criteria since its main purpose is to evaluate the environmental impact of a certain activity. On the other hand, LCA is not much integrated within other appraisal tools—even though there have been attempts to do it through the social life cycle assessment (SLCA) approach. For this reason, it is an incomplete method to fully assess the triple bottom line of sustainability. Furthermore, the significant changes in the environmental effects captured through the LCA scarcely include the design phase since it does not consider how energy consumption varies with different design parameters. According to Bueno et al. (2015a), "LCA can be regarded as a particular step to define a complete sustainability impact assessment tool."

3.4 Techniques to assess social impacts

Measuring social impacts is the most difficult part for a proper sustainability assessment basically because there is not a common agreement on the most important social aspects to consider, neither are there universally acknowledged methodological tools to conduct the analysis. Actually, the Evaluation Partnership and the Centre for European Policy Studies (TEP and CEPS, 2010) pointed out two limitations to assess social aspects. The first one is the fact that the term "social" is too broad and there is not a consensus on the specific items that it should include. The second one is the lack of tools to quantitatively measure social impacts since most of the social aspects are just measured on a qualitative and sometimes rather superficial basis. In this respect, the European Commission (2009) warned that greater attention is given to economic and environmental aspects compared to social ones. Evaluating the latter requires a greater public participation.

The LCA approach, mentioned above, has been recently extended to social aspect through what is called social life cycle assessment (SLCA).

However, these methodologies are still at an early stage since consensus building happens to be complicated. Jørgensen et al. (2008) claim that "some agreement regarding which impacts are most relevant to include in the SLCA in order to cover the field sufficiently seems paramount if the SLCA is to gain any weight as a decision support tool."

4. A suggested methodological approach to appraise sustainability

Sections 2 and 3 concluded that, currently, all the available tools are limited to thoroughly address sustainability. Therefore, composite decision tools for combining different methodologies seems sensible in order to preserve the strengths of some these traditional ways of measuring sustainability, while at the same time improving them. In this line, Bueno et al. (2015a) suggested an integrated approach which merges the multi-criteria approach with the single criterion approach (i.e., the combination of CBA and MCA). Based on this assumption (see Bueno et al., 2015a), this section is intended to present a novel methodology, based on the idea that the CBA and the MCA can be combined along with other techniques, to seek a suitable solution to measure sustainability, especially when it comes to setting trade-offs to account for environmental, social and economic impacts.

The model was originally developed by the authors of this paper in a former project for the European Investment Bank entitled "Road Infrastructure Design for Optimizing Sustainability"—see Bueno et al. (2013a). The main objective of that research was to investigate how transport projects are appraised and what alternatives are recommended to improve sustainability assessment. As a result of the research work, a model called STAR (Sustainability Tool for the Appraisal of Road projects) was developed to help decision-makers when selecting the most sustainable infrastructure design. Although STAR was initially focused on roads, its applicability may cover other types of infrastructure and transport interventions.

The method heavily relies on the results and conclusions drawn by Bueno et al. (2015a) and Bueno and Vassallo (2015) and is structured in three steps briefly described in the following paragraphs—see Fig. 1. The first step consists of identifying and quantifying, within the context of the project or intervention to be evaluated, appropriate criteria necessary to characterize sustainability. Since it requires compiling a thorough list of criteria

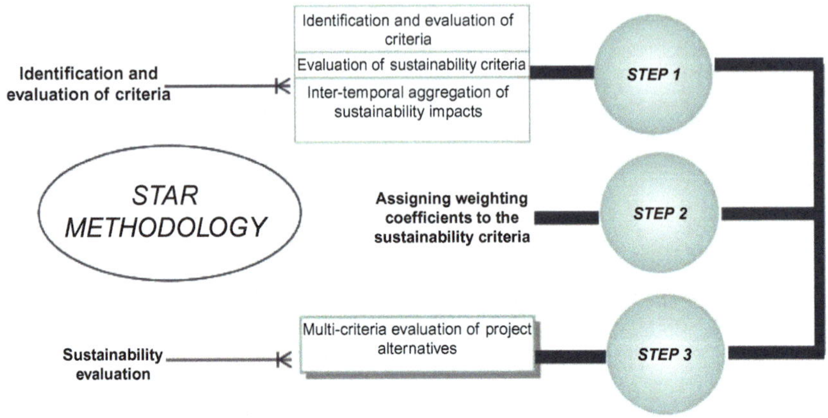

Fig. 1 Structure of the STAR model.

covered by sustainable requirements, one contribution of this section is that we broadened the table originally presented in Bueno et al. (2015a), which summarizes the main sustainability items to be considered for infrastructure projects throughout their life cycle. The methodology is also based on a suitable and straightforward approach for the inter-temporal aggregation of environmental, social and economic impacts.

The second step addresses the relatively limited number of real applications to determine proper and consistent weights for each sustainability criterion previously identified. The proposed weighting process was published by Bueno and Vassallo (2015). It uses the REMBRANDT technique, a pairwise comparison method for determining the relative importance of different criteria, and it also incorporates decision-makers' judgments in the decision-making process. The third step is the sustainability performance ranking of the alternatives in order to select the option with the best global sustainability score.

The main sustainability assessment limitations overcome by this new approach are summarized below:

i. By expressing the assessment of different criteria into a common language (MCA), it tackles the problem associated with incomparable quantities. It should be noted that this is a fundamental premise of the novel methodology.

ii. It suggests a standard approach to enhance the credibility to the entire assessment process, thereby limiting the inherent subjective nature of qualitative assessment.

iii. The methodology proposes a simple approach for the inter-temporal aggregation of environmental, social and economic impacts, including alternative discounting methods according to the characteristics of specific sustainability criteria.

iv. By accounting for expert preferences and the context-sensitive nature of sustainability, the model increases the scientific rigor and objectivity in setting the weights of sustainability criteria.

It should be noted that the purpose of this approach is not to set up a completely new method capable of estimating the sustainability impact of transport projects. Instead, it intends to use existing methodologies more wisely, based on a thorough understanding of the concept of sustainability and its application in the transport context. This process also required a previous identification of the advantages, limitations, strengths, and weaknesses of conventional appraisal methods and other sustainability assessment methods—see Sections 2 and 3.

4.1 Identification and evaluation of criteria

The first step is intended to identify basic fundamentals to judge the sustainability of the project assessed. After the identification, a proper quantification should also be performed. This quantification should be completed on an alternative-basis, which implies that each identified criterion should be evaluated for each of the alternatives either in monetary units or other qualitative units. As described below, this step is divided into the following three tasks.

4.1.1 Identifying sustainability criteria throughout different project stages

Ideally, criteria to measure sustainability should take into account the well-known triple bottom line of sustainability: economic efficiency, environmental protection, and social and distributional aspects. These criteria should be evaluated throughout the different project stages (construction, maintenance and operation). In this step, it is necessary to distinguish those criteria that can be set in monetary units from those that can only be measured in a qualitative scale.

In this section, we adapt the proposed set of major sustainability criteria to be considered for transport infrastructure projects over their life cycle developed by Bueno et al. (2015a). Although this list was initially created for road projects, it is designed to be easily adapted to other transport infrastructure interventions. The set of sustainability criteria shown in Table 4 was originally developed by reviewing reporting guidelines, frameworks and more than 100 relevant academic studies—see Bueno et al. (2013b). An explanation of each criterion is provided below to supplement the list provided in the original paper. However, it should be noted that this is only a framework example as bespoke sustainability criteria must be selected depending on the characteristics of the project being appraised.

4.1.2 Evaluation of sustainability criteria to identify impacts for each alternative

The purpose of this step is to measure specific project impacts by quantifying/qualifying each of the identified criteria. This exercise is intended to be based on the differential values between the without scheme case (i.e., do-nothing) and the with intervention case (i.e., do-something scenario).

The methodology recommends a different approach depending on the type of assessment to be carried out (qualitative assessment or quantitative assessment). Where possible, a quantitative approach (in monetary or other units) should be used. In this case, it is recommended to estimate the monetary impact with accurate shadow prices considering sustainability aspects. The method also suggests using physical/original units for those items with no market prices (e.g., accidents saved, tons of NO_2 saved).

It is expected that in many cases, sustainability criteria cannot be quantified. This is the case for most of the social impacts derived by the project, including aspects such as security and community disruption (severance). Then, a qualitative assessment should be conducted based on a seven-point assessment scale, consistent with other published appraisal schemes (Fig. 2).

4.1.3 Inter-temporal aggregation of sustainability impacts

The inter-temporal aggregation of sustainability impacts is still a work in progress. This is because valuing the future costs and benefits of some items occurring over long periods is still debated. According to the STAR methodology, it is recommended to use:

i. An appropriate discount rate for items which can be quantified in monetary terms. The analyst should convert future impacts to present-day values or aggregated impacts (AI). Then, in order to combine CBA with MCA, the qualitative scale shown in Fig. 3 should be used to obtain homogenized aggregated impacts (HAI).

Table 4 Sustainability criteria for infrastructure projects throughout their life cycle.

Sust. area	Sustainability criteria	Reasoning
Economic	Infrastructure costs	Considers all the investment costs of the project, generally comprising land acquisition, design/legal/administration and construction costs. Maintenance and operating costs should be included in the analysis
	Travel time cost	Represents the cost of time spent traveling and waiting. Also identifies the project's contribution when reducing congestion
	Vehicle operating cost	Considers fixed costs (e.g., insurance) and operating costs (e.g., fuel consumption and lubricants) derived from operating the vehicle
	Accident cost	Covers transport accidents (fatal accidents/injuries/damage-only accidents) that should be assessed according to their severity
	Macroeconomic impacts	Represents all economic benefits or costs that are not captured directly when evaluating user benefits. Should be incorporated as wider economic impacts (such as competition, agglomeration and labor market effects)
Environmental	Energy consumption, resource use and CO_2 emissions	Includes the total energy consumed in the processes of extraction, processing, transportation and fabrication of construction materials and resources. Should also include the most important carbon emissions from the construction-maintenance-operation of the road
	Habitat fragmentation and negative effects on species	Considers the overall effect of the project on biodiversity and earth heritage attributes, from the construction stage to the service period. The analysis should include mitigation/compensation/substitution measures, relocation of species, etc.
	Air pollution	Covers short-term air quality effects caused by construction/maintenance activities (e.g., dust nuisance). Other air pollutant emissions must be considered during the operation stage (local air pollution/global air pollution)

Continued

Table 4 Sustainability criteria for infrastructure projects throughout their life cycle.—cont'd

Sust. area	Sustainability criteria	Reasoning
	Noise pollution	Assesses noise associated with the road development, including vehicle noise, frictional noise, and activities derived from road construction and maintenance
	Landscape degradation and negative visual impacts	Considers all impacts on aesthetics and landscape resulting from construction activities that adversely affect landforms
Social	Community disruption (also called severance)	Covers changes to local interactions caused by a new road. The analysis may include necessary measures to maintain social and economic interactions or an assessment of the impacts on community relations (community split, modifications to travel routes, impacts on tourism, etc.)
	Impacts on businesses and community services	Evaluates impacts on businesses and community services (e.g., hospitals, churches, schools, parks) when a new road is built, including relocation, loss of clients, etc.
	Employment and labor standards	Includes a range of indirect effects such as changes in economic, climate and labor/materials markets due to the construction of a new infrastructure. Temporary effects such as job creation should be included in the analysis
	Distributional effects of the project	Considers significant potential equity impacts, particularly for neighboring communities and users. The assessment must include how disadvantaged people benefit in terms of time savings, convenience, safety, affordability and health. Connectivity must be specifically considered with a view to transporting disadvantaged people (low-income, disabled, isolated, by gender) and in terms of access to education, employment, and economic opportunities
	Occupational and community health and safety	Covers the effects of work on health, including working conditions and also considers safety and health impacts on the surrounding community

Author's elaboration based on Bueno, P.C., Vassallo, J.M., Cheung, K., 2015a. Sustainability assessment of transport infrastructure projects: a review of existing tools and methods. Transplant. Rev. 35 (5), 622–649.

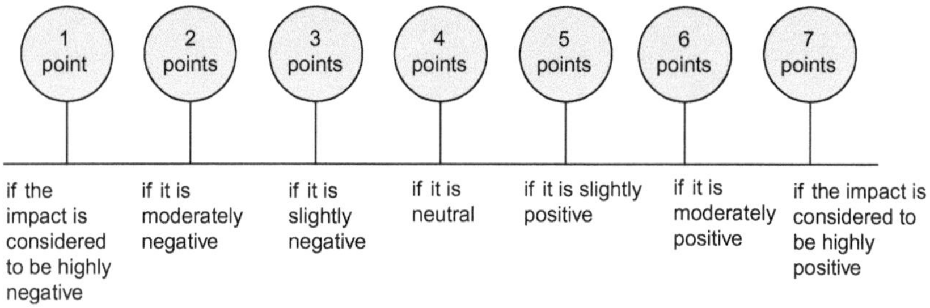

Fig. 2 Seven-point assessment scale to be used for the evaluation of qualitative items (do-something vs do-nothing scenario).

ii. The original units for items not expressed in monetary terms. As there is no well-known time preference for those items, it is also suggested to obtain a "cumulative value" which needs to be converted from physical units into the seven-point assessment scale for obtaining the previously explained homogenized aggregated impacts (HAI), as indicated in Fig. 3.

iii. No discounting technique for items that can only be measured in a qualitative fashion.

For this process, assumptions have to be made about whether each criterion is a "benefit" or "cost" criterion. This means whether it is preferable to have more (more is better) or less of a certain criterion (less is better) from the sustainability viewpoint. An indicative numerical interpretation of what is much, moderately and slightly better or worse is also shown in the figure. However, these thresholds should be treated with some caution by the decision-maker. For example, for a "less is better" criterion, the $(AI)_i$ of one project option may be considered to be much worse than the average of the alternatives when it is 45% higher than this average.

4.2 Assigning weighting coefficients to the sustainability criteria

The purpose of the second step is to determine appropriate weights for each of the homogenized impacts obtained from Step 1. As acknowledged in the literature, there are currently few studies addressing the relative impact of each sustainability criterion (hereinafter referred to as sustainability weights).

To propose a new weighting methodology is beyond the scope of this chapter. The reader is referred to Bueno and Vassallo (2015), who provided

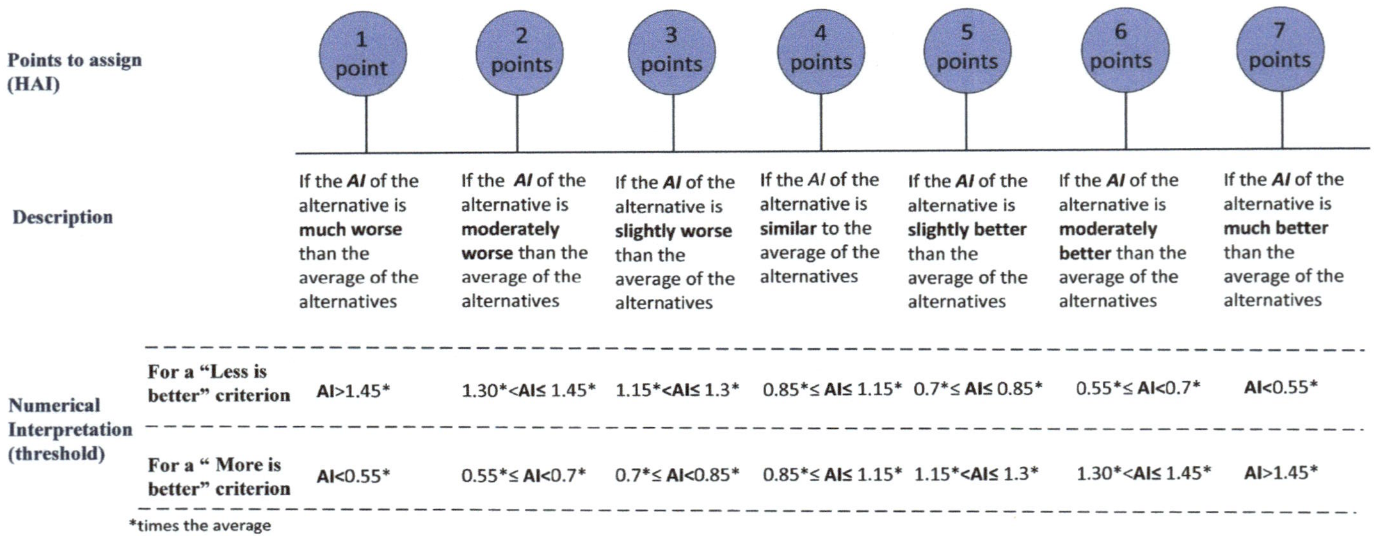

Fig. 3 Proposed seven-point assessment scale for obtaining HAI.

one of the most comprehensive and practical studies to set the weights of sustainability criteria used in a multi-criteria decision analysis. The proposed weighting process uses the REMBRANDT system (*Ratio Estimation in Magnitudes or deci-Bells to Rate Alternatives which are Non-DominaTed system*) and an objective evaluation of all the criteria in the project context. In summary, weighting coefficients are obtained for each of the sustainability criteria based on:

i. The project context, meaning that the method recognizes the sensitivity of sustainability evaluation to the context where the project will be developed;

ii. Points of view from key stakeholders by including experts' opinion and preferences for pairwise comparisons of sustainability criteria.

Other methodologies to obtain sustainability weights can also be applied to complete this step, as long as they are compliant with the "rigorous trade-offs" requirement for the suitable appraisal of transport projects previously explained in Section 2.1. Some recent methodologies based on the multi-actor multi-criteria analysis (MAMCA) approach are also an alternative to be considered by decision-makers when completing this step—see, for example, Bergqvist et al. (2015), Geudens et al. (2009) and Macharis et al. (2009).

4.3 Sustainability evaluation of project options

Finally, the objective of this step is to proceed to the full sustainability evaluation for each project option. Step 3 investigates the sustainability performance of each alternative, which is required to support the selection of the preferred scheme scenario.

4.3.1 Multi-criteria evaluation of project alternatives

The STAR methodology recommends the weighted sum method as a simple and well-known approach to obtain the ranking order of project alternatives from the sustainability viewpoint. However, there are other methods available in the literature, which the analyst should consider. Justification should be provided within the appraisal report. The following equation should be used to obtain the final sustainability evaluation of a certain alternative (*alternative a*). The final score has to be then considered when ranking the alternatives in the final selection process.

$$\text{Sustainability Performance of alternative}_a = \sum_{i=1}^{n} SW_i \times HAI_i \quad (1)$$

where

- Sustainability Performance of alternative$_a$ = Sustainability performance of alternative *a*
- SW_i = Sustainability weight for the sustainability criterion *i*
- HAI_i = Homogenized aggregated impact for sustainability criterion *i*
- n = Total number of sustainability criteria in alternative *a*

It is recommended to select the alternative with the highest sustainability performance. However, decision-makers are encouraged to keep in mind that this type of analysis may "hide" potential compensations across impacts. Displaying a summary table including the assessment of each of the impacts may be considered as a potential solution for this limitation. In this way decision-makers can analyze the "whole picture" without missing a disaggregated view across the impacts and options under consideration.

The main drawbacks of the STAR methodology are described below:

i. For each project, a specific identification of sustainability criteria should be undertaken. Although allowing some flexibility, it also means that this step of the methodology is open to the criteria of the analyst, undermining its standard nature.

ii. The process of including experts' opinion and preferences for pairwise comparisons of sustainability criteria can be time-consuming and laborious.

iii. In practice, many sustainability criteria cannot be quantified in a proportional way (given the size and scope of the project). This problem may end up in a merely qualitative assessment of the different criteria which can lead to a loss in credibility.

4.4 Application to a case study

4.4.1 Project description

As part of the STAREBEI project delivered by the authors of this chapter, an application to a case study was carried out to demonstrate the applicability of the STAR methodology. As the purpose of this section is only to illustrate the explained methodology, the reader is referred to Bueno et al. (2015b) for a full description of the results.

The case study is the ex-ante design of a new road planned to be built in north-western Spain. The motorway was included in the Strategic Infrastructure and Transport Plan of the Spanish Ministry of Public

Works (2015). The pre-feasibility report has identified three project options including the provision of an additional lane (option 1), the construction of a new North-road to replace the existing one (option 2), and the construction of a new South-road to replace the existing old road (option 3). A number of issues have been identified in the existing road including congestion and delay disrupting journeys, a considerable number of accidents and consequent poor air quality. Table 5 presents a description of each one of the project options. Again, the reader is referred to Bueno et al. (2015b) for further details. It should be noted that values presented below correspond to differential values (difference between the do-something compared to the do-nothing scenario).

In terms of the qualitative items, a previous assessment has been completed to determine the "score" of each item according to the seven-point assessment scale. A description of this assessment is also shown in Table 6.

4.4.2 Results

This section briefly summarizes the results of the sustainability appraisal applied to the project alternatives, following the STAR methodology previously outlined. Key points are as follows:

- Appropriate sustainability criteria were identified based on the guidance provided in Table 4.
- Investment costs and maintenance cost are expressed in monetary terms. Vehicle operating costs are also quantified using shadow prices.
- Travel time savings, accident savings and energy consumption were quantitatively assessed in physical units (i.e., hours, total number of accidents saved, kg fuel/veh-km).
- Most of the environmental, social and distributional impacts are presented qualitatively.[a]

Building on the inputs provided in Table 5, the following steps have been completed:

i. Quantification of sustainability criteria for each project option, assuming a 25-year appraisal period. As indicated above, items were quantified in monetary terms to obtain specific project impacts. A traditional cost-benefit analysis was used to convert future cost and benefits into their present values.

[a] For simplicity purposes, environmental impacts are assessed and presented qualitatively in this illustrative case study. However, it should be noted that in reality many environmental impacts can be quantified.

Table 5 Project options.

Description (differential value)	Option 1 in comparison to the do-nothing scenario	Option 2 in comparison to the do-nothing scenario	Option 3 in comparison to the do-nothing scenario
Length (m)	0	−3	−10
Vehicle operating costs (€ veh/km)	−0.06	−0.03	−0.08
Maintenance cost (€/Km)	12,000	12,000	22,000
Road management and operating cost (€/km)	8000	8000	18,000
Investment (million €/Km)	2.0	3.0	4.0
AADT (veh/daily)	−2000	−2000	−2000
Accidents (accidents/million veh*km)	0.2	0.4	0.8
Travel time (min)	9.6	11.3	15.3

ii. For the criteria for which the market does not provide an acceptable economic value, impacts were not measured in monetary units, and present-day values were calculated by using a simple addition of physical units.

iii. The final homogenized aggregated impacts (HAI)—see Fig. 4—were obtained based on the guidance provided in Fig. 3.

In order to obtain sustainability priorities (weighting) to be used in the appraisal, the methodology presented in Section 4.2 was used. This method was applied as part of the same case study so the results were directly taken from this study. Detailed results are presented in the cited research work, and in this section only the main results are illustrated to avoid duplications. Table 7 shows the sustainability weights obtained when applying the mentioned weighting method. As shown, the weight importance found for the "accident cost savings" criterion was significantly higher when compared to the rest of the environmental and social items. The overall importance obtained for environmental and social criteria was quite similar.

Table 6 Qualitative assessment of the options.

Description (differential value)	Option 1 in comparison to the do-nothing scenario	Option 2 in comparison to the do-nothing scenario	Option 3 in comparison to the do-nothing scenario
Habitat fragmentation and impacts on species			
Landscape degradation and visual impacts			
Employment effects			
Noise pollution			
Community disruption			
Social and distributional impacts			
Negative impacts on businesses and residents			

Legend

Highly negative	
Moderately negative	
Slightly negative	
Neutral	
Slightly positive	
Moderately positive	
Highly positive	

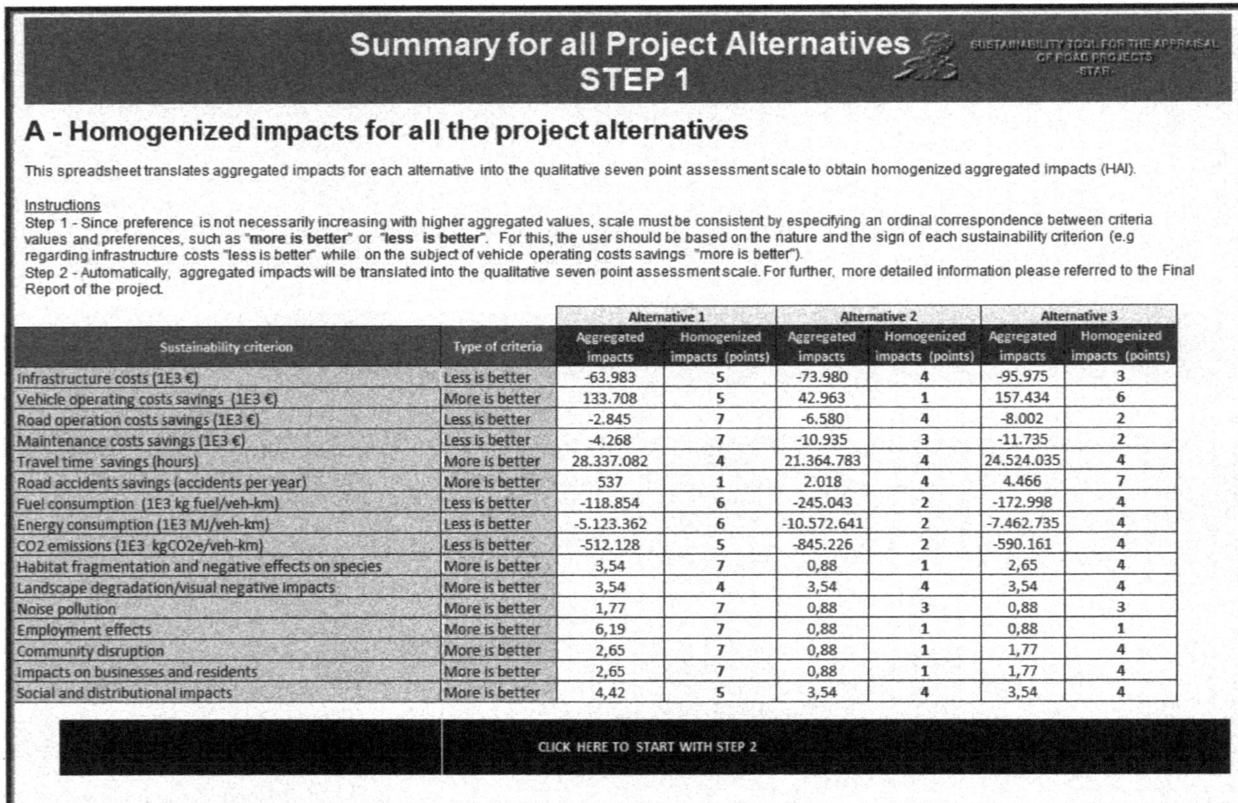

Summary for all Project Alternatives
STEP 1

SUSTAINABILITY TOOL FOR THE APPRAISAL OF ROAD PROJECTS -STAR-

A - Homogenized impacts for all the project alternatives

This spreadsheet translates aggregated impacts for each alternative into the qualitative seven point assessment scale to obtain homogenized aggregated impacts (HAI).

Instructions
Step 1 - Since preference is not necessarily increasing with higher aggregated values, scale must be consistent by especifying an ordinal correspondence between criteria values and preferences, such as "**more is better**" or "**less is better**". For this, the user should be based on the nature and the sign of each sustainability criterion (e.g regarding infrastructure costs "less is better" while on the subject of vehicle operating costs savings "more is better").
Step 2 - Automatically, aggregated impacts will be translated into the qualitative seven point assessment scale. For further, more detailed information please referred to the Final Report of the project.

Sustainability criterion	Type of criteria	Alternative 1		Alternative 2		Alternative 3	
		Aggregated impacts	Homogenized impacts (points)	Aggregated impacts	Homogenized impacts (points)	Aggregated impacts	Homogenized impacts (points)
Infrastructure costs (1E3 €)	Less is better	-63.983	5	-73.980	4	-95.975	3
Vehicle operating costs savings (1E3 €)	More is better	133.708	5	42.963	1	157.434	6
Road operation costs savings (1E3 €)	Less is better	-2.845	7	-6.580	4	-8.002	2
Maintenance costs savings (1E3 €)	Less is better	-4.268	7	-10.935	3	-11.735	2
Travel time savings (hours)	More is better	28.337.082	4	21.364.783	4	24.524.035	4
Road accidents savings (accidents per year)	More is better	537	1	2.018	4	4.466	7
Fuel consumption (1E3 kg fuel/veh-km)	Less is better	-118.854	6	-245.043	2	-172.998	4
Energy consumption (1E3 MJ/veh-km)	Less is better	-5.123.362	6	-10.572.641	2	-7.462.735	4
CO2 emissions (1E3 kgCO2e/veh-km)	Less is better	-512.128	5	-845.226	2	-590.161	4
Habitat fragmentation and negative effects on species	More is better	3,54	7	0,88	1	2,65	4
Landscape degradation/visual negative impacts	More is better	3,54	4	3,54	4	3,54	4
Noise pollution	More is better	1,77	7	0,88	3	0,88	3
Employment effects	More is better	6,19	7	0,88	1	0,88	1
Community disruption	More is better	2,65	7	0,88	1	1,77	4
Impacts on businesses and residents	More is better	2,65	7	0,88	1	1,77	4
Social and distributional impacts	More is better	4,42	5	3,54	4	3,54	4

CLICK HERE TO START WITH STEP 2

Fig. 4 Homogenized aggregated impacts (HAI) for project options.

Table 7 Weighting exercise results.

Sustainability component	Sustainability criterion	Normalized weights
Economic	Infrastructure costs	3.820
	Vehicle operating costs	3.215
	Road operation costs	3.820
	Maintenance costs	3.820
	Travel time savings	4.136
	Accidents savings	14.523
Environmental	Fuel consumption	5.411
	Energy consumption	5.411
	CO_2 emissions	5.411
	Habitat fragmentation and e effects on species	5.490
	Landscape degradation/visual impacts	5.951
	Noise pollution	5.658
Social	Employment effects	8.129
	Community disruption	8.412
	Impacts on businesses and residents	8.942
	Social and distributional impacts	7.850

The sustainability performance of project alternatives is given by Eq. (1). The resulting performance for each alternative is then used to rank and choose the option with the highest credits. Table 8 details the results and presents alternative 1 as the preferred option given its final sustainability performance in comparison to the rest of the alternatives.

5. Future challenges

Unlike other appraisal techniques such as CBA and MCA, sustainability assessment of transport projects and policies is still at an early stage. First, because even though the term sustainability appears to be very appealing for politicians and decision-makers, there is not a unanimous interpretation of

Table 8 Sustainability performance of project options.

Sustainability component	Sustainability criterion	Sustainability evaluation: option 1	Sustainability evaluation: option 2	Sustainability evaluation: option 3
Economic	Infrastructure costs	22.58	18.06	13.55
	Vehicle operating costs	19.01	15.21	11.40
	Road operation costs	31.61	18.06	13.55
	Maintenance costs	31.61	18.06	13.55
	Travel time savings	6.52	6.52	4.89
	Road accidents	17.17	68.68	51.51
Environmental	Fuel consumption	19.19	12.80	9.60
	Energy consumption	12.80	8.53	6.40
	CO_2 emissions	5.33	4.27	3.20
	Habitat fragmentation and negative effects on species	45.44	25.97	19.47
	Landscape degradation/visual negative impacts	28.14	28.14	21.11
	Noise pollution	31.22	17.84	13.38
Social	Employment effects	78.49	44.85	33.64
	Community disruption	69.62	39.78	29.84
	Impacts on businesses and residents	74.01	42.29	31.72
	Social and distributional impacts	38.67	30.94	23.20
Final sustainability performance		531.41	400.00	300.00

the concept, which remains being too broad and context specific. And second, because as shown in this chapter, there is no universally accepted method available yet to thoroughly address the sustainability assessment of transport plans and projects. As shown throughout the chapter, specific tools designed to measures sustainability, such as rating systems and guidelines, have important limitations because they are mostly designed for practical purposes such as providing certifications, or just as a set of guidelines aimed at helping designers to account for the main sustainability impacts of certain projects (Bueno et al., 2015a).

Setting a specific definition of the sustainability concept is becoming challenging. Actually, over the last few years, the concept has been broadening rather than getting more and more precise. The sustainable development goals promoted by United Nations is a clear example of such a trend. It seems as if the concept of sustainability was turning toward a set of human desires irrespective of the need to conciliate economic, social and environmental goals in the long-term and in a context of budgetary restriction. This is the reason why it is recommended that sustainability tools take account of the context they are applied in, and where possible include stakeholders in their design.

In spite of that, measuring sustainability at the time of appraising transport projects and policies remains being a challenge that governments and transport authorities have to address given the fact that most of the decisions adopted nowadays are mostly based on economic tools, such as CBA, complemented through MCA to add other impacts, especially environmental ones, which cannot be expressed in monetary units. Unfortunately, little attention is still paid to social impacts that go far beyond the effects usually captured by conventional project appraisal methods; and also to setting up rigorous trade-offs between economic, social and environmental impacts from a long-term perspective.

Regarding sustainability appraisal of transport projects, the proposal of the authors is not to build a completely new tool from scratch isolated from the traditional appraisal methods such as CBA and MCA. Rather, a combination of traditional and sustainable-specific tools would likely be the best option to come up with a robust solution for a thorough appraisal of transport projects and policies. The authors suggest to build sustainability appraisal tools upon the basis of already existing methods that rightly measure economic and environmental impacts, by completing them with additional aspects that the concept of sustainability incorporates, such as the need to account for social impacts (equity, job creation, regional balance, security, gender, etc.), and the need to consider in a more precise way the consequences that present decisions may end up having on future generations.

In order to address such an evaluation, there are many challenges that require further investigations. There is still a lot of work ahead to identify and quantify social impacts by capturing those aspects that are not included in conventional economic analyses. Another crucial aspect to keep on doing research is the way of considering the impact of nonrenewable resources and the consequences that they may have on future generation, which is very much related to the concept of the social discount rate, and to what extent human-made capital and natural resources are interchangeable. Particularly interesting is also to study the impact of uncertainty in assessing sustainability given the rapid evolution of technological solutions and the impact they may have on current sustainability problems such as the creation of renewable substitutes. Finally, it is necessary to develop transparent approaches to evaluate similar impacts within different economic, social and environmental contexts.

References

Almansa, C., Calatrava, J., 2007. Reconciling sustainability and discounting in cost-benefit analysis: a methodological proposal. Ecol. Econ. 60 (4), 712–725. https://doi.org/10.1016/j.ecolecon.2006.05.002.

Awadh, O., 2017. Sustainability and green building rating systems: LEED, BREEAM, GSAS and Estidama critical analysis. J. Build. Eng. 11, 25–29.

Baker, J.W., Lepech, M.D., 2009, September. Treatment of uncertainties in life cycle assessment. In: Paper Presented at the 10th International Conference on Structural Safety and Reliability (ICOSSAR09), Osaka.

Bergqvist, R., Macharis, C., Meers, D., Woxenius, J., 2015. Making hinterland transport more sustainable a multi actor multi criteria analysis. Res. Transp. Bus. Manag. 14, 80–89.

Browne, D., Ryan, L., 2011. Comparative analysis of evaluation techniques for transport policies. Environ. Impact Assess. Rev. 31 (3), 226–233.

Bueno, P.C., Vassallo, J.M., 2015. Setting the weights of sustainability criteria for the appraisal of transport projects. Transport 30 (3), 298–306.

Bueno, P.C., Vassallo, J.M., Cheung, K., 2013a. Road Infrastructure Design for Optimizing Sustainability. Final Report. European Investment Bank. StareBEI Programme.

Bueno, P.C., Vassallo, J.M., Cheung, K., 2013b. Road infrastructure design for optimizing sustainability. Literature review. In: TRANSyT Working Paper 2013-01-EN.

Bueno, P.C., Vassallo, J.M., Cheung, K., 2015a. Sustainability assessment of transport infrastructure projects: a review of existing tools and methods. Transplant. Rev. 35 (5), 622–649.

Bueno, P.C., Vassallo, J.M., Cheung, K., 2015b. Road infrastructure design for optimizing sustainability. In: TRANSyT Working Paper 2015-01-EN. Universidad Politécnica de Madrid, Spain.

Chaharbaghi, K., Willis, R., 1999. The study and practice of sustainable development. Eng. Manag. J. 9 (1), 41–48. https://doi.org/10.1049/em:19990115.

Daly, H.E., Cobb Jr., J.B., 1989. For the Common Good: Redirecting the Economy Toward Community, the Environment, and a Sustainable Future. Beacon Press.

Dean, M., 2020. Multicriteria analysis. Chapter 6. In: Mouter, N. (Ed.), Standard Appraisal Methods. Advances in Transport Policy and Planning, vol. 6. Elsevier, Amsterdam.

European Commission, 2009. Impact Assessment Guidelines. Published Reports of the European Commission. Retrieved from: http://ec.europa.eu/smart-regulation/impact/commission_guidelines/docs/iag_2009_en.pdf.

European Commission, 2020. Taxonomy: Final Report of the Technical Expert Group on Sustainable Finance. Published Reports of the European Commission. Retrieved from: https://ec.europa.eu/info/sites/info/files/business_economy_euro/banking_and_finance/documents/200309-sustainable-finance-teg-final-report-taxonomy_en.pdf.

Frey, S.D., Harrison, D.J., Billett, E., 2000. Environmental assessment of electronic products using LCA and ecological footprint. In: Joint International Congress and Exhibition, Electronics Goes Green, Berlin.

Geudens, T., Macharis, C., De Brucker, K., Van Malderen, F., 2009. Multi-actor multi-criteria analysis (MAMCA) as a technique for the evaluation of traffic safety measures. In: Macharis, Turcksin (Eds.), Proceedings of the BIVEC-GIBET Transport Research Day Part I. VUBPRESS, pp. 943–957.

Gilmour, D., Blackwood, D., Banks, L., Wilson, F., 2011. Sustainable development indicators for major infrastructure projects. Proc. Inst. Civ. Eng. Munic. Eng. 164 (1), 15–24.

Graedel, T.E., Klee, R.J., 2002. Getting serious about sustainability. Environ. Sci. Technol. 36, 523–529.

Gudmundsson, H., Höjer, M., 1996. Sustainable development principles and their implications for transport. Ecol. Econ. 19 (3), 269–282.

Gühnemann, A., Laird, J.J., Pearman, A.D., 2012. Combining cost-benefit and multi-criteria analysis to prioritise a national road infrastructure programme. Transp. Policy 23, 15–24.

Hirsch, G., 1999. Nachhaltige Entwicklung und der Wert der Natur [Sustainable development and the value of nature]. Gaia 8 (4), 269–274.

Hirsch, A., 2012. Overview of sustainability rating system trends in transportation. In: Presented at 92nd Annual Meeting of the Transportation Research Board, Washington, D.C.

Huang, I.B., Keisler, J., Linkov, I., 2011. Multi-criteria decision analysis in environmental sciences: ten years of applications and trends. Sci. Total Environ. 409 (19), 3578–3594. https://doi.org/10.1016/j.scitotenv.2011.06.022.

Iacono, M., Levinson, D., 2015. Methods for estimating the economic impact of transportation improvements: an interpretive review. In: Hickman, R., Givoni, M., Bonilla, D., Banister, D. (Eds.), Handbook on Transport and Development. Edward Elgar, Cheltenham, UK/Northhampton, MA, USA, pp. 243–258.

International Federation of Consulting Engineers, 2012. State of the World Report 2012. Sustainable Infrastructure. Published Reports of the International Federation of National Member Associations of Consulting Engineers (FIDIC). Retrieved from: http://fidic.org/books/state-world-report-2012sustainable-infrastructure.

Janic, M., 2003. Multicriteria evaluation of high-speed rail, transrapid maglev and air passenger transport in Europe. Transp. Plan. Technol. 26 (6), 491–512. https://doi.org/10.1080/0308106032000167373.

Jansson, A., Hammer, M., Folke, C., Costanza, R., 1994. Investing in natural capital—why, what and how? In: Jansson, A., Hammer, M., Folke, C., Costanza, R. (Eds.), Investing in Natural Capital—The Ecological Economics Approach to Sustainability. Island Press, Covelo, FL, pp. 1–20.

Jesinghaus, J., 2014. Bellagio principles for assessing sustainable development. In: Michalos, A. (Ed.), Encyclopedia of Quality of Life and Well-Being Research. Springer Publishers.

Jones, H., Moura, F., Domingos, T., 2014. Transport infrastructure project evaluation using cost-benefit analysis. Procedia. Soc. Behav. Sci. 111, 400–409. https://doi.org/10.1016/j.sbspro.2014.01.073.

Jørgensen, A., Le Bocq, A., Nazarkina, L., Hauschild, M., 2008. Methodologies for social life cycle assessment. Int. J. Life Cycle Assess. 13 (2), 96–103. https://doi.org/10.1065/lca2007.11.367.

Kabir, G., Sadiq, R., Tesfamariam, S., 2013. A review of multi-criteria decision-making methods for infrastructure management. Struct. Infrastruct. Eng. 10, 1176–1210. https://doi.org/10.1080/15732479.2013.795978.

Kates, R.W., Clark, W.C., Corell, R., Hall, J.M., Jaeger, C.C., Lowe, I., McCarthy, J.J., Schellnhuber, H.J., Bolin, B., Dickson, N.M., et al., 2001. Sustainability science. Science 292 (5517), 641–642.

Keoleian, G.A., Spitzley, D.V., 2006. Life cycle based sustainability metrics. In: Abraham, M. (Ed.), Sustainability Science and Engineering: Defining Principles. Elsevier B.V, Amsterdam, pp. 127–159.

Koopmans, C.C., Mouter, N., 2020. Cost-Benefit Analysis. Chapter 1. In: Mouter, N. (Ed.), Standard Appraisal Methods. Advances in Transport Policy and Planning, vol. 6. Elsevier, Amsterdam.

Kowalski, K., Stagl, S., Madlener, R., Omann, I., 2009. Sustainable energy futures: methodological challenges in combining scenarios and participatory multi-criteria analysis. Eur. J. Oper. Res. 197 (3), 1063–1074. https://doi.org/10.1016/j.ejor.2007.12.049.

Lee, J., Edil, T., Benson, C., Tinjum, J., 2011, January. Evaluation of variable affecting sustainable highway design using the BE^{2}ST-in-HighwaysTM system. In: The 90th Annual Meeting of the Transportation Research Board, Washington, DC.

Liang, S., 2012. International experiences on sustainable scoring system: comparisons and applications. In: Paper Presented at the 6th International Association for China Planning Conference, Wuhan.

Loiseau, E., Junqua, G., Roux, P., Bellon-Maurel, V., 2012. Environmental assessment of a territory: an overview of existing tools and methods. J. Environ. Manage. 112, 213–225. https://doi.org/10.1016/j.jenvman.2012.07.024.

Macharis, C., De Witte, A., Ampe, J., 2009. The multi-actor, multi-criteria analysis methodology (MAMCA) for the evaluation of transport projects: theory and practice. J. Adv. Transp. 43 (2), 183–202.

Marshall, J.D., Toffel, M.W., 2019. Framing the elusive concept of sustainability: a sustainability hierarchy. Environ. Sci. Tech. 39 (3), 673–682.

Mieg, H.A., 2010. Sustainability and innovation in urban development: concept and case. Sustain. Dev. 20 (4), 251–263.

Mouter, N., 2018. A critical assessment of discounting policies for transport cost-benefit analysis in five European practices. Eur. J. Transp. Infrastruct. Res. 18 (4), 389–412.

Mouter, N., Dean, M., Koopmans, C., Vassallo, J.M. 2020. Comparing cost-benefit analysis and multi-criteria analysis. Chapter 7. In: Mouter, N. (Ed.), Standard Appraisal Methods. Advances in Transport Policy and Planning, vol. 6. Elsevier, Amsterdam.

Muench, S.T., Armstrong, A., Allen, B., 2012. Sustainable roadway design and construction in federal lands highway program. J. Transp. Res. Board 2271 (1), 19–30. https://doi.org/10.3141/2271-03.

Munasinghe, M., 2001. Sustainable development and climate change: applying the sustainomics transdisciplinary meta-framework. Int. J. Global. Environ. Issues 1, 13–55. https://doi.org/10.1504/IJGENVI.2001.000970.

Munasinghe, M., Sunkel, O., Miguel, C.D., 2001. The Sustainability of Long-Term Growth: Socioeconomic and Ecological Perspectives. Edward Elgar Publishing Ltd. Retrieved from: http://www.cabdirect.org/abstracts/20023109930.html.

Munda, G., Nijkamp, P., Rietveld, P., 1998. Environmental decision making: a comparison between cost-benefit analysis and multicriteria decision aid. In: Faucheux, S., O'Connor, M., van der Straaten, J. (Eds.), Sustainable Development: Concepts, Rationalities and Strategies. Economy & Environment, vol. 13. Springer, Dordrecht, pp. 227–238.

Nattrass, B., Altomare, M., 1999. The Natural Step for Business: Wealth, Ecology and the Evolutionary Corporation. New Society Publishers, Gabriola Island, BC.

OECD, 2010. Guidance on Sustainability Impact Assessment. OECD Publishing, Paris, https://doi.org/10.1787/9789264086913-en.

O'Riordan, T., 1988. The politics of sustainability. In: Turner, R.K. (Ed.), Sustainable Environmental Management: Principle and Practice. Belhaven Press; Boulder: Westview Press, London, pp. 29–50.

Parkin, S., 2000. Sustainable development: the concept and the practical challenge. Proc. Inst. Civ. Eng. 138 (6), 3–8.

Parkin, S., Sommer, F., Uren, S., 2003. Sustainable development: understanding the concept and practical challenge. Proc. Inst. Civ. Eng.-Eng. Sustain. 156 (1), 19–26.

Paul, B.D., 2008. A history of the concept of sustainable development: literature review. Ann. Univ. Oradea Econ. Sci. Ser. 17 (2), 576–580.

Pezzey, J., 1989. Economic analysis of sustainable growth and sustainable development. In: World Bank Environment Department Working Paper No. 15. Washington, D.C. The World Bank.

Radermacher, W., 1999. Indicators, green accounting and environment statistics—information requirements for sustainable development. Int. Stat. Rev. 67 (3), 339–354.

Ramani, T.L., Zietsman, J., Gudmundsson, H., Hall, R.P., Marsden, G., 2011. Framework for sustainability assessment by transportation agencies. J. Transp. Res. Board 2242, 9–18. Transportation Research Board of the National Academies, Washington, D.C.

Reap, J., Roman, F., Duncan, S., Bras, B., 2008. A survey of unresolved problems in life cycle assessment. Int. J. Life Cycle Assess. 13 (5), 374–388. https://doi.org/10.1007/s11367-008-0009-9.

Reid, L., Davis, A., Bevan, T., 2012. An approach for integrating sustainability into roadway project development. In: Paper Presented at the 92nd Annual Meeting of the Transportation Research Board, Washington, DC.

Säynäjoki, A., Heinonen, J., Junnila, S., 2011. Carbon footprint assessment of a residential development project. Int. J. Environ. Sci. Dev. 2 (2), 116–123.

Scholz, R.W., 2011. Environmental Literacy in Science and Society: From Knowledge to Decisions. Cambridge University Press, Cambridge (UK).

Schoolman, E.D., Guest, J.S., Bush, K.F., Bell, A.R., 2012. How interdisciplinary is sustainability research? Analyzing the structure of an emerging scientific field. Sustain. Sci. 7 (1), 67–80.

Sev, A., 2011. A comparative analysis of building environmental assessment tools and suggestions for regional adaptations. Civ. Eng. Environ. Syst. 28, 231–245. https://doi.org/10.1080/10286608.2011.588327.

Sharma, S., Geerlings, H., 2017. Sustainability benefits assessment in urban transport project appraisal: a new method of transport project appraisal. 2017, In: Bisello, A., et al. (Eds.), Smart and Sustainable Planning for Cities and Regions, Green Energy and Technology. Springer International Publishing, Switzerland, pp. 185–203.

Shelbourn, M., Bouchlaghem, D., Anumba, C., Carrillo, P., Khalfan, M., Glass, J., 2006. Managing knowledge in the context of sustainable construction. Electron. J. Inf. Technol. Constr. 11, 57–71.
Sijtsma, F.J., 2006. Project Evaluation, Sustainability and Accountability: Combining Cost-Benefit Analysis (CBA) and Multi-Criteria Analysis (MCA). Doctoral Dissertation, University of Groningen. Retrieved from: http://www.waddenacademie.nl/fileadmin/inhoud/pdf/06-wadweten/Proefschriften/Thesis_Sytsma.pdf.
Spanish Ministry ofPublic Works, 2015. Plan Estratégico de Infraestructuras Y Transporte (PEIT). https://www.fomento.gob.es/MFOM/LANG_CASTELLANO/_ESPECIALES/PEIT/.
Stamford, L., Azapagic, A., 2011. Sustainability indicators for the assessment of nuclear power. Energy 36 (10), 6037–6057.
Stripple, H., 2001. Life Cycle Assessment of Road: A Pilot Study for Inventory Analysis. (Report 96). Swedish Environmental Research Institute, Sweden.
Stripple, H., Erlandsson, M., 2004. Methods and Possibilities for Application of Life Cycle Assessment in Strategic Environmental Assessment of Transport Infrastructures (Report B1661). Swedish Environmental Research Institute, Stockholm.
TEP, CEPS, 2010. Study on Social Impact Assessment as a Tool for Mainstreaming Social Inclusion and Social Protection Concerns in Public Policy in EU Member States. Published Reports of the European Commission, London. Retrieved from: http://csdle.lex.unict.it/docs/labourweb/Study-on-Social-Impact-Assessment-asa-tool-for-mainstreaming-social-inclusion-and-social-protection/2459.aspx.
Thomopoulos, N., Grant-Muller, S., Tight, M.R., 2009. Incorporating equity considerations in transport infrastructure evaluation: current practice and a proposed methodology. Eval. Program Plann. 32 (4), 351–359. https://doi.org/10.1016/j.evalprogplan.2009.06.013.
Treloar, G.J., Love, P.E., Crawford, R.H., 2004. Hybrid life-cycle inventory for road construction and use. J. Constr. Eng. Manag. 130 (1), 43–49. https://doi.org/10.1061/(ASCE)0733-9364(2004)130:1(43).
Tsai, C.Y., Chang, A.S., 2012. Framework for developing construction sustainability items: the example of highway design. J. Clean. Prod. 20 (1), 127–136.
Tudela, A., Akiki, N., Cisternas, R., 2006. Comparing the output of cost benefit and multi-criteria analysis. Transp. Res. A Policy Pract. 40 (5), 414–423. https://doi.org/10.1016/j.tra.2005.08.002.
Turner, R.K., 1993. Sustainable Environmental Economics and Management: Principles and Practice. Bellhaven Press, London.
University of Leeds, 2013. International Comparisons of Transport Appraisal Practice: Overview Report. Institute for Transport Studies, Faculty of Environment.
Veeravigrom, M., Muench, S.T., Kosonen, H., 2015, January. A global framework for sustainable roadway rating system. In: Paper Presented at the 94th Annual Meeting of the Transportation Research Board, Washington, DC.
Walker, G., 2010. Environmental justice, impact assessment and the politics of knowledge: the implications of assessing the social distribution of environmental outcomes. Environ. Impact Assess. Rev. 30 (5), 312–318.
Wang, J.-J., Jing, Y.-Y., Zhang, C.-F., Zhao, J.-H., 2009. Review on multi-criteria decision analysis aid in sustainable energy decision-making. Renew. Sustain. Energy Rev. 13 (9), 2263–2278. https://doi.org/10.1016/j.rser.2009.06.021.
World Commission on Environment and Development, 1987. Our Common Future (Brundtland Report). Oxford University Press, Oxford (UK).

CHAPTER THREE

Deliberative appraisal methods

Ruth Shortall*
TU Delft, Delft, The Netherlands
*Corresponding author: e-mail address: r.m.shortall@tudelft.nl

Contents

Abstract

Deliberative appraisal methods have gained popularity in recent years, due to an increased demand for public participation in government decision-making. There is a recognition that transportation policy appraisals need to take account of a diversity of views and disciplines, for which deliberative approaches are considered ideal. In comparison with other forms of citizen consultation or participation, deliberative approaches are regarded as the most promising in terms of fulfilling democratic ideals such as inclusiveness, equity and transparency. They are hence also likely to increase the legitimacy of decisions. Due to their unique characteristics, deliberative appraisal methods hold the potential to resolve some of the issues associated with commonly used traditional appraisal methods. Because of this, approaches that combine both traditional analytic and deliberative aspects are increasingly sought after, but remain in the early stages. Deliberation is based on the premise that a diverse group of citizens, if given adequate information, resources and time to deliberate on a given topic, can produce a rational, informed judgment. Participants must consider a question from multiple viewpoints, exchange perspectives, opinions, and understandings and think critically about all possible options. This process has been shown to build civic capacity, produce better decisions and provide unique and useful insights for policy-makers. A deliberative event may include a small group of participants or many hundreds. Purely deliberative approaches

Advances in Transport Policy and Planning, Volume 7
ISSN 2543-0009
https://doi.org/10.1016/bs.atpp.2020.07.003

may result in qualitative outputs such as a verdict or report, whereas analytic-deliberative approaches may involve monetizing values, voting or ranking in order to reach workable recommendations. While the application of deliberative approaches in the transport domain is still in its early stages, this chapter provides an overview of the best-known deliberative approaches in use in policy-making today as well as introducing new developments in the physical and online spaces.

Keywords: Deliberative methods, Analytic-deliberative methods, Deliberative appraisal, Collective decision-making, Deliberative democracy, Digital deliberation

1. Introduction

The broadening context of policy appraisal in the last few decades, from that of simpler project-based approaches to the more complex consideration of plans, programs or policies (Owens et al., 2004), and a greater emphasis on communicative planning (Healey, 1999) has seen deliberative appraisal methods rising in popularity in many policy sectors. They have been used in policy appraisals on issues as diverse as geoengineering (Bellamy et al., 2014) to biodiversity policy (Lienhoop et al., 2015) to public health (Paul et al., 2008) or urban agriculture (Miccoli et al., 2014). Even so, while their potential for enhancing policy appraisals (Owens et al., 2004; Raymond et al., 2014), promoting sustainable transportation policy (Whitmarsh et al., 2007) and for providing decision-support on complex or wicked problems (Cascetta et al., 2015; Hoppe, 2011) is widely acknowledged, in many countries, transportation policy-making has been slow to integrate deliberative practices (Murray, 2011). For the most part, deliberative methods have been developed by non-governmental organizations or academics, rather than governments themselves (Gregory et al., 2008). Nonetheless, use of these approaches is gradually increasing (Vigar, 2017) in the EU (Aparicio, 2018) and elsewhere. Governments in countries such as the UK (Vigar, 2017) or US (Quick and Zhao, 2011) Australia (Gregory et al., 2008) are taking clear steps in this direction.

This chapter provides an overview of various deliberative appraisal methods that may be used in the appraisal of transportation plans or policies. Let us clarify here what we mean by deliberative methods, since the terms "participatory" and "deliberative" are often used interchangeably. The main differences between participatory methods and deliberative methods relate to the type of participation, the numbers of participants and how participants are selected (Carson and Elstub, 2019). Participatory methods encompass a diverse array of opportunities to participate with varying levels of citizen empowerment or influence on the final decision, including for instance information provision and consultation (Arnstein, 1969). Deliberative methods are a small subset of participatory methods—they involve only one very specific means of participation: deliberation, where citizens must become well informed about a topic and exchange views with others. In general, participatory methods can involve large numbers of participants, whereas deliberative methods tend toward smaller, but representative, groups, to ensure high quality deliberations occur (since this is unlikely to be possible with large groups) (Carson and Elstub, 2019). Participatory methods tend to favor self-selection by participants, whereas deliberative methods use techniques of random selection to ensure a group is representative of the wider population (Courant, 2017).

In the introduction, we will first take a brief look at reasons for the rising popularity of deliberative methods for transportation policy appraisal. In Section 2, current deliberative methods are described in detail. In Section 3, deliberative methods are compared with other appraisal methods and potential advantages, disadvantages and synergies are identified. Criticisms of deliberative methods are also outlined. Finally, in Section 4, some future research challenges are discussed.

1.1 A growing interest in deliberative methods for transportation policy appraisal

Public participation in policy-making has been on the rise since the 1980s, when a clear shift toward involving the public in decision-making, with increasing emphasis on deliberative methods, took place in the developed world (Dryzek, 2002). In a general sense, this shift can be attributed to a combination of factors. Firstly, declining public trust in institutions has led to a search for ways to regain legitimacy (Fishkin and Mansbridge, 2017). Secondly, the increasing complexity of social systems, with their multiplicity of value systems and worldviews means that decision-making has in turn become more complex (Cass, 2006).

There is a growing recognition that different types of knowledge or information may legitimately inform policy appraisal methods (Vigar, 2017). Until recently, transportation policy appraisals have been dominated by a utilitarian/efficiency paradigm, but there is an increasing realization that this needs to change to reflect a more complex policy environment and to include the broader public (Handy, 2008). Transport planning is no longer separate from other planning processes and overlaps with other economic, social, environmental and spatial aspects of planning (Beukers et al., 2015).

A far greater diversity of perspectives and goals than in the past must now be taken into account, especially when assessing the sustainability of transportation policy (Lindenau and Böhler-Baedeker, 2014; Sagaris, 2018; Whitmarsh et al., 2007). Likewise, growing criticisms of the narrow scope or theoretical assumptions of common "technical-rational" approaches to transport policy appraisal like CBA (Cass, 2006; Næss, 2006), the four-step model (FSM) (Evans et al., 2007) and MCDA (Frame and O'Connor, 2011; Le Pira et al., 2017) have lead governments to rethink their suitability for addressing broader, complex and uncertain issues (Bellamy et al., 2014). Numerous scholars (Aparicio, 2018; Beukers et al., 2015; Healey, 1999; Lowry, 2010; Owens et al., 2004; Vigar, 2017) advise of the need to make more room for communicative planning, citizen dialogue and learning alongside a technical-rational perspective in transportation policy-making. Deliberative methods can facilitate this need and can furthermore bridge the gap between the broader public and representative institutions (Jonsson, 2015), by expanding and democratizing the decision-making process (Kelemen and Saarikoski, 2015). This provides a way to increase legitimacy and address declining trust (Fishkin and Mansbridge, 2017).

2. Deliberative appraisal methods

Deliberative appraisal methods can be applied at various stages of the policy cycle, from agenda setting to policy development to decision-making or implementation. This section will explain the basic principles and workings of deliberative appraisal methods, and then introduce, with examples, a selection of tried and tested deliberative methods that have been applied in transportation and various other policy arenas, in the last few decades. The newest developments in deliberative methods are also discussed.

2.1 How do deliberative methods work?

Deliberative appraisal methods can be applied in diverse decision contexts: from priority setting to mediating conflicts. Such methods may use a variety of tools and techniques from different disciplines, and may be used on either small or large spatial scales (Kelemen and Saarikoski, 2015). First, let us distinguish deliberative appraisal methods from analytical or technical rational methods. Analytical or technical-rational appraisal methods place an emphasis on factual perspectives and ensuring that these are based on valid methods and procedures. Their outputs may involve monetizing, ranking or rating. Deliberative appraisal methods, on the other hand, emphasize diverse values, communication, argumentation and combining expert and lay knowledge (Raymond et al., 2014). Because each type of appraisal offers unique insights and benefits, many scholars now advocate for the integration of deliberative methods with analytical technical-rational approaches in order to have the best of both worlds (Chilvers, 2008; Nyerges and Aguirre, 2011; Raymond et al., 2014).

The Deliberative Democracy Consortium defines deliberation as "*an approach to decision-making in which citizens consider relevant facts from multiple points of view, converse with one another to think critically about options before them and enlarge their perspectives, opinions, and understandings.*" The basic reasoning behind deliberative approaches is that a diverse group of citizens, if given adequate information, resources and time to deliberate on a given topic, can produce a rational, informed judgment. Furthermore, ordinary citizens are less likely to make decisions based on political interests or be subjected to pressure from interest groups (Fishkin et al., 2017). Deliberation can in theory be carried out with any group of people and if using online tools can theoretically involve very large numbers of people.

Although a wide variety of approaches exist, the best-known methods, such as citizen's juries, consensus conferences or deliberative polling center around mini-publics. A mini-public is intended to provide a demographically representative sample of the greater public, which is regarded by decision-makers as a proxy or microcosm for the views of the general public. Normally, citizens are recruited via (quasi)random sampling or sortition. Total attendance for one such event can range from 15 to 1000 participants. Deliberation is usually carried out in small groups of maximum 15 people, within an organized setting. This may or may not occur alongside elected representatives. Groups are usually provided with information or submissions from interest groups providing arguments for or against various options. They may also have access to experts which hold different points of view (Fishkin and Mansbridge, 2017). While deliberative methods embody the principles of deliberative democracy, they may also act as a bridge between deliberative and direct democracy if, for example, they are followed by a referendum or popular vote.

Deliberative methods may be categorized into purely deliberative or analytic-deliberative (UK National Ecosystem Assessment, 2014). Purely deliberative methods involve reflection on exchanged information and points of view, with a view to cooperatively constructing the views of participants. These methods, some of which are mentioned above, may be stand-alone or used as one of a number of appraisal approaches that will inform a policy decision. Outcomes of purely deliberative approaches tend to be qualitative and be expressed in the form of recommendations or verdicts.

Analytic-deliberative methods integrate deliberative approaches with formal decision-support tools and have combined or quantitative outcomes which may include rankings or ratings (Kenter, 2014). However, numerous formats are possible, each with their own advantages and disadvantages. For example, large-scale data collection (e.g., via surveys) could be followed by deliberation to address trade-offs and incommensurable values, whereas a deliberative event could be followed by representative democratic validation to enhance legitimacy (Raymond, 2014). While pragmatic use of this type of approach may make sense, it is also important to carefully consider the design of the process. The different underlying assumptions or rationalities, valuation processes, types of representation and the degree of involvement of the decision-maker can have a huge bearing on the outcome of this kind of integrated appraisal (Raymond, 2014). The methods presented in this chapter are not intended to form an exhaustive list but more of a "sampling menu" of deliberative methods that have so far been used for transportation policy appraisal today.

2.2 Purely deliberative methods

Purely deliberative methods may be used in various planning or policy arenas. The methods presented here differ somewhat from each other in terms of number of participants and timeframe, but generally adhere to the same basic format of participation selection, followed by learning, deliberation and decision-making. These methods provide qualitative outputs in the form of citizen verdicts or recommendations, which may or may not be binding, and may be used to inform strategies, plans or policies. However, in practice, some methods mentioned here may not always be "*purely*" deliberative. For example, in a citizen's jury, if a large number of recommendations are produced during the decision phase, they may need to be reduced by using voting methods (Huitema et al., 2007). The most well-known of these methods, citizen's juries, consensus conferences, citizen's assemblies (and their variations) which have been used in transportation policy appraisal, are described in this section.

2.2.1 Citizen's juries

First developed in 1971 by Ned Crosby of the Jefferson Centre in the USA, citizen's juries, a form of mini-public, have since expanded to many other countries and are applied in a variety of policy areas. Citizen's juries have been used for providing citizen verdicts on transportation policy. Several examples re available from Baumann and White (2010), including the use of citizen's juries for controversies regarding traffic limitation in Italy, bypass roads in Germany, and highway extensions in Australia.

Further examples can be found in Ontario, Canada, where the citizen's juries gave a verdict on the Hamilton Light Rail in Ontario in 2016, in Australia where they provided recommendations on road safety measures and biking and in London where they provided recommendations for disabled passengers for Transport for London (TfL) in 2011 for the Mayor's Transport Strategy and Accessibility Implementation Plan.

In a citizen's jury, as a general rule a small group (12–25) of citizens is randomly selected or stratified to be representative of the broader community. However, much larger numbers have been involved in some cases. The group deliberates on a policy issue and provides a recommendation or verdict in the form of a report to the organizing body. The decision on the issue is reached either by consensus or voting. Citizen's juries are often used along with or as part of a greater participatory process, which could include other forms of participation such as surveys or online forums. Normally a specific question or scope as well as their commitment regarding the response is defined by the decision-maker and the results are used in an advisory capacity and decision-makers may or may not agree to implement the recommendations. A jury event may be held over 1–5 days, over a number of weekends or spread over a number of months. In some cases, members of the general public may sit in or observe some or all of the process (Jefferson Centre, 2020). The process for a citizen's jury may vary but consists of four main phases: selection of participants, information provision, deliberation and decisions and recommendations.

For the selection of participants, independent professional practitioners are commissioned to organize the citizen's jury. They are mostly responsible for recruiting participants, selecting witnesses, facilitation and other logistical tasks. Experts and other stakeholders are recruited to present balanced evidence (from different viewpoints) to the jury for consideration. In the information phase, jurors receive information which builds their understanding of the issue at hand. Prior to the first meeting, jurors will receive background information and during the meeting, they attend presentations from experts on the topics, where they have opportunities to ask questions. Witnesses may include technical experts, or stakeholders representing particular positions on an issue. Jurors receive training on working in groups and on critical questioning techniques to ensure they can process the information in an unbiased way. The deliberation phase involves jurors working in small groups to discuss evidence and work on producing final recommendations, or a collective verdict.

2.2.1.1 Regional resident's reference panels

A Canadian variation on citizen's juries, regional residents references panels are non-compulsory public juries that provide policy advice to public and elected officials. They are generally organized by the government and meet over a longer time than citizen's juries (weeks or months) to learn about, discuss, and provide non-binding recommendations on a contentious public issue. They may have between 14 and 54 members, representative of the region they represent.[a] Regional residence reference panels have been used numerous times to provide transportation policy advice in Canada. Examples include the Metrolinx Regional Residents' Reference Panel on Transportation Investment (MASSLBP, 2013), the Greater Toronto Airports Authority Residents' Reference Panel on Airport Growth and Noise Fairness[b] and the Metrolinx Residents' Reference Panel on the Davenport Community Rail Overpass.[c]

2.2.1.2 Planning cells

A variation on citizen's juries is the planning cell. Planning cells were developed in the 1970s in Germany by Peter Dienel, of the Research Institute for Citizens' Participation at the University of Wuppertal in Germany. Planning cells involve a small group of members of the public that help develop solutions for a specific planning or policy problem. In contrast to citizen's juries, they tend to be used to find solutions for urgent problems for which a number of options are available, and for issues without a large degree of polarization in public attitudes. The majority of planning cells have been used in urban planning in Germany with some examples to be found in Austria, Switzerland, Spain and the USA. In contrast to citizen's juries, a number of planning cells tend to be held concurrently with around 25 participants each. Furthermore, facilitation is mainly done by issue specialists, rather than process specialists (Escobar and Elstub, 2017).

[a] https://participedia.net/method/635.
[b] https://www.masslbp.com/work-projects.
[c] https://participedia.net/case/4605.

2.2.2 Consensus conferences

First developed in Denmark in the 1980s by the Danish Board of Technology, consensus conferences were intended to provide parliament with citizen advice on emerging technologies on topics that tend to be controversial or expert-dominated. To date, consensus conferences have been used in various countries by technology assessment institutes, science museums, ethical committees, research committees, parliamentary offices, advisory agencies, policy centers/think-tanks, independent or private foundations and NGOs (Nielsen et al., 2006) on topics such as plant biotechnology, medical technology or health policy.[d] Essentially, the consensus conference is similar to a jury, except that lay citizens and experts deliberate on technical problems.

The goals of a consensus conferences can range from broadening and qualifying the public debate to informing policy making or legislative decision-making to altering the power balance between e.g., technical experts and lay people (Nielsen et al., 2006). Consensus conferences have been used in diverse policy arenas in Denmark and a number of countries including Australia, Argentina, New Zealand, Korea, Israel, Japan, Canada, UK and the USA. As an example of how consensus conferences can be used in transportation policy appraisal, in 2001 Danish consensus conferences on traffic and road pricing was held by the Technology Council in with the Transportation Council (Denmark) 2001.[e] The process for a consensus conferences may vary but consists of several phases: selection of participants, preparation, selection of experts and witnesses, information provision and questioning, deliberation, decisions and recommendations (Nielsen et al., 2006).

Participants are recruited by inviting a random sample of 1000 or more lay citizens, with no prior knowledge of the topic, which is stratified to reflect a variety of socio-demographic criteria. The final panel is made up of 10–25 participants. This group takes part in two preparatory weekends and then a 4-day conference. A unique feature of this method is that the initiative lies with the citizens in defining the topics to be discussed. Like

[d] http://people.ucalgary.ca/~pubconf/Education/grundahl.htm.

[e] The question to the citizen panel was: "*For many people it is a necessity to have and use a car. The traffic has increased with 60% over the last 20 years and it is the traffic in cars, which has the biggest growth. At the same time there is a significant increase in the crowd problems on the roads in and around the bigger cities and air pollution, accidents and noise still make problems. If there is a need to reduce the traffic growth several point out that variable road pricing are a possible means. Should road pricing be introduced in Denmark? And if so, how should the system be organized?.*"

citizen's juries, consensus conferences are organized by an independent advisory committee. This committee selects the citizens, compiles the list of experts from which the citizens choose, develops information packs and selects facilitators. In recent cases, the organizing committee has allowed participants to compile the list of experts (Escobar and Elstub, 2017). The committee is responsible for maintaining impartiality and deliberative quality throughout the entire process. Consensus conferences take place in the public view: press and members of the public are permitted to attend.

The selected panel receives a detailed information pack and has time to prepare for the conference in advance. The first stage of the consensus conference involves citizens meeting for a series of preparatory weekends to learn about the topic at hand and the conference process. At this stage, citizens also select experts and interest groups who will present to the citizens in the second stage of the conference. The second stage of a consensus conference involves citizens attending around 4 days of presentations from various experts or interest groups. Citizens may question the experts during the presentations. Finally, citizens deliberate and produce a report which reflects their decision.

2.2.3 Citizen's assemblies

Citizen's assemblies are a relatively novel democratic innovation which has seen success in various countries such as Ireland, Canada, Estonia, France and Belgium. A well-known recent outcome of a citizen's assembly was the referendum on same-sex marriage in Ireland. Citizen's assemblies have been held in order to provide input to policy-making on diverse topics from tackling climate change (France) to reforming the electoral system (Canada, The Netherlands). The cross-cutting 2017 Irish citizen's assembly on climate change[f] requested 99 citizens to explicitly focus on the transport sector (among others) in their deliberations (Devaney et al., 2020). The recommendations were reached by ballot paper voting and followed two weekends of deliberation. Recommendations to the state[g] included having low carbon public vehicles, increase spending on public transport, increasing the number of bus lanes, cycle lanes, park and ride facilities within 5 years

[f] https://www.citizensassembly.ie/en/how-the-state-can-make-ireland-a-leader-in-tackling-climate-change/.

[g] https://www.citizensassembly.ie/en/how-the-state-can-make-ireland-a-leader-in-tackling-climate-change/recommendations/.

and increasing the resilience of public land and infrastructure. In particular, they recommended that the state immediately support the transition to electric vehicles, by developing a national network of charging points or providing incentives for the purchase of electric vehicles. They also recommended that the state undertake a comprehensive assessment of the vulnerability of all critical transport infrastructure with a view to building resilience to ongoing climate change and extreme weather events.

Citizen's assemblies can last for several months and until now have included 100–150 participants (Escobar and Elstub, 2017); significantly more than citizen's juries or consensus conferences. Citizens are selected randomly from an electoral register and invited to participate. Those who express interest in participation are further sampled at random, with the aim of ensuring the assembly is representative of the broader population in terms of age, gender and geographical location. The agenda for the citizen's assembly is usually set by the government (although this is not a requirement). The process for a citizen's assembly is not entirely standardized but normally occurs in several (5–6) phases (Escobar and Elstub, 2017):

1. Learning phase: Over several weekends participants hear presentations by experts, take part in group discussions and have access to a range of source materials. The goal is that citizens may fully grasp the complexities of the issues under consideration.
2. Public consultation phase: Over several weeks, the chosen citizens run public hearings in their local constituencies to gather information and opinions from other members of the public.
3. Deliberative phase: The citizens discuss the evidence and agree their final proposal.
4. Voting on options: Following the deliberation, a vote among the participants is usually conducted to decide a final outcome.
5. Presentation of results: Final proposal is sent to legislature or parliament (policy decision may or may not be binding, depending on the country).
6. In some cases a referendum for entire country, on proposed recommendations or changes may be held.

Although citizen's assemblies have never been permanent fixtures in government decision-making, this may be changing. In February 2019, the Ostbelgien community in Belgium voted to embed permanent citizen participation into legislation. They have established a Citizen's Council to complement the elected parliament. This makes them the first region in the world to institutionalize randomly selected citizens in political decision-making. The G1000 group, known for their work on organizing citizen summits,[h] was instrumental in the design of this democratic innovation. Citizens are drawn by lot to sit on the Citizen Council which will decide each year on the topics needing consultation. These topics are then discussed by a temporary, independent citizen's assembly (also drawn by lot), and will lead to concrete policy recommendations. The parliament of the community has committed to using the results of the citizen's assembly in their policy-making process. The Citizen Council is assigned a permanent secretariat and an annual budget by the parliament and consists of 24 members who hold their seat for 1½ years. The council can propose policy recommendations to the elected parliament on its own initiative or after a request. These recommendations will be based on the outcomes of regular citizen's assemblies. Each citizens' assembly should last about three weekends over 3 months and will have a maximum of 50 members. Participants are compensated for their participation (Dejaeghere, 2019).

2.3 Analytic-deliberative methods

Analytic-deliberative methods remain somewhat experimental and may take on a variety of forms. The term "analytic-deliberative" describes processes that reconcile "technocratic" and "citizen-centric" approaches (Burgess et al., 2007). These methods aim to balance traditional scientific or technical analysis with deliberation involving a diverse group of participants (Chilvers, 2008). Incorporating deliberation into appraisal can help participants express their preferences in various ways, for instance in terms of moral values as well as in monetary terms (Lo and Spash, 2013). For this reason, methods like deliberative monetary valuation, deliberative multi-criteria analysis and deliberative polling can be considered as analytic-deliberative methods. In this section, some examples of analytic-deliberative methods used in transportation policy appraisal are described.

2.3.1 Deliberative monetary valuation

Deliberative methods can be used to elicit economic values if they are combined with monetary approaches. Any method that generates monetary values in a group-based setting can be considered as deliberative monetary valuation (DMV). A DMV process can be carried out to elicit individual monetary values (individual willingness to pay or accept (WTP/A)) from

[h] In 2011, G1000 organized an experimental deliberative event, what they term a "citizen summit," in Brussels, independently of the Belgian government as an awareness-raising experiment in citizen participation in policy-making. Based on their experiences, they were consulted for the design of the Ostbelgien model.

a group, or social monetary values (social WTP/A estimates). Put simply, the final outputs depend on whether a group or an individual expresses the WTP/A values. A more detailed explanation can be found in (Fish et al., 2011).

An example of the use of a DMV approach in transportation policy appraisal is described in (Miccoli et al., 2015), who carried out a variation of deliberative monetary evaluation related to creating an alternative route for the East Elevated Expressway of Rome. The method was intended for measuring the social appreciation of community goods (old structures that the community wanted to repurpose into a recreational area) using a combination of stated preference techniques and deliberative methods. To value the community good, the researchers combined deliberative methods, based on an informed discussion of a sample of the community with stated preference methods (SPM). The deliberative phase was held first, involving a random sample of citizens, known as the valuation group (VG), which was statistically representative of the community in question. During a series of meetings, members of the VG were provided with necessary information and then discussed the social appreciation of the community good in question as a group. They were given the chance to ask experts and stakeholders questions to clarify their understanding of different viewpoints. The VG then stated their preference on the social importance attached to the community good. The members of the VG were asked to state value for the community good in terms of collective interest, rather than individual preference. This process produced a shared WTP value.

2.3.2 Deliberative multi-criteria analysis

Multi-criteria analysis (MCA) is a family of methods that may be more or less deliberative, depending on the design of the process, how stakeholders are involved and facilitated and how results are presented (Saarikoski et al., 2016). MCA in general is seen as methodologically suitable for dealing with plural value dimensions and hence for deliberative appraisal. However, the need for the integration of a transparent, participative dialogue process among stakeholders in MCA been increasingly acknowledged (Macharis and Bernardini, 2015; Saarikoski et al., 2016; Baudry et al., 2018). Dean (2019) point out that MCA involving stakeholders can vary greatly along a spectrum from analyst-led to fully participatory. Participants may be experts, citizens or stakeholders chosen by the researchers. Although research relating to more "participative" MCA is common (Macharis and Bernardini, 2015), examples of integrating deliberation into MCA for decision-making in the transportation sector are quite few. Dean (2019) tested the application of their proposed "participatory MCA" for choosing between potential project options for the South Fylde railway line in North West England. In this example, the researchers involved "multi-actors" in two middle stages of the process, i.e., criteria weighting and impact assessment. For mega transport infrastructure appraisal, Ward (2016) propose what they term "policy-led multi-criteria analysis," in which stakeholder groups may get involved at various stages of the process, although not at the initial problem-definition stage. In other sectors, further examples exist which could potentially be used in the transport sector. For instance, Munda (2004) proposed social multi-criteria analysis (SMCA) to tackle decision problems that represent a public choice. He argues that social problems are multidimensional and the evaluation of public plans or projects should be based on procedures that explicitly require the integration of a broad set of various and conflicting points of view. Another approach from the health sector, the deliberative mapping method proposed by Burgess et al. (2007) combines both the qualitative stakeholder analysis group based process and the quantitative multi-criteria mapping (MCM). During deliberative mapping, a group of citizens have regular meetings to discuss a particular problem, define options and criteria to measure each option. The options are then weighted and ranked in order to create a "map" of how each option performs compared to other views in the group. More recently, Williams and Fang (2018) proposed the "multiple participant multi-criteria" (MPMC) approach to policy formulation, which places emphasis on value-based rather than alternative based decision-making while performing a multi-criteria analysis. This is achieved by taking into account multiple participant perspectives, prior to identifying alternatives, along with their associated criteria during the MCA.

2.3.3 Deliberative polling

Developed by Professor James Fishkin of Stanford University in 1988, deliberative surveys or polls were initially developed in order to overcome the problem of a lack of citizen knowledge on public issues or trade-offs between different policy options. In order to make an informed decision, citizens must spend time and energy to educate themselves but often they lack incentives to do so. The method also offers more accurate insights into citizen opinion on complex issues compared with traditional polling and can aid politicians in public planning. Deliberative polling is furthermore a useful indicator for policy-makers whether access to comprehensive information and deliberation will change the community's views on a particular issue of concern (Gregory et al., 2008). Governments (local and regional) in a number of countries worldwide have used this method to poll public opinion more accurately on a variety of topics. Deliberative polling has been used in transport policy appraisal for example in Italy on the issue of high speed railways[i] or at the federal level in Canada,[j] where it was used by the Road Safety Authority to consult the public on options for reducing driver distraction. A further example Schweigert (2010) concerns the use of deliberative polling following the collapse of the Interstate 35W Bridge in Minneapolis, Minnesota in 2007. Researchers polled a random sample of 1003 residents of the seven-county metropolitan area of Saint Paul and Minneapolis to discover their level of support for a variety of transportation priorities and funding options. All those responding to the survey were invited to participate in an all-day deliberation on these topics. 70 people attended, and met in randomly-assigned small groups to discuss the issues and formulating questions to pose to panels of transportation experts and local policy-makers.

Deliberative polling measures the opinion of citizens before and after deliberation, which provides conditions where citizens are exposed to fair and balanced information and the views of other citizens. Citizens are given enough time to reflect on the information and also have access to expert panels of policy-makers. Citizens are selected randomly from the public and are remunerated for their participation. A deliberative poll may consist of several hundreds of participants, who are compensated for their time, though usually no more than 450 participate. The duration of events may vary, but normally they are completed in 1–2 days. Normally a deliberative poll follows a six-step process (Fishkin and Fishkin, 2018):

1. First poll: a random, representative sample of the public is contacted and asked to provide feedback on an initial questionnaire aimed at evaluating the knowledge, perceptions, and preferences of the general public on a specific question.
2. Recruitment: another random representative sample of citizens are contacted and asked to participate in a deliberative event to be held over the course of 1 or 2 days.

[i] https://cdd.stanford.edu/2007/results-of-deliberative-polling-on-immigrant-voting-and-high-speed-rail-in-italy/.

[j] https://www.iapss.org/2015/10/19/deliberative-democracy-at-the-federal-level-in-canada/.

3. Learning: before the event, selected participants receive balanced briefing materials that have been checked by a panel of experts on the topics to be discussed.
4. Deliberation: on the day of the deliberative event, participants are randomly assigned to small groups with trained moderators. During the group sessions, the participants are urged to developing questions to be posed to a panel of experts and policymakers at a final plenary session.
5. Second poll: participants fill out a second questionnaire on their opinions on the topic at hand. The results of the first and second poll are compared, and any changes in opinion are measured and analyzed.
6. Dissemination of results: the findings of the final poll are publicly circulated through the media and may be used to stimulate further debate and deliberations by politicians or policy-makers.

2.3.3.1 21st Century Town Meeting

A variation on deliberative polling, the 21st Century Town Meeting is a 1-day deliberative method developed in the late 1990s by America Speaks, a non-governmental organization based in the USA. The method was developed with the aim of increasing the number of people that can participate, without compromising the quality of deliberation. A unique feature of the method is the use of technology during an event.

21st Century Town Meetings have been held for diverse topics, including transportation. For instance, in 2002, the Hamilton County, Ohio, Regional Planning Commission used a 21st Century Town Meeting to develop a comprehensive plan for issues including employment, housing, transportation, and education. The event was attended by 1300 participations. As well as this, 11 community forums, one youth forum, and a weeklong online forum were held. The results were used to produce 160 specific strategies for helping the county reach its goals. The county commissioners endorsed the citizens' vision statement, and in November 2004, started implementing the citizen's priorities (Lukensmeyer and Brigham, 2002).

A 21st Century Town Meeting is held during 1 day and includes small groups (10 people) engaging in simultaneous face-to-face deliberations. In one event, hundreds or even thousands of people may participate. At the end of the event, a shared message is passed on to decision-makers. Technologies used include keypad polling, groupware computers, large screen projections and teleconferencing. Meetings may be held simultaneously across multiple locations. The representativeness of each group is checked via polling at the beginning of the meeting (America Speaks, 2020).

Professional facilitators lead the discussions in each group. Participants quickly record their ideas or responses to discussion questions on laptops and these results are reviewed by issues experts in real time, who identify key messages and themes coming from each table in the town hall. Participants use polling keypads to vote on key concerns or issues. The results of these votes are instantly visible to everyone on large projection screens. Citizens have access to decision-makers on various topic areas throughout the day. A summary report is prepared at the end of the day and distributed to all participants. Decision-makers must comment on how the results of the event will influence their actions going forward (Lukensmeyer, 1995).

2.4 Digital deliberation

Digital or online deliberation has been marked as a promising new approach to deliberation in transportation appraisal (Lowry, 2010). The internet could provide a virtual space with the ideal conditions for scaling up deliberation and facilitating the "public sphere" that deliberative theorists such as Jürgen Habermas advocate. For instance, Lowry (2010) created an online platform for policy decision-making on transportation improvement. A moderated asynchronous structured discussion tool was provided for participants who made a final proposal of projects and taxes. Wilson and Ramsey (2008) also provided an online deliberative GIS tool on a website which enabled 200 or more participants to asynchronously collaborate in the construction, evaluation, and selection of their own transportation improvement program. Similarly, Nyerges and Aguirre (2011) designed an online platform making use of GIS tools and deliberative aspects for an experiment involving a large group of participants in an analytic-deliberative process about regional transportation improvement programming in the central Puget Sound region.

Online deliberation tools offer the chance for asynchronous deliberation (text/argument representations), synchronous (real-time) chat-based (text) or video deliberation, sometimes with the use of automatic facilitation. Although both synchronous and asynchronous approaches to online deliberation have their own particular advantages and disadvantages, these tools offer some clear advantages over "physical" deliberation for either small or large groups, such as greater flexibility, convenience or lower costs. However, depending on how they are implemented they may at the same time may result in "social loss," for instance, they may suffer from a lower perceived effectiveness of collaboration (Iandoli et al., 2016).

Asynchronous text-based deliberation tools include (among others) conversation-centric tools and representation-centric tools (Iandoli et al., 2016). Conversation-centric tools are the most commonly used, due to the prevalence of social media platforms, forums, wikis and blogs. However, their facility to promote fair and transparent discussion is debatable (Black, 2011; Fishkin et al., 2018; Klein, 2015). Hence, new collaborative platforms have sprung up which use representation-centric approaches to visualize knowledge. Among these new innovations are collaborative computer-supported argument visualization (CCSAV) tools. Some well-known recent examples include Kialo or ConsiderIt.

These tools allow the representation of arguments in the form of a shared argument map/visualizations, which result from a collaborative process. Although argument-based interactions lack the benefits of conversational interactions found in forums, comparisons nonetheless show that CCSAV technologies are likely less easily manipulated to support propaganda diffusion and more likely to promote fair and rational assessment of alternative policy proposals (Iandoli et al., 2018).

With the availability of communication APIs for voice, video and messaging, real-time chat-based and video-based deliberation is also possible. Facilitation can also be automated through machine-learning techniques like case-based reasoning (CBR) (Yang et al., 2019). This can address some of the challenges associated with human facilitation. Recently, Fishkin et al., 2018 developed the Stanford Online Deliberation Platform, described as "*a web-based platform that facilitates constructive discussions on civic issues with the use of an automated moderator.*" The automated moderator encourages participants to consider arguments from both sides of all proposals, maintain civility in the discussion, and encourages equitable participation by all participants. A structured collaboration phase also takes place where participants formulate a final set of questions or action items.

Advances in text analytics and sentiment analysis can also enhance the usefulness of the results of online deliberation and promote better decision-making. Various software tools are now available that open up new possibilities for mass deliberation, understanding its dynamics and the impact of system design. It is also possible, for example, using speech recognition, argument mining or visual data analytics, for the results of deliberations to be presented as they take place, rather than afterwards. These dynamic updates can be used to display visualizations publicly to participants in real time (Gold et al., 2018) and this can further improve the deliberative quality of the communication as well as provide rich insights into the views and interaction of participants as the deliberation evolves.

In summary, online deliberation offers various advantages over physical deliberation. However, the way moderation, information, identification, time and location are managed has an impact on the process of online deliberation and hence the quality of the deliberation (Friess and Eilders, 2015). Various software tools exist, each with different functionality. More research with regard to the optimal design of software tools to ensure high quality online deliberation (Iandoli, 2016), timing in the decision process and combination with physical deliberation (Lowry, 2010) is called for. Further research is also needed to determine the effect of different approaches to analyzing the outputs of online, especially large-scale, deliberation and how these may be used to inform policy or be used to communicate with citizens as well as influencing deliberations themselves if published in real-time.

3. Comparison with other appraisal methods

Most of the well-known deliberative methods such as citizen's juries or consensus conferences, have as their basis a step-by-step process that can be largely described as (1) learning (2) discussion or deliberation (3) reaching a collective decision and providing recommendations. These steps are what distinguish deliberative events from other types of appraisal. Citizens are given time to absorb and reflect on informational resources, in the form of documentation or via access to experts. They also interact with the views of others before forming a final opinion. Since they are generally idealized as involving the contribution or exchange of information and knowledge, mutual respect and equal democratic participation (Mansbridge et al., 2012), deliberative approaches are appealing in their strong adherence to democratic principles in comparison with other appraisal methods, including other participatory methods. Deliberative appraisal methods offer the possibility of outcomes that are well-balanced, inclusive and representative of the entire population (Fishkin and Mansbridge, 2017). Additional, indirect benefits may arise from using deliberative approaches. One is the creation of an "audience effect" where deliberations are observed by the public, providing an opportunity for more outside inputs alongside the process at the same time increasing the transparency of the process. Another is the building of the capacity of the community for future deliberative events since selected participants become experts in the topic at hand and spread this knowledge to the wider community (Michels, 2012). They also become more adept at critically analyzing opposing arguments and understanding trade-offs that must be made. Deliberative events may also be useful in navigating conflict between divergent views or polarizing topics (Kenter et al.,

2016a, 2016b), and through repeated meetings trust can be built between participants, or else through appropriate facilitation conflict can be managed.

The substantive results of deliberative processes are also unique. Rather than being based on a statistical aggregation of the opinions of the greater public, deliberative methods instead tap into individual opinions formed during a collective process based on informed reasoning and mutual exchange. In this regard, deliberative processes may offer far richer insights compared to other technical appraisal methods.

Apart from providing richer insights, using deliberative approaches, it is argued, can lead to better decisions. Since citizens have time to construct or potentially modify their views, they are more likely to carefully consider balanced arguments for a given options. As well as this, the cognitive diversity found in deliberating groups (Landemore, 2012) also promotes better decisions. As Quick and Zhao (2011) argue, deliberating with a diverse selection of participants can alert experts to previously unconsidered types of knowledge, lived experience or emotions, leading to new understandings of problems.

As touched upon in the introduction, differences in policy appraisal methods can be attributed to their key underlying assumptions. These assumptions dictate the way how and in what roles people may participate, which type of data and knowledge will be gathered, whether or not value types will be similar or incommensurable, how information is conveyed to the participants and how they reach conclusions (Vatn, 2009). Methods, such as CBA assume values or preferences to be individual and fixed and that assume rational outcomes do not require social exchange. Such methods will seek to objectively measure and quantify these values in a clear and impartial way. They pay more attention to statistical requirements such as sample sizes and demographic representation (Raymond, 2014). Methods, such as deliberation, that assume social values to be formed through reflection, mutual understanding and exchange of views, will rather seek to facilitate the construction of values for the right context (Vatn, 2009) during the appraisal process. These methods pay most attention to providing balanced arguments for all relevant interests and ensuring a fair and egalitarian process (Raymond, 2014).

When is it appropriate to use deliberative methods? In general, deliberation is said to be best used when the issue in question involves complexity, uncertainty or conflicting values or viewpoints (Kenter, 2014). Deliberative methods are said to be most suitable when sociocultural or values related to human well-being are at stake (Kelemen and Saarikoski, 2015) or when there is a high plurality of values (Frame and O'Connor, 2011). In contrast, analytic methods like CBA could be more appropriate when there is clarity about the winners and losers resulting from a policy, with greater certainty about the major consequences, where the arguments for different policy options are already widely understood and the alternatives to be evaluated are highly comparable (Frame and O'Connor, 2011; van Wee, 2012).

However, as Nyerges and Aguirre (2011) point out, within an overall decision process, analysis and deliberation have distinct goals and each activity will involve different types of knowledge and outputs. In practice, a more pragmatic approach to transportation appraisal may be needed, where both analytic methods and deliberative methods are integrated. Deliberative appraisal is therefore not restricted to one particular method, but is a rather a paradigm (Raymond, 2014) that can be used for the appraisal or valuation of policies. Owens et al. (2004) recommend a sensitive combination of approaches, depending on the objective of the appraisal.

3.1 Advantages over other appraisal methods

CBA and MCA are the most commonly used appraisal methods for transportation projects in the developed world (Berechman, 2018). Deliberative methods offer some particular unique advantages over these methods, particularly CBA. Although it is beyond the scope of this chapter to delve into all existing criticisms of CBA or MCA, some of these criticisms are discussed here, in order to demonstrate how they may be remedied through the use of deliberative approaches. Criticism of CBA center around the following arguments (van Wee, 2012; Wegner and Pascual, 2011):

1. CBA is not based on a pluralistic ethical framework that reflects the pluralism of societal values
2. CBA ignores certain externalities such as distribution effects
3. CBA lacks transparency in that the process of defining options is controlled by certain people in positions of power.

3.1.1 Pluralistic perspective

CBA seeks to appraise the net economic value of alternatives, which are then prioritized based on welfare-economic principles. However, problems exist in relation to how neoclassical economics conceptualizes value. Since economic methods focus on aggregating individual values to measure policy effects in monetary terms only, they neglect the pluralistic values of our complex societies or communities and fail to recognize other measures of societal well-being (Wegner and Pascual, 2011). Economic valuation methods are based on notions of willingness-to-pay (i.e., the value an individual holds for something is reflected by how much they would spend on it) however, this assumption has been widely disputed on a number of grounds. Essentially, individual preferences or values are far more diverse (van Wee, 2012) and depend on the context (Kenter et al., 2016b). For example, people will assign different values to something depending on whether they are asked to do so as a consumer or a citizen (Mouter et al., 2017a). Furthermore, neoclassical economics assumes that values rely on rational, pre-formed utilitarian preferences, whereas ample evidence exists within other disciplines such as psychology that preferences and values are not pre-formed are instead constructed through a process of deliberation (Kenter, 2014). In contrast, deliberative approaches conceptualize value from a pluralistic perspective and aim for the construction of societal values in a particular social context, making them suited to valuing public goods. Deliberative methods hence offer a way to address the complexities inherent in transportation policy appraisal and take account of a variety of values, such as, for instance, culture and practices related to mobility (Murray, 2011).

3.1.2 Externalities and distribution effects

In transportation policy appraisal, CBA has also been criticized for not taking non-welfare effects into account. These effects include distributional and externality effects, which comprise economic development and environmental impacts. Equity concerns, for instance, are cited as the most neglected (and difficult to measure) in transport policy (Berechman, 2018). Although CBAs may include a discussion of distributional effects, by e.g., reporting the net present value of a project for specific regions, or by providing a "winners and losers table" in the report, this may not in fact affect the final outcomes of a CBA (Mouter et al., 2017b).

Deliberative approaches may remedy this shortcoming since it can identify previously unknown values that people attribute to certain amenities, nature or infrastructure, including sense of place, traditional knowledge, spiritual and cultural values. Vigar, (2017), for instance, calls for the use of deliberative methods in transport planning in order to ensure the integration of what he refers to as the "four knowledges" of transport planning: embodied or local knowledge, technical or codified knowledge, practice-centered knowledge and political knowledge. Proponents of equity in transport also argue that the "communicative rationality" and democratic qualities of deliberative methods promote fairer outcomes (Aparicio, 2018), since properly facilitated deliberative methods can help to counteract power imbalances that may occur when certain interest groups have more time or resources to influence policy decisions (Baumann and White, 2010).

3.1.3 Transparency and balance of power

CBA is further criticized based on the potential for manipulation. This can occur via the selection of unit values (e.g., VoT) or cost estimates, or by strategic selection of scenarios or models (van Wee, 2012). Preferences could also be manipulated via social norms or advertisement (Wegner and Pascual, 2011). In this regard, Vigar (2017) highlights the need for greater transparency regarding the advice given to and used by politicians and argues that an "engage-deliberate-decide" rather than a "decide-announce-defend" approach builds greater transparency and trust. Although potential for manipulation is also a possibility in deliberative methods, for instance during the selection of participants, information or experts, there is still a far lower possibility of takeover by political interests because randomly selected citizens are less likely to be aligned with interest groups. Some further remedies for manipulation are described in Section 3.2.

With regards to MCA, although it is often proposed as a complement to CBA, since it addresses the utilitarian and monistic approach of CBA, it is also criticized regarding the subjectivity of weights and for the potential for manipulation (van Wee, 2012). Although MCA allows for the prioritization of multiple objectives and the inclusion of incommensurable values it still produces an aggregated result only and may suffer from power imbalances between participants (Wegner and Pascual, 2011). The same problems with regard to value formation exist in relation to MCA as they do with CBA. MCA does not incorporate values that arise from a discursive, social process (i.e., deliberation). New approaches which combine deliberation with MCA may help to overcome these issues. Section 2.3.2 discusses some of these possible approaches.

In comparison to other participatory methods, deliberative methods have also been shown to offer advantages. An extensive review of participatory processes in transportation policy-making in the USA revealed that deliberative methods were considered to be the most effective compared to methods based on basic consultation (Quick and Zhao, 2011). Another study Dabney (2013) on transportation planning methods found that transportation decisions reflect public input more often when deliberative public participation techniques are used.

3.2 Criticisms

Various concerns or criticisms of deliberative methods have been put forward in the literature. These criticisms relate to inclusivity and accessibility, representativeness, facilitation and moderation, the usefulness of the outputs, the costs, power issues and potential for manipulation and lack of empirical study. Criticisms apply to both physical and online deliberation approaches. In this section each criticism is explained and solutions offered where possible.

3.2.1 Inclusivity and accessibility

Although deliberative methods should aim to include a diverse group of citizens, in practice difficulties may arise with including certain social groups (minorities, the poor or less-educated) in deliberations (Asenbaum, 2016). Even online deliberation, with its potential for greater inclusivity may not deliver if certain social groups are not computer literate or do not have access to computers or internet. It may be difficult to get some people to take part at all without significant offline outreach efforts in the first place. Nonetheless, evidence exists to suggest that once they receive initial support and encouragement, citizens can build their capacity and interest to engage in future deliberations (Fishkin et al., 2017).

During deliberation itself, the less vocal or less politically experienced may be marginalized and social pressure may impact already marginalized groups like women, or ethnic and sexual minorities (Asenbaum, 2016). Special facilitation methods, such as "dynamic facilitation" can be used to overcome these issues. Dynamic facilitation, as an example, is a facilitation style that avoids constraining the group to agendas or exercises and focuses on creating choices rather than deciding between solutions. Facilitators remain open to different modes of communication such as narratives, rather than solely rational arguments. As well as this, additional training on the deliberative process or topic at hand can be provided to help reduce the gap between the lower educated and participants. Translators and materials in multiple languages can also be provided.

3.2.2 Representativeness

There may be a tension between holding a good deliberation and ensuring representativeness. In terms of representativeness, deliberative methods may include only small numbers of citizens, which although representative in terms of diversity, may be perceived by some as less representative than a large sample of the population and therefore as less legitimate. Even crowdsourced online deliberation involving very large numbers of participants may rely on self-selection and suffer from biases (Aitamurto, 2016). Apart from organizers correcting for selection bias, various innovations have sought to expand participation in deliberative events and ensure adequate representation. For example, 21st century town halls use technology to allow greater numbers to participate in several physical locations and make efforts to ensure representative groups are formed. Mass deliberation is possible by dividing the larger group into smaller ones. Alternatively, new internet tools now hold the potential to allow individuals to access deliberations in greater numbers and powerful analytical tools can deal with the large corpus of discussion produced. Further solutions include providing adequate compensation, accommodation or childcare, so that the representation of lower income groups can be improved (Lee, 2011).

3.2.3 Power issues and potential for manipulation

In spite of the aspiration toward democratic ideals of equity and inclusivity, there is potential for power imbalances or manipulation to occur during the organization or running of deliberative events. Public deliberative initiatives may in reality simply reproduce the power relations found in society (Blue and Dale, 2016). Interest groups may even hijack the deliberative decision-making processes (Blue and Dale, 2016; Spada and Vreeland, 2013). Those involved in selecting participants, providing information or organizing the event may selectively choose information, experts or even participants. For instance, mini-publics are often "front-loaded" whereby the event is convened by policy makers or elected officials, who set the agenda and hence could steer the process toward a particular goal (Beauvais and Warren, 2019). Efforts to include citizens in agenda setting can alleviate this problem. The framing of issues is particularly important and there is a risk that technical or instrumental reasoning may be prioritized, particularly in relation to policy-issues that require technical knowledge. This can lead to the reinforcement of status quo by marginalizing other perspectives (Blue and Dale, 2016). In this regard, the quality of facilitation is paramount (Escobar and Elstub, 2017).

3.2.4 Facilitation or moderation

It is generally agreed that deliberative approaches ideally require trained facilitators. Without moderation, there is a high risk of domination by strong personalities, discussions going off topic or that groups will splinter (Fishkin and Fishkin, 2018). However, deliberative approaches may suffer from human resource constraints and facilitators themselves are not immune to human bias, or restrictions of location and time. Research shows that biased moderators can significantly influence the attitudes and behaviors of participants by expressing their views (Spada and Vreeland, 2013). Ensuring independent and properly trained facilitation is available can help to alleviate these issues. Automated facilitation online is also an important upcoming avenue of research (Yang et al., 2019).

3.2.5 Outputs and their usefulness

Deliberative methods do not always provide a neat and tidy result that allows easy comparison between options since outputs tend to be qualitative and lengthy. However, the outcomes of deliberative appraisal may include more than particular outputs and the process may be an end in itself, for instance as a way of facilitating learning, communication, trust building (Beukers et al., 2014), or civic capacity building (Michels, 2012). As mentioned in Section 3, rather than trading off between succinct results and richer discourse, there is hence much recognition in the literature of the value of combining technical or analytical assessments, that produce a "bottom line" figure, and deliberative elements in practice (Cass, 2006). With regard to deliberation aiming for consensus as an outcome, this goal has been criticized because, as some theorists argue, pushing for consensus may suppress the diversity of opinions and result in worse decisions (Lowry, 2010). In practice, though, deliberative theorists rarely aspire for full consensus, and usually settle for metaconsensus (Fishkin et al., 2017). As Huitema et al. (2007) point out, deliberative methods may use some form of voting or aggregation of viewpoints to come to a final decision, rather than aiming for consensus. Instead of seeking full consensus, deliberative approaches may instead seek to find "workable agreements" or consensual states (Fishkin et al., 2017). In cases where consensus *is* sought, voices of those not in agreement can still be expressed in the form of a minority report which is presented to policy-makers (Beauvais and Warren, 2019).

3.2.6 Lack of empirical study

Other criticisms of deliberative approaches relate to the fact that they are relatively nascent and that the empirical study of deliberation lacks richness and depth. Deliberative methods have yet to be widely institutionalized. In most cases, there is no binding decision for decision-makers to act on the final recommendation of the citizens, aside from a handful of cases.

Further research on deliberative approaches is needed to address outstanding theoretical questions before approaches can be fully brought into the mainstream. Some avenues for future research are elaborated in the next section.

4. Future research challenges

As shown in the previous section *Criticisms*, research is ongoing on major procedural or design issues relating to deliberative methods in general, such as how to improve representativeness, how to include marginalized groups, how to avoid manipulation or power imbalances and increase transparency, how to reduce cost or increase convenience, e.g., through online deliberation platforms. Further questions remain as to the best way to scale up deliberation online while still adhering to democratic principles (Kadlec and Friedman, 2007; van den Hoven and Dignum, 2016).

For transportation policy appraisal in particular, Lowry (2010) identifies gaps in the research as relating to which point in decision-making is deliberation most appropriate and whether it should replace or complement other types of appraisal or participation. Also, to what extent is internet deliberation beneficial and when should it be used? Chilvers (2008)and Lindenau and Böhler-Baedeker (2014) point out that research is still needed to determine how exactly we should integrate the results of deliberative approaches technical transport planning processes or into decision-making in general. Furthermore, if the public comes to a decision that is unrealistic or financially unfeasible, how can this be dealt with? Similarly, Isaksson et al. (2009) show the need for further research into how emerging practices of deliberative appraisal and traditional analytical models can coexist in a meaningful way within institutions. Baumann and White (2010) have called for further research into improving the quality of deliberations and the impact this can have on transportation policies that promote sustainability, since these tend to involve conflicting values and interests among civil society and policy communities that create barriers in the policy process.

References

Aitamurto, T., 2016. Crowdsourced democratic deliberation in open policymaking: definition, promises, challenges. Int. Rep. Soc. Inf. 13 (1), 67–78.

America Speaks, 2020. America Speaks. Available at: www.AmericaSpeaks.org. (Accessed: 25 January 2020).

Aparicio, Á., 2018. Equity challenges in major transport plans. Transp. Res. Proc. 31, 121–135. https://doi.org/10.1016/j.trpro.2018.09.054. Elsevier B.V.

Arnstein, S., 1969. A ladder of citizen participation. J. Am. Inst. Plann. 34 (4), 216–224.

Asenbaum, H., 2016. Facilitating inclusion: Austrian wisdom councils as democratic innovation between consensus and diversity. J. Public Deliberation 12 (1), 7.
Baudry, G., Macharis, C., Vallée, T., 2018. Range-based multi-actor multi-criteria analysis: a combined method of multi-actor multi-criteria analysis and Monte Carlo simulation to support participatory decision making under uncertainty. Eur. J. Oper. Res. 264 (1), 257–269. https://doi.org/10.1016/j.ejor.2017.06.036. Elsevier B.V.
Baumann, C., White, S., 2010. Learning from the world—adding a strategic dimension to lesson-drawing from successful sustainable transport policies. In: ATRF 2010: 33rd Australasian Transport Research Forum, pp. 1–9 (October).
Beauvais, E., Warren, M.E., 2019. What can deliberative mini-publics contribute to democratic systems? Eur. J. Polit. Res. 58 (3), 893–914. https://doi.org/10.1111/1475-6765.12303.
Bellamy, R., Chilvers, J., Vaughan, N.E., 2014. Deliberative mapping of options for tackling climate change: citizens and specialists "open up" appraisal of geoengineering. Public Underst. Sci. 25 (3), 269–286. https://doi.org/10.1177/0963662514548628.
Berechman, J., 2018. The Infrastructure We Ride on Decision Making in Transportation Investment. Palgrave Macmillan, Cham. https://doi-org.tudelft.idm.oclc.org/10.1007/978-3-319-74606-7.
Beukers, E., Bertolini, L., Te Brömmelstroet, M., 2014. Using cost benefit analysis as a learning process: identifying interventions for improving communication and trust. Transp. Policy 31, 61–72. https://doi.org/10.1016/J.TRANPOL.2013.12.002. Pergamon.
Beukers, E., Bertolini, L., te Brömmelstroet, M., 2015. An assessment of interventions for improving communication and trust in cost benefit analysis processes. Impact Assess. Proj. Apprais. 33 (1), 28–42. https://doi.org/10.1080/14615517.2014.941142. Taylor & Francis.
Black, L.W., 2011. The Promise and Problems of Online Deliberation. Charles F. Kettering Foundation Inc.
Blue, G., Dale, J., 2016. Framing and power in public deliberation with climate change: critical reflections on the role of deliberative practitioners. J. Public Deliberation 12 (1), 2.
Burgess, J., et al., 2007. Deliberative mapping: a novel analytic-deliberative methodology to support contested science-policy decisions. Public Underst. Sci. 16 (3), 299–322. https://doi.org/10.1177/0963662507077510.
Carson, L., Elstub, S., 2019. Comparing Participatory and Deliberative Democracy, https://doi.org/10.2307/j.ctvbkk41f.8.
Cascetta, E., et al., 2015. A new look at planning and designing transportation systems: a decision-making model based on cognitive rationality, stakeholder engagement and quantitative methods. Transp. Policy 38, 27–39. https://doi.org/10.1016/J.TRANPOL.2014.11.005. Pergamon.
Cass, N., 2006. Participatory-Deliberative Engagement: A Literature Review. School of Environment and Development. Manchester University, Manchester, UK. http://www.manchester.ac.uk/sed/research/beyond_nimbyism.
Chilvers, J., 2008. In: Deliberating Competence Theoretical and Practitioner Participatory Appraisal Practice, Change, third ed. 33. Sage Publications, pp. 421–451.
Courant, D., 2017. Les Cahiers de l' IEPHI IEPHI Working Paper Series Thinking Sortition Frameworks and Democratic Principles.
Dabney, U.B., 2013. Public Participation in Transportation Planning: How Does the Level of Engagement and Deliberation Affect Transportation Decisions in Virginia's MPOs? ProQuest Dissertations and Theses, p. 298. Available at: http://ezproxy.umuc.edu/login?url=https://search.proquest.com/docview/1447009096?accountid=14580%0Ahttp://sfx.umd.edu/uc?url_ver=Z39.88-2004&rft_val_fmt=info:ofi/fmt:kev:mtx:dissertation&genre=dissertations+%26+theses&sid=ProQ:ProQuest+Dissertations+%26+T.

Dean, M., et al., 2019. Testing the application of participatory MCA: the case of the South Fylde Line. Transp. Policy 73, 62–70. https://doi.org/10.1016/j.tranpol.2018.10.007.

Dejaeghere, Y., 2019. German-Speaking Community of Belgium Becomes World's First Region With Permanent Citizen Participation Drafted by Lot: Ambitious Model for Innovating Democracy Designed by G1000. Available at: https://www.newdemocracy.com.au/wp-content/uploads/2019/02/Eupen-Press-Release.pdf.

Devaney, L., et al., 2020. Ireland's citizens' assembly on climate change: lessons for deliberative public engagement and communication. Environ. Commun. 14 (2), 141–146. https://doi.org/10.1080/17524032.2019.1708429.

Dryzek, J.S., 2002. Deliberative Democracy and Beyond: Liberals, Critics, Contestations. Oxford University Press, Demand.

Escobar, O., Elstub, S., 2017. Forms of Mini-Publics: An Introduction to Deliberative Innovations in Democratic Practice. newDemocracy.

Evans, R., Burke, M., Dodson, J., 2007. Clothing the emperor? Transport modelling and decision-making in Australian cities. In: State of Australian Cities National Conference, pp. 418–426.

Fishkin, J., et al., 2018. Deliberative Democracy with the Online Deliberation Platform. The 7th AAAI Conference on Human Computation and Crowdsourcing (HCOMP 2019). HCOMP.

Fishkin, J., Fishkin, J., 2018. Deliberative polling. In: Bächtiger, A., Dryzek, J., Mansbridge, J., Warren, M. (Eds.), The Oxford Handbook of Deliberative Democracy. Oxford University Press, pp. 314–328.

Fishkin, J.S., Mansbridge, J., 2017. Introduction. Daedalus 146 (3), 6–13. https://doi.org/10.1162/DAED_x_00442.

Fish, R., et al., 2011. Participatory and Deliberative Techniques to Support the Monetary and Non-Monetary Valuation of Ecosystem Services: An Introductory Guide (Deftra Project Code: NR124) (May). Department for Environment Food and Rural Affairs, United Kingdom.

Fishkin, J.S., et al., 2017. The prospects and limits of deliberative democracy. J. Am. Acad. Arts Sci. 146 (3), 6–13. https://doi.org/10.1162/DAED_ x_00442.

Frame, B., O'Connor, M., 2011. Integrating valuation and deliberation: the purposes of sustainability assessment. Environ. Sci. Pol. 14 (1), 1–10. https://doi.org/10.1016/j.envsci.2010.10.009. Elsevier Ltd.

Friess, D., Eilders, C., 2015. A systematic review of online deliberation research. Policy Internet 7 (3), 319–339. https://doi.org/10.1002/poi3.95.

Gold, V., et al., 2018. Towards deliberation analytics: stream processing of argument data for deliberative communication. In: Proceedings of COMMA Workshop on Argumentation and Society, pp. 1–3. Available at: http://comma2018.argdiap.pl/wp-content/uploads/Gold.pdf.

Gregory, J., Hartz-Karp, J., Watson, R., 2008. Using deliberative techniques to engage the community in policy development. Aust. New Zealand Health Policy 5, 1–9. https://doi.org/10.1186/1743-8462-5-16.

Handy, S., 2008. Regional transportation planning in the US: an examination of changes in technical aspects of the planning process in response to changing goals. Transp. Policy 15 (2), 113–126. https://doi.org/10.1016/j.tranpol.2007.10.006. Elsevier.

Healey, P., 1999. Institutionalist analysis, communicative planning, and shaping places. J. Plan. Educ. Res. 19 (2), 111–121. https://doi.org/10.1177/0739456X9901900201.

Hoppe, R., 2011. Institutional constraints and practical problems in deliberative and participatory policy making. Policy Polit. 39 (2), 163–186. https://doi.org/10.1332/030557310X519650.

Huitema, D., van de Kerkhof, M., Pesch, U., 2007. The nature of the beast: are citizens' juries deliberative or pluralist? Pol. Sci. 40 (4), 287–311. https://doi.org/10.1007/s11077-007-9046-7.

Iandoli, L., et al., 2016. On online collaboration and construction of shared knowledge: assessing mediation capability in computer supported argument visualization tools. J. Assoc. Inf. Sci. Technol. 67 (5), 1052–1067. https://doi.org/10.1002/asi.23481.

Iandoli, L., et al., 2018. Supporting argumentation in online political debate: evidence from an experiment of collective deliberation. New Media Soc. 20 (4), 1320–1341. https://doi.org/10.1177/1461444817691509.

Isaksson, K., Richardson, T., Olsson, K., 2009. From consultation to deliberation? Tracing deliberative norms in EIA frameworks in Swedish roads planning. Environ. Impact Assess. Rev. 29 (5), 295–304. https://doi.org/10.1016/j.eiar.2009.01.007. Elsevier Inc.

Jefferson Centre, 2020. Retrieved January 25 from https://jefferson-center.org/.

Jonsson, M., 2015. Democratic innovations in deliberative systems: the case of the Estonian citizens' assembly process. J. Public Deliberation 11 (1), 7.

Kadlec, A., Friedman, W., 2007. Deliberative democracy and the problem of scope. J. Public Deliberation 3 (1), 8.

Kelemen, E., Saarikoski, H., 2015. Method Factsheet Deliberative Valuation. Openness Project, pp. 4–7.

Kenter, J.O., 2014. Deliberative and non-monetary valuation: a review of methods. In: Laurence Mee Centre for People and the Sea, pp. 1–43, https://doi.org/10.13140/RG.2.1.1430.7606 (October).

Kenter, J.O., et al., 2016a. Shared values and deliberative valuation: future directions. Ecosyst. Serv. 21, 358–371. https://doi.org/10.1016/J.ECOSER.2016.10.006. Elsevier.

Kenter, J.O., Reed, M.S., Fazey, I., 2016b. The deliberative value formation model. Ecosyst. Serv. 21, 194–207. https://doi.org/10.1016/J.ECOSER.2016.09.015. Elsevier.

Klein, M., 2015. A critical review of crowd-scale online deliberation technologies. SSRN Electron. J., 1–10. https://doi.org/10.2139/ssrn.2658811.

Landemore, H.E., 2012. Why the many are smarter than the few and why it matters. J. Public Deliberation 8 (1), 7. Available at: http://www.publicdeliberation.net/cgi/viewcontent.cgi?article=1190&context=jpd.

Le Pira, M., et al., 2017. Towards a decision-support procedure to foster stakeholder involvement and acceptability of urban freight transport policies. Eur. Transp. Res. Rev. 9 (4), 54. https://doi.org/10.1007/s12544-017-0268-2.

Lee, C.W., 2011. Five assumptions academics make about public deliberation, and why they deserve rethinking. J. Public Deliberation 7 (1), 7.

Lienhoop, N., Bartkowski, B., Hansjürgens, B., 2015. Informing biodiversity policy: the role of economic valuation, deliberative institutions and deliberative monetary valuation. Environ. Sci. Policy 54, 522–532. https://doi.org/10.1016/j.envsci.2015.01.007.

Lindenau, M., Böhler-Baedeker, S., 2014. Citizen and stakeholder involvement: a precondition for sustainable urban mobility. Transp. Res. Proc. 4, 347–360. https://doi.org/10.1016/J.TRPRO.2014.11.026. Elsevier.

Lo, A.Y., Spash, C.L., 2013. Deliberative monetary valuation: in search of a democratic and value plural approach to environmental policy. J. Econ. Surv. 27 (4), 768–789. https://doi.org/10.1111/j.1467-6419.2011.00718.x.

Lowry, M.B., 2010. Online public deliberation for a regional transportation improvement decision. Transportation 37 (1), 39–58. https://doi.org/10.1007/s11116-009-9219-7.

Lukensmeyer, C., 1995. 21 st century town meeting ®. In: Business. America Speaks, pp. 1–12.

Lukensmeyer, C.J., Brigham, S., 2002. Taking democracy to scale: creating a town hall meeting for the twenty-first century. Natl. Civ. Rev. 91 (4), 351–366. https://doi.org/10.1002/ncr.91406.

MASSLBP, 2013. Residents' Reference Panel on Regional Transportation Investment.
Macharis, C., Bernardini, A., 2015. Reviewing the use of multi-criteria decision analysis for the evaluation of transport projects: time for a multi-actor approach. Transp. Policy 37, 177–186. https://doi.org/10.1016/J.TRANPOL.2014.11.002. Pergamon.
Mansbridge, J., et al., 2012. A systematic approach to deliberative democracy. In: Parkinson, J., Mansbridge, J. (Eds.), Deliberative Systems: Deliberative Democracy at the Large Scale. Cambridge University Press, pp. 1–41. Available at: http://www.cambridge.org/gb/knowledge/isbn/item6796478/?site_locale=en_GB%5Cnhttp://www.worldcat.org/title/deliberative-systems-deliberative-democracy-at-the-large-scale/oclc/784577135&referer=brief_results.
Miccoli, S., Finucci, F., Murro, R., 2014. A monetary measure of inclusive goods: the concept of deliberative appraisal in the context of urban agriculture. Sustainability 6 (12), 9007–9026. https://doi.org/10.3390/su6129007.
Miccoli, S., Finucci, F., Murro, R., 2015. Measuring shared social appreciation of community goods: an experiment for the east elevated expressway of Rome. Sustainability 7 (11), 15194–15218. https://doi.org/10.3390/su71115194.
Michels, A., 2012. Citizen participation in local policy making: design and democracy. Int. J. Public Adm. 35 (4), 285–292. https://doi.org/10.1080/01900692.2012.661301.
Mouter, N., van Cranenburg, S., van Wee, B., 2017a. Do individuals have different preferences as consumer and citizen? The trade-off between travel time and safety. Transp. Res. A Policy Pract. 106, 333–349.
Mouter, N., van Cranenburgh, S., van Wee, B., 2017b. An empirical assessment of Dutch citizens' preferences for spatial equality in the context of a national transport investment plan. J. Transp. Geogr. 60, 217–230. https://doi.org/10.1016/j.jtrangeo.2017.03.011. Elsevier Ltd.
Munda, G., 2004. Social multi-criteria evaluation: methodological foundations and operational consequences. Eur. J. Oper. Res. 158 (3), 662–677. https://doi.org/10.1016/S0377-2217(03)00369-2. North-Holland.
Murray, L., 2011. Deliberative research for deliberative policy making: creating and recreating evidence in transport policy. Soc. Policy Soc. 10 (4), 459–470. https://doi.org/10.1017/S1474746411000212.
Næss, P., 2006. Cost-benefit analyses of transportation investments. J. Crit. Realism 5 (1), 32–60. https://doi.org/10.1558/jocr.v5i1.32. Routledge.
Nielsen, A.P., et al., 2006. Consensus Conference Manual (February), p. 40.
Nyerges, T., Aguirre, R.W., 2011. Public participation in analytic-deliberative decision making: evaluating a large-group online field experiment. Ann. Assoc. Am. Geogr. 101 (3), 561–586. https://doi.org/10.1080/00045608.2011.563669. Routledge.
Owens, S., Rayner, T., Bina, O., 2004. New agendas for appraisal: reflections on theory, practice, and research. Environ. Plan. A 36 (11), 1943–1959. https://doi.org/10.1068/a36281.
Paul, C., et al., 2008. Making policy decisions about population screening for breast cancer: the role of citizens' deliberation. Health Policy 85 (3), 314–320. https://doi.org/10.1016/j.healthpol.2007.08.007.
Quick, K.S., Zhao, Z., 2011. Suggested Design and Management Techniques for Enhancing Public Engagement in Transportation Policymaking., p. 52. Available at http://www.cts.umn.edu/Publications/ResearchReports/reportdetail.html?id=2066.
Raymond, C.M., et al., 2014. Comparing instrumental and deliberative paradigms underpinning the assessment of social values for cultural ecosystem services. Ecol. Econ. 107, 145–156. https://doi.org/10.1016/j.ecolecon.2014.07.033. Elsevier, B.V.
Saarikoski, H., et al., 2016. Multi-criteria decision analysis and cost-benefit analysis: comparing alternative frameworks for integrated valuation of ecosystem services. Ecosyst. Serv. 22, 238–249. https://doi.org/10.1016/J.ECOSER.2016.10.014. Elsevier.

Sagaris, L., 2018. Citizen participation for sustainable transport: Lessons for change from Santiago and Temuco, Chile. Res. Transp. Econ. 69 (April), 402–410. https://doi.org/10.1016/j.retrec.2018.05.001. Elsevier.

Schweigert, F., 2010. Strengthening citizenship through deliberative polling. J. Community Pract. 18 (1), 19–39. https://doi.org/10.1080/10705421003761223.

Spada, P., Vreeland, J.R., 2013. Who moderates the moderators? The effect of non-neutral moderators in deliberative decision making. J. Public Deliberation 9 (2), 1.

UK National Ecosystem Assessment, 2014. UK national ecosystem assessment follow-on. In: UK National Ecosystem Assessment Follow-on: A synthesis of Key Findings, pp. 1–100, https://doi.org/10.13140/RG.2.1.4683.5281 (January).

van den Hoven, J., Dignum, V., 2016. MOODs: Massive Open Online Deliberation (August). https://doi.org/10.13140/RG.2.1.3030.8085.

van Wee, B., 2012. How suitable is CBA for the ex-ante evaluation of transport projects and policies? A discussion from the perspective of ethics. Transp. Policy 19 (1), 1–7. https://doi.org/10.1016/J.TRANPOL.2011.07.001. Pergamon.

Vatn, A., 2009. An institutional analysis of methods for environmental appraisal. Ecol. Econ. 68, 2207–2215.

Vigar, G., 2017. The four knowledges of transport planning: enacting a more communicative, trans-disciplinary policy and decision-making. Transp. Policy 58 (February), 39–45. https://doi.org/10.1016/j.tranpol.2017.04.013.

Ward, J., et al., 2016. Theory and background of multi-criteria analysis: toward a policy-led approach to mega transport infrastructure project appraisal. Res. Transp. Econ. 58, 21–45. https://doi.org/10.1016/j.retrec.2016.08.003.

Wegner, G., Pascual, U., 2011. Cost-benefit analysis in the context of ecosystem services for human well-being: a multidisciplinary critique. Glob. Environ. Chang. 21 (2), 492–504. https://doi.org/10.1016/J.GLOENVCHA.2010.12.008. Pergamon.

Whitmarsh, L., Haxeltine, A., Wietschel, M., 2007. Sustainable transport visions: expert and non-expert stakeholder perspectives on sustainable transport. In: International Conference on Whole Life Urban Sustainability and its Assessment.

Williams, C., Fang, L., 2018. A value-focused multiple participant-multiple criteria (MPMC) decision support approach for public policy formulation. Group Decis. Negot. 28 (1), 99–126. https://doi.org/10.1007/s10726-018-9597-3. Springer Netherlands.

Wilson, M.W., Ramsey, K.S., 2008. Integrating online deliberation into transportation investment decision-making: preliminary reflections on a field experiment. Transp. Res. Rec. 1645, 52–59.

Yang, C., Ito, T., Gu, W., 2019. Toward machine learning-based facilitation for online discussion in crowd-scale deliberation. The 33rd Annual Conference of the Japanese Society for Artificial Intelligence. Japanese Society for Artificial Intelligence, pp. 2–5.

CHAPTER FOUR

Willingness to allocate public budget and Participatory Value Evaluation

Niek Mouter*
Faculty of Technology, Policy and Management, Engineering Systems and Services Department, Transport and Logistics Group, Delft, The Netherlands
*Corresponding author: e-mail address: n.mouter@tudelft.nl

Contents

Abstract

Particularly in western countries Cost-Benefit Analysis (CBA) is the most widely used appraisal method supporting government decision-making on transport projects. A CBA expresses the impacts of a government project in monetary metrics based on the number of euros affected individuals and parties are willing to pay from their private income. However, the private WTP valuation approach is contested in the literature. One central critique is that this approach fails to consider that private choices may not fully reflect citizens' preferences over public goods and means. In response to this critique, academics developed three types of preference elicitation methods: (1) Collective willingness to pay; (2) Willingness to allocate public budget; (3) Participatory Value Evaluation. This chapter elaborates on these preference elicitation methods. We provide empirical examples of the application of these methods in the transport literature and we pay attention to the fact that these three classes of preference elicitation methods give individuals the opportunity to express a broader range of preferences compared to private WTP-based valuation methods.

Advances in Transport Policy and Planning, Volume 7
ISSN 2543-0009
https://doi.org/10.1016/bs.atpp.2021.01.001

Keywords: Preference elicitation, Willingness to pay, Willingness to allocate public budget, Participatory Value Evaluation, Stated preference, Transport appraisal, Cost-benefit analysis

1. Introduction

Particularly in western countries Cost-Benefit Analysis (CBA) is the most widely used appraisal method supporting government decision-making on transport projects (Mackie et al., 2014). A CBA expresses the impacts of a government project in monetary metrics based on the number of euros affected individuals and parties are willing to pay from their private income (Persky, 2001). Analysts derive such willingness to pay (WTP) estimates, among other things, directly from individuals' market behavior. For example, impacts of transport projects on landscape, nature and noise pollution are evaluated by investigating the private decisions people make in the real estate market (e.g., Allen et al., 2015; Seo et al., 2014). In cases where market behavior is absent, monetary values can be inferred from hypothetical consumer choices. For example, the conventional empirical approach used to infer the value of travel time savings accruing from government projects relies on (hypothetical) route choice experiments (see also Abrantes and Wardman, 2011). In these experiments, respondents are asked to make a series of private choices between routes which differ in terms of travel time, travel costs and possibly other attributes such as reliability and accident risk.

However, the private WTP valuation approach is contested in the literature (e.g., Ackerman and Heinzerling, 2004; Kelman, 1981; Sagoff, 1988). One central critique is that this approach fails to consider that private choices may not fully reflect citizens' preferences over public goods and means (Mouter et al., 2018). That is, the ways in which individuals balance their own after-tax incomes against the attributes of government projects when making private choices may be a poor proxy for how the same individuals believe that their government should trade-off public budget and impacts of public projects. In response to this critique, academics developed three types of preference elicitation methods: (1) Collective willingness to pay; (2) Willingness to allocate public budget; (3) Participatory Value Evaluation. This chapter elaborates on these methods. We provide empirical examples of the application of these preference elicitation methods in the transport literature and we pay attention to the fact that these three classes of methods give individuals the opportunity to express a broader range of preferences compared to private WTP-based valuation methods.

2. Collective willingness to pay

2.1 Critique on private willingness to pay

As alluded to in the introduction, the practice of inferring parameters like the value of travel time (VTT) and the Value of Statistical Life (VOSL) from the number of euros individuals are willing to pay from their own income when making private choices—and establishing the societal welfare effect of transport policies and projects through aggregating changes in travel time and safety with these money metrics—has been contested by numerous academics (e.g., Ackerman and Heinzerling, 2004; Hauer, 1994; Kelman, 1981; Sagoff, 1988). These academics acknowledge that the amount of money individuals are willing to pay from their after tax income in (hypothetical) markets provides crucial information for setting the price of private goods offered by companies such as food, drinks and the price that a toll company asks for travelers that want to use the road. However, these academics argue that the private WTP valuation paradigm fails to consider that private choices may not fully reflect citizens' preferences toward public policy (Mouter et al., 2018). For instance, Alphonce et al. (2014) state that individuals' willingness to pay for private goods provides valuable decision support for marketers and producers, but studies investigating private WTP through observing people's behavior in real (or hypothetical) markets are unlikely to reflect people's preferences regarding public decision-making. Moreover, Jara-Díaz and co-workers assert that there can be a difference between the values for use in public sector appraisal and the values which a commercial operator would wish to use in an analysis of the same project (Jara-Díaz, 2007; Jara-Díaz et al., 2000; Mackie et al., 2001). When a project is directly financed by users, their willingness to pay for this project from their private income will determine whether or not a commercial operator builds a project (Jara-Díaz, 2007). However, Mackie et al. (2001) argue that there is no good reason for the value that the individual is willing to pay to reduce travel time to be equal to the value that society at large attaches to the reassignment of time of that individual to other activities. Ackerman and Heinzerling (2004) provide a concrete example to illustrate why they believe that private willingness to pay inferred from (hypothetical) market behavior might be a poor proxy for informing government decisions. They contest the decision of the US Government against banning cellphone use in the car based on calculations that people who are talking while driving are willing to pay a lot to talk on the phone more than many people who face deadly risks are willing to pay to avoid the risk of being killed. In their view, the private willingness to pay for talking while driving cannot legitimize that some US citizens will die because they are hit by other US citizens distracted by their cellphone while driving a car: "using private market behavior as a standard for public policy overlooks the possibility that people will have different preferences when they take on different roles" (Ackerman and Heinzerling, 2004, p. 191).

The literature lists several reasons why it is problematic to infer the welfare of a government policy through individuals' private willingness to pay in the context of private consumer choices. A first reason why private choices may not reflect people's preferences regarding the social impacts of public policies is that private choices can be distorted through collective action problems (e.g., Hestermann et al., 2018; Ivehammer, 2009; Lusk and Norwood, 2011; Sen, 1995). For instance, people may not be willing to contribute individually because the impact of their individual contribution is negligible, but people may be willing to contribute when the whole community is forced to contribute through a new law or a tax increase because the impact of this coordinated contribution can be substantial (Lusk and Norwood, 2011; Sen, 1995). For example, Californians voted in support of a ballot prohibiting battery-produced eggs, which at the time of the vote were the most popular type of eggs purchased and consumed in California (Lusk and Norwood, 2011). Hestermann et al. (2018) argue that one reason why individuals' voting decisions differed from their aggregate decisions in the grocery store is that individuals have the opportunity to coordinate their actions in a voting context. However, an alternative explanation is that individuals value the same impact, in this case animal welfare, differently in a private sphere (grocery store) and a public sphere (ballot box) as moral considerations might be more salient in the latter context (e.g., Sagoff, 1988). The idea that individuals can entertain different kinds of valuations in different spheres is, among others, covered in the contributions of Sunstein (1993) and Anderson (1993). For instance, Sunstein (1993, p. 784) states: "distinctions among kinds of valuation are highly sensitive to the particular setting in which they operate. People do not value goods acontextually. In one setting—say, the workplace—the prevailing kinds of valuation might be quite different from what they are elsewhere—say, the home or the ballot box." Furthermore, Sunstein (1993) asserts that because of the highly contextual nature of choice it is incorrect to assume that an individuals' private choices can be simply adaptable for policy use. Although transport economists already recognize the importance of context by valuing travel time savings for business trips in a different way from the value of time for commuting and leisure trips, they ignore the fact that these travel time savings materialize in the context of a government decision and not in the context of a private route choice (Mouter and Chorus, 2016). The literature proposes two other reasons for the divergences of people's preferences in a private context and a public context. First, Jara-Díaz (2007) establishes that tax money will go proportionally more to high income groups when social appraisal is based on private willingness to pay. Second, Weimer (2017) asserts that valuing impacts of a government project through observing their consumer choices ignores that people may place a value on the way collective decisions are made.

2.2 Introduction of collective willingness to pay

Mouter et al. (2019) assert that a solution to the problems with private WTP addressed above is valuing impacts of transport projects in a collective setting in which overall burdens and benefits of proposed transport projects are considered together in the context of a government decision. These so-called collective WTP experiments express the impacts of government projects to the entire community but are financed, for example, by a uniform tax increase or comparable payment vehicle. Collective willingness to pay experiments are also called "social choice valuation experiments" and "holistic valuation experiments" (Ackerman and Heinzerling, 2004; Mouter et al., 2019). The idea to infer individuals' willingness to pay in a collective instead of private context has also been suggested by Jara-Díaz (2007) who argues that a government's decision (not) to finance a project with tax money should be grounded in society's willingness to pay to improve its members' mobility, a sum which may differ from the aggregate amount that individuals are willing to pay for the same improvement. Moreover, Jara-Díaz (2007, p. 106) argues that, "society has its own budget and its own priorities, and clearly total welfare is not necessarily the simple sum of all users' benefits." Collective willingness to pay experiments are particularly conducted in the environmental economics literature because in this field it is sometimes not even possible to identify private choices that provide any information about people's preferences for environmental goods. For instance, Arrow et al. (1993), Carson et al. (2003) and Johnston et al. (2017) recommend to value environmental goods using experiments adopting a referendum format. Since everyone is asked to contribute, the coordination problem associated with private WTP studies is resolved (Mouter et al., 2019). In addition, collective

WTP experiments allow individuals to express a broader range of preferences compared to private WTP-based valuation methods as participants are facilitated to express (altruistic and moral) considerations regarding the way government should trade-off burdens and benefits of public policies (Posner and Sunstein, 2017).

2.3 Examples of collective WTP experiments in the transport domain

In the transport literature various collective WTP-based valuation studies have been conducted (e.g., Chorus et al., 2018; Daniels and Hensher, 2000; Mouter et al., 2017a, 2019; Svensson and Johansson, 2010). Daniels and Hensher (2000) conducted a study in which participants evaluated the overall societal impacts of a proposed urban road project such as travel time savings, noise pollution, bushland lost, open space lost and a tax increase for 2 years to finance the project costs. In their study, participants were asked whether they thought that the government should build the M5 East, a 13-km extension of an existing tolled motorway. Hence, respondents participating in this experiment did not value impacts such as travel time savings in isolation, but in the context of the overall positive and negative impacts of a government project. Mouter et al. (2019) asked respondents to choose between alternatives for a new road, trading off overall travel time savings, three environmental impacts (noise, recreation and biodiversity) and a one-time tax increase. They showed that there is a stark deviation between the values respondents assigned to travel time savings and the three environmental variables in the collective willingness to pay experiment and the values that are currently applied in the Netherlands which are based on the private WTP valuation paradigm. For instance, Mouter et al. (2019) established that individuals prefer a project preventing 300 households from experiencing 63 dB of noise pollution over one which saves between 7 min of travel time for 10,000 trips per day, all else being equal. This drastically contrasts with the current Dutch practice in which a project saving 30 s of travel time for 10,000 trips per day performs better in a CBA than a project preventing 300 households from experiencing 63 dB of noise pollution. Hence, Mouter et al. (2019) conclude that a collective WTP valuation approach to the analysis of a project resulting in travel time savings and noise pollution produces substantially different outcomes than an analysis of the same project using private WTP-based valuation. Moreover, in a collective WTP-setting, individuals assigned monetary values to environmental impacts that are not (or only qualitatively) considered in CBAs that depart from private WTP.

In their experiments they also asked respondents to provide written motivations for their choices. Based on an analysis of the qualitative data they established that a collective WTP choice context allows individuals to express (moral) considerations regarding the way government should trade off the costs and benefits of government projects that cannot be included in private WTP-based valuation studies. Chorus et al. (2018) asked respondents whether they support or oppose a massive national transport infrastructure investment scheme among car commuters in the Netherlands which impacted the number of traffic fatalities, number of people seriously injured in traffic, travel time savings as well as the national vehicle ownership tax. They find that participants dislike choosing an alternative which embodies an implicit trading off of a "sacred" value such as a human life against a "secular" value such as money or travel time. They propose to account for this so-called taboo trade-off aversion in conventional linear random utility models by including taboo trade-off penalties. Svensson and Johansson (2010) asked respondents how much they would be willing to pay for renting a safety device which reduces their own mortality and morbidity risk (private WTP) and respondents were also asked whether they would support a coercive lump-sum tax increase to finance a public road safety investment that would reduce the mortality and morbidity risks (collective WTP). Interestingly, they found that the mean WTP in the private WTP setting was three times higher than in the collective WTP setting. They argue that the difference between private WTP and collective WTP might be explained by the fact that the only elicitation mechanism for a new public good which is incentive compatible concerns a (collective) WTP experiment with coercive payment as a private good framing implies that it is always rational for the respondent to overstate the WTP, since when the good is on the market the individual can always choose whether or not to actually purchase the good (see also Carson and Groves, 2007). Another explanation of their finding might be that individuals believe that a public safety project should not be financed by a new tax increase but through a re-allocation of public funding from other sectors to public safety. That is, when individuals believe that public money is currently wasted by spending it on bad policies, they might be hesitant toward a new tax increase as they think that the government should first do a better job by refraining from investing in poor policies. Andersson and Lindberg (2009) analyzed people's willingness to pay for reducing mortality risk through a private willingness to pay experiment in which people were asked about their willingness to pay for a traffic safety device that aims to reduce the fatality and severe injury risk to zero within an urban area and a collective willingness to pay experiment in which respondents were asked about their willingness to pay for an unspecified safety program with the same purpose. In the latter experiment, the payment vehicle for the public good was an annual fee earmarked contribution for a traffic safety fund within the municipality. It was highlighted that all other individuals within the municipality also had to pay the fee. Just like Svensson and Johansson (2010), they found a higher willingness to pay in the private willingness to pay experiments than in the collective willingness to pay experiments. They argue that one reason for this result is that individuals may prefer private rather than public provision of safety when they believe that public provision of safety will be inefficient. As alluded to before, an alternative explanation is that participants in the private willingness to pay experiments are incentivized to overstate their purchase proclivities for a new private good in stated preference studies because this will encourage the production of the good and the individual can always decide later whether or not to purchase the good in question without experiencing any negative consequences when defecting (Carson and Groves, 2007). Hultkrantz et al. (2006) conducted a similar experiment as Andersson and Lindberg (2009) and also found that the WTP for risk reduction within a collective willingness to pay setting is considerably lower than within a private willingness to pay setting. The condition in their collective willingness to pay experiment was a bit different than in the Andersson and Lindberg (2009) study as it was described as follows: "*A requirement for the traffic safety programme to be implemented is that you and at least 70% of the inhabitants in Orebro contribute with a fee to a special road traffic fond used for funding the programme. The Orebro municipality will administrate the fund.*" They also make a normative claim about which type of preference elicitation setting would be more appropriate for the evaluation of a government project: *"As infrastructure planning is made in the public-good context, we find it natural to consider such a value for CBA models that are used for assessing public infrastructure programs"* (Hultkrantz et al., 2006; p. 14). Andersson et al. (2019) argue that the divergence between outcomes of collective WTP experiments and private WTP experiments in the Swedish studies discussed above is problematic as the value of statistical life that are adopted in CBAs is often derived from private willingness to pay experiments, whereas the projects that are evaluated in these CBAs are normally public projects that are financed from the collective budget.

3. Willingness to allocate public budget

Valuing impacts of government projects using the collective WTP approach instead of the private WTP approach does not solve all criticisms raised against (private) WTP-based valuation. The most important remaining critique concerns that (private or collective) WTP-based valuation postulates that private euros and public euros cannot have a different purpose, i.e., they are completely fungible (Hess et al., 2012; Mouter et al., 2017a). This principle is also known as the "a euro is a euro principle." Under complete fungibility, it is possible to establish the social welfare effect of a public good that is financed with government funds (public euros) through aggregating the number of euros that individuals are (collectively) willing to pay from their after-tax income (private euros). However, a crucial issue with this assumption is that, "complete fungibility" does not fit with what is observed in reality (e.g., Thaler, 1999; Tversky and Kahneman, 1981). Thaler (1999), for instance, observes that euros contained within a given sub-budget can indeed have a specific purpose. As a result, they are at best imperfect substitutes for euros from other budgets, even for the same individual. Hence, a more defensible notion is to assume that individuals might view their private income and public budget as constituting two separate budgets: even if individual A is measurably willing to pay X euros from their own budget for government project Z, we cannot then simply conclude that this individual also believes that X euros should be taken from the government budget. More specifically, when the analyst observes that individuals are willing to pay for presents, beers, going on a holiday to Italy and travel time reductions from their private income, this implies that they gain utility from these goods when they are financed with their private income. However, this does not have to imply that they experience the same level of utility when the presents, beers, travel time reductions and the holiday to Italy are financed from the public budget. When it indeed makes a difference whether public projects are paid for by private euros (e.g., private or collective WTP) or public euros, WTP-based valuation is no longer useful for the evaluation of government projects financed from public revenues. Instead, the welfare effects of such projects should be derived from individuals' preferences regarding the expenditure of public euros.

Scholars developed so-called willingness to allocate public budget experiments (WTAPB) specifically for this purpose (Mouter et al., 2019).

In WTAPB experiments individuals make choices concerning alternative allocations of government budget across different government projects. The WTAPB approach thus aspires to infer welfare effects of (impacts of) government projects from individuals' preferences regarding the expenditure of public euros. As said, the most important benefit of the WTAPB valuation approach is that preferences of individuals who believe that government funds should be spend on different purposes than their own money can be expressed (Mouter et al., 2020). A second advantage of the WTAPB valuation approach is that it bypasses the concern that WTP-based valuation is an inappropriate way to value impacts of government projects that are incommensurable with private income (Aldred, 2006; Clark et al., 2000). For instance, Sunstein (1993) asserts that values which are not traded in a real-life market setting, such as free speech, biodiversity and landscape might be valued in the wrong way when they are expressed in private income. Raz (1986) argues that values such as friendship and our relationship with the natural world, cannot be valued in terms of private income without somehow corroding or degrading them. Crucially, WTAPB does not require translation of government project impacts into private income. Instead, an impact of a government project is valued through the extent to which individuals are willing to sacrifice other impacts of government projects. For instance, in a WTAPB experiment, individuals are asked to trade-off environmental impacts against other impacts of governmental policy (e.g., reduction of mortality risk) which contrasts the WTP valuation approach in which individuals are asked to trade-off environmental impacts against private income.

3.1 Willingness to allocate and willingness to re-allocate

A distinction can be made between two types of WTAPB experiments. First, various studies in the literature investigate people's preferences regarding a tax *reallocation* towards a public good (e.g., Barak and Katz, 2015; Bergstrom et al., 2004; Dalrymple et al., 2012; Ivehammer, 2009; Huang et al., 2018; Kontoleon et al., 2005; Mouter and Chorus, 2016; Nunes and Travisi, 2009; Swallow and McGonagle, 2006). In the willingness to reallocate public budget experiments, the financing of the public good under study is to be paid for by a decrease in the amount of a household's taxation money that was previously spent on other government projects that are not explicitly considered in the choice experiment (Nunes and Travisi, 2009). For instance, Bergstrom et al. (2004) asked respondents whether they agreed with a project which improved groundwater quality protection that would be financed from a re-allocation from taxes from other public services (e.g., spending on roads, bridges, schools, parks, police protection, health care). A clear downside of a "reallocation" context is that it is difficult for participants to make an assumption regarding what will happen precisely when they choose to re-allocate taxes toward the public good under investigation. For instance, Bergstrom et al. (2004) did not provide any information on the impacts of retracting money from school or park budgets to the protection of groundwater quality. Ivehammer (2009) suggests that the re-allocation context does not work as good as a payment vehicle because respondents do not fully interpret it as a cost. They might, for instance, believe that the reallocation would be made from what they think is least valuable. A second cluster of WTAPB studies, particularly applied in health economics, investigate citizens' preferences between two or more alternative tax allocations of the government (e.g., Anand and Wailoo, 2000; Dolan and Tsuchiya, 2005; Johannesson and Johansson, 1997; Johansson-Stenman and Martinsson, 2008; Mouter et al., 2017a,b). In such experiments, respondents are asked to choose between different projects which do not differ in terms of allocation of public budget. A feature of this approach is that the respondents only need to consider the effects of two or more alternative allocations of taxes. Both the respondent's disposable income and the provision of other public goods (other than the ones a respondent could choose in the experiment) will not be affected. This allows for a direct measurement of individuals' trade-offs between the effects of these alternative public investments: i.e., individuals' trade-offs between travel time and environmental effects. In some studies (e.g., Mouter et al., 2017a) this marginal rate of substitution is explicitly computed.

3.2 Willingness to allocate public budget and the consumer-citizen duality

In the transport literature WTAPB experiments have often been labeled as "citizen stated choice experiments" and WTP valuation experiments have been coined "consumer experiments" (e.g., Mouter and Chorus, 2016; Mouter et al., 2017a,b, 2018). For instance, Mouter and Chorus (2016) define citizen preferences as: individuals' preferences toward the allocation of (expected) taxes and consumer preferences as an individual's preferences within his/her personal budget constraint (e.g., after tax income). The most important reasons to not adopt the labels "consumer" and "citizen" for these type of experiments is that these labels are defined in various different ways in the literature. For instance, Curtis and McConnell (2002) and

Ovaskainen and Kniivilä (2005) define "citizen preferences" as consumer preferences with altruism and Balbontin et al. (2020), Blamey et al. (1995), Daniels and Hensher (2000) and Nyborg (2000) equate the concept "consumer" with "Homo Economicus"—who only pursues personal interests—and the concept "citizen" with "Homo Politicus"—who judges matters from society's point of view.

3.3 Empirical examples in the transport literature

Mouter et al. (2017a) conducted five stated choice experiments to investigate the extent to which individuals make different trade-offs between travel time and safety in a private WTP-setting, collective WTP-setting and WTAPB-setting. In the two private WTP-settings respondents were asked to choose—as a car driver—between two hypothetical routes which differed in terms of travel time, accident risk and toll costs. In the collective WTP-setting respondents were informed that the government considers a one-time tax increase to finance a new road between two cities. Next, the respondents were asked whether they would recommend the government to build a new road and if so, which route they would recommend. The routes differed in terms of reductions in travel time and accident risk. Finally, respondents participating in the two WTAPB experiments were informed that the government had decided to allocate taxes to the construction of a new road and wanted the advice of the respondents in choosing between two routes that differed in terms of travel time and accident risk. The results of this study suggest that individuals participating in the WTAPB experiment assign substantially more value to safety than travel time when compared to the respondents participating in the WTP-based valuation experiments. Individuals participating in the two private WTP-based valuation experiments show a marginal rate of substitution of 2.5 min per a reduction of 1 traffic casualty, the marginal rate of substitution of participants of the collective WTP-experiment was 5.4 min of travel time savings for 80,000 trips per day per a reduction of 1 traffic casualty on the road per year. However, when individuals are put in a WTAPB setting their marginal rate of substitution ranges between 10.7 and 16.4 min of travel time savings for 80,000 trips per day per a reduction of 1 traffic casualty on the road per year. To illustrate the interpretation of these results, let's consider a government which must decide between two route options being Route A: 32 min and 3 traffic casualties per year and Route B: 40 min and 2 traffic casualties per year. All else being equal, the outcomes of the WTP-based valuation experiments would suggest that the social desirability of Route A is higher than Route B, since participants in the experiments derive more utility from 8 min of travel time savings than a reduction of the numbers of traffic deaths on the road with one per year. However, when using the results of the WTAPB experiments the government should conclude that the social desirability of Route B is higher than Route A as citizens derive more utility from a reduction of 1 traffic casualty on the road per year than 8 min of travel time savings for 80,000 trips per day. These results confirm that the selection of a particular valuation approach to evaluate transport policies impacting accident risk and/or travel time can substantially affect the results of an appraisal study.

In a follow-up study, Mouter et al. (2018) aimed to provide explanations for this finding by asking respondents to conduct one private WTP-based experiment and one WTAPB experiment conducted in the Mouter et al. (2017a) study. In both cases, they were asked to choose between routes which differed in travel time and accident risk. However, in the first experiment they made choices as a car driver, whereas in the second experiment they were asked to recommend the government regarding a choice that needs to be made between two route options that differed in terms of travel time and accident risk. Importantly, respondents were also prompted to elaborate on the reasons underlying their choices. Mouter et al. (2018) identified 10 reasons for why individuals assigned a higher value to reducing accident risk than reducing travel time in the WTAPB-setting than in the private WTP-setting (five cognitive explanations and five normative explanations). The cognitive explanations suggest that individuals make diverging choices because their perceptions of accident risk differ between the two roles. For instance, individuals assign a lower value to accident risk in the private WTP-based valuation experiments because as a car driver they, for instance, perceive that their personal risk is controllable and trivial on an individual level. Moreover, participants assigned a relatively low value to accident risk because they conceived their personal risk to be lower than the average risk. The normative explanations consist of several reasons why individuals believe that the government should assign more value to safety compared to individual drivers. For instance, individuals believe that the government should assign a specifically high value to safety because it has a duty of care concerning the safety of the transportation network, whereas respondents think the government should not assign a very high value to travel time reductions because car drivers have a relatively high degree of responsibility to reduce their own travel times.

In the experiment of Mouter et al. (2017b) respondents were asked to choose between three alternative transport investment programs of the government which did not differ in terms of the amount of public budget needed to finance the project. The investment programs differed in terms of the size of the travel time savings/traffic safety improvements accruing to the rural areas and urban areas of the Netherlands. Mouter et al. (2017b) shows that in the context of travel time savings, a vast majority of citizens has a strong preference for spatial equality. When the investment program involves traffic safety improvements, the share of citizens that has a preference for spatial equality is considerably smaller. In the experiment of Johansson-Stenman and Martinsson (2008) respondents were asked to choose between two safety-enhancing road investment projects that target different age groups and road user types. Both options required the same public investments. An important difference between the study of Johansson-Stenman and Martinsson (2008) and the studies of Mouter et al. (2017a,b, 2018) is that participants in the former study are framed as third-party decision-makers who choose allocations for other households, implying that their decision will have real effects for other households but not for themselves, whereas the Mouter et al. studies put individuals in a "veil of ignorance" situation informing the respondent that it is not made clear whether or not they would experience any effects (positive or negative) from the road projects among which they can choose. Which of the two experimental settings is more auspicious, is an interesting topic for further research.

4. Participatory Value Evaluation

As addressed, the WTAPB approach infers preferences for impacts of government projects from individuals' choices regarding the expenditure of public euros. However, one clear downside of the WTAPB approach is that respondents are forced to spend the public budget. That is, they have to make a choice between two or three alternative allocations of public budget. Therefore, preferences of individuals who believe that it is better to do nothing and/or reduce taxes instead of allocating public budget to one of the proposed projects are not respected. Participatory Value Evaluation (PVE) is a valuation method which has been developed to address this limitation of WTAPB. PVE establishes the desirability of government projects based on an experiment in which individuals select their preferred portfolio of government projects given a constrained public budget (Mouter et al., 2021).

The crucial difference between PVE and WTAPB is that participants in a PVE have the option to advise the government against allocating the budget to any (or some) of the projects that are considered in the PVE and shift the remaining budget to the next year (Mouter et al., 2020). Recent studies present two variants of PVE-experiments. First, the "fixed budget PVE format" which allows participants to allocate an earmarked amount of public budget. As said, respondents can also decide against allocating public budget to any of the projects and shift the public budget to the next year. To provide a stylized example of a "fixed-budget" PVE-experiment, assume that respondents can allocate a budget of 4 million euro to 8 projects all costing 1 million euro. In this context, respondents can allocate the budget to 4 or less projects. The second type of PVE experiment is called "the flexible budget PVE format." In this format, participants are also allowed to change the public budget which will imply a change in taxes thereby affecting their after tax income. In our stylized example participants would also be allowed to decrease the budget to, for instance, 0 euro and this would imply an increase in private income thereby reducing taxes. On the other hand, respondents can also increase the budget which allows them to select more projects. This would result in a tax increase and a reduction in their private income. Another difference between WTAPB experiments and PVE is that participants in a PVE allocate public budget to a portfolio of projects and, as a result, they can consider positive and negative synergies between projects and potential spatial equity concerns (Mouter et al., 2021). This is not possible in a WTAPB experiment were respondents select only one project from a limited set of projects. Hence, PVE allows individuals to express a broader set of preferences than WTAPB experiments (e.g., positive and negative synergy effects, preferences of individuals who believe that it is better to do nothing and/or reduce taxes instead of allocating public budget to one of the proposed projects).

The innovations of the PVE appraisal method are described in various papers (Dekker et al., 2020; Mouter et al., 2020, 2021). Mouter et al. (2020) explains that the conceptual innovation of the introduction of flexible budget PVEs is that the collective WTP valuation paradigm and the WTAPB valuation paradigm are integrated in one valuation framework. Although the experimental set-up of the flexible budget PVE re-introduces private income into the mix, the issues of WTP-based valuation which WTAPB-based valuation aims to resolve are not re-introduced (Mouter et al., 2020). For instance, preferences of individuals who believe that government funds should be spend on different purposes than their own money can be expressed in flexible budget PVEs and not in WTP-based valuation experiments. Moreover, the problem in WTP-based approaches that respondents protest because they think that the government should pay from (a reallocation of) expected or previously collected taxes is non-existent in a flexible budget PVE.

Mouter et al. (2021) explain that PVE cannot only be considered as a preference elicitation approach which provides input for a CBA, but that the outcomes of a PVE can also be directly used for establishing the social welfare effects of government policy options. In that case, PVE can be considered as a full-fledged alternative to CBA. Dekker et al. (2020) present the technical details of such a welfare analysis. Mouter et al. (2021) also establish the extent to which CBA and PVE provide different policy recommendations and finally they aim to generate empirical insights into potential reasons why PVE and CBA produce different outcomes.

At present, only one large scale PVE has been conducted for the evaluation of transport projects (Mouter et al., 2021). In this PVE, 2498 inhabitants from the Transport Authority Amsterdam (TAA) were presented with 16 transport projects and related societal impacts. The total costs of the 16 projects was 386.5 million euros but with only 100 million euros to spend, it was not possible for the respondents to include all projects in their portfolio. The authors find that projects which focus on improving traffic safety and cycling perform relatively good in the PVE, whereas car projects perform relatively good in the CBA analysis. The authors find two potential reasons why PVE and CBA provide different rankings in the context of the urban mobility investment projects: (1) conventional CBAs value impacts of government projects through observing people's past consumer choices (e.g., hypothetical route choices and behavior in the housing market). Instead, PVE allows individuals to include normative ideas regarding their preferred future urban mobility system. Many of these forward-looking normative statements referred to the importance of fostering cycling and traffic safety (e.g., the normative belief of citizens that the mobility system of Amsterdam should be cycling friendly with less place for the car) (Mouter et al., 2021); (2) a conventional CBA uses standardized approaches to estimate and value impacts of an urban mobility investment, whereas a PVE experiment allows participants to include specific (local) characteristics of a project that are not on the radar of policy makers when valuing the impacts of a project. Especially for the safety projects participants grounded their judgments in personal experiences that policy makers were unaware of prior to the completion of the PVE which might explain why these projects ranked relatively high in the PVE-analysis (Mouter et al., 2021).

5. Future research

The number of collective WTP experiments, WTAPB experiments and PVE experiments conducted in the literature is relatively low compared to the number of private WTP experiments that have been conducted. Hence, we recommend more applications of these three classes of preference elicitation methods to learn more about their merits and the extent to which they produce different outcomes. Secondly, it would be interesting to start new research projects which aim to further explain why these different approaches produce different results. Some potential explanations for differences between private WTP experiments and collective WTP experiments have been offered by Svensson and Johansson (2010). Mouter et al. (2018) provide potential reasons why individuals make different choices in a private WTP and WTAPB setting and Mouter et al. (2021) provide a list of potential reasons why outcomes of CBAs differ from outcomes of PVE-experiments. However, much more research is needed to decipher the mechanisms underlying the empirical differences. Another avenue for further research involves investigating the extent to which different variations of the design of the collective willingness to pay experiments, WTAPB experiments and PVE experiments provide different results. For instance, we have seen that respondents in Johansson-Stenman and Martinsson (2008) are framed as third-party decision-makers, whereas the participants in the experiments of Mouter et al. (2017b) allocated public budget in a "veil of ignorance" context. It is interesting to conduct follow-up research projects which explores the impact of both formats on choices of individuals.

It goes without saying that investigating the normative question of which type of valuation approach (private WTP, collective WTP, WTAPB, PVE) enables "better" economic evaluations of transport-related policies is an important direction for future research. Mouter et al. (2020) state that the answer to this question perhaps depends on the economic question that is being posed. For instance, it is conceivable that PVE is a much more useful tool for analyzing preferences over a fixed set of public projects using existing public funds than in the case of the evaluation of a public project that might be financed through voluntary private contributions of citizens. In the latter case, it might be desirable to evaluate the policy using a private WTP-based valuation approach. A particularly strong argument for basing the appraisal of government projects on the outcomes of other preference elicitation techniques than private willingness to pay studies is that respondents in the study of Mouter et al. (2018) cited various reasons for why the government should not use their own consumer behavior as a model for public policy. However, a potential downside of collective WTP, WTAPB and PVE studies is that it allows respondents to express altruistic preferences and equity concerns which potentially blurs the distinction between efficiency and equity considerations.

A research project which might provide useful input for answering the question which preference elicitation technique is most auspicious for the evaluation of (types of) transport projects involves surveying policy makers' perceptions on this question which can be done using focus groups, interviews or questionnaires.

References

Abrantes, P.A.L., Wardman, M., 2011. Meta-analysis of the UK values of time: an update. Transp. Res. A 45, 1–17.

Ackerman, F., Heinzerling, L., 2004. Priceless: On Knowing the Price of Everything and the Value of Noting. The New Press, New York.

Aldred, J., 2006. Incommensurability and monetary valuation. Land Econ. 82 (2), 141–161.

Allen, M.T., Austin, G.W., Swaleheen, M., 2015. Measuring highway impacts on house prices using spatial regression. J. Sustain. Real Estate 7 (1), 83–98.

Alphonce, R., Alfnes, F., Sharma, A., 2014. Consumer vs. citizen willingness to pay for restaurant food safety. Food Policy 49, 160–166.

Anand, P., Wailoo, P., 2000. Utilities versus rights to publicly provided goods. Arguments and evidence from health care rationing. Economica 67, 543–577.

Anderson, E., 1993. Value in Ethics and Economics. Harvard University Press.

Andersson, H., Lindberg, G., 2009. Benevolence and the value of road safety. Accid. Anal. Prev. 41, 286–293.

Andersson, H., Levivier, E., Lindberg, G., 2019. Private and public willingness to pay for safety: a validity test. Accid. Anal. Prev. 123, 170–175.

Arrow, K., Solow, R., Portney, P.R., Leamer, E.E., Radner, R., Schuman, H., 1993. Report of the NOAA panel on contingent valuation. Fed. Regist. 58, 4601–4614.

Balbontin, C., Hensher, D.A., Ho, C., et al., 2020. Do preferences for BRT and LRT change as a voter, citizen, tax payer, or self-interested resident? Transportation 47 (6), 2981–3030.

Barak, B., Katz, D., 2015. Valuing instream and riparian aspects of stream restoration – a willingness to tax approach. Land Use Policy 45, 204–212.

Bergstrom, J.C., Boyle, K.J., Yabe, M., 2004. Trading taxes vs. paying taxes to value and finance public environmental goods. Environ. Resour. Econ. 28 (4), 533–549.

Blamey, R.K., Common, M., Quiggin, J., 1995. Respondents to contingent valuation surveys: consumers or citizens? Aust. J. Agric. Econ. 39, 263–288.

Carson, R.T., Groves, T., 2007. Incentive and informational properties of preference questions. Environ. Resource Econ. 37, 181–210.

Carson, R.T., Mitchell, R.C., Hanemann, M., Kopp, R.J., Presser, S., Ruud, P.A., 2003. Contingent valuation and lost passive use: damages from the Exxon Valdez oil spill. Environ. Resource Econ. 25, 257–286.

Chorus, C.G., Pudane, B., Mouter, N., Campbell, D., 2018. Taboo trade-off aversion: a discrete choice model and empirical analysis. J. Choice Model. 27, 37–49.

Clark, J., Burgess, J., Harrison, C.M., 2000. I struggled with this money business: respondents' perspectives on contingent valuation. Ecol. Econ. 33, 45–62.

Curtis, J.A., McConnell, K.E., 2002. The citizen versus consumer hypothesis: evidence from a contingent valuation survey. Aust. J. Agric. Econ. 46, 69–83.

Dalrymple, C.J., Peterson, M.N., Cobb, D.T., Sills, E.O., Bondell, H.D., Dalrymple, D.J., 2012. Estimating public willingness to fund nongame conservation through state tax initiatives. Wildl. Soc. Bull. 36 (3), 483–491.

Daniels, R.F., Hensher, D.A., 2000. Valuation of environmental impacts of transport projects. The challenge of self-interest proximity. JTEP 34 (2), 189–214.

Dekker, T., Koster, P.R., Mouter, N., 2020. The economics of participatory value evaluation. Tinbergen institute discussion papers 19-008/VIII.

Dolan, P., Tsuchiya, A., 2005. Health priorities and public preferences: the relative importance of past health experience and future health prospects. J. Health Econ. 24, 703–714.

Hauer, E., 1994. Can one estimate the value of life or, is it better to be dead than stuck in traffic? Transp. Res. A 28 (2), 109–118.

Hess, S., Orr, S., Sheldon, R., 2012. Consistency and fungibility of monetary valuations in transport. Transp. Res. A 46 (10), 1507–1516.

Hestermann, N., Le Yaouanq, Y., Treich, N., 2018. An Economic Model of the Meat Paradox. (Working Paper).

Huang, D., Andersson, H., Zhang, S., 2018. Willingness to pay to reduce health risks related to air quality: evidence from a choice experiment survey in Beijing. J. Environ. Plan. Manag. 61 (12), 2207–2229.

Hultkrantz, L., Lindberg, G., Andersson, C., 2006. The value of improved road safety. J. Risk Uncertain. 32 (2), 151–170.

Ivehammer, P., 2009. The payment vehicle used in CV studies of environmental goods does matter. Agric. Resour. Econ. Rev. 34 (3), 450–463.

Jara-Díaz, S.R., 2007. Transport Economic Theory. Elsevier Science, Amsterdam.

Jara-Díaz, S.R., Gálvez, T., Vergara, C., 2000. Social valuation of road accident reductions using subjective perceptions. JTEP 34 (2), 215–232.

Johannesson, M., Johansson, P.O., 1997. Is the valuation of a QALY gained independent of age? Some empirical evidence. J. Health Econ. 16 (5), 589–599.

Johansson-Stenman, O., Martinsson, P., 2008. Are some lives more valuable? An ethical preferences approach. J. Health Econ. 27 (3), 739–752.

Johnston, R.J., Boyle, K.J., Adamowicz, W., Bennett, J., Brouwer, R., Cameron, T.A., Hanemann, W.M., Hanley, N., Ryan, M., Scarpa, R., Tourangeau, R., Vossler, C.A., 2017. Contemporary guidance for stated preference studies. J. Assoc. Environ. Resour. Econ. 4 (2), 319–405.

Kelman, S., 1981. Cost-benefit analysis: an ethical critique. In: Donaldson, T., Werhane, P.H., Cording, M. (Eds.), Ethical Issues in Business: A Philosophical Approach, pp. 559–564.

Kontoleon, A., Yabe, M., Darby, L., 2005. Alternative payment vehicles in contingent valuation: the case of genetically modified foods. In: Munich Personal RePEcArchive. MPRA Paper No. 1827.

Lusk, J.L., Norwood, F.B., 2011. Animal welfare economics. Appl. Econ. Perspect. Policy 33 (4), 463–483.

Mackie, P.J., Jara-Díaz, S.R., Fowkes, A.S., 2001. The value of travel time savings in evaluation. Transp. Res. E 37, 91–106.

Mackie, P.J., Worsley, T., Eliasson, J., 2014. Transport appraisal revisited. Res. Transp. Econ. 47, 3–18.

Mouter, N., Chorus, C.G., 2016. Value of time: a citizen perspective. Transp. Res. A 91, 317–329.

Mouter, N., van Cranenburgh, S., van Wee, G.P., 2017a. Do individuals have different preferences as consumer and citizen? The trade-off between travel time and safety. Transp. Res. A 106, 333–349.

Mouter, N., van Cranenburgh, S., van Wee., G.P., 2017b. An empirical assessment of Dutch citizens' preferences for spatial equality in the context of a national transport investment plan. J. Transp. Geogr. 60, 217–230.
Mouter, N., van Cranenburgh, S., van Wee, G.P., 2018. The consumer-citizen duality: ten reasons why citizens prefer safety and drivers desire speed. Accid. Anal. Prev. 121, 53–63.
Mouter, N., Ojeda Cabral, M., Dekker, T., van Cranenburgh, S., 2019. The value of travel time, noise pollution, recreation and biodiversity: a social choice valuation perspective. Res. Transp. Econ. 76, 100733.
Mouter, N., Koster, P.R., Dekker, T., 2020. An introduction to participatory value evaluation. Working paper Tinbergen institute 19-024/V.
Mouter, N., Koster, P., Dekker, T., 2021. Contrasting the recommendations of participatory value evaluation and cost-benefit analysis in the context of urban mobility investments. Transp. Res. A Policy Pract. 144, 54–73.
Nunes, P., Travisi, C., 2009. Comparing tax and tax reallocation payments in financing grail noise abatement programmes: results from a stated choice valuation studying Italy. Environ. Resource Econ. 43 (4), 503–517.
Nyborg, K., 2000. Homo Economicus and Homo Politicus: interpretation and aggregation of environmental values. J. Econ. Behav. Organ. 42, 305–322.
Ovaskainen, V., Kniivilä, M., 2005. Consumer versus citizen preferences in contingent valuation: evidence on the role of question framing. Aust. J. Agric. Res. Econ. 49, 379–394.
Persky, J., 2001. Retrospectives. Cost-benefit analysis and the classical creed. J. Econ. Perspect. 15 (4), 199–208.
Posner, E.A., Sunstein, C.R., 2017. Moral Commitments in Cost-Benefit Analysis. Coase-Sandor Institute for Law and Economic Working Papers. No. 802.
Raz, J., 1986. The Morality of Freedom. Clarendon, Oxford, U.K.
Sagoff, M., 1988. The Economy of the Earth: Philosophy, Law, and the Environment. Cambridge University Press.
Sen, A., 1995. Environmental evaluation and social choice: contingent valuation and the market analogy. Jpn. Econ. Rev. 46 (1), 23–37.
Seo, K., Golub, A., Kuby, M., 2014. Combined impacts of highways and light rail transit on residential property values: a spatial hedonic price model for Phoenix, Arizona. J. Transp. Geogr. 41, 53–62.
Sunstein, C.R., 1993. Incommensurability and valuation in law. Mich. Law Rev. 92, 779.
Svensson, M., Johansson, M.V., 2010. Willingness to pay for private and public road safety in stated preference studies: why the difference? Accid. Anal. Prev. 42, 1205–1212.
Swallow, S.K., McGonagle, M.P., 2006. Public funding of environmental amenities: contingent choices using new taxes or existing revenues for coastal land conservation. Land Econ. 82 (1), 56–67.
Thaler, R., 1999. Mental accounting matters. J. Behav. Decis. Mak. 12, 183–206.
Tversky, A., Kahneman, D., 1981. The framing of decisions and the psychology of choice. Science 211, 453–458.
Weimer, D.L., 2017. Behavioral Economics for Cost-Benefit Analysis: Benefit Validity when Sovereign Consumers Seem to Make Mistakes. Cambridge University Press.

CHAPTER FIVE

Evaluating transport equity

Bert van Wee* and Niek Mouter
Delft University of Technology, Delft, The Netherlands
*Corresponding author: e-mail address: g.p.vanwee@tudelft.nl

Contents

Abstract

This chapter reviews and discusses the literature on how equity is operationalized for the purpose of evaluating the impacts of transport policies. It concludes that the equity of accessibility is the most evaluated topic studied. The Gini index is by far the most frequently used index for distributions of accessibility and other effects, probably because of ease of interpretability and communication. The literature on ethical preferences of people, at least as far as related to the distribution of effects of candidate transport policy options, is in its infancy. Interesting topics for future research include distributions in the area of safety, the environment, mobility, changes in distributions over time, preferences of potential users with respect to equity analyses, and the integration of equity analyses in wider evaluation frameworks.

Keywords: Transport policy, Equity, Fairness, Cost-benefit analyses, Gini index, Research agenda

Advances in Transport Policy and Planning, Volume 7
ISSN 2543-0009
https://doi.org/10.1016/bs.atpp.2020.08.002

1. Introduction

Transport policy and planning aim to improve the transport system via implementing policies. Policies include infrastructure policies (roads, bike lanes, rail, ports, airports, ...), pricing (such as levies on fuels, subsidies on public transport or environmentally friendly road vehicles, road pricing), land-use policies, specific public transport policies (such as service hours, time tables), and marketing, information and communication policies. Policies have many different types of effects, on travel times travel time reliability, accessibility levels, safety, the environment, and costs for the public sector, as well as for citizens and companies. This makes evaluating transport policies a very important but also challenging task.

How to evaluate policies, which criteria should apply? In the policy analysis literature there is consensus that "sound" policies have to meet three criteria: they should be effective, efficient and fair (Young and Tilley, 2006). Effectiveness implies that if a policy intervention aims to change the value of any indicator, it should indeed do so. For example, if a policy aims to reduce the number of fatalities, the first criteria implies that it indeed should reduce the number of fatalities. The second criterion, efficiency, implies that the aim should be reached at relatively low "costs." In the case of our example, if a policy measure to reduce the number of fatalities would costs 10 million euro per reduced fatality, and there are other policies that reduce the number of fatalities for, say 100,000 euro, the policy is not efficient. Costs do not have to be financial costs only, but could also include non-financial factors, such as travel times.

Fairness is more difficult to tackle, and rather normative as perceptions of fairness might differ across people (Graham et al., 2013; Haidt and Joseph, 2004). This might explain why fairness has received way less attention in the transport literature than effectiveness and efficiency. Until about 2010 a lively debate on fairness and transport was absent in the literature, the main exception being the social exclusion literature (e.g., Lucas, 2012) but most of that literature is about (local or regional) case studies. Another explanation for the scant attention to the evaluation of equity impacts of transport projects and policies until the 2010s could be that in many countries it is obligatory to assess candidate policy measures, such as transport infrastructure projects or road pricing, using a Cost-Benefit Analysis (CBA). CBA is an economic appraisal method which aims to list all pros and cons of a project, quantifies them, expresses them in monetary terms (Euros, Dollars, ...)

and finally aggregates them in one or a few indicators, such as Benefits minus Costs, or the Benefit Cost Ratio (Koopmans and Mouter, 2020). Subsequently, projects are ranked according to their efficiency. The analyses generally have a national focus: all costs and benefits are calculated at the national level. Fairness is often, but not exclusively, about distributions of effects across (groups of) people, such as income groups, or regions, within a country. Best practice CBA studies nevertheless describe the distributional effects of a transport policy. For instance, in the Norwegian practice distributional consequences may be summarized as a list of winners and losers, supplementing the findings from a CBA (Hagen et al., 2012). However, in a CBA distributional effects are deliberately not evaluated and as a result they also do not affect its final indicators. One reason is that distributional effects are hard to evaluate based on economics alone as the evaluation of distributions depends strongly on the ethical paradigm one adopts (Nyborg, 2012). Thus, the argument goes, the evaluation of equity should be left to policy makers and there is no clear role for researchers (Nyborg, 2012). Another well-known argument against incorporating individuals' distributional concerns in CBA conveyed by Harberger (1978) is that if policy makers want to consider distributional concerns in their decisions, they should always consider to achieve this goal through amending the tax policy because from a societal point of view amending the tax policy is more efficient than handling this particular distributional goal via specific government projects such as building roads or public parks. More specifically, the preference of citizens for a certain distribution of wealth should be handled—when one follows the line of arguing of Harberger—by the tax system and the results should have no implications for the evaluation of specific transport projects.

So it may be understandable that fairness did not receive a lot of attention in the transport appraisal literature, at least not until the 2010s, but on the other hand it is also a bit surprising, because the pros and cons of transport policy measures are generally unequally distributed over (groups of) people. And a lack of (perceived) equity could even be a showstopper for implementing policies, such as road pricing policies (Vonk Noordegraaf et al., 2014). The importance of equity in the public's acceptance of transport policies might have been an underlying reason for the demand of policy makers for more precise evidence on the equity impacts of transport policies which resulted in an increasing demand for academic research revolving around this topic. However, the increasing attention to transport equity in academia might also be triggered by an increase in attention for justice and inequality outside the transport domain. For instance, reducing inequality is nowadays the tenth global goal of the United Nations and the French economist Thomas Piketty reached international fame with his research on wealth concentration (Piketty, 2015).

This chapter reviews and discusses the literature on how fairness is operationalized for the purpose of evaluating the impacts of transport policies. It is limited to distribution effects, first because such effects are a very important subcategory of fairness, and secondly because this is the focus of most of the literature in the area of transport and fairness. We excluded literature that only presents results for distinguished groups, not using a metric to compare groups.

It is important to realize that fairness is not limited to distributions only. For example, it could be that a minister or parliament promised a region to finance a railway line. Regardless of the question if the decision to build the line is a good idea, most people will agree that it is not fair if the minister of parliament would not keep its promise (especially when there does not seem to be a good reason to do so).

More specifically, this chapter aims to answer the following research questions: (1) which topics for which distributions are evaluated? (2) which evaluation methods/indices are used to quantitatively express distributions? (3) which methods are used to evaluate citizens' preferences regarding distributions? (4) how to select a metric to assess distributions quantitatively? (5) which research challenges remain?

If would have been possible to also systematically review the distinctions between groups of people that are made, but the book of Lucas et al. (2019) already gives a clear overview of such distinctions, concluding that dominant distinctions are those based on (1) residential location, (2) mode, (3) income, (4) age, (5) gender, (6) (Dis)ability, and (7) ethnicity. Because the focus of this chapter is on the quantitative indicators used, we do not elaborate on this topic.

The methodology we apply is reviewing the literature. We searched in SCOPUS using several combinations of the keywords EQUITY, FAIRNESS, DISTRIBUTION, ACCESSIBILITY, SAFETY, ENVIRONMENT—see below for more details.

Section 2 discusses the concept of equity, followed by Section 3 presenting the most common metrics to express inequalities of distributions, and Section 4 showing the results of a review of the literature in the areas of accessibility, safety and the environment. Subsequently, Section 5 presents a research agenda, and Section 6 summarizes the most important conclusions of this chapter.

2. What is equity or fairness, and which equity types do exist?

Even though fairness (or equity) is an important concept, it is very difficult to define. The Stanford Encyclopedia of Philosophy does not even provide a definition. It does discuss the concept of fair allocation—see https://plato.stanford.edu/entries/economic-justice/#FaiAll (accessed 9-12-2019), and the terms fairness and equity are used interchangeably. It refers to Kolm (1972) who defines equity as "no envy," and states that "an allocation is envy-free if no individual would prefer having the bundle of another." This does not necessarily mean that "an egalitarian distribution in which everyone has the same bundle" is the only option.

The World Health Organization (WHO) defines equity as: "The absence of avoidable or remediable differences among groups of people, whether those groups are defined socially, economically, demographically, or geographically" (Davis and Pilkington, 2019: 161). We consider the addition of "avoidable or remediable" as extremely important for transport related distributive justice, because differences in levels of accessibility are to a large extent unavoidable and non-remediable. Consider access to, for example, a theater or swimming pool: it is unavoidable that people living nearby have better access to such destinations than people living at a larger distance. And building many theaters and swimming pools across cities would be extremely expensive. In other cases, differences can be reduced by policies, the planning of shopping centers being a clear example.

It is beyond the aim of this chapter to further discuss the concept of fairness, and more specifically distributive justice. And it is not necessary either. This because the majority of the academic papers that discuss transport and fairness do not come to a final conclusion about the level of fairness of a distribution, as their results only provide input to facilitate policy makers to judge the (un)fairness of transport policy options. In other words, it provides information about the level of (un)equality of distributions. Others can use it to come to a final verdict. This is a fundamental difference with the two other criteria of "sound" policies, effectiveness and efficiency, because evaluations can directly address if a policy is effective and efficient. In Section 3 we discuss a small number of studies which attempt to evaluate citizens' preferences regarding distributions. These studies aspire to provide policy makers with information regarding the extent to which a transport policy lines up with the public's fairness judgments.

In line with common practice in this chapter we limit ourselves to methods to quantitatively assess distributions of any output indicator.

A next question is: which equity types are discussed in the literature. Thomopoulos et al. (2009) provide an excellent, and to the best of our knowledge the most extensive overview, at least in the literature on transport and equity. Table 1 gives an overview.

Table 1 shows that many equity types exist, some of which relate to distributions over (groups of) people. This at least applies to equity types 1, 2, 3, 8 and 9. Assessing quantitatively related distributions is very useful to come to a final judgment of these equity types.

Table 2 links these five equity types to the three dominant effect types of transport policies: accessibility, safety and the environment. Health effects

Table 1 Equity types and principles.

Equity types	Nr	Features
Horizontal equity	1	Comparable individuals, groups or regions should be treated in a comparable way
Vertical equity	2	Disadvantaged individuals, groups or regions deserve protection. People should be burdened according to their ability to contribute, and this may lead to schemes where taxes may be progressive
Territorial equity	3	Results from the notion of individual equity, when it is projected on relatively homogeneous regions, and the need to get similar funds for (public) transport
Territorial cohesion	4	Refers to balanced development of human activities across the EU
Level playing field	5	Transport sectors should be treated in similar ways according to taxation, payment for the use of infrastructure, etc
Transport users should pay their way	6	This concept is usually interpreted in terms of average costs implying that the collective of all transport users exactly pays for the aggregate costs
Individuals that are negatively affected by policies need to be compensated	7	This principle has its starting point in the status-quo situation, and implies that winners have to compensate losers
Egalitarianism	8	All individuals are treated equally, making the same contribution, disregarding their financial (or other) ability

Table 1 Equity types and principles.—cont'd

Equity types	Nr	Features
Spatial equity	9	It refers to the geographical location of an individual, group or region affected by a transport infrastructure project
Social equity	10	It refers to the impacts on personal, economic or social characteristics of an individual, group or region
Solidarity	11	It is anticipated that an increased focus on solidarity issues will be facilitated by setting the EU transport policy in the context of the wider EU cohesion policy

Source: Thomopoulos, N., S. Grant-Muller, M.R. Tight, 2009, Incorporating equity considerations in transport infrastructure evaluation: current practice and a proposed methodology. Eval. Program Plann. 32 (4), 351–359.

Table 2 Examples of equity types, applied to accessibility, safety and the environment.

Equity type	Accessibility	Safety	Environment
Horizontal	Accessibility levels of comparable (groups of) people or regions should be about equal	Comparable (groups of) people should have roughly the same safety risks	Comparable (groups of) people should have comparable (maximum) levels of exposure to pollutants
Vertical	Disadvantaged individuals, groups or regions should be treated with priority to increase their accessibility levels	The transport system should prioritize the safety of disadvantaged individuals, groups or regions	The environmental quality of disadvantaged individuals, groups or regions should be improved with priority
Territorial	(European) regions that lag behind should be prioritized via policies that improve accessibility	(European) regions that lag behind should be prioritized via policies that improve safety	(European) regions that lag behind should be prioritized via policies that improve the environment
Egalitarianism	Policies should reduce differences in levels of accessibility between people	Policies should reduce differences in levels of safety between people	Policies should reduce differences in levels of environmental quality between people
Spatial equity	Covered by the regional component of the equity types above		

could be distinguished as a separate category, but because the dominant health effect found in the literature is the exposure to pollutants, we include health effects under the label "environment."

Table 2 shows that at least five of the equity types of Thomopoulos et al. (2009) are useful for the areas of accessibility, safety and the environment.

3. Which evaluation methods are used to express distributions?

Equity analysis is complex because there are several types of equity, various ways to categorize people for equity analysis, numerous impacts to consider, and various ways of measuring these impacts (van Wee and Geurs, 2011). And equity analyses can focus at the level of all persons affected by a project, or at the level of a region or even state or country. The first focus also boils down to a specific geographical area (where changes will be observable), but the area can be flexible, depending on the occurrence of changes. The latter focus generally departs from a predefined geographical area, such as a region or country/state, and is particularly of interest if the focus is on the equity impacts of a combination of policies. Next, we discuss the methods and metrics used for the levels of (in)equality of distributions in transport. Based on our literature search we found the following indicators: the Gini index (and indicators based on the Gini index), the Theil index, the Palma ratio (and comparable indices), the Atkinson index and the Suit index. Below we discuss these indices.

Finally, there are many other methods to qualitatively or quantitatively express distributions across (groups of) people, generally developed in the context of a specific case. Rubensson (2020) for instance identified the Generalized Entropy index and the Robin Hood index. In the book *Measuring transport equity* (Lucas et al., 2019) 16 chapters presenting case studies can be found, and only one of these chapters used one of the indices described below, the Gini index (Pritchard et al., 2019a). It is beyond the aim of this chapter to discuss these methods. We limit ourselves to the generally used quantitative indices as presented below.

3.1 The Gini index

The Gini index is a quantitative indicator expressing the level of (un)equality of a distribution. It expresses the index graphically. It sorts the unit of analyses (individuals, regions, …) on the X-axis, based on the unit of the variable for which the distribution is shown. That unit is expressed on the Y-axis, and shows the sum of that indicator up to any point on the X-axis. The graph also shows the Lorenz curve which is the line representing a 100% equal distribution. Assuming an equal length of the X-axis and the Y-axis, that line is the 45 degree line. The Gini index is the surface between the Lorenz curve and the equal distribution curve, divided by the triangle between the Lorenz curve the X-axis, and the right hand positioned Y-axis. The larger the Gini index, the more unequal the distribution. An often-used indicator for which distributions are visualized this way and expressed in terms of a Gini index is income. Fig. 1 visualizes this distribution of income and the Gini index.

The indicator to be evaluated for the evaluation of distributions relevant for transport could be any quantitative indicator, such as accessibility indicators, indicators for the exposure to air pollution or noise, or risk levels. Note that in case of accessibility a high value is to be preferred, but in case of exposure to pollution, noise or risks a low level is to be preferred. For reasons of interpretation it is possible to sort unit of the X-axis (people, regions ...) in the reversed way, from a high level of exposure (left) to a low level exposure (right), and to transpose values using for the Y-axis the maximum level minus the actual level. For example, if the indicator aims to express the exposure to concentrations of particulate matter, and the maximum level would be 80 microgram per cubic meter, the value for a person

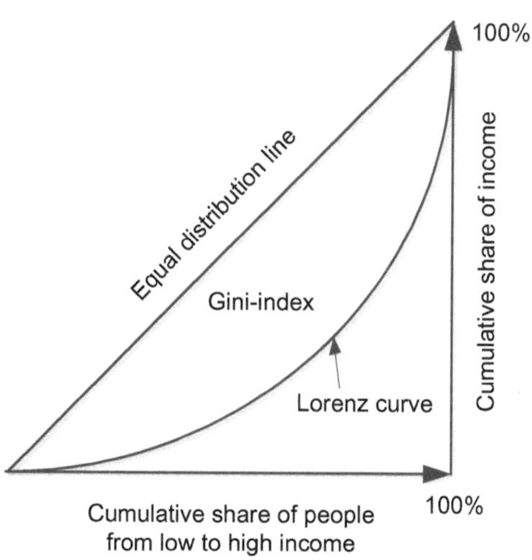

Fig. 1 The Lorenz curve and the Gini coefficient. *Source: Silber, J. (Ed.), 1999. Handbook on Income Inequality Measurement. Norwell, Massachusetts, Dordrecht, The Netherlands, Kluwer.*

exposed to the maximum level would be 0, a person exposed to 60 microgram per cubic meter would receive the value of20, and a person exposed to 20 microgram per cubic meter would receive the value of 60. Transposing the values implies that, as with income, those at the left hand side of the X-axis are worst off, and those at the right hand side are best off.

Such indicators could be expressed at the individual level, but also for areas. The index can also be used to express, for example, per capita CO_2-emissions for travel.

3.2 The Suits index

The Suits index (Suits, 1977), is heavily familiar to the Gini index. The main difference is that units (for example: people) are not sorted based on the value of the variable expressed at the Y-index, but based on income (from low to high). Therefore the slope of the curve is not necessarily increasing continuously, and values above the 45 degree line are possible. It originally was developed to assess tax progressiveness. If low income people would pay a relatively large share of taxes, the value becomes negative, if their share is relatively low it becomes positive.

In the transport arena it can be used to assess to what extent the distribution of any output indicator (accessibility, noise exposure, ...) is distributed over income groups.

3.3 The Palma index

The Gini index includes the distribution over all units, for example, all people in a country, or all municipalities in a country. The Palma index (Palma, 2011) only includes the top 10% and the lowest 40% and expresses the ratio between both groups. In case of income it would divide the income of the top 10% of people by the income of the 40% of the population with the lowest incomes. The Palma index, in other words, ignores the middle income categories, and focuses on the extremes.

As the Gini index, the Palma index can also be used to express levels of accessibility, exposure to air pollution or noise, or risk levels. Again, transposing values could increase the ease of interpretation.

3.4 The Theil index

As the Gini index, the Theil index is also an index to express the level of (in) equality of a distribution (Conceição and Ferreira, 2000). A high value implies a high level of inequality. It is developed to compare groups, for example, geographical units (countries, regions, zones). The value of the Theil index consists of a part expressing the inequality within the groups, and a part expressing the differences between the groups. The index is calculated based on comparing the share of each unit (such as a region) in the total population for which the index is calculated, with the share of that unit in the output indicator. For example, it compares the share of a US state in the population with the share of that state in Gross Domestic Product (GDP). The formula and further explanation can be found at, for example, Wikipedia.

It could potentially be useful to express the level of (in)equality of accessibility across a geographical area. For example, it could be used to express the level of (in)equality of accessibility of all four digit postal codes or local municipalities within one country.

A problem with the Theil index is that it is not easy to communicate, making it a less suitable indicator to communicate to, for example, policy makers.

3.5 The Atkinson index

The Atkinson index (Atkinson, 1970) was originally developed to measure income inequalities. It quantitatively expresses the increase of social utility that would result from a redistribution of resources. As the Palma ratio, the Atkinson index (Atkinson, 1970) is sensitive to the parts of a distribution relevant for inequality since it assesses which ends of a distribution contribute most to the measured inequality. Again the formula can be found on Wikipedia.

The index could be used in the area of transport to show what gains would result from a redistribution of accessibility levels, but this would be a quite theoretical exercise because it would remain unclear which policy actions could lead to such a redistribution.

As with the Theil index a problem with the Atkinson index is that it is not easy to communicate, making it a less suitable indicator to communicate to, for example, policy makers.

3.6 Percentile ratio

This metric compares the level of an indicator of a specific group expressed as a percentile, with the median value for the full populations. An example is comparing the accessibility level of disadvantaged groups relative to all people, as done by Chen et al. (2019b).

3.7 Coefficient of Variation and comparable distribution indices

This standard statistic can be interpreted as an indicator presenting the variability of any quantitative output indicator. A related metric is the standard deviation.

4. Which topics and distribution indices for equity evaluations?

We checked the literature in the areas of accessibility, safety and the environment, to explore which topics were studied, and which metrics for distribution effects were used. We searched for literature in SCOPUS.

4.1 Accessibility

The search strings we used for accessibility is (equity OR equality OR fairness) AND (accessibility). We found 4322 hits, but after checking the first 200 hits we conclude that the large majority of the publications are not about quantitative indicators for the distribution of accessibility. We selected the 10 most recent papers that do have this focus. We excluded papers that only presented results in the form of direct comparisons of groups or regions without any metric for distributions. See for an example: Boisjoly et al. (2020), who studied vertical (income groups based) equity of access to public transport services in four metropolitan areas in Brazil. We first checked via the title and abstract if it would be likely that the paper would focus on distributions of accessibility, and if so, we checked it this was the case. If positive, we included the paper. We summarize our findings in Table 3.

Table 3 can only be used indicatively, it does not include all studies on accessibility and distributions. It shows that the Gini index and Coefficient of Variation (CV) are the most frequently used metrics to quantify inequality of distributions of accessibility. None of the other metrics discussed above were used in these examples. In addition, it shows that some studies present their own indicator. Table 3 also reveals that six out of the ten studies have as the area of application a developing country, and four a developed country.

To find out if the preliminary conclusion that the Gini index is way more popular than the Theil or Palma index, we searched for the combination of Accessibility and Gini, Theil and Palma respectively and found 136, 16 and 7 hits, confirming our preliminary conclusion. We did not do an equal check for the Suits index, because we received many positive hits with the word "suit" or "suits," not referring to the Suits index.

Table 3 Ten recent examples of studies on distributions of accessibility.

Sources	Area	Topic	Metrics used
Chen et al. (2019a)	Tampa, USA	Distribution of benefits of bike sharing systems, horizontal and vertical equity	Gini index Mapping
Mayaud et al. (2019)	Vancouver, Seattle and Portland	healthcare access via public transit	Gini index
Chen et al. (2019b)	Shenzhen, China	Travel time uncertainty/ distributions. Road	Coefficient of Variation, Gini index, percentile ratio
Panagiotopoulos and Kaliampakos (2019)	Greece	Remoteness of service centers	Accessibility/ remoteness index, developed for this study
Tahmasbi et al. (2019)	Isfahan, Iran	Access to urban public facilities, horizontal and vertical equity	Gini index
Grisé et al. (2019)	Montreal and Toronto, Canada	Accessibility by public transport, jobs	Accessibility ratio: job accessibility for people in a wheelchair compared to others
Pucci et al. (2019)	Buenos Aires	Job accessibility by public transport	A synthetic index based on five indices
Liu et al. (2019)	Henan province, China	Access to medical facilities	Coefficient of Variation
Wang and Zhang (2019)	Central Plains Economic Region, China	High Speed Rail travel times between cities	Coefficient of Variation weighted average travel time
Pritchard et al. (2019a,b,c)	São Paulo, Brazil	Bike and ride job accessibility	Gini index

4.2 Safety

Table 4 presents the results for safety. The first search string we used is: ((equity OR equality OR fairness) AND (road safety)). Excluding "road" in the search string would result in many non-transport studies. Because road safety is by far the most important cause of injuries and fatalities in the

Table 4 Studies on distributions of safety.

Sources	Area	Topic	Metrics used
Noland and Zhou (2017)	USA	Impact of recession on traffic fatalities	Gini, but not to measure inequality in safety or risk, but the Gini index for income as an explanatory variable
Chen et al. (2013)	China	Traffic-related disability	Specifically developed indicator: concentration index. Familiar to the Gini index, but population is sorted by income, so even more familiar to the Suits index
Bidgoli et al. (2011)	Iran	Injuries and fatalities	Gini
Elvik (2009)	Norway	Fatalities	Gini
Gaygisiz (2009)	OECD	Fatalities	Gini, as Noland and Zhu
Bener and Farooq (2007)	Qatar	Injuries	Gini
Abdalla (2020)	Dubai	Fatalities	Gini

transport sector we limit our search to road safety. The gross number of hits is 163, only about 4% of the number of hits on accessibility. Only two of the hits used metrics to evaluate inequalities in road safety. Next, we continued our search via the search string ((Gini OR Theil OR Palma OR Atkinson) AND (road AND safety)). Again, we excluded Suits, because this resulted in many hits with the word "suit" or "suits" in the abstract. Five more hits were found, but two of those do use the Gini index without expressing safety impacts in the Gini index. They only use the Gini index for income as an explanatory variable. Table 4 shows the results.

A first conclusion is that measuring inequalities in the area of safety is way less common than in the area of accessibility. Next, all but one study used the Gini index, and one used an index strongly familiar with the Suits index.

4.3 The environment

Finally, we searched for literature in the area of the environment using as the search string.

((Equity OR equality OR fairness) AND (environment) AND (transport*))

Table 5 Studies on distributions of environmental impacts.

Sources	Area	Topic	Metrics used
Ma et al. (2018)	China	Composite measures for sustainable transport efficiency	Gini, Coefficient of Variation
Luo et al. (2016)	China	Freight transport CO_2 emissions	Gini

Because none of the first 50 hits was what we were searching for we changed the search string into:

((Gini OR Theil OR Atkinson OR Palma) AND (environment) AND (transport*))

We only found two successful hits—see Table 5.

The two studies we found both use the Gini index, and one of the two also uses the Coefficient of Variation.

Summarizing the findings of Tables 3–5 we conclude that there are way more applications in the area of accessibility, than in the areas of road safety and the environment. This echoes the observation of various researchers (Brodie, 2015; Martens, 2016; Pereira et al., 2017) that the equitable distribution of accessibility is at the core of the literature regarding transport justice. We could easily find ten papers on accessibility and equity metrics published in 2019, and there were several more even in the same year. A second conclusion is that the Gini index is by far the most used metric, followed by the Coefficient of Variation. We found one application of the Suits index, and no applications of the Theil, Atkinson and Palma ratio. This does not mean they are absent in the transport literature—we only reported the first 10 hits in the area of accessibility. For example, Banister (2018) uses the Palma ratio to compare mode use of dominant transport modes by income class in the UK. And Souche et al. (2016) used the Gini, Theil and Atkinson index to express the distribution of accessibility impacts of urban pricing policies in Lyon, France.

It could be that the use of these indices in the area of transport differs from other areas. To find out we searched for the Gini, Theil and Atkinson index, and the Palma ratio, in Scopus. Again we exclude the Suits index, for the reason explained above. Table 6 presents the results.

Table 6 shows that the Gini index has more hits than the other three metrics together, confirming the conclusion that it is by far the most popular metric used.

An important question is: why is the Gini index way more popular than its competitors? It is a bit speculative, but expect interpretability and ease

Table 6 Use of inequality indices—gross findings from SCOPUS.

Metric	Number of hits
Gini	1767
Theil	504
Atkinson	211
Palma	391

of communication to be the dominant reason. Geurs and van Wee (2004) discuss criteria to select an accessibility indicator, and suggest that the choice should be made based on (1) theoretical basis, (2) interpretability and communicability, (3) data requirements, and (4) usability in social and economic evaluations. The latter criteria is specifically added because of the fact that accessibility impacts are one of several implications of interventions in the transport system, and for the evaluation of all impacts Social Cost-Benefit Analysis (SCBA) and Multi Criteria Analysis (MCA) are often used tools—see Koopmans and Mouter (2020) and Dean (2020). We think that the Gini index and the Palma ratio are way easier to interpret and communicate than the Theil and Atkinson index. Because inequality evaluations generally aim to inform non-experts like policy makers and the wider public, the use of the Theil and Atkinson index probably is chosen way less frequently, because they are difficult to explain. The Palma index is easy to interpret, but focuses on the extremes of a distribution, not the full range, which could be a reason for the higher popularity of the Gini index.

In addition to the ease of communication there are more criteria to choose a metric, the scientific quality and the specific research purpose being probably the most important. It is beyond our aim to fully discuss the pros and cons of indicators in general and for specific cases. Moreover, it is important to realize that there is no consensus about which metric is "best" (Pritchard et al., 2019a,b,c). But there certainly are differences between what the metrics measure. For example, the Gini index (and the related Suits index) includes all measurements, whereas the Palma ratio compares the highest and lowest values. This makes the Gini index more sensitive to the distribution in the middle categories. If one is mainly interested in the differences between the extremes, the Palma ratio thus is the more auspicious metric. But if one is interested in the full distribution, the Gini index is.

It is also important to realize that not only the choice of the metric matters, also the choice of the indicator chosen. Pritchard et al. (2019a,b,c) compare different indicators for accessibility for a specific case using the Gini index and Palma ratio to evaluate the distributions of accessibility levels, and conclude that the outcome of both indices are quite sensitive for the accessibility indicator chosen. In their case this applies more for the Gini index than the Palma ratio.

5. Which methods are used to evaluate citizens' preferences regarding distributions?

The methods discussed in Section 2 are used to quantitatively express the distributional impacts of transport policy options. This can already be useful decision-support to inform the viewpoints of policy makers and other stakeholders such as citizens. Some studies go one step further by evaluating the distributional impacts of transport policy options through a specific or multiple ethical framework (e.g., utilitarianism, Rawls' egalitarianism, sufficientarianism or the capability approach). For policy makers it might be difficult to choose between the ethical frameworks they can adopt to evaluate the fairness of a specific distribution of burdens and benefits resulting from a transport policy. Some scholars defend why a specific framework might be the most auspicious one for evaluating distributional impacts. For instance, Martens (2016), drawing on the philosophical analysis of Dworkin, concludes that a transportation system is fair, if persons struck by various forms of accessibility-related brute bad luck (e.g., travel-related impairments) are provided with a sufficient level of accessibility. Because there is no consensus about which ethical framework to use in which cases, we consider empirical research into preferences of people a useful "solution," and we expect that policy makers in general, and politicians in particular, might find it useful to be informed about the ethical preferences (groups or) citizens. Hence, a small number of contributions in the academic literature aims to study citizens' preferences regarding the desirability of distributions of impacts of transport policy options.

We are only aware of two studies which ask citizens to explicitly assess distributions of transport impacts between individuals. Both studies conduct stated choice experiments in which citizens can choose between alternatives which differ in the way burdens and benefits are distributed among citizens. In Johansson-Stenman and Martinsson (2008) citizens are asked to choose between different safety enhancing road investments that target different age groups. More specifically, they ask respondents to choose between policy options that differ in terms of the number of lives saved, the age of the saved individuals and the type of road users that are saved (pedestrians or car drivers). They find that citizens value a saved life of a pedestrian higher than saving the life of a car driver. Mouter et al. (2017) investigate citizens' preferences for spatial equality in the context of decision-making regarding the composition of a national transport investment plan. They conducted two stated choice experiments: one involving an investment plan for travel time savings, the other involving an investment plan for traffic safety. In the choice experiments, respondents were asked to choose between investment alternatives that differ in terms of the total travel time savings (or safety impacts) for citizens accruing from the investment program, and the extent to which the travel time savings (or safety impacts) accruing from the investment program are distributed in an equal way across two regions (Region A and Region B). Mouter et al. (2017) show that in the context of travel time savings, a vast majority of citizens has a strong preference for spatial equality. Many citizens are willing to sacrifice aggregate travel time savings accruing from a transport investment scheme to ensure a more equal distribution of travel time savings between regions. When the investment program involves traffic safety improvements, the share of citizens that has a preference for spatial equality is considerably smaller. Mouter et al. (2017) assert that these results can inform policy makers who have to evaluate the fairness of the distribution of effects accruing from a transport investment program. For instance, the observation that a larger proportion of citizens' has a preference for spatial equality when the benefits involve travel time savings than when the benefits involve safety improvements might facilitate a more informed and nuanced discussion regarding the importance of spatial equality in the design and appraisal and decision-making regarding transport policies.

But the literature on ethical preferences of people, at least as far as related to the distribution of effects of candidate transport policy options, is in its infancy, and consequently we consider such research are important—see next section.

6. Research agenda

We next present a research agenda for the quantitative evaluation of inequalities in the transport sector.

The most fundamental gap in the scientific literature on transport equity concerns insights into the preferences of potential users of (in)equality studies, such as policy makers, politicians, the wider public, and interest groups. In our study we identified that the equitable distribution of accessibility is at the core of the literature regarding transport equity, but it is not clear whether this is caused by a researcher's preference to study this topic (supply driven research) or because potential users of (in)equality studies value this information (demand driven research). We think that it is particularly important to study this topic. For instance, we observe that people's preferences for the spatial distribution of impacts of transport schemes are hardly studied, whereas researchers who did investigate political decision-making regarding transport projects established that politicians particularly regard "spatial equity" of transport investments as a key consideration in their decisions (e.g., Fridstrøm and Elvik, 1997; Mouter, 2017; Sager, 2016; van der Hoeven, 2015). We do not want to argue that researchers should only investigate topics that are directly useful for practitioners, but in our view more insight into practitioners' preferences with regard to the relevance of information on distributional impacts of transport policies can be a useful starting point for researchers who do want to align their research effort with the needs of practitioners. The same argument holds for the metrics provided by transport equity researchers. We established that the Gini index is the most popular metric deployed by researchers, but we do not know whether and in which contexts policy makers prefer this metric over other metrics.

A closely related topic could be expanding the research which aims to understand citizens' preferences for distributions of transport impacts. It is quite surprising that citizens' preferences regarding this topic are understudied and that the transport literature seems to take a quite technocratic approach when investigating the value-laden topic of transport ethics. It is possible to build upon the studies of Johansson-Stenman and Martinsson (2008) and Mouter et al. (2017) through conducting additional stated choice methods. These two studies investigate citizens' preferences for equity at a very abstract level and it might be more relevant to scrutinize concrete (and real-life) transport policies from this perspective. However, it might also be interesting to investigate this topic using qualitative methods such as interviews and focus groups to gain deeper insight in citizens' fairness intuitions in the transport domain. We consider the combination of qualitative explorative research in the first phase, followed by larger scale quantitative (stated preference) research in the second phase as particularly promising.

Although we think that the research agenda should be affected by needs of practitioners, we believe that it is safe to recommend more research in other areas than accessibility. In the area of safety candidate topics include the distribution of fatalities over population groups in general but also by income group, region, or mode. Such analyses could focus on fatalities per million inhabitants, but also per kilometer driven. In the area of the environment candidate topics include the exposure to concentrations of pollutants and noise, in general, by income group, or geographical area (region, category of municipalities, for example, by urbanization level). Also CO_2 emissions per capita are of interest, to show the inequality in the contribution to climate change. In the area of mobility in general research could focus on the share of income spent on mobility, either in general, or by mode, and the number of kilometers traveled in general and by mode.

Secondly, we observe that most of the research focuses on the distributions in a given year, but we recommend to investigate the changes over years, showing trends in inequalities.

Finally, research could focus on the integration of inequality indices in wider evaluation frameworks. In case of an MCA this is relatively easily because the Gini index and several other indices are normalized (between zero and one). And even non-normalized indices can easily be normalized, for example, on a scale ranging from zero to one. In case of a CBA a monetary value needs to be linked to changes in distributions. The concept of the Willingness To Pay For Fairness (WTPFF) is an interesting option. Researchers could ask respondents for their WTPFF for a more equal distribution in general, or for the trade-off between a more equal distribution and another indicator that can be expressed in monetary terms. For example, researchers could ask for the decrease in overall levels of accessibility or the increase of overall travel times they would consider acceptable for a more equal distribution of accessibility levels or travel times. In case of travel times converting the results in monetary terms is relatively easy because of the standard use of the concept of the Marginal Value of Travel Time Savings (De Jong and Kouwenhoven, 2020). The economic evaluation of accessibility is still in its infancy, the logsum indicator being the most common accessibility indicator used to convert accessibility levels into monetary terms (e.g., Geurs et al., 2010; Rubensson et al., 2020). A third option is a cost-effectiveness analysis (CEA). In that case policy measures can directly be compared on the improvement in any metric per monetary unit (Euro, Dollar, Renminbi, ...) invested. If the concept of the WTPFF would be used, it is important to realize that the research suggested only monetizes the value of change in (perceived) fairness levels. The policies aimed to improve fairness could of course also have negative impacts on others, i.e., those who benefit from the current status, relative to the scenario after the implementation of the policies suggested, and those impacts should be included in a full-fletched CBA as well. If those people are included in a survey on the WTPFF it could be that their answers are influenced by such negative impacts, influencing their responses to questions about their willingness to pay for fairness. Designing good questionnaires and interpreting the results therefore is very important.

7. Conclusions

The most important conclusions of this chapter are first that several metrics exist to express quantitatively the distribution of effects of the transport system, more specifically: accessibility, safety and environmental effects. Secondly, horizontal, vertical, territorial and spatial equity are equity types that can easily linked to quantitative metrics for equity. Third, most applications can be found in the area of accessibility. Studies on the distributions of effects in the area of safety and the environment using quantitative metrics are scarce. Fourth, the Gini index is by far the most frequently used index. We think that the fact that this index is easy to understand and communicate contributes to its popularity. Finally, interesting topics for future research include distributions in the area of safety, the environment, mobility, changes in distributions over time, preferences with respect to distribution analyses of clients, and the integration of distribution analyses and wider evaluation frameworks.

References

Abdalla, I.M., 2020. Fatality risk assessment and modeling of drivers responsibility for causing traffic accidents in Dubai. J. Safety Res. 33 (4), 483–496.

Atkinson, A.B., 1970. On the measurement of inequality. J. Econ. Theory 2 (3), 244–263.

Banister, D., 2018. Inequality in Transport. Alexandrine Press, Marcham, Oxfordshire, UK.

Bener, A., Farooq, A., 2007. Analysis of road traffic crashes data: applying the Lorenz curve and associated Gini index. Middle East J. Emerg. Med. 7 (1), 18–23.

Bidgoli, H.H., Bogg, L., Hasselberg, M., 2011. Pre-hospital trauma care resources for road traffic injuries in a middle-income country—a province based study on need and access in Iran. Injury 42 (9), 879–884.

Boisjoly, G., Serra, B., Oliveira, G.T., El-Geneidy, A., 2020. Accessibility measurements in São Paulo, Rio de Janeiro, Curitiba and Recife, Brazil. J. Transp. Geogr. 82, 102551.

Brodie, S.R., 2015. Equity Considerations for Long-Range Transportation Planning and Program Development. Dissertation, Georgia Institute of Technology.

Chen, H., Du, W., Li, N., Chen, G., Zheng, X., 2013. The socioeconomic inequality in traffic-related disability among Chinese adults: the application of concentration index. Accid. Anal. Prev. 55, 101–106.

Chen, Z., Guo, Y., Stuart, A.L., Zhang, Y., Li, X., 2019a. Exploring the equity performance of bike-sharing systems with disaggregated data: a story of southern Tampa. Transp. Res. A 130, 529–545.

Chen, B.Y., Wang, Y., Wang, D., Lam, W.H.K., 2019b. Understanding travel time uncertainty impacts on the equity of individual accessibility. Transp. Res. Part D: Transp. Environ. 75, 156–169.

Conceição, P., Ferreira, P., 2000. The Young Person's Guide to the Theil Index: Suggesting Intuitive Interpretations and Exploring Analytical Applications. UTIP Working Paper Number 14.

Davis, A., Pilkington, P., 2019. A public health approach to assessing road safety equity—the RoSE cycle. In: Lucas, K., Martens, K., Di Ciommo, F., Dupont-Kieffer, A. (Eds.), Measuring Transport Equity. Elsevier, Amsterdam/Oxford (UK)/Cambridge (USA), p. 328.

De Jong, G., Kouwenhoven, M., 2020. Value of travel time and travel time reliability. Chapter 2. In: Mouter, N. (Ed.), Appraisal Methods. Series: Advances in Transport Policy and Planning, vol. 6. Elsevier, Amsterdam.

Dean, M., 2020. Multicriteria analysis. Chapter 6. In: Mouter, N. (Ed.), Standard Appraisal Methods. Advances in Transport Policy and Planning, vol. 6. Elsevier, Amsterdam.

Elvik, R., 2009. The trade-off between efficiency and equity in road safety policy. Saf. Sci. 47 (6), 817–825.

Fridstrøm, L., Elvik, R., 1997. The barely revealed preference behind road investment priorities. Public Choice 92, 145–168.

Gaygisiz, E., 2009. Economic and cultural correlates of road-traffic accident fatality rates in OECD countries. Percept. Mot. Skills 109 (2), 531–545.

Geurs, K.T., van Wee, B., 2004. Accessibility evaluation of land-use and transport strategies: review and research directions. J. Transp. Geogr. 12 (2), 127–140.

Geurs, K., Zondag, B., de Jong, G., de Bok, M., 2010. Accessibility appraisal of land-use/transport policy strategies: more than just adding up travel-time savings. Transp. Res. Part D: Transp. Environ. 15 (7), 382–393.

Graham, J., Haidt, J., Koleva, S., Motyl, M., Iyer, R., Wojcik, S., Ditto, P.H., 2013. Moral foundations theory: the pragmatic validity of moral pluralism (PDF). Adv. Exp. Soc. Psychol. 47, 55–130. https://doi.org/10.1016/b978-0-12-407236-7.00002-4. ISBN 9780124072367.

Grisé, E., Boisjoly, G., Maguire, M., El-Geneidy, A., 2019. Elevating access: comparing accessibility to jobs by public transport for individuals with and without a physical disability. Transp. Res. A 125, 280–293.

Hagen, K.P., Berntsen, S., Bye, B., Hultkrantz, L., Nyborg, K., Pedersen, K.R., Sandsmark, M., Volden, G.H., Avitsland, G., 2012. Cost-Benefit Analysis. Official Norwegian Report NOU 2012, 16.

Haidt, J., Joseph, C., 2004. Intuitive ethics: how innately prepared intuitions generate culturally variable virtues (PDF). Daedalus 133 (4), 55–66. https://doi.org/10.1162/0011526042365555.

Harberger, A, 1978. On the use of distributional weights in social cost-benefit analysis. J. Polit. Econ. 86, S87–S120.

Johansson-Stenman, O., Martinsson, P., 2008. Are some lives more valuable? An ethical preferences approach. J. Health Econ. 27 (3), 739–752.

Kolm, S.C., 1972. Justice et équité, Paris. In: du CNRS (Ed.), Translated as Justice and Equity. MIT Press, Cambridge, Massachusetts, p. 2000.

Koopmans, C., Mouter, N., 2020. Cost-benefit analysis. Chapter 1. In: Mouter, N. (Ed.), Appraisal Methods. Series: Advances in Transport Policy and Planning, vol. 6. Elsevier, Amsterdam.

Liu, S., Qin, Y., Xu, Y., 2019. Inequality and influencing factors of spatial accessibility of medical facilities in rural areas of China: a case study of Henan province. Int. J. Environ. Res. Public Health 16 (10), 1833.

Lucas, K., 2012. Transport and social exclusion: where are we now? Transp. Policy 20, 105–113.

Lucas, K., Martens, K., Di Ciommo, F., Dupont-Kieffer, A. (Eds.), 2019. Measuring Transport Equity. Elsevier, Amsterdam/Oxford (UK)/Cambridge (USA).

Luo, X., Dong, L., Dou, Y., Liang, H., Ren, J., Fang, K., 2016. Regional disparity analysis of Chinese freight transport CO_2 emissions from 1990 to 2007: driving forces and policy challenges. J. Transp. Geogr. 56, 1–14.

Ma, F., Li, X., Sun, Q., Wang, W., Bai, L., 2018. Regional differences and spatial aggregation of sustainable transport efficiency: a case study of China. Sustainability 10 (7), 2399.

Martens, K., 2016. Transport Justice: Designing Fair Transportation Systems. Routledge, London.

Mayaud, J.R., Tran, M., Nuttall, R., 2019. An urban data framework for assessing equity in cities: comparing accessibility to healthcare facilities in Cascadia. Comput. Environ. Urban. Syst. 78, 101401.

Mouter, N., 2017. Dutch politicians' attitudes towards Cost-Benefit Analysis. Transp. Policy 54, 1–10.

Mouter, N., van Cranenburgh, S., van Wee., G.P., 2017. An empirical assessment of Dutch citizens' preferences for spatial equality in the context of a national transport investment plan. J. Transp. Geogr. 60, 217–230.

Noland, R.B., Zhou, Y., 2017. Has the great recession and its aftermath reduced traffic fatalities? Accid. Anal. Prev. 98, 130–138.

Nyborg, K., 2012. The Ethics and Politics of Environmental Cost-Benefit Analysis. Routledge.

Palma, J.G., 2011. Homogeneous middles vs. heterogeneous tails, and the end of the 'Inverted-U': the share of the rich is what it's all about. In: Cambridge Working Papers in Economics (CWPE), p. 1111. http://www.econ.cam.ac.uk/research-files/repec/cam/pdf/cwpe1111.pdf.

Panagiotopoulos, G., Kaliampakos, D., 2019. Accessibility and spatial inequalities in Greece. Appl. Spat. Anal. Policy 12 (3), 567–586.

Pereira, R.H.M., Schwanen, T., Banister, D., 2017. Distributive justice and equity in transportation. Transp. Rev. 37 (2), 170–191.

Piketty, T., 2015. About capital in the twenty-first century. Am. Econ. Rev. 105 (5), 48–53.

Pritchard, J.P., Stepniak, M., Geurs, K.T., 2019a. Equity analysis of dynamic bike-and-ride accessibility in the Netherlands. In: Lucas, K., Martens, K., Di Ciommo, F., Dupont-Kieffer, A. (Eds.), Measuring Transport Equity. Elsevier, Amsterdam/Oxford (UK)/Cambridge (USA).

Pritchard, J.P., Tomasiello, D.B., Giannotti, M., Geurs, K., 2019b. Potential impacts of bike-and-ride on job accessibility and spatial equity in São Paulo, Brazil. Transp. Res. A 121, 386–400.

Pritchard, J.P., Tomasiello, D., Giannotti, M., Geurs, K., 2019c. An international comparison of equity in accessibility to jobs: London, São Paulo and the Randstad. Transp. Find. https://doi.org/10.32866/7412.

Pucci, P., Vecchio, G., Bocchimuzzi, L., Lanza, G., 2019. Inequalities in job-related accessibility: testing an evaluative approach and its policy relevance in Buenos Aires. Appl. Geogr. 107, 1–11.

Rubensson, I.J., 2020. Making Equity in Public Transport Count. Doctoral Thesis in Transport Science. Stockholm, January 2020.
Rubensson, I., Susilo, Y., Cats, O., 2020. Fair accessibility—operationalizing the distributional effects of policy interventions. In: Submitted to Journal of Transport Geography. TRB Annual Meeting, Washington, USA 12–16 January.
Sager, T., 2016. Why don't cost-benefit results count for more? The case of Norwegian road investment priorities. Urban Plan. Transp. Res. 4 (1), 101–121. https://doi.org/10.1080/21650020.2016.1192957.
Souche, S., Mercier, A., Ovtracht, N., 2016. The impacts of urban pricing on social and spatial inequalities: the case study of Lyon (France). Urban Stud. 53 (2), 373–399.
Suits, D.B., 1977. Measurement of tax progressivity. Am. Econ. Rev. 67 (4), 747–752.
Tahmasbi, B., Mansourianfar, M.H., Haghshenas, H., Kim, I., 2019. Multimodal accessibility-based equity assessment of urban public facilities distribution. Sustain. Cities Soc. 49, 101633.
Thomopoulos, N., Grant-Muller, S., Tight, M.R., 2009. Incorporating equity considerations in transport infrastructure evaluation: current practice and a proposed methodology. Eval. Program Plann. 32 (4), 351–359.
van der Hoeven, N., 2015. The Use of Argumentation in Transport Infrastructure Debates: An Analysis. Delft University of Technology. Thesis Repository.
van Wee, B., Geurs, K.T., 2011. Discussing equity and social exclusion in accessibility evaluations. EJTIR 11 (4), 350–367.
Vonk Noordegraaf, D., Annema, J.A., van Wee, B., 2014. Policy implementation lessons from six road pricing cases. Transp. Res. A Policy Pract. 59, 172–191.
Wang, X., Zhang, W., 2019. Efficiency and spatial equity impacts of high-speed rail on the central plains economic region of China. Sustainability 11 (9), 2583.
Young, W., Tilley, F., 2006. Can businesses move beyond efficiency? The shift toward effectiveness and equity in the corporate sustainability debate. Bus. Strateg. Environ. 15 (6), 402–415.

CHAPTER SIX

Innovations in the appraisal of public transport projects

Niels van Oort* and Menno Yap
Smart Public Transport Lab, Delft University of Technology, Delft, The Netherlands
*Corresponding author: e-mail address: n.vanoort@tudelft.nl

Contents

Abstract

Public transport is an effective tool to address multiple societal challenges, regarding mobility, sustainability and livability. When looking at typical public transport projects and traditional appraisal methods, the main type of benefits that are considered for

Advances in Transport Policy and Planning, Volume 7
ISSN 2543-0009
https://doi.org/10.1016/bs.atpp.2020.07.008

public transport projects are passenger travel time savings, additional revenues due to increased ridership or a new fare policy and timetable savings (due to shorter trip times and less timetable hours). These current approaches provide insights into the expected performance and benefits of public transport to *some* extent, but they often disregard many other (positive) effects. This is partly due to a limited focus, but also due to a lack of a framework and knowledge. In this chapter, we present a framework, the 5E model, that supports the assessment of the broader benefits of public transport projects. Specifically, we show how to quantify and monetize the improvements of service reliability, robustness and crowding relief.

Keywords: Public transport, Appraisal, Service reliability, Crowding, Robustness, Wider benefits

1. Introduction

Public transport is an effective "tool" to address multiple societal challenges, regarding for instance mobility, sustainability and livability (see for instance Manville and Cummins, 2015 and Nicolaisen et al., 2017). Public transport is often related to multiple policy goals. One obvious objective of introducing, extending and consolidating public transport systems is to enable people to move from A to B with a specific quality level. The customer satisfaction pyramid (Van Hagen and van Oort, 2019) shows the multiple quality attributes of public transport that are appreciated by users (see Fig. 1).

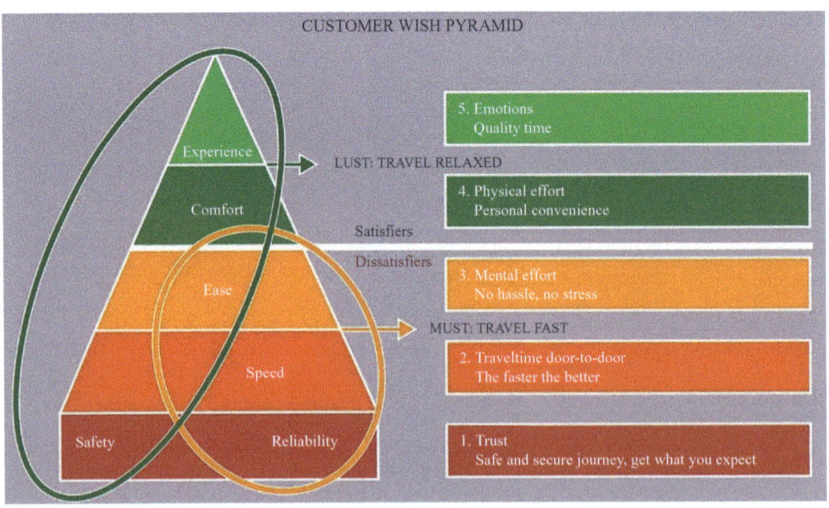

Fig. 1 Customer satisfaction pyramid (Van Hagen and van Oort, 2019).

All attributes of the pyramid influence passenger perceptions and thus need to be of a sufficient quality level to attract people to use the system. In Peek and van Hagen (2002) it is shown that both the basic needs (dissatisfiers) and additional ones (satisfiers) should be considered when investing in (improving) public transport. Depending on many variables, such as context and current performance, it might be more efficient to invest in alleviating the dissatisfiers in one case, and promoting the satisfiers in another case.

In addition to the mobility related goals as mentioned above, other policy goals served by (good) public transport could be:

- Climate goals
- Reducing congestion
- Social inclusion

On a more strategic level, one could say that public transport could help to develop sustainable, accessible and livable cities and regions. When discussing objectives, stakeholders are important to consider as well. Multiple stakeholders are involved in both public transport projects and operations, having different interests and stakes. In addition to the passenger, important stakeholders are transit authorities, operators, infrastructure providers and last but not least, citizens. They might not use the specific system, but they can be affected nevertheless, for instance in their living area or while using other modes.

To decide whether to start with a public transport project, aiming at goals such as mentioned above, appraisal of the expected costs and benefits is essential. This is independent of the type of project, ranging from very large projects such as a new metro line (the Elizabeth Line in London for instance) to small ones, such as adjusting traffic lights to give priority to public transport. Other types of public transport projects relate to the (re)design of the network, concerning services and infrastructure (including stops and stations), schedules, operations and control. In general, two types of assessments exist: ex ante and ex post. This chapter addresses ex ante analysis, showing methods and challenges to assess the expected impacts of a project before the actual implementation. Ex post analysis (evaluating the actual impacts after the implementation of a project) yields valuable input to assess these expected impacts, taking into account all lessons learnt, revealed preferences and behavior (see e.g., Hensher, 2014; Tirachini et al., 2016), and actual construction times and costs (see for instance Flyvbjerg, 2007). The type of impacts could vary greatly among different projects. Obviously, on an aggregated level, (societal) costs and benefits are the two main components when assessing these impacts. These could be divided however in multiple disaggregated attributes. For costs, that concerns investment costs and operation costs, for all kinds of elements of public transport, such as tracks, roads, stops, stations, depots, workshops, signaling and safety systems, power supply, in addition to the service itself, provided by vehicles and crew. The number of trips and total trip times determine the total number of offered schedule hours and depending on the mode (and its specific cost per hour to operate) that yields total operating costs. Costs, however wide, are relatively easy to assess. Benefits are even broader and are often harder to grasp. In addition, the importance of some benefits greatly depends on the objectives set (by multiple stakeholders). For these reasons, this chapter provides insights in ex ante appraisal of the (potential) benefits of public transport systems. This chapter specifically considers the assessment of broader benefits of public transport projects, in addition to traditional travel time benefits. The outline of the chapter is as follows: In Section 2 the general framework of the chapter is explained, being the 5Es. Sections 3–7 elaborate on all E's individually. Sections 8–10 provide more details about three specific, potential benefits of public transport projects, being service reliability, robustness and crowding. This complete chapter is based on (project) experiences, literature and multiple research projects and publications (Van Oort, 2016; Van Oort et al., 2017; Yap, 2020).

2. Assessing public transport benefits: The 5E framework

When looking at typical public transport project and traditional appraisal methods (see for instance Annema et al., 2007), the main type of benefits that are considered for public transport projects are passenger travel time savings (using the Value of Time; see e.g., Li et al., 2013; De Jong and Kouwenhoven, 2020), additional revenues due to increased ridership or a new fare policy and timetable savings (due to shorter trip times and less timetable hours).

Current approaches, such as CBAs (cost-benefit analysis; see e.g., Mouter et al., 2013; Koopmans and Mouter, 2020), provide insights into the expected performance and benefits of public transport to *some* extent, but they often disregard many other (positive) effects, such as space efficiency and equity related impacts (Van der Bijl et al., 2018). This is partly due to a limited focus, but also due to a lack of a framework and knowledge. The (potential) underestimation of the benefits might result in the postponement or even cancellation of plans, since justification of the (high level of) costs are necessary. To allow for a better and fair assessment of public transport projects, more insights are required into (the value of) its "broader" benefits. All the effects related to the goals mentioned in the introduction should be taken into account when assessing public transport projects.

To outline the "broader" effects that could be taken into account while assessing public transport projects, we developed a methodology to illustrate and to quantify the value of public transport using five E's (Van Oort et al., 2017). The five domains of argumentation are listed below and illustrated by Fig. 2:

- Effective mobility—effectiveness of transport and mobility;
- Efficient city—suitability of spatial use and spatial/urban (re)development;
- Economy—prosperity and wellbeing in/for cities;
- Environment and health—decreasing carbon footprints; sustainable cities; public health;
- Equity—socially inclusive cities.

All five domains are discussed in Sections 3–7. These sections do not aim to provide a full review, but they provide insights and inspiration for every "E" supporting application in appraisal schemes. More details and

Fig. 2 The 5E framework (Van Oort et al., 2017).

references regarding all "E's" may be found in Van Oort et al. (2017). The model is also useful and applied for assessments of projects of other modes, such as bicycle projects.

3. Effective mobility

Public transport is able to transfer a large number of people from A to B in a fast, comfortable and reliable manner and could reduce congestion on roads in the process. However, in traditional assessment methods, the main focus is mostly only on travel time gains. Other related impacts get limited attention and are discussed below (based on findings in Van Oort et al., 2017).

3.1 Comfort, robustness and service reliability

High-quality public transport has the potential to increase travel quality. Examples to achieve this are higher frequencies, more comfort brought about by new vehicles and upgrading stops. Mobility reliability and resilience have become more important over the years (see e.g., Anderson and Daganzo, 2019; Snelder and Tavasszy, 2010) and similarly, reliability and robustness are important aspects to consider when assessing projects. Also, enhanced passenger comfort and experience are more frequently discussed (see for instance Yap, 2020, Tirachini et al., 2013, Van Hagen and van Oort, 2019). However, important and on the political agenda, service reliability, robustness and comfort are often neglected and underestimated in cost-benefit analyses (as shown by for instance Van Oort, 2016). Therefore, we discuss these topics in detail in Sections 8–10.

3.2 Rail bonus

Another aspect often absent in assessments of public transport projects is the so-called Rail bonus. Provision of rail bound public transport might lead to greater benefits than comparable road bound public transport, identified by Bunschoten et al. (2013) as the "rail bonus." This bonus is the added value causing more travelers to use rail than bus while levels of service are equal. To better understand this phenomenon, they conducted a choice experiment among inhabitants of Dutch cities. The choice experiment required respondents to choose between a bus alternative and a rail alternative. Both alternatives differ in the same aspects, so the difference in mode-specific constants indicates the difference in preference. The perceptions of a number of mode characteristics of bus and light rail were measured to explain the difference in preference. Finally, the transition from difference in preference to the number of travelers was made using a transport model.

The ratio indicated that when a minute traveled by bus is valued as 1 min, this minute in light rail is valued as 47 s. Traveling by rail is therefore on average perceived 22% shorter than traveling by bus. Applying this number in a study of transforming a bus line into a light rail line in Utrecht, it resulted in a prospect of an increase in travelers of 4.3%, solely by this rail bonus (Bunschoten et al., 2013). More recent research of the rail bonus by Gaspardo (2019) confirms these findings, showing that passengers appreciate rail over bus, due to, for instance, better driving and seating comfort and capacity.

3.3 Modal shift and congestion reduction

The potential of public transport to reduce traffic congestion also stems from the fact that a relatively small reduction in vehicle use can lead to a significantly larger reduction in hinder, once roads reach their maximum capacity. For example, a reduction of traffic volumes from 90% to 85% of a road's capacity can reduce delays for all users by 20% or more (Litman, 2009). Considering the societal costs of congestion, estimated at an annual €2.3–€3 billion in the Netherlands (Stichting Wetenschappelijk Onderzoek Verkeersveiligheid (SWOV), 2017) or between £7 and £30 billion per annum in the UK (Shaw and Dochterty, 2014) there is an enormous potential.

At a minimum, shifting from private cars to public transport saves fuel and oil, which typically results in about 10¢ per vehicle-mile reduction in the USA (Litman, 2015). In addition, depreciation, insurance and parking costs are partly variable, since increased driving increases the frequency of vehicle repairs and replacement, reduces vehicle resale value, and increases the risks of crashes, traffic and parking sides. These additional mileage-related costs are typically 10–15¢ per mile, implying total cost savings of 20–25¢ per mile. More savings are available when better public transport incentivizes vehicle ownership reductions. For example, if improved public transport services allow 10% of users to reduce their households' vehicle ownership (e.g., from two vehicles to one), the savings average $300 annually per user, or 6¢ per public transport travel passenger-mile in addition to vehicle operating cost savings (Van Oort et al., 2017).

Because public transport riders tend to travel on congested urban corridors, they tend to have much larger congestion reduction impacts than their regional mode share. For example, although only 11% of Los Angeles commutes use public transport, when a strike halted public transport service for 5 weeks, average highway congestion delay increased 47%, and regional congestion costs increased 11–38% (Anderson, 2013). Large speed reductions were observed particularly on roads parallel to rail corridors (Lo and Hall, 2006), indicating that higher quality, grade-separated service is particularly effective at reducing congestion (Anderson, 2013; Lo and Hall, 2006).

Another example in Baltimore showed that the roadway congestion index increased on average 2.8% annually before light rail service started in 1992, but only 1.5% afterwards. Similarly, Sacramento's congestion increased 4.5% annually before and 2.2% after light rail service started in 1987; St. Louis congestion increased 0.89% before and 0.86% after light rail service started in 1993; while Dallas experienced no change after rail service commenced in 1996 (Litman, 2015).

3.4 Option value

The option value refers to the value people place on having a transport option available even if they do not currently use it (ECONorthwest and PBQD, 2002; Laird et al., 2009). Public transport can provide critical transportation services during personal and community-wide emergencies, such as when a personal vehicle has a mechanical failure, or an incident limits car traffic. This involves assigning an additional value to each public transport trip made by infrequent users, taking into account the cost to consumers of each trip, the volatility of demand and the expected frequency of such trips. In typical conditions this appears to be in the range of $1–10 annual per resident who expects to use public transport a few times each year (ECONorthwest and PBQD, 2002; Litman, 2015).

4. Efficient cities

The second E of our framework addresses the impacts of public transport projects on space efficiency, considering the challenge of land use planning facing limited space in most cities. We discuss them both in this section, based on Van Oort et al. (2017). Public transport is efficient in its use of space and spurs and sustains urban (re)development and improvements of public realm by accessing areas (see e.g., Van der Bijl, 2006). A previous study found that gross urban population densities would be

27% lower without public transport systems to support compact development, and this increased density reduces urban vehicle travel, transport fuel use and GHG emissions by 8% (Gallivan et al., 2015). Based on fixed infrastructure, high-quality public transport modes can play an important role in urban planning/design and traffic planning/design. Knowles and Ferbrache (2015) appreciate these qualities because public transport in this respect can attract "inward investment, employers, business and tourist visitors." Various new tramways and BRT (Bus Rapid Transit) systems show the iconic effect and value of public transport. Hence, cities may develop their own brands around their public transport system. In addition, public transport is able to (re)structure and to (re)shape the city. We mention four perspectives here (obtained from Van der Bijl, 2006):

Firstly, high-quality public transport can play a decisive part in designing public space. Over the past years many examples have been gathered (Van der Bijl et al., 2005, 2018), in which principles and strategies were developed to create high-quality public transport in cities and urban regions. Belden et al. (2004) report that USA consumers place a high value on urban amenities such as shorter commute time and neighborhood walkability. Sixty percent of prospective homebuyers reported that they prefer a neighborhood that offered a shorter commute, sidewalks and amenities like local shops, restaurants, libraries, schools and public transport over a more automobile-dependent community with larger lots but longer commutes and poorer walking condition. About 46% find being in walking distance of public transportation "very" or "somewhat important."

Secondly, public transport is an efficient tool for urban and regional planning (Van der Bijl et al., 2018). High-quality public transport turns out to be able to restructure the city and urban region. The same goes for neighborhoods, quarters and precincts, including declining areas. Public transport as urban-regional public transport is a powerful tool to oppose unrestrained urban growth.

Thirdly, public transport can be considered a major condition for urban development. High-quality public transport on embedded and fixed infrastructure (like metros) can improve urban connections and local accessibility. Their fixed infrastructure guarantees a technical and economic life span of at least 30 years. This ensures that the connections and local accessibilities can be useful for a very long time. More remote areas further away can be connected and accessed when the infrastructure is extended. This could be helpful to create new, favorable conditions for further (re) development of these areas.

The fourth function of public transport is its support to Transit Oriented Development (TOD, see Marti et al., 2018). The fixed infrastructure that comes with for instance rail systems provide structure, which is useful for TOD as it helps to steer real estate investments around stations, hubs (see e.g., Torabi et al., 2019) and stops.

5. Economy

High-quality public transport could improve the competitiveness of an area by attracting companies and inhabitants to its direct surroundings (Hensher et al., 2012). These benefits should be considered while assessing the impacts of public transport projects. In this section, we will discuss multiple examples of the economy related benefits (obtained from Van Oort et al., 2017). Pogonyi (2020) also addressed some of these (wider) economic benefits.

Well served public transport stops and stations present favorable conditions that can elicit investments or other economic incentives. Particularly improved accessibility of sites is very meaningful for development, hence for the (future) land and property value. Hass-Klau et al. (2004) report that public transport can represent an important condition for creating urban situations with positive economic effects, but always in combination with other interventions, such as investments, supportive policies, etc.

In many cases, the introduction or improvement of public transport is seen as a key success factor when developing (new) sites, for instance because many companies see it as an essential element before relocating to a new site. For example, a public investment in the MediaCity UK light rail-extension in Manchester was a perquisite for BBC to become a local tenant of the newly developed area (Conventz et al., 2013).

The impact of public transport on urban development is especially apparent at the former Docklands area in East London, which was redeveloped into business district Canary Wharf. A public investment of £77 million in the Docklands Light Railway, intended to provide the area with fast connections to the City of London and, among others, London City Airport, enabled Canary Wharf to be developed by Olympia and York (Conventz et al., 2013). The firm also invested itself in the public transport development: £25 million in the construction of Canary Wharf station and £68 million in the DRL-extension to Bank underground station (Carter, 1991). Subsequently, land values in the Isle of Dogs area (located in the

Docklands area) rose from of £70,000 an acre in 1981 to £4.9 million in 1988 (Knowles, 1992). This theory is confirmed by other cases; for instance in Bremen, where sites adjacent to tram lines had land prices roughly 50% higher than those with no direct public transport access. In the Rouen area, housing prices rose more than 10% when public transport was improved and the same happened in Portland (+6.5%) (Hass-Klau et al., 2004).

Concerning commercial values, several sources report on impacts (see e.g., Dubé et al., 2014). In San Jose, for instance, rents on commercial lease transactions between 1984 and 2000 were 13% higher within 400 m of light rail stations than those more than 1200 m away. In Dallas it was 22.7% and in Santa Clara it was 7–10% (Crocker et al., 2008; Hass-Klau et al., 2004; Mohammad et al., 2013; Weinberger, 2001).

Conventz et al. (2013) discuss similar situations of high-quality public transport stimulating inward investment occurring in Ørestad (relocation of Denmark's Radio), West Midlands, Montpellier, Rouen, Calgary, Vancouver, St. Louis.

6. Public transport impacts on environment and health

The fourth E of the 5E model concerns the potential benefits of public transport projects on environment and health. In this section, we provide examples and literature regarding these aspects (obtained from Van Oort et al., 2017).

6.1 Environment

Public transport is considered an environmentally friendly mode, regardless of some differences between specific modes (Mulley et al., 2017). Together with walking and cycling, public transport is essential for keeping cities and urban areas livable. A modal shift from individual to active and collective transport forms the foundation of sustainable transport, which in this regard is more efficient for all related issues, such as energy consumption and greenhouse emissions. This does not only concern the operations, but the complete life cycle, from construction to recycling (Kapetanović et al., 2019).

Public transport could lower emissions mostly in the urban areas, where the problems are most profound. Compared to car traffic, it is estimated that public transport consumes about half the energy and only produces 5% as much CO and 50% of the CO_2 and NOx emissions per passenger-mile (Shapiro et al., 2002). This is even without involving current developments regarding zero-emission buses. Typical households can reduce their greenhouse gas emissions by 25–30% when they shift from two cars to one car (Davis and Hale, 2007). When shifting to public transport entirely, a typical household can reduce its energy consumption and harmful emissions by about 45% (Bailey, 2007).

In addition, shifts from automobile to public transport directly reduce vehicle mileage, transport fuel use and GHG emissions by 2%, indicating that indirect emission reductions leveraged by land use changes are four times larger than the direct benefits from mode shifting.

6.2 Health

The impact of public transport on public health is in general positive. As identified above, more public transport use (if replacing private car trips) leads to lower carbon emissions and hence reduces the risk on several diseases and premature deaths. This can have an enormous impact, as recent European (EU) figures show that 400,000 premature deaths per year can be attributed to air pollution, be it from all sources and thus not limited to transport (European Environment Agency, 2015). To put this figure in perspective; the annual death toll by traffic accidents is around 25,000 (Eurostat, 2016).

Apart from reducing the risk on pollution related diseases, there are more health benefits associated with using public transport. As most public transport trips involve walking or cycling to access stops or stations, passengers walk about three times more than people who rely on car transport. Recent developments and trends show more attention to ridership growth of the combined bicycle and transit mode (e.g., Shelat et al., 2018). One of the reasons is, among others, the introduction of shared bike schemes as a last mile solution (Ma et al., 2020). Besser and Dannenberg (2005) report that public transport users perform nearly 22 min of moderate physical activity on average. An Australian study revealed that in Melbourne, public transport users spend 41 daily minutes on walking or cycling, which is 5 times more than the 8 min by people traveling entirely by car (BusVic, 2010). Lachapelle et al. (2011) confirm this, as they found that public transport commuters on average 5–10 times more daily minutes of moderate-intensity physical activity. As a result, the odds of becoming obese for elder (60+) public transport users are up to 25% lower than for those who do not use public transport in the same age group (Webb et al., 2011).

7. Equity

Public transport could have large beneficial social impacts in establishing an inclusive society with equal opportunities for all inhabitants. Public transport systems allow people that cannot use private transport, e.g., due to lower incomes or a disability, to access education, employment centers or healthcare facilities. This raises, among others, the employment levels and aides social inclusion. This could also lead to significant overall cost reductions in the public funding of health care and welfare. This section provides examples and literature regarding these effects, related to the last E of our framework, being Equity (as discussed in more detail in Van Oort et al., 2017; van Wee and Mouter, 2021).

Crain & Associates (1999) discuss that many commuters would not be able to continue their current job when public transport services would cease. Therefore, it is no surprise that the availability of public transport plays a major role in the decision of many people whether to apply for, to accept or stay in employment. In some cases, almost half of the job seekers say that a lack of personal transport or poor public transport is a key barrier from preventing them from getting a job (Social Exclusion Unit, 2003). Looking at this from a company perspective, this also implies that a lack of public transport services has a direct negative impact on the labor pool available (Knowles and Ferbrache, 2015).

Public transport can support government agency activities and reduce their costs. For example, without public transport services some people are unable to reach medical services, sometimes resulting in more acute and expensive medical problems. The Social Exclusion Unit (2003) found that nearly one third of all people without a car have difficulties accessing their local hospital (compared to 17% of people owning a car). Public transport can have a crucial role in improving this accessibility. This is illustrated by a study in Rural North Carolina, where public transport users averaged four more chronic health care visits than non-users (Arcury et al., 2005). This use of transport services for preventive medical trips (therewith avoiding hospital stays) in a study in Florida was estimated to result in a social benefit of $11.08 per dollar invested (Cronin et al., 2008). Given the costs involved, it is no surprise that the social benefit of health care-related public transport trips (in relation to home health care costs) was found to be around \$5.66 per trip in Wisconsin; much higher as the benefit per work-related trip, which "only" came to about \$1.55 (HLB Decision Economics Inc, 2003).

8. Assessing service reliability benefits

In Sections 8–10, we discuss approaches how to assess the benefits of three important public transport aspects in cost-benefit analyses, namely reliability benefits (Section 8), crowding relief (Section 9) and robustness benefits (Section 10). In current state-of-the-practice, potential benefits resulting from these aspects are often incorporated only in a simplified or qualitative manner in cost-benefit analyses, hence justifying a more detailed discussion how to quantify these benefits.

8.1 Introduction

Both passengers and operators benefit from more reliable services and therefore service reliability is found among the most important quality characteristics of public transport (Crocker et al., 2008), leading to many projects aiming to improve its level. However, until recently, this attribute is rarely incorporated explicitly in ex ante assessments. OECD/ITF (2009) stated that until then incorporating reliability in CBAs was only applied in a limited number of countries and the main applications were focusing on road traffic instead of public transport.

Fig. 3 presents the findings of an analysis of over 20 randomly selected cost-benefit analyses (CBA) of public transport projects in the Netherlands

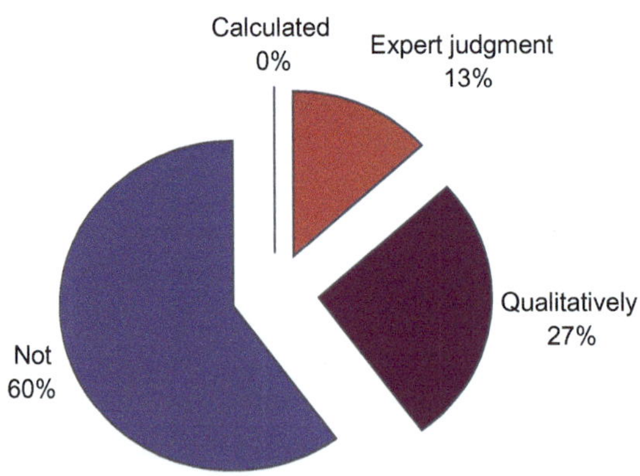

Fig. 3 Results of survey on incorporating service reliability impacts in Dutch CBAs (Van Oort, 2016).

(Van Oort, 2016), that explicitly aimed at improved service reliability. It is demonstrated that no explicit calculation of expected service reliability effects is performed at all and in 60% of the projects it is not even mentioned as a benefit.

So until recently, quantifying service reliability effects of projects on passengers was not common practice. In general, the focus of service reliability indicators lied (is) often on vehicle effects (Van Oort, 2014), while the passenger effects are also of importance when assessing costs and benefits.

In this section, we share a framework to calculate these passenger effects and will show how to incorporate them into a CBA (based on Van Oort, 2011 and Van Oort, 2016). We also show an application of the method to a case study of a new tram line in Utrecht in the Netherlands (obtained from Van Oort, 2016).

In preparation of quantifying service reliability related benefits, we introduce the impacts of service unreliability on passengers, being (Noland and Small, 1995; Van Oort and van Nes, 2009):

- Extension of in-vehicle time and waiting time, which lead to arriving late;
- Increased variability of departure times, arrival times, in-vehicle times and waiting times, which lead to uncertainty of the actual arrival time.

The third impact, being the probability of finding a seat and crowding, will be discussed in Section 9.

8.2 Three steps to incorporate service reliability effects in CBAs

To consider service reliability related impacts in CBAs, we developed a three-step approach (Fig. 4; Van Oort et al., 2016). The previous section

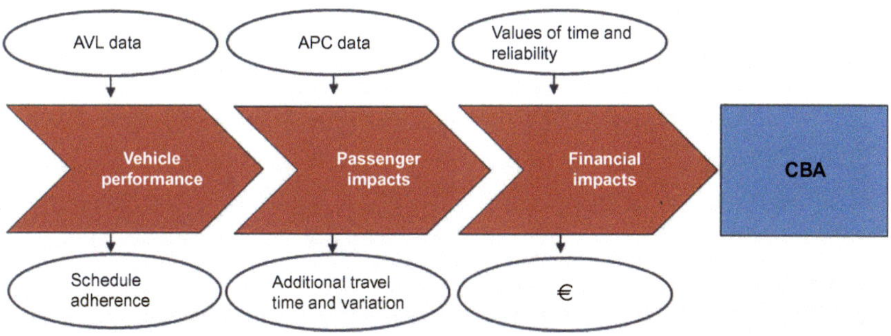

Fig. 4 Three steps to incorporate passenger impacts of service reliability into CBAs (Van Oort, 2016).

already showed the passenger effects of service unreliability, namely the additional travel time per passenger and its distribution. These impacts may be calculated by the methods described in Van Oort (2011). These methods imply translating the vehicle impacts (e.g., punctuality) into passenger impacts (e.g., additional travel time). These are respectively step 1 and step 2 of our method, as shown by Fig. 4. These passenger impacts may be expressed as monetary values by using the values of time and reliability (see for instance Li et al., 2010, 2013), see de Jong and Kouwenhoven (2020). In that format, they may be directly incorporated into CBAs.

8.3 Case study: CBA Uithoflijn

In addition to setting up this three-step approach, we performed a case study in the city of Utrecht, being the fourth largest city in The Netherlands with over 300,000 inhabitants. The Dutch government required a CBA to financially support the construction of a tram line in Utrecht between the central station and the university and hospital campus (Uithof). The case gives an example of applying our method and is illustrated in the remainder of this section.

In the CBA of the case study, we calculated the service reliability benefits of transforming the existing bus system into a tram system. We compared five future situations (in 2020), including bus and tram. A detailed description of all alternatives and their costs and benefits may be found in Goudappel Coffeng (2011) and Van Oort (2016). In this section we will only focus on the reference and the tram alternative, being:

Reference case (2020)

No additional infrastructure will be constructed and the capacity is limited. Since ridership will increase and the number of buses accordingly, it is expected that unreliability will increase.

Tram case (2020)

In this case the service is operated by trams with high-quality via for instance own right of way. Due to sufficient capacity on the track and at the stops and little interaction with other traffic, the expected level of service reliability will be high.

To support the CBA with insights in the passenger impacts of service reliability, we analyzed the current (2008) performance, which we used as the base for the 2020 predictions of all scenarios and all steps of Fig. 5. The level of service was determined by investigating vehicle data (illustrating for instance punctuality; find more details of these so-called Automatic

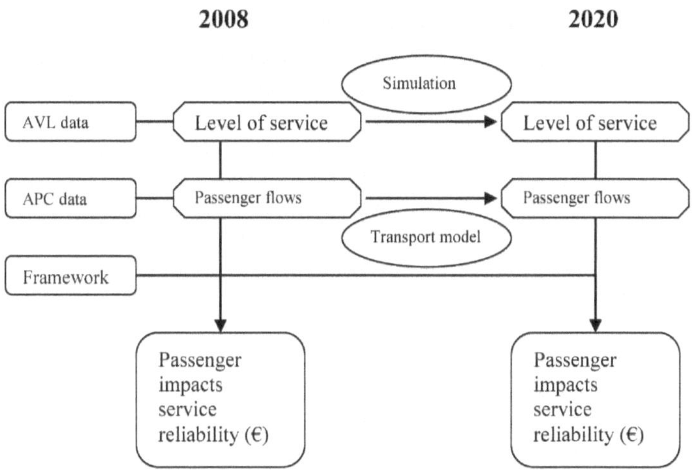

Fig. 5 Calculation steps toward service reliability impacts per case in 2020 (Van Oort, 2016).

Vehicle Location (AVL) data in Van Oort et al., 2015b). Passenger data, showing passenger movements (more details in Van Oort et al., 2015a), was used to illustrate passenger flows. Both data sources were combined using our three-step approach.

Step 1

In step 1 the passenger effects concerning the change of waiting times (from 2008 to 2020) and the change of distribution of total travel times were calculated. Applying a simulation method similar to the one described in Van Oort (2011) we predicted the new operations, yielding the new (distribution of) trip times, dwell times, delays and the level of bunching. The simulated AVL and passenger data enabled us to calculate the passenger effects (both extension and variation of travel times). In the reference case, the level of service is very low due to high passenger demand and insufficient bus infrastructure. In case of the tram line, sufficient infrastructure is provided and tram services require fewer vehicles thereby reducing the probability of bunching. Table 1 summarizes the details of the (expected) level of service in the investigated cases (step 1 of our framework shown by Fig. 4). The level of irregularity is expressed as the average deviation of the headway as a percentage of the scheduled headway (see Van Oort and van Nes, 2009). These numbers show a poor level of reliability in 2008, which will even decrease substantially in the reference case.

Table 1 Actual and expected level of service.

	2008	Reference case	Tram case
Level of irregularity (%)	100%	150%	10%
Coefficient of variation (CoV)	1	1.5	0.1
Average additional trip time (delays per trip)	1.5 min	2 min	≈0 min
Distribution of trip time (standard deviation)	1.5 min	2 min	≈0 min

Table 2 Passenger effects of unreliability of services in reference and tram case.

	Reference case	Tram case
Average additional waiting time per passenger	2.9 min	≈0 min
Average additional in-vehicle time per passenger	4.9 min	≈0 min
Distribution of travel times (standard deviation)	2.4 min	≈0 min

Step 2

In the following step, we calculated the passenger impacts: the average additional travel time per passenger and the distribution of travel times, as shown in Table 2. The additional travel time consists of additional waiting time and the additional in-vehicle time. For the calculation of the distribution of the waiting and in-vehicle times we applied the methods of Van Oort (2011) and the simulated AVL data. Due to the high level of service reliability in the tram case, the expected negative passenger effects of unreliability are small.

Step 3

After the calculation of these passenger impacts, the monetary values of these effects were calculated (step 3 of our framework shown by Fig. 5), using values of time and values of reliability (more details and specific values may be found in Van Oort (2016).

After this step, all costs and benefits are compared, including the findings of our three-step approach. Table 3 shows the total costs and benefits of the project, showing the substantial contribution of improved reliability to the positive score of the CBA, resulting in a benefit-cost ratio of 1.2 (i.e., the benefits are 20% higher than the costs). The impact of less additional waiting time due to enhanced service reliability of the tram line is €123 million (calculated over the complete life cycle) and the reduction of distribution in travel time results in €78 million less societal costs. As a result, service reliability related benefits account for 2/3 of the total project benefits of €336 million.

Table 3 Additional costs and benefits of tram line compared to reference case.

	Value compared to reference case (millions in 2011)
Investment costs	−€222
Operating costs	€66
Total costs	*€288*
Additional ticket revenues	€40
Increased travel time	€67
Service reliability effects	
Less waiting time	*€123*
Reduction in distribution	*€78*
Increased probability of finding a seat in the vehicle	€4
External effects (emissions, safety, etc.)	€8
Total benefits	*€336*
Benefits-costs	*+€48*
Benefit cost ratio	*1.2*

Since the CBA result was 1.2, the Dutch Minister of Infrastructure and Environment supported the project and the tram system started to operate in December 2019. Without our three-step approach, it would not have been possible to calculate the benefits of enhanced service reliability, which proved to be a major part of the total benefits.

9. Assessment of benefits from crowding relief

9.1 Introduction

Over the last decades, the percentage inhabitants living in urban areas has been increasing continuously. In 2018, 55% of the entire population worldwide was living in urban agglomerations, which is expected to increase to 68% by 2050 (United Nations (UN), Department of Economic and Social Affairs, 2018). This tendency is expected to have implications for public transport (PT) systems in cities. Metro systems in many cities worldwide, such as London, Tokyo, Santiago, Beijing, are currently subject to severe crowding. Because of the expected increase in concentration of people and activities within urban agglomerations, PT crowding is expected to become an even more dominant factor for urban PT systems in the future.

Crowding in public transport affects passengers' journey in three different ways (Tirachini et al., 2013):

- Increase in perceived in-vehicle time. Passengers generally perceive one-minute traveling in a crowded PT vehicle as more negative compared to traveling in an uncrowded PT vehicle. The perceived PT in-vehicle time increases as function of the on-board crowding level.
- Increase in dwell time. In case of more severe crowding, a larger volume of boarding and alighting passengers can increase the required dwell time of PT services at the stops. This results in longer in-vehicle times for all on-board passengers, and longer waiting time for downstream waiting passengers caused by this prolonged dwell time. In addition, this can result in the well-known bunching phenomenon: the longer dwell time increases the headway with the previous PT trip, while the headway with the subsequent PT trip becomes smaller. As this next PT service will have fewer passengers waiting at the stop, this dwell time becomes shorter, resulting in irregular headways, service unreliability and potentially bunching. The service reliability impacts can be quantified using the method as discussed in Section 8.
- Increase in waiting time due to denied boarding. In the event of severe crowding, passengers might not be able to board the first PT trip serving their stop. When passengers are being denied boarding due to crowding levels, this will extend their waiting time with (at least) one headway until the next service arrives.

As a consequence of current and expected future crowding levels in cities, governments, PT agencies and service providers employ several types of measures developed to realize crowding relief, particularly for urban PT. We provide a few examples of crowding relief schemes developed for the crowded London Underground network:

- Increase in service frequency: increase the frequency of the busy Victoria Line from 33 to 36 trains per hour in the peak hours.
- Introduction of Automatic Train Operation (ATO): transforming the manual operated District, Circle, Hammersmith & City and Metropolitan Lines to an ATO service, together with an updated signaling system. This enables a frequency increase from 24 to 32 trains per hour, hence providing 33% more capacity to alleviate crowding levels (Transport for London, 2020).

- Construction of new lines: one of the main purposes of the newly constructed Elizabeth Line—connecting Reading in the west with Shenfield and Abbey Wood in the east of London—is reducing crowding on the busy Central Line. The line runs parallel to the Central Line in central London, thereby directly providing additional capacity.

9.2 Methods

The abovementioned schemes are exemplary measures to reduce crowding in urban PT systems. For these schemes to be implemented, it is essential that its benefits can be quantified in an accurate and complete manner, to be contrasted with its costs in a cost-benefit analysis framework. However, traditional project assessments do typically not cover and quantify the three types of benefits as stipulated above (reducing perceived on-board times, reducing dwell times and unreliability, reducing waiting times in the event of passengers being left behind). Traditionally, only direct journey time benefits are quantified in project assessments. In the case of the service frequency increase measure on the Victoria Line mentioned above, this would result in a reduction of average waiting time from 55 s (for 33 trains per hour, assuming that passengers arrive randomly at the stops) to 50 s (for 36 trains per hour): only a 5 s journey time benefit for passengers. However, this would substantially underestimate the benefits of this scheme on crowding relief, potentially resulting in a negative benefit-cost ratio if not properly assessed.

Guidelines how to perform cost-benefit analyses in the Netherlands for long-term infrastructure and transport projects (Rijkswaterstaat, 2018) indicate that benefits resulting from a higher seat probability in PT could be incorporated. This only partially captures the reduction in perceived in-vehicle time of crowding relief schemes, while the second and third benefit component are not addressed. An exact description how these benefits should be calculated is not provided. In the United Kingdom, the Passenger Demand Forecasting Handbook (PDFH) prescribes in detail how costs and benefits of PT appraisal studies should be quantified (Rail Delivery Group, 2018). In line with scientific literature (e.g., Wardman and Whelan, 2011), they recommend to use an in-vehicle time multiplier as function of expected crowding levels to reflect perceived in-vehicle time benefits. The use of variable demand and PT assignment models which do incorporate public transport crowding is recommended (see van Nes and de Jong, 2020). These models perform an iterative assignment procedure, where the perceived in-vehicle time of each alternative PT route is updated based on the passenger volume (and hence the crowding levels) assigned to each route. This results in an equilibrium state where passengers distribute over the different routes available to them. Perceived in-vehicle times are calculated using crowding multipliers from MVA Consultancy (2008). Perceived in-vehicle times are expected to deviate from nominal in-vehicle times when more than 60% of all seats are occupied. Crowding multipliers are then recommended to be calculated as function of the load factor (passenger volume/seat capacity) until all seats are occupied, and as function of the density of standing passengers per sq. meter standing space available onwards. This captures the impact of different stock types (with different ratios between seated and total capacity, e.g., when comparing a long-distance intercity train and a metro). A lower generalized journey time is considered a societal benefit of a crowding relief scheme, and can be translated to expected PT ridership increases via a variable demand model or using an elasticity based approach. Quantification of the second and third impact of crowding schemes as mentioned above are not explicitly addressed in the PDFH.

To be able to quantify crowding relief benefits related to perceived in-vehicle times, two inputs are required. The first input is the expected impact on crowding levels. Most conventional public transport models are able to capture this when an equilibrium based, crowded assignment procedure is applied (as discussed above). The second input is how this new crowding level is perceived by passengers: i.e., estimating the in-vehicle time crowding multiplier. Over the last decades, many researchers studied how in-vehicle time is perceived as a function of on-board crowding levels. Extensive meta-analyses of in-vehicle time crowding multipliers as function of load factor or standing density were performed by Wardman and Whelan (2011) and Li and Hensher (2011). However, these crowding multipliers are typically based on stated preference (SP) research, rather than using observed choice behavior. SP research has the inherent limitation that there might be a discrepancy between the behavior stated by respondents and their realized behavior, the latter being used in revealed preference (RP) research. Therefore, there is a risk of potential bias when estimating crowding multipliers based on SP research, as suggested by studies where selected RP data was used to validate SP results (Batarce et al., 2015; Kroes et al., 2014).

The availability of large amounts of passenger data from Automated Fare Collection (AFC) (ticketing) data and Automated Vehicle Location (AVL) (timetable) data nowadays does provide an opportunity to re-estimate models on how passengers value on-board crowding based on realized (RP) choices instead of stated choices. More recently, such studies are performed for the metro network of Singapore (Tirachini et al., 2016), the MTR network in Hong Kong (Hörcher et al., 2017) and the urban tram and bus network in The Hague, the Netherlands (Yap et al., 2018a). AFC data contains information about the boarding and observed/inferred alighting location of passenger journeys made by public transport based on smart card data transactions. Therefore, AFC data shows the different route alternatives passengers choose for a given origin-destination pair. AVL data on the other hand enables calculating the attributes of the observed route alternatives. AVL data consists of the scheduled and realized departure and arrival times of each PT vehicle trip at each PT stop. It thus provides the expected travel time for each route alternative. Crowding levels of each PT route can be obtained directly from Automated Passenger Count (APC) systems, which provide an estimate of the number of passengers on-board via (for example) infrared sensors or load-weight systems. Alternatively, AFC and AVL data can be fused: when passenger journey transactions from the AFC data are assigned to individual PT trips (by matching trips, or by matching the smart card tap in and tap out times with the realized arrival and departure times of a PT trip), loads and crowding levels can also be obtained or inferred. This enables the estimation of perceived in-vehicle time benefits as function of crowding in a more accurate way, which can be incorporated in a cost-benefit analysis.

Fig. 6 shows the resulting crowding multipliers as function of the standing density (the number of standing passengers per m^2) based on a Revealed Preference study performed for urban tram and bus journeys in the Netherlands. We distinguished between frequent, experienced passengers and infrequent passengers. As can be seen, on average the crowding multiplier equals 1.16 when all seats are occupied. In case the occupancy level increases to three standing passengers per m^2 on average, the crowding multiplier equals 1.34. For frequent travelers, the crowding multiplier equals 1.31 when all seats are occupied. In case of three standing passengers per square meter on average, this results in a crowding multiplier of 1.75. On the other hand, results indicate that infrequent travelers do not incorporate anticipated crowding levels in their route choice. This is

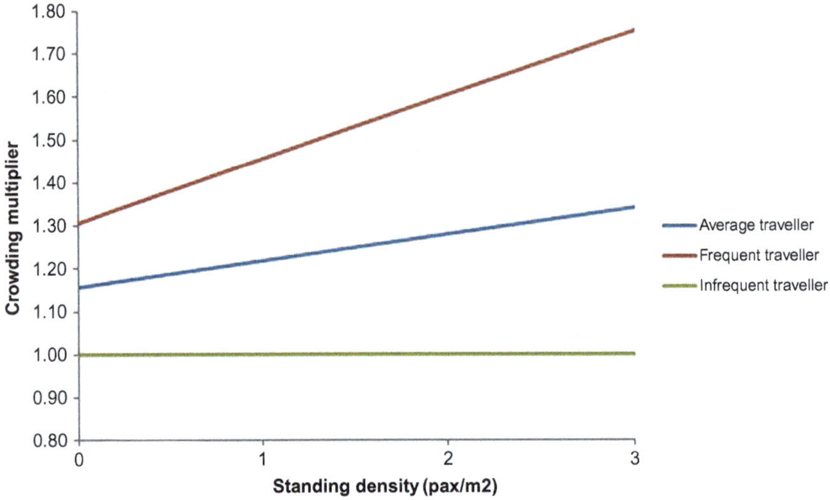

Fig. 6 Crowding multipliers as function of the standing density (Yap et al., 2018a).

plausible, given their lack of prior knowledge and experience regarding expected crowding levels (Yap et al., 2018a).

Quantifying benefits of crowding relief schemes on reduced dwell times and denied boarding is typically less straightforward. In strategic transport models, it is often possible to reflect unreliability in a simplified way using the effective (or perceived) frequency (see Van Oort and van Nes, 2009). This is a corrected headway compared to the scheduled headway due to irregularity between PT services on a line, thereby increasing the average passenger waiting time (and hence, reducing the effective service frequency provided to passengers). This might be used as a proxy to reflect extended dwell times at stops due to crowding, although it does not provide a complete picture. Dynamic, simulation-based PT models are required to accurately reflect the relation between crowding levels and dwell times. These models, typically agent-based models built in software packages as MatSIM (see Horni et al., 2016) or BusMezzo (see Cats et al., 2016a), specify passenger flow-dependent dwell time functions for different stock types, and can simulate individual train and passenger movements. This provides a detailed insight how crowding affects dwell times and unreliability, and how this delay propagates down the line and over the wider PT network. Furthermore, these models incorporate capacity constraints of individual PT services, so that impacts on left behind passengers can be calculated. Using dynamic PT assignment models can however be computationally expensive, as detailed model inputs are required and in some cases several model replications are required due to the stochastic nature of demand and supply characteristics.

9.3 Case study

We illustrate how crowding benefits can be incorporated in public transport appraisal studies using a case study in The Hague, the Netherlands (obtained from Van Oort et al., 2016). The Hague has more than 500,000 inhabitants and is part of the Randstad, the most important economic area of the Netherlands. The urban PT system consists of 12 tram lines and 10 bus lines. The purpose of this particular case study was to evaluate the benefits of a potential increase in the service frequency of one tram line from 6 to 8 trams per hour during the AM and PM peak period.

As a first step, we used AFC and AVL data from this PT system to estimate crowding in-vehicle time multipliers based on revealed passenger behavior. These estimated crowding multipliers were used as input to quantify the benefits of the aforementioned service frequency increase using a PT ridership prediction model in the transport planning software OmniTRANS (Brands et al., 2014) as a second step. As an illustration, we compare the impact of this scheme on the forecast increase in passenger ridership on the tram network of The Hague for a scenario with and without consideration of crowding benefits. Table 4 only reports the expected increase in ridership in the AM and PM when only benefits related to waiting time reduction are considered (left), and when crowding relief benefits are added (right). Notwithstanding, the majority of the benefits are related to lower generalized journey costs for existing PT passengers: this table only illustrates the underestimation of benefits related to new PT demand. It can be concluded that not incorporating crowding benefits underestimates ridership benefits by up to 30% (in the AM peak) for this case study. As PT demand is particularly concentrated during the

Table 4 Forecast ridership increase for case study.

	Model without crowding benefits	**Model with crowding benefits**
Morning peak	+165	+240
Evening peak	+165	+200

Obtained from Van Oort, N., de Brands, T., Romph, E., Yap, M., 2016. Ridership evaluation and prediction in public transport by processing smart card data: a Dutch approach and example, chapter 11. In: Kurauchi, F., Schmöcker, J.D. (Eds.), Public Transport Planning With Smart Card Data. CRC Press.

AM peak—demand in the PM is more uniformly distributed—most crowding benefits can be expected during the AM. This explains that a largest demand underestimation is expected during this period and emphasizes the importance of quantifying crowding benefits in cost-benefit analyses to forecast the benefits of these schemes in an accurate and a complete manner. The network-wide impacts are visualized in Fig. 7. More detailed results may be found in Van Oort et al. (2016).

10. Assessment of robustness benefits

10.1 Introduction

As discussed in Section 8, disruptions in public transport have negative impacts on passengers. Disruptions can result in additional travel time, more distributed travel times and extra and/or longer transfers for passengers (see for instance Lee et al., 2014). Besides, perceived journey times might increase due to higher crowding levels on alternative PT services.

It is important to note that "disruptions" in this chapter relate to different disruption types. Unplanned disruptions can be categorized as recurrent or non-recurrent. Recurrent disruptions (discussed in Section 13.8.8) are smaller, more frequently occurring disruptions (e.g., a delayed tram), while non-recurrent disruptions—being the focus of this section—relate to more severe, less frequent types (e.g., a broken down train). The distinction is shown in Fig. 8, which illustrates there is no hard distinction between these types. Instead, they can be considered as two ends of one scale. A distinction can also be made between planned and unplanned disruptions. In scientific research, most attention is typically paid to unplanned disruptions, while planned disruptions are relatively understudied (Shires et al., 2018). The impact of planned disruptions—such as planned track maintenance works—is generally smaller than the impact this same disruption would have if unplanned. This is due to awareness and route and mode choice adjustments by passengers, as well as due to planned resource allocation by the service provider in anticipation of this disruption. Hence, the unplanned disruption impact can be considered an upper bound for the disruption impact of the same planned disruption. However, the duration of planned disruptions can substantially exceed the duration of unplanned disruptions, and hence result in severe disruption impacts over time. While most unplanned disruptions often last relatively short, planned disruptions can result in track closures for full days, weekends or even multiple

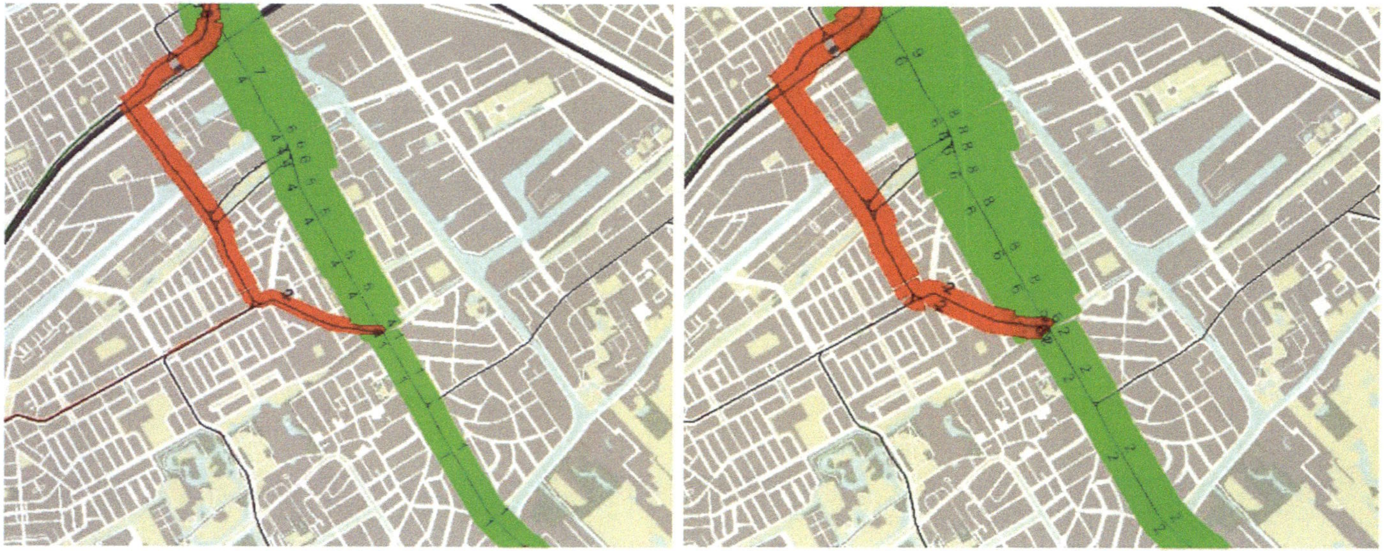

Fig. 7 Network impacts of case study frequency increase without (left) and with (right) crowding impacts incorporated. *Obtained from Van Oort, N., de Brands, T., Romph, E., Yap, M., 2016. Ridership evaluation and prediction in public transport by processing smart card data: a Dutch approach and example. In: Kurauchi, F., Schmöcker, J.D. (Eds.), Public Transport Planning With Smart Card Data. CRC Press (Chapter 11).*

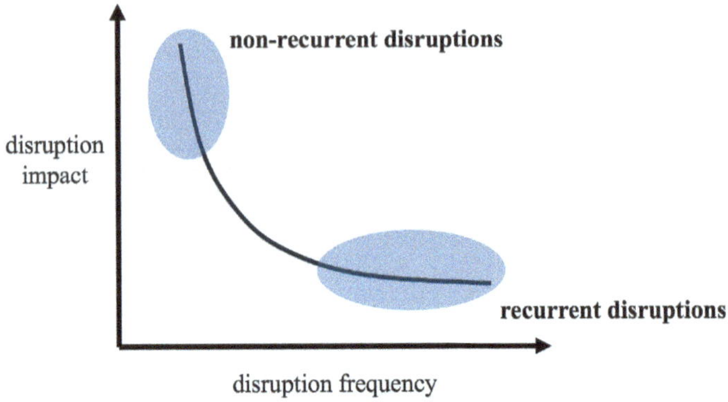

Fig. 8 Conceptual framework of recurrent and non-recurrent disruptions.

weeks or months (see e.g., Yap et al., 2018b). Neglecting the robustness benefits of measures in relation to planned disruptions can therefore incorrectly underestimate benefit-cost ratios.

Disruptions could cause substantial costs. For example, in Cats et al. (2016b), we calculated that yearly passenger disruption costs resulting from disruptions on one single light rail link in the metropolitan PT network of The Hague and Rotterdam, the Netherlands, can exceed €900,000. In addition, in London all disruptions on Transport for London's underground network during a 4-week period from April 28 to May 25, 2019 have resulted in 2.2 million lost customer hours (Transport for London, 2019b), which illustrates the severity of the impact PT disruptions can have on passengers.

PT disruptions can also result in revenue losses, rescheduling costs, reimbursement costs and fines for the PT service provider. Several service providers refund the fare to passengers if a delay exceeds a certain threshold. For example, the PT agency in Washington D.C., WMATA, fully reimburses passengers whose journey is delayed by more than 10 min during rush hours (WMATA (Washington Metropolitan Area Transit Authority), 2019). Transport for London automatically refunds passengers in case selected disruption types result in a delay of 15 min or more (Transport for London, 2019a). Besides, PT service providers can be required to pay a fine to the PT authority in the event of delays or disruptions, depending on the contractual agreements between authority and service provider. For example, in 2016 MTR—service provider of the Hong Kong metro—was required to pay HK$14.5 million (€1.7 million) due to delays (Straits Times, 2017). Additionally, service providers can suffer from temporary or systematic revenue losses when passengers decide not to travel by public transport in response to a disruption. Saberi et al. (2018) found an 85% increase in usage of bicycle-sharing schemes during a strike on the London Underground network, while Shires et al. (2018) found that planned rail closures resulted in a temporary PT demand reduction ranging from 5% up to 32%. These examples illustrate the financial impact PT disruptions might have for the PT service provider involved.

The examples above illustrate that PT disruptions result in financial and societal costs for passengers and PT service provider. Measures can be developed to improve the robustness of a PT system: i.e., to reduce the frequency and/or impact of PT disruptions. Robustness measures can be deployed on a strategic level (e.g., robust terminal configuration: Van Oort and Van Nes, 2010), a tactical level (e.g., robust timetable design: Gkiotsalitis and Cats, 2018; robust driver schedule design: Yap and Van Oort, 2018), or on an operational level (see for instance Ibarra-Rojas et al., 2015). While computing the costs of these measures is relatively straightforward, it is important to be able to quantify and monetize the robustness benefits of these measures as well. The impact a certain scheme has on reducing the abovementioned costs should therefore ideally be included as a monetized component in a cost-benefit analysis. Quantification of robustness benefits is however not standard practice in PT appraisal studies or cost-benefit analyses. In many CBA frameworks, these benefits are only incorporated in a qualitative or simplified way. For example, in the Dutch guidelines for societal cost-benefit analyses, robustness benefits are not explicitly mentioned (Rijkswaterstaat, 2018). The robustness benefits of a new rail connection in the UK is typically quantified via an assumed improvement in the train on-time performance. This measure does however not consider the full passenger and operator costs it can mitigate, potentially underestimating robustness benefits and the benefit-cost ratio of the project as a whole.

10.2 Methods

This section addresses how robustness benefits of schemes can be monetized and incorporated in CBA frameworks. For this, we define the *vulnerability* of a PT network based on Rodriguez-Nunez and Garcia-Palomares (2014) and Oliveira et al. (2016): the degree of susceptibility of a PT network to disruptions and the ability of the PT network to cope with these disruptions. *Robustness* indicates its antonym: 100% robustness yields 0%

vulnerability and vice versa (Snelder and Tavasszy, 2010). This definition indicates that robustness is composed of two components: the disruption frequency and disruption impact. In its most basic form, vulnerability of a PT network can be computed using Eq. (1), which multiplies the predicted frequency $\breve{f}_{d,s}$ of each disruption type $d \in D$ (expressed in disruptions per year) at each network location $s \in S$ with the predicted (monetized) disruption impact $\breve{w}_{d,s}$. When calculating robustness benefits in a CBA for a certain year, this implies that PT network vulnerability should be computed for a scenario with and without the robustness scheme of interest in place, where the difference ΔV per year provides the yearly robustness benefits to be incorporated in a CBA.

$$V = \sum_{s \in S} \sum_{d \in D} \breve{f}_{d,s} * \breve{w}_{d,s}. \tag{1}$$

The disruption frequency can be derived from empirical data, for example, from incident log files typically kept by the PT service provider. These empirical data sources can be used directly to obtain the disruption frequencies, or can be fit to a distribution function to estimate the future number of disruptions (see, for example, Yap et al., 2018c). Alternatively, machine learning models can be developed to predict future disruption frequencies, as typically there will be no empirical data available for all disruption types $d \in D$ at each network location (node or link) $s \in S$ (see, for example, Yap and Cats, 2019). Disruption frequencies might also be derived from statistics regarding the mean time between failures (MTBF) for different assets.

Quantification or prediction of passenger disruption impacts with and without a certain scheme in place consists of several components. Typically, the generalized journey costs are calculated for this, which is a summation of the different components of a PT journey (walking time, waiting time, (perceived) in-vehicle time, number of transfers), multiplied with each respective coefficient which reflects how passengers perceive each component. This entails that benefits are not only related to the nominal travel time difference between two scenarios, but also relate to perceived journey times, for example, resulting from higher crowding levels on alternative services during a PT disruption. Generalized journey time impacts can then be monetized using a Value of Time conversion.

The change in generalized journey costs can be obtained from PT assignment models. Traditionally static, frequency-based or schedule-based, PT assignment models are used to predict PT disruption impacts (Gentile et al., 2016; van Nes and de Jong, 2020), in some cases combined with variable demand models to capture mode choice impacts in the event of planned disruptions in particular. The disadvantage of using static assignment models for this purpose is their assumption that passenger route choice is determined before the journey starts, based on knowledge on how PT services are amended in response to a disruption. This means that these models might be used to predict the impact of planned disruptions, where passengers can be assumed to be aware of the disruption when commencing their journey. These models are however unable to incorporate the dynamics of especially unplanned PT disruptions. Typically, passengers become aware of unplanned disruptions during their journey, requiring them to adjust their route during their journey, often based on limited information of the service adjustments or disruption duration. To predict impacts of unplanned disruptions—assuming a fixed PT demand—there is a need for more advanced, dynamic PT assignment models, which are able to capture the demand and supply dynamics and their interactions during disruptions. In recent years, there have been several developments to use mesoscopic, agent-based simulation-based assignment models to predict disruption impacts (e.g., MatSIM, (see Horni et al., 2016) or BusMezzo: see Cats et al., 2016a), instead of the aforementioned traditional static assignment models. In addition, machine learning approaches can be adopted to predict disruption impacts (Yap and Cats, 2019) or to infer disruption impacts from empirical data (Marra and Corman, 2019).

In addition to calculating generalized journey costs, it is also possible to quantify the impact of passengers who change their travel mode or cancel their journey when confronted with disruptions. Yap et al. (2018b), for example, calibrated route and mode choice parameters for a PT ridership prediction model, specifically for planned disruptions. The Rule of Half—reflecting the change in consumer surplus (see, for example, Winkler, 2015)—can be used as an approximation of costs for passengers who do not make their journey with PT during a disruption (as, for example, applied in Yap et al., 2018c). Most studies assume a fixed PT demand during unplanned disruptions. However, the rise of new mobility options, acceptance of flexible working arrangements in several countries, and provision of real-time information via smartphones does result in this assumption potentially being violated. Passengers might decide to cancel their trip and work from home, or to make use of bicycle-sharing schemes or services provided by transport network companies (TNC's), such as *Uber* or *Lyft*.

While this is currently not explicitly considered in most CBA frameworks, it is recommended to account for the additional expenses for passengers resulting from this when calculating disruption impacts (and hence, when calculating robustness benefits of measures), as well as for the external costs, for example, caused by higher road congestion levels caused by TNC's during PT disruptions.

10.3 Case study

We illustrate the incorporation of robustness benefits of schemes in a CBA using a case study in The Hague, the Netherlands (obtained from Yap et al., 2018c). This study considered the vulnerability of the main tram link in this city, which is located in a tunnel under the city center. Above ground, there was a disused tram track available, which was not suitable to accommodate the recently introduced new tram types in The Hague at the time of consideration. The question here was to quantify the robustness benefits of upgrading this disused tram route above ground in such a way, that it could be used by all trams in the event of a disruption within the tram tunnel. This would result in an additional 5 min detour for all affected tram lines compared to the route via the tunnel. However, in the reference case without this route being available, the majority of these tram lines needed to be split in two parts and short-turn at both ends of the tunnel.

An empirical dataset containing historical information about disruption type and duration was used as input, considering both planned and unplanned disruptions. A probability density function was fit to this data, based upon which Monte Carlo simulation was used to simulate the number of future disruptions for a 10-year time horizon. To model the disruption impact with and without the rerouting option being available, the transport planning software OmniTRANS (see Brands et al., 2014) was used to model this disruption and to quantify the generalized passenger costs for both scenarios. Based on this, also trip cancellation costs were computed using the Rule of Half. The disruption impacts were multiplied with the simulated number of future disruptions in order to obtain the total robustness benefits of this measure, which were offset against expected costs of this measure.

The results of the CBA are presented in Fig. 9. It illustrates that the expected societal disruption costs for this 10-year time horizon (disruption impact multiplied by the expected number of disruptions) are reduced from >€2.0 million by 62%. Accumulated over 10 years, the total expected benefits equal €1.35 million, while required infrastructure investment

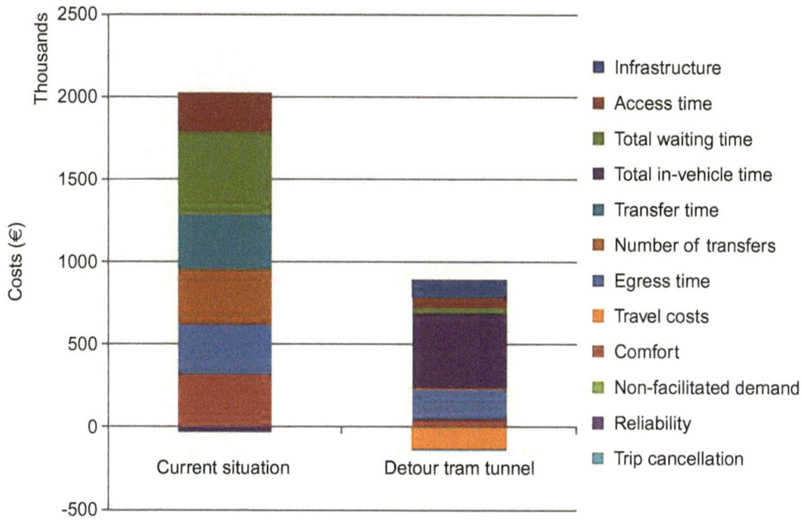

Fig. 9 Vulnerability costs during tram disruptions without (left) and with (right) detour measure in place.

and maintenance costs were expected to equal €0.1 million, thereby incorporating the residual value of the infrastructure after the 10-year time horizon. This resulted in a strongly positive Net Present Value of €1.24 million, based upon which it was recommended to proceed with this scheme. This case study illustrates the importance of incorporating the robustness benefits explicitly, thereby supporting proper decision making in relation to robustness schemes.

References

Anderson, M.L., 2013. Subways, Strikes, and Slowdowns: The Impacts of Public Transit on Traffic Congestion. Working Paper No. 18757, National Bureau of Economic Research.

Anderson, P., Daganzo, C.F., 2019. Effect of transit signal priority on bus service reliability. Transp. Res. B Methodol. 132, 2–14.

Annema, J.A., Koopmans, C., van Wee, B., 2007. Evaluating transport infrastructure investments: the Dutch experience with a standardized approach. Transp. Rev. 27 (2), 125–150.

Arcury, T.A., et al., 2005. Access to transportation and health care utilization in a rural region. J. Rural Health 21 (2005), 31–38.

Bailey, L., 2007. Public Transportation and Petroleum Savings in the U.S.: Reducing Dependence on Oil. ICF International for the American Public Transportation Association.

Batarce, M., Munoz, J.C., Ortuzar, J., Raveau, S., Mojica, C., Rios, R.A., 2015. Valuing crowding in public transport systems using mixed stated/revealed preference data: the case of Santiago. Transp. Res. Rec. 2535, 73–78.

Belden, Rusonello, Stewart, 2004. 2004 American Community Survey—National Survey on Communities. Washington, DC.
Besser, L.M., Dannenberg, A.L., 2005. Walking to public transit: steps to help meet physical activity recommendations. Am. J. Prev. Med. 29 (4), 273–280.
Brands, T., de Romph, E., Veitch, T., Cook, J., 2014. Modelling public transport route choice with multiple access and egress modes. Transp. Res. Procedia 1, 12–23.
Bunschoten, T., Molin, E., van Nes, R., 2013. Tram or bus; does the tram bonus exist? In: European Transport Conference.
BusVic, 2010. Public Transport Use a Ticket to Health. Briefing Paper, Bus Association Victoria.
Carter, D., 1991. London Docklands: the DLR's dash for growth. Light Rail Rev. 2, 67–77.
Cats, O., West, J., Eliasson, J., 2016a. A dynamic stochastic model for evaluating congestion and crowding effects in transit systems. Transp. Res. B 89, 43–57.
Cats, O., Yap, M.D., Van Oort, N., 2016b. Exposing the role of exposure: public transport network risk analysis. Transp. Res. A 88, 1–14.
Conventz, S., Derudder, B., Thierstein, A., Witlox, F. (Eds.), 2013. Hub Cities in the Knowledge Economy: Seaports, Airports, Brainports. Ashgate Publishing Ltd., Farnham, UK.
Crain & Associates, 1999. Using Public Transportation to Reduce the Economic, Social, and Human Costs of Personal Immobility, Report 49 TCRP. TRB.
Crocker, S., Dabinett, G., Gore, T., Haywood, R., Hennebury, J., Herrington, A., Kirkpatrick, A., Currie, G., Shalaby, A., 2008. Active transit signal priority for streetcars: experience in Melbourne, Australia, and Toronto, Canada. Transp. Res. Rec. 2042, 41–49. Washington D.C.
Cronin, J.J., Hagerich, J., Horton, J., Hotaling, J., 2008. Florida Transportation Disadvantaged Programs: Return on Investment Study. The Marketing Institute, Florida State University College of Business.
Davis, T., Hale, M., 2007. Public Transportation's Contribution to Greenhouse Gas Reduction. American Public Transportation Association.
De Jong, G., Kouwenhoven, M., 2020. Value of travel time and travel time reliability. Chapter 2. In: Mouter, N. (Ed.), Standard Appraisal Methods. Series: Advances in Transport Policy and Planning, vol. 6. Elsevier, Amsterdam.
Dubé, J., Legros, D., Thériault, M., Des Rosiers, F., 2014. A spatial difference-in-differences estimator to evaluate the effect of change in public mass transit systems on house prices. Transp. Res. B Methodol. 64, 24–40.
ECONorthwest and PBQD, 2002. Estimating the Benefits and Costs of Public Transit Projects, TCRP Report 78.
European Environment Agency, 2015. Air Quality in Europe—2015 report.
Eurostat, 2016. Road Safety Statistics at Regional Level. Eurostat.
Flyvbjerg, B., 2007. Cost overruns and demand shortfalls in urban rail and other infrastructure. Transp. Plan. Technol. 30 (1), 9–30.
Gallivan, F., Rose, E., Ewing, R., Hamidi, S., Brown, T., 2015. Quantifying Transit's Impact On GHG Emissions and Energy Use—The Land Use Component, Report 176. Transit Cooperative Research Program.
Gaspardo, A., 2019. The BRT-LRT Dilemma: A Public Transport Users' and Policymakers' Perspective on Differences in Preferences and Perceptions Between BRT and LRT. M. Sc. Thesis, Delft University of Technology.
Gentile, G., Florian, M., Hamdouch, Y., Cats, O., Nuzzolo, A., 2016. The theory of transit assignment: basic modelling frameworks. In: Gentile, G., Noekel, K. (Eds.), Modelling Public Transport Passenger Flows in the Era of Intelligent Transport Systems. Springer International Publishing, Cham, Switzerland, pp. 287–386.

Gkiotsalitis, K., Cats, O., 2018. Reliable frequency determination: incorporating information on service uncertainty when setting dispatching headways. Transp. Res. C 88, 187–207.

Goudappel Coffeng, 2011. Demand Forecasting and Service Reliability Analysis Uithoflijn Utrecht. (In Dutch).

Hass-Klau, C., Crampton, G.R., Benjari, R., 2004. Economic Impacts of Light Rail: The Results for 15 Urban Areas in France, Germany, UK and North America. Environmental and Transport Planning, Brighton, UK.

Hensher, D.A., 2014. The relationship between bus contract costs, user perceived service quality and performance assessment. Int. J. Sustain. Transp. 8 (1), 5–27.

Hensher, D.A., Truong, T.P., Mulley, C., Ellison, R., 2012. Assessing the wider economy impacts of transport infrastructure investment with an illustrative application to the North-West Rail Link project in Sydney, Australia. J. Transp. Geogr. 24, 292–305.

HLB Decision Economics Inc, 2003. The Socioeconomic Benefits of Transit in Wisconsin. HLB Decision Economics Inc.

Hörcher, D., Graham, D.J., Anderson, R.J., 2017. Crowding cost estimation with large scale smart card and vehicle location data. Transp. Res. B 95, 105–125.

Horni, A., et al. (Eds.), 2016. The Multi-Agent Transport Simulation MATSim. Ubiquity Press, London. https://doi.org/10.5334/baw.

Ibarra-Rojas, O.J., Delgado, F., Giesen, R., Muñoz, J.C., 2015. Planning, operation, and control of bus transport systems: a literature review. Transp. Res. B Methodol. 77, 38–75.

Kapetanović, M., van Oort, N., Nunez, A., Goverde, R., 2019. Sustainability of railway passenger services: a review of aspects, issues, contributions and challenges of life cycle emissions. In: Peterson, A., Joborn, M., Bohlin, M. (Eds.), Proceedings of the 8th International Conference on Railway Operations Modelling and Analysis: Rail Norrköping 2019.

Knowles, R.D., 1992. Light rail transport. In: Whitelegg, J. (Ed.), Traffic Congestion: Is There a Way Out? Leading Edge Press, Hawes, pp. 107–133.

Knowles, R.D., Ferbrache, F., 2015. Evaluation of wider economic impacts of light rail investment on cities. J. Transp. Geogr. 54, 430–439.

Koopmans, C.C., Mouter, N., 2020. Cost-benefit analysis. Chapter 1. In: Mouter, N. (Ed.), Standard Appraisal Methods. Series: Advances in Transport Policy and Planning, vol. 6. Elsevier, Amsterdam.

Kroes, E., Kouwenhoven, M., Debrincat, L., Pauget, N., 2014. On the Value of Crowding in Public Transport for Ile-de-France. Transport Research Arena, Paris, France.

Lachapelle, U., Frank, L., Saelens, B.E., Sallis, J.F., Conway, T.L., 2011. Commuting by public transit and physical activity: where you live, where you work, and how you get there. J. Phys. Act. Health 8 (Suppl. 1), S72–S82.

Laird, J., Geurs, K., Nash, C., 2009. Option and non-use values and rail project appraisal. Transp. Policy 16 (4), 173–182.

Lee, A., van Oort, N., van Nes, R., 2014. Service reliability in a network context. Transp. Res. Rec. 2417, 18–26.

Li, Z., Hensher, D., 2011. Crowding and public transport: a review of willingness to pay evidence and its relevance in project appraisal. Transp. Policy 18, 880–887.

Li, Z., Hensher, D.A., Rose, J.M., 2010. Willingness to pay for travel time reliability in passenger transport: a review and some new empirical evidence. Transp. Res. E 46, 384–403.

Li, Z., Hensher, D.A., Rose, J.M., 2013. Accommodating perceptual conditioning in the valuation of expected travel time savings for car and public transport. Res. Transp. Econ. 39, 270–276.

Litman, T., 2009. Transportation Cost and Benefit Analysis Guidebook. Victoria Transport Policy Institute.
Litman, T., 2015. Evaluating Public Transit Benefits and Costs—Best Practices Guidebook. Victoria Transport Policy Institute.
Lo, S., Hall, R.W., 2006. Effects of the Los Angeles transit strike on highway congestion. Transp. Res. A 40 (10), 903–917.
Ma, X., Yuan, Y., van Oort, N., Hoogendoorn, S., 2020. investigating impact of bike-sharing systems on modal shift: a case study in Delft, the Netherlands. J. Clean. Prod. 259. https://doi.org/10.1016/j.jclepro.2020.120846.
Manville, M., Cummins, B., 2015. Why do voters support public transportation? Public choices and private behavior. Transportation 42, 303–332. https://doi.org/10.1007/s11116-014-9545-2.
Marra, A.D., Corman, F., 2019. From delay to disruption: the impact of service degradation on public transport network. In: Proceedings of the 8th Symposium of the European Association for Research in Transportation (hEART), Budapest, Hungary.
Marti, C.M., Betolini, L., Weidmann, U., 2018. Transit orientation: more than just coverage—a new method for the assessment of transit and development co-location. Transp. Res. Rec.
Mohammad, S.I., Graham, D.J., Melo, P.C., Anderson, R.J., 2013. A meta-analysis of the impact of rail projects on land and property values. Transp. Res. A 50, 158–170.
Mouter, N., Annema, J.A., van Wee, B., 2013. Attitudes towards the role of cost–benefit analysis in the decision-making process for spatial-infrastructure projects: a Dutch case study. Transp. Res. A Policy Pract. 58, 1–14.
Mulley, C., Hensher, D.A., Cosgrove, D., 2017. Is rail cleaner and greener than bus? Transp. Res. D: Transp. Environ. 51, 14–28.
MVA Consultancy, 2008. Valuation of Overcrowding on Rail Services. Report Prepared for the UK Department of Transport.
Nicolaisen, M.S., Olesen, M., Olesen, K., 2017. Vision vs. evaluation—case studies of light rail planning in Denmark. Eur. J. Spatial Dev. 65, 1–26.
Noland, R., Small, K.A., 1995. Travel time uncertainty, departure time and the cost of the morning commute. In: Proceedings of 74th Annual Meeting of Transportation Research Board, Washington D.C.
OECD/ITF, 2009. Improving Reliability on Surface Transport Networks. OECD.
Oliveira, E.L., Portugal, L.S., Junior, W.P., 2016. Indicators of reliability and vulnerability: similarities and differences in ranking links of a complex road system. Transp. Res. A 88, 195–208.
Peek, G.J., van Hagen, M., 2002. Creating synergy in and around stations: three strategies in and around stations. Transp. Res. Rec. 1793, 1–6.
Pogonyi, C., 2020. Wider economic benefits. Chapter 5. In: Mouter, N. (Ed.), Standard Appraisal Methods. Series: Advances in Transport Policy and Planning, vol. 6. Elsevier, Amsterdam.
Rail Delivery Group, 2018. Passenger Demand Forecasting Handbook. United Kingdom, London.
Rijkswaterstaat, 2018. Werkwijze MKBA bij MIRT-verkenningen. The Hague, The Netherlands. (In Dutch).
Rodriguez-Nunez, E., Garcia-Palomares, J.C., 2014. Measuring the vulnerability of public transport networks. J. Transp. Geogr. 35, 50–63.
Saberi, M., Ghamami, M., Gu, Y., Shojaei, M.H., Fishman, E., 2018. Understanding the impacts of a public transit disruption on bicycle sharing mobility patterns: a case of tube strike in London. J. Transp. Geogr. 66, 154–166.
Shapiro, R.J., Hassett, K.A., Arnold, F.S., 2002. Conserving Energy and Preserving the Environment: The Role of Public Transit. APTA.

Shaw, J., Dochterty, I., 2014. The Transport Debate. Policy Press, Bristol.
Shelat, S., Huisman, R., van Oort, N., 2018. Analysing the trip and user characteristics of the combined bicycle and transit mode. Res. Transp. Econ. 69, 68–76.
Shires, J.D., Ojeda-Cabral, M., Wardman, M., 2018. The impact of planned disruptions on rail passenger demand. Transportation 46, 1807–1837. https://doi.org/10.1007/s11116-018-9889-0.
Snelder, M., Tavasszy, L.A., 2010. Quantifying the full reliability benefits of road network improvements. In: Proceedings of WCTR 2010, Lisbon, Portugal.
Social Exclusion Unit, 2003. Making the Connections: Final Report on Transport and Social Exclusion.
Stichting Wetenschappelijk Onderzoek Verkeersveiligheid (SWOV), 2017. Factsheet: Kosten van verkeersongevallen. (In Dutch).
Straits Times, 2017. Hong Kong's MTR Faces $3.5m Fine for 10-Hour Train Delay. Retrieved from: https://www.straitstimes.com/asia/east-asia/hks-mtr-faces-35m-fine-for-10-hour-train-delay.
Tirachini, A., Hensher, D.A., Rose, J.M., 2013. Crowding in public transport systems: effects on users, operations and implications for the estimation of demand. Transp. Res. A 53, 36–52.
Tirachini, A., Sun, L., Erath, A., Chakirov, A., 2016. Valuation of sitting and standing in metro trains using revealed preferences. Transp. Policy 47, 94–104.
Torabi, F., van Oort, N., Hoogendoorn, S.P., 2019. The future of intermodal hubs. Chapter, In: Triggianese, Cavallo, Baron, Kuijper (Eds.), Stations as Nodes Exploring the Role of Stations in Future Metropolitan Areas, From a French and Dutch Perspective. TU Delft Open, pp. 56–62.
Transport for London, 2019a. Tube and DLR Delays. Retrieved from: https://tfl.gov.uk/fares/refunds-and-replacements/tube-and-dlr-delays.
Transport for London, 2019b. Underground Service Performance. Retrieved from: https://tfl.gov.uk/corporate/publications-and-reports/underground-services-performance.
Transport for London, 2020. Four Lines Modernisation. Retrieved from: https://tfl.gov.uk/travel-information/improvements-and-projects/four-lines-modernisation.
United Nations (UN), Department of Economic and Social Affairs, 2018. 68% of the World Population Projected to Live in Urban Areas by 2050, Says UN. Retrieved from: https://www.un.org/development/desa/en/news/population/2018-revision-of-world-urbanization-prospects.html.
Van der Bijl, R.A.J., 2006. Portland: Urban Planning by Streetcar, Scape 2. pp. 8–81.
Van der Bijl, R.A.J., et al., 2005. Development of Principles and Strategies for Introducing High Quality Public Transport in Medium Sized Cities and Regions (HITRANS). Best Practice Guides 1–5. HiTrans, Stavanger, Norway.
Van der Bijl, R., van Oort, N., Bukman, B., 2018. Light Rail Transit Systems: 61 Lessons in Sustainable Urban Development. Elsevier.
Van Hagen, M., van Oort, N., 2019. Improving railway passengers experience: two perspectives. J. Traffic Transp. Eng. 7, 97–110.
Van Nes, R., de Jong, G., 2020. Transport models. Chapter 4. In: Mouter, N. (Ed.), Standard Appraisal Methods. Series: Advances in Transport Policy and Planning, vol. 6. Elsevier, Amsterdam.
Van Oort, N., 2011. Service Reliability and Urban Public Transport Design. T2011/2, TRAIL, Ph.D. Thesis Series, Delft.
Van Oort, N., 2014. Incorporating service reliability in public transport design and performance requirements: international survey results and recommendations. Res. Transp. Econ. 48, 92–100.
Van Oort, N., 2016. Incorporating enhanced service reliability of public transport in cost-benefit analyses. Public Transp. 8 (1), 143–160.

Van Oort, N., van Nes, R., 2009. Regularity analysis for optimizing urban transit network design. Public Transp. 1 (2), 155–168.
Van Oort, N., Van Nes, R., 2010. Impact of rail terminal design on transit service reliability. Transp. Res. Rec. 2146, 109–118.
Van Oort, N., Sparing, D., Brands, T., Goverde, R.M.P., 2015a. Data driven improvements in public transport: the Dutch example. Public Transp. 7 (3), 369–389.
Van Oort, N., Brands, T., de Romph, E., 2015b. Short-term prediction of ridership on public transport with smart card data. Transp. Res. Rec. 2535, 105–111.
Van Oort, N., de Brands, T., Romph, E., Yap, M., 2016. Ridership evaluation and prediction in public transport by processing smart card data: a Dutch approach and example, chapter 11. In: Kurauchi, F., Schmöcker, J.D. (Eds.), Public Transport Planning With Smart Card Data. CRC Press, pp. 197–224.
Van Oort, N., vd Bijl, R.A.J., Verhoof, F.C.A., 2017. The wider benefits of high quality public transport for cities. In: European Transport Conference, Barcelona,.
van Wee, B., Mouter, N., 2021. Evaluating transport equity. Chapter 5. In: Mouter, N. (Ed.), New Methods, Reflections and Application Domains in Transport Appraisal. Series: Advances in Transport Policy and Planning, vol. 7. Elsevier, Amsterdam, pp. 103–126.
Wardman, M., Whelan, G., 2011. Twenty years of rail crowding valuation studies: evidence and lessons from British experience. Transp. Rev. 31, 379–398.
Webb, E., Netuveli, G., Millett, C., 2011. Free bus passes, use of public transport among older people in England. J. Epidemiol. Community Health 66 (2), 176–180.
Weinberger, R., 2001. Light rail proximity: benefit or detriment in the case of Santa Clara County, California? Transp. Res. Rec. 1747, 104–113.
Winkler, C., 2015. Transport user benefits calculation with the 'rule of a half' for travel demand models with constraints. Res. Transp. Econ. 49, 36–42.
WMATA (Washington Metropolitan Area Transit Authority), 2019. Rush Hour Promise. Retrieved from: https://www.wmata.com/fares/smartrip/rush-hour-promise.cfm.
Yap, M.D., 2020. Measuring, Predicting and Controlling Disruption Impacts for Urban Public Transport. T2020/3, February 2020, TRAIL Thesis Series, the Netherlands.
Yap, M.D., Cats, O., 2019. Analysis and prediction of disruptions in metro networks. In: Proceedings of the 6th International Conference on Models and Technologies for Intelligent Transportation Systems (MT-ITS), Krakow, Poland,.
Yap, M.D., Van Oort, N., 2018. Driver schedule efficiency vs. public transport robustness: a framework to quantify this trade-off based on passive data. In: Proceedings of the 14th Conference on Advanced Systems in Public Transport (CASPT), Brisbane, Australia.
Yap, M.D., Cats, O., Van Arem, B., 2018a. Crowding valuation in urban tram and bus transportation based on smart card data. Transportmetrica A 16 (1), 23–42. https://doi.org/10.1080/23249935.2018.1537319.
Yap, M.D., Nijënstein, S., Van Oort, N., 2018b. Improving predictions of public transport usage during disturbances based on smart card data. Transp. Policy 61, 84–95.
Yap, M.D., Van Oort, N., Van Nes, R., Van Arem, B., 2018c. Identification and quantification of link vulnerability in multi-level public transport networks: a passenger perspective. Transportation 45, 1161–1180.

CHAPTER SEVEN

Appraisal of cycling and pedestrian projects

Paolo Ruffino* and Matteo Jarre*
Decisio BV, Amsterdam, The Netherlands
*Corresponding authors: e-mail address: p.ruffino@decisio.nl; m.jarre@decisio.nl

Contents

Abstract

Cycling and walking have gained a prominent role in the mobility policy agenda as awareness has risen over the growing unsustainability of the current transport system and the multiple co-benefits of active mobility. As interest and investments for cycling and walking increase, how active mobility can be appraised becomes a crucial question, which has been tackled over the years through different methods and tools. The aim of this chapter is to provide a structured review of the methods and the practices of appraisal of walking and cycling policies and projects, focusing on both traditional and emerging assessment techniques. At present, much attention has been paid to the application of four main traditional methods: Balance Sheet Calculations, Cost-Benefit Analysis, Cost-Effectiveness Analysis and Multi-Criteria Analysis. We compare and discuss these methods to identify strengths and weaknesses for each of them, as well as their main limitations and knowledge gaps in their application. We conclude that over the last decades much effort has been undertaken to further expand and

Advances in Transport Policy and Planning, Volume 7
ISSN 2543-0009
https://doi.org/10.1016/bs.atpp.2020.08.005

develop these tools thanks to an increased attention to walking and cycling. However, much research is still needed, particularly in the quantification and valuation of specific effects within Cost-Benefit Analysis and in better integrating different appraisal techniques. Finally, the impact of appraisals on decision-making outcomes is still underexplored.

Keywords: Walking, Cycling, Cost-Benefit Analysis, Appraisal, Evaluation, Multi-Criteria Analysis, Cost-effectiveness

1. Introduction

Over the last two decades, interest in the promotion of active mobility, namely walking and cycling, as alternative form of urban transport has grown consistently (Banister, 1990; Buehler and Dill, 2016; Buehler et al., 2017; Pucher and Buehler, 2008). On one hand, concerns have risen about externalities of the current (car-centric) transport system; on the other hand, a better understanding and awareness of the multiple co-benefits of active mobility in terms of health, efficiency and social inclusion is emerging (Banister, 2005; Gärling et al., 2014; Gössling et al., 2019; Mueller et al., 2015). Increased planning and financing activity has followed, targeting larger infrastructure projects such as bicycle and pedestrian networks, cycling highways, mass bicycle parking, diffused traffic calming measures and car-free areas, as well as the experimentation of behavioral interventions such as (non) monetary incentives such as bike-to-work or walk-to-school programs (Banister, 1990; Bertolini and le Clercq, 2003; Braun et al., 2016; Martens, 2007; Pucher and Buehler, 2012; Pucher et al., 2010).

More recently, the COVID-19 pandemic has urged public authorities in many countries to promote walking and cycling even more vigorously as a way to limit the spread of the virus, address physical inactivity and also prevent a mass shift from public transport to private car that would worse pre-existing traffic conditions (IEA, 2020; World Health Organization, 2020). For example, in 2020 alone the UK government approved a £2 billion package for active mobility and green transportation (UK Government, 2020), the Italian Ministry of Transport allocated over € 137 million for urban cycling infrastructure (Italian Government, 2020), and many other countries have taken similar initiatives.

These developments pose two main challenges:

(1) A planning challenge: as investments and projects' size increase, questions arise on the feasibility, efficiency, and prioritization of measures (Aldred et al., 2019; Bloyce and White, 2018).

(2) A political challenge: as changes in the functions of public space (e.g., the removal of car parking to add bicycle lanes) have historically been met with suspicion and sometimes public outcry, a need to build greater stakeholder support and acceptance using rational arguments emerges (see for instance: Aldred et al., 2019; Bloyce and White, 2018; Oldenziel and Albert de la Bruhèze, 2011).

Transport appraisal attempts to address these challenges by supporting decision-makers in forming a rational opinion about the strengths and weaknesses of alternative options (Priemus and van Wee, 2013). In many countries in Europe, the US and Australia, standardized frameworks exist to appraise "traditional" transport infrastructure projects, such as highways or railways lines, using methods such as Cost-Benefit Analysis (CBA) (Geurs et al., 2009; Mackie et al., 2014). However, it is neither a common nor an institutionalized practice to appraise cycling and walking projects, as they usually entail lower costs and risks (Van Wee and Börjesson, 2015). This is especially the case for countries with low cycling and/or walking rates, but also in The Netherlands and Denmark—where active mobility is widespread—thorough evaluations are not regularly performed (ibid.). This can be self-defeating, as either too much or too little resources may be allocated, possibly preventing the realization of greater benefits (Börjesson and Eliasson, 2012).

Nevertheless, interest on how active mobility projects could be appraised is growing rapidly among governments, practitioners and academics, and multiple approaches are being explored. Recently, governments are starting to include walking and cycling in their own evaluation frameworks (see, for example, UK Department for Transport, 2014); countries such as Denmark, the Netherlands, Germany and Sweden have commissioned guidelines and studies to identify applicable unit costs for CBA to cycling and walking schemes within their own territories (see for instance COWI and City of Copenhagen, 2008; Decisio, 2012, 2017). A number of transnational research projects have been funded that among others focus (or have focused) on walking and cycling projects and policies appraisal, such as the EU projects PASTA, FLOW, HANDSHAKE. International agencies have published tools (such as the HEAT tool from the World Health Organization) to support urban planners, professionals, and community leaders in performing economic assessment of the health effects of projects aiming to increase walking and cycling rates (Deenihan and Caulfield, 2014).

In this chapter, we examine how appraisal methods commonly used in the transport sector are applied to evaluate walking and cycling projects.

The main goal is to observe what strengths, weaknesses, and limitations these appraisal methods entail when applied to walking and cycling. For doing so, we first provide an overview of the main tools used to assess transport policies and projects. Secondly, we examine the literature and provide examples of where such techniques have been applied, together with a critical discussion of such application(s). Finally, we draw some concluding remarks and implications for further research and policies.

2. Transport appraisal methods and assessment criteria

2.1 Overview of appraisal methods for transport policies

Transportation networks provide multiple benefits in terms of accessibility to people, goods and services but they may also be the source of social, environmental and economic impacts. For this reason, decision-makers should, appraise how different policy options trade-off when planning new infrastructure. In a nutshell, project appraisal is the process of evaluating (i.e., attaching a value to) a policy or project outcome with the intent to assess its particular desirability condition (efficiency, effectiveness, etc.) before the implementation, in order to judge the strengths and weaknesses of a particular course of action using a common framework (Rossi et al., 2004). This should enable decision-makers to rank their preferences and deal with multiple stakeholder interests and perspectives over the same issue.

In the field of transport, scholars have proposed several techniques to appraise projects and policies (Bakker et al., 2010; Browne and Ryan, 2011; Grant-Muller et al., 2001; Mackie et al., 2014), with the most widely used being:

1. Balance Sheet Calculations.
2. Cost-Benefit Analysis.
3. Cost-Effectiveness Analysis.
4. Multi-Criteria Analysis.

BSC is typically the first step of any assessment upon which other methods are built, while CBA, CEA and (in most cases) BSC belong to "*Mono-Criterion*" assessment methods, as they consider a single and specific objective, MCA is "*Multi-Criteria*" as it attempts to deal with a plurality of objectives (Dean, 2020). The main characteristics of each method are summarized in Table 1, and a short description is provided, while we refer to the specific chapters for a more in-depth discussion.

Table 1 Appraisal methods and their characteristics.

Method	Observed indicators	When used	Decision criterion
Balance Sheet Calculations (BSC)	Multiple; Mainly financial	Mostly Ex-ante	No integral criterion
Cost-Benefit Analysis (CBA)	Socio-economic	Ex-ante and ex-post	Welfare expressed as sum of all Willingness-to-Pay (WTP)
Cost-Effectiveness Analysis (CEA) or Cost-Utility Analysis (CUA)	Economic	Ex-ante	Ratio of main effects to costs
Multi-Criteria Analysis (MCA)	Multiple	Ex-ante and ex-post	Weighted sum of effects

Inspired by Bakker et al. (2010).

2.1.1 Balance Sheet Calculation

The Balance Sheet Calculation (BSC) is the simplest among transport appraisal methods. It consists of the separate observation of a number of selected criteria and effects upon which decision-makers draw their own conclusions (typically the intervention costs, supplied by extra information about specific effects, such as traffic impacts) (Bakker et al., 2010). Balance sheets—particularly the cost-analysis, business cases and technical-financial feasibility studies—represent the basic input to other assessment methodologies discussed in this chapter. In general, this approach has the benefit of being quick and cheap, but the assessment of the broader consequences is often limited to the decision-makers' intuition.

2.1.2 Cost-Benefit Analysis

Cost-Benefit Analysis (CBA, or Social Cost-Benefit Analysis for completeness) stands out traditionally as the most common appraisal method for large transport infrastructure projects (see Boardman and Pearson Education, 2014). CBA is grounded in welfare economic theory and it measures changes in society's welfare (expressed as the aggregation of all individual utilities or willingness-to-pay) resulting from the implementation of a specific project or policy (Boadway and Bruce, 1984). The analysis' object is said to be "*desirable*" or "*socially efficient*" if it satisfies the Kaldor-Hicks criterion, namely if the sum of gains outweighs the sum of losses and therefore losers are theoretically compensated by winners (Hicks, 1939; Kaldor, 1939). Hence, in performing a CBA, all the quantifiable effects (direct and indirect) revolving around a policy or a project are listed and monetized (as costs and benefits) during a specific timeframe (usually the project lifespan). These monetized effects, and the associated investment costs, are then discounted to the present value of money (or net present value, NPV) and results are typically expressed as a benefit-cost ratio, which is the means to verify if the Kaldor-Hicks criterion is met (Boadway, 2006). A CBA may be used to compare either an intervention scenario with a do-nothing (or do-minimum) scenario or different courses of action. CBA may also be performed ex-post in order to verify the accuracy of the initial predictions and/or to monitor the effects and promote policy learning (i.e., Eliasson et al., 2015).

In the field of transport, the quantification of the effects often relies on transport models, which provide the necessary inputs for a CBA (such as changes in travel times, emissions, etc.) (Priemus and van Wee, 2013).

2.1.3 Cost-Effectiveness Analysis

Cost-Effectiveness Analysis (CEA), also known as Cost-Utility Analysis (CUA) in health economics (Robinson, 1993), is a form of Cost-Benefit Analysis that focuses on a single, non-monetized effect or outcome which is compared to the costs of different courses of action (Browne and Ryan, 2011). In this way, decision-makers are informed about which measure ensures that a goal will be reached at the minimum cost. CBA and CEA follow similar research techniques and principles; the latter, however, is limited to a narrowly defined goal.

In the field of transport and environmental policy, CEA is used especially for the so called "*optioneering*," i.e., the comparison of multiple options with a specific set of outputs in order to rank priorities by cost-effectiveness (Bakker et al., 2010). A typical example of CEA application in transport is the ranking of projects by cost per unit of emission reduced (see Kampman et al., 2006, for example).

2.1.4 Multi-Criteria Analysis

Multi-Criteria Analysis (MCA) allows to select alternative projects by considering multiple weighted monetary and non-monetary criteria (Bakker et al., 2010; Beinat, 2001; Browne and Ryan, 2011). The weighing of criteria can be performed in a participatory setting to include expert and stakeholders' opinions in order to balance trade-offs among different goals and needs advocated by different actors (Dean, 2020). Several approaches to MCA exist, ranging from formal (continuous and discrete) to simplified methods, the most common being: Analytical Hierarchy Process (AHP), Analytical Network Process (ANP) and REGIME, ELECTRE (etc.) (see Dean, 2018 for a classification of methods). Each method presents unique features as well as advantages and disadvantages (ibid.). The process to draft a MCA follows in general five main steps: (1) The project and its alternative(s) are defined; (2) the judgment criteria, weighing and ranking method are determined; (3) the impacts of the project and its alternatives are analyzed; (4) the impacts are categorized in as list of criteria that are weighted; (5) the judgments may be aggregated into a single criteria depending on the chosen approach (ibid.). In the field of transport appraisal, MCA is the most common alternative to Cost-Benefit Analysis as it allows to consider effects that are typically difficult to quantify and monetize (such as social inclusion, aesthetics, image, equity, etc.) (Browne and Ryan, 2011).

2.2 Literature search and method

A significant body of literature has analyzed appraisal methods for active mobility in the past. As the aim of this paper is to focus on strengths and weaknesses of the different methods, we selected relevant papers to illustrate the application of appraisal tools and focused on the methodology and process of construction of the appraisal technique more than on the results of each application to the context of cycling and walking. In this perspective, the results of the evaluations are of less interest than the applicability of the proposed methods. Therefore, the selection has discarded papers which did not offer new insights on the choice of appraisal method or discussed its applicability and limitations; the initial selection has built upon previous systematic reviews (mainly Brown et al., 2016; Cavill et al., 2008; Mueller et al., 2015) that have addressed appraisal methods and similar research questions in the past. In addition, such sources were integrated and corroborated by:

(a) Performing a new database search on both Google Scholar and Elsevier in order to fill the 2016–2020 temporal gap.

(b) Adding missing papers through the snowball method and expert suggestions.

(c) Integrating academic publications with gray literature and publicly available professional reports for a more comprehensive perspective.

Table 2 Selection criteria used.

Assessment method	**Criteria**
BS	There is, at least, a financial overview of the costs of a measure
CBA	The expected benefits of an intervention are measured in monetary terms and compared to the costs of the intervention. Results are reported as cost per unit of benefits
CEA/CUA	The expected outcomes (health, traffic reductions, etc.) of an intervention are measured against the costs and expressed in terms of cost per adverted/gained outcome
MCA	Several (weighted) indicators is used to determine the relative importance/priority of measures

(d) Interviewing active mobility experts from several municipalities within the project CIVITAS Handshake in order to have a more comprehensive understanding of how decisions are formed within municipalities and obtain relevant examples.

The inclusion criteria that were adopted for selecting papers about each method are summarized in Table 2.

3. Applications

3.1 Balance Sheet Calculations

Despite being the most common way in which public authorities perform appraisals on walking and cycling projects, the academic debate on BSC is surprisingly scarce. In part, this might be due to the fact that BSC usually represents only the first phase of a more thorough appraisal. Much of the publicly available knowledge is gray literature in the form of technical-financial feasibility studies (see for instance Centraal Utrecht 2030, 2012; St. Luis (City Government), 2014; Opus Consultants, 2016). Study designs also vary depending on the laws and standards applied in each country, as well as the context-specific needs. In general, the content of such studies can be narrowed down to three main components:

1. A general description of the intervention site.
2. A preliminary technical design and cost estimate of the proposed solution, and its alternative(s).

3. Occasionally, the previous steps are supplemented by qualitative judgments on strengths and weaknesses, sensitivity analyses, traffic impact studies, environmental assessments, etc.

Typical examples of "*Balance Sheet Calculations*" are the financial analyses performed on bicycle sharing projects and large bicycle parking facilities to verify costs and revenues of their operation in order to determine adequate budgeting.

For instance, in 2012 the Municipality of Utrecht, Dutch Railways, and ProRail (the owner of the railway lines) performed a business cases and scenario analyses when redesigning Utrecht's train station; such redesign included the construction of several large bicycle parking facilities. The BSC was necessary to estimate the financial impacts of different daily/monthly tariffs under several assumptions (daily users, parking duration, quality of service) in order to quantify the costs and revenues and determine a possible management agreement (Centraal Utrecht 2030, 2012). The resulting costs for the different scenarios are summarized in Table 3.

This type of analysis considers mainly financial effects. In the reported example, the construction, maintenance, enforcement, exploitation costs, incidental costs etc., were included, while revenues consisted of tariffs, taxes, sales etc. Sensitivity analyses were included in order to allow decision-makers to understand the order of magnitude of the financial implications.

Bicycle share programs are another example that is typically evaluated using BS studies (St. Luis (City Government), 2014). These studies start by analyzing the potential demand in the area to identify adequate locations of bicycle docking stations; next, the costs of the program for a variable number of years are estimated as well as the revenues of multiple financial plans using scenarios. In most cases, since the demand for such infrastructure projects is complex to determine, significant hypotheses must be introduced and then tested through sensitivity analyses on key parameters (such as duration, trip frequency and modal shift) (ibid.).

Through BSC the broader social, economic, and environmental effects are not systematically captured, thus leaving the judgment about the merits and flaws of the proposal to intuitive assessments.

3.2 Cost-Benefit Analysis

CBA is currently among the assessment techniques that have received the most attention from both practice and academia over the last two decades (Van Wee and Börjesson, 2015). A "*typical*" CBA study applied to walking

Table 3 Balance sheet results example.

Exploitation results (x1.000)	Scenario 1: All free		Scenario 2: All paid		Scenario 3: Different pricing		Scenario 4: Different quality	
	Min	Max	Min	Max	Min	Max	Min	Max
2014	–€ 1.300	–€ 1.600	–€ 900	–€ 1.100	–€ 1.400	–€ 1.700	–€ 900	–€ 1.100
2016	–€ 3.500	–€ 4.300	–€ 1.800	–€ 2.200	–€ 3.700	–€ 4.600	–€ 2.000	–€ 2.500
2021	–€ 5.200	–€ 6.400	–€ 2.200	–€ 2.700	–€ 5.600	–€ 6.800	–€ 2.600	–€ 3.200
2031	–€ 6.400	–€ 7.800	–€ 2.600	–€ 3.200	–€ 6.800	–€ 8.300	–€ 3.100	–€ 3.800

Centraal Utrecht 2030 (2012).

and cycling does not substantially differ from its counterpart applied to other modes, as it consists of:

1. A general description of the intervention site.
2. An analysis of the reference scenario (which usually accounts for a "do-nothing" or "do-minimum" policy intervention) to be used as benchmark.
3. A description of the intervention scenario (including costs and risks), alternatives, and a causal model to quantify the effects.
4. A monetarization of the expected effects that revolve around a project's lifetime, and a comparison to the costs at the NPV.
5. A (optional) sensitivity analyses to test the effect of some key parameters to the end result.

In contrast to BSC, which is limited to an analysis of financial cash flows only, a CBA provides a more comprehensive picture of all the welfare effects revolving around a measure which would otherwise be underexposed.

An example of CBA that included walking and cycling among other modes is the study performed by the City of Amsterdam in 2016 to appraise different solutions to improve the connection between the City Centre and the expanding neighborhood of Amsterdam-Noord across the river IJ (Hoefsloot et al., 2016). The explored solutions included the improvement of the current ferry system, the construction of a pedestrian and bicycle bridge (including different design variants), the construction of a tunnel under the river IJ, the construction of a metro station and pedestrian tunnel, and several "packages" of different measures. In total, 14 (combinations of) measures were tested in two development scenarios (high and low growth scenario) using Amsterdam's transport model. Table 4 is an excerpt that illustrates some of the results.

In the scientific literature, Elvik (2000) was among the first scholars to critically discuss the application of CBA on measures designed to improve safety or mobility for pedestrians and cyclists. In doing so, he applied the best available knowledge of the time to a hypothetical case in order to identify a research agenda. What he found is still relevant nowadays and concerns four main aspects:

(a) how to determine changes in the amount of walking and cycling;
(b) how to value changes in travel time for pedestrians and cyclists;
(c) how to measure changes in road user insecurity and feeling of safety;
(d) how to determine and value changes in the health state.

His analysis indicated that the inclusion of these effects could make a major difference in the results of CBA. Later, Sælensminde (2004) published one of

Table 4 CBA results example.

NPV results (in Mln €)	Alternative 1a: Optimization of the ferry system		Alternative 2a: IJ-plein tunnel		Alternative 3a: Java tunnel		Alternative 3b: Java bridge (9.7 m)		Alternative 6c: Pedestrian tunnel + Optimization of ferry system		Others
Growth scenarios	**Low**	**High**	**Low**	**High**	**Low**	**High**	**Low**	**High**	**Low**	**High**	…
Financial effects	−€78.7	−€106.4	−€264.6	−€241.8	−€240	−€216.8	−€290	−267.5€	€270	−266.6€	…
Accessibility effects	+€79.6	+€347.1	+€154.2	+€674.9	+€154.7	+€473.4	+€199.8	+625.3€	+€128.8	+510.8€	…
External effects	+€12.6	−€1.3	+€15.4	+€101.5	+€9.4	+€36.1	+€25.1	+91.5€	-€3.9	+44.1€	…
Indirect effects	+€4.3	+€50.1	+€15.5	+€68	+€17.4	+€58.2	+€18.4	+66.9€	+€18	+58.9€	…
Total	+€17.8	+€289.5	−€79.5	+€603.2	−€58.5	+€350.8	−€47.3	+516.1€	−€127.4	+347.2€	…
Benefit-cost ratio	**1.2**	**3.7**	**0.7**	**3.5**	**0.8**	**2.6**	**0.8**	**2.9**	**0.5**	**2.3**	…

Hoefsloot et al. (2016)—Reworked by authors (simplified to improve readability).

the first "*complete*" CBA study on walking and cycle tracks in three Norwegian cities. The study included for the first time (a) the health benefits associated with increased active mobility rates, (b) reduced external costs from motorized traffic and (c) reduced parking costs. As hypothesized by Elvik (2000), the inclusion of these social effects meant that the benefits of investment in active travel networks could be as high as 4–5 times the costs. However, the study also acknowledged that improvements in the valuation of some effects as well as more information on the relationship between physical activity and the incidence and costs of different diseases were needed in order to make more accurate estimates. Finally, the traffic accidents effects of a modal shift from car and public transport to cycling were deemed unclear (ibid.).

Multiple studies have since been published that have further explored the application of CBA to walking and cycling infrastructure in different contexts and attempted to address various knowledge gaps. Three systematic reviews of the literature have been published between 2008 and 2016 (see Brown et al., 2016; Cavill et al., 2008; Mueller et al., 2015). In general, most studies have found that investing in cycling and walking usually carries a positive effect on society because of lower road externalities, particularly when the shift occurs from car travels(ibid.). When losses occur, these are usually due to the missed collection of car and fuel taxes or when a policy fails to generate enough demand for a project (Gössling et al., 2019; Litman, 2020).

The effects with the most significant impact are the reduced health-related costs and travel time gains (especially due to decongestion). Hence, the results of CBAs have been used to harness support among stakeholders by showing that promoting more walking and cycling would create a win-win situation and deconstruct policy frames that marginalize cycling and walking as recreational activities (Aldred, 2015; Bloyce and White, 2018). However, it is unclear from the literature how these results affect the outcomes of decision-making processes.

Over the years, a relevant body of research has attempted to fill the knowledge gaps about the estimation and valuation of specific effects of active mobility and other consequences of changes in travel habits. Notably, Hopkinson and Wardman (1996), Wardman et al. (2007), Ramjerdi et al. (2010) and Börjesson and Eliasson (2012) have focused on estimating the value of travel time reductions and improvements in perceived safety for different types of roadway improvements, finding that cyclists have higher value of times than other mode users due to the physical effort involved. Studies in the health and epidemiology domain have found positive effects of walking and cycling in reducing all-cause mortality (Kelly et al., 2014), lowering absenteeism (de Hartog et al., 2010), improving fitness and productivity levels (Etemadi et al., 2016; Walker et al., 2017; Wattles et al., 2003), and reducing the cost of several illnesses (Kahlmeier et al., 2017).

A push to the development and use of CBA for walking and cycling projects has indeed come from the health sector. Notably, the WHO made an important contribution by publishing the Health Economic Assessment Tool (HEAT) for walking and cycling (Kahlmeier et al., 2017; World Health Organization, 2014) which is grounded in some of the studies cited before (Kelly et al., 2014 in particular). This planning-support tool, based on CBA principles, aids planners and advocates in estimating the value of reduced mortality and other externalities that results from a shift to regular walking and cycling and compare the monetized effects with the costs of a measure. Despite the limitation arising from its "simplified" dashboard-like functioning, the HEAT tool has contributed to increasing the popularity in both academia and practice of health-economic assessments. For instance, Fishman et al. (2015) used HEAT to quantify the population-level health benefits of cycling in the Netherlands, finding that over 6500 deaths are prevented each year and Dutch people have half-a-year-longer life expectancy thanks to high cycling levels with respect to a non-cycling base. Maizlish et al. (2013), Deenihan and Caulfield (2014), Götschi et al. (2015), Sá et al. (2015), de Sá et al. (2017) and Rodrigues et al. (2019) have all performed similar studies using HEAT or HEAT-like approaches.

CBA has also seen applications to assess non-infrastructure projects such as mandatory helmet laws (Sieg, 2014; Taylor and Scuffham, 2002), programs that encourage active travel habits (Beale et al., 2012), changes to the built environment (Guo and Gandavarapu, 2010), bicycle share programs (Bullock et al., 2017) as well as integrated active travel policies (Chapman et al., 2018). Moreover, CBA has been used to appraise measures at different levels: from site-specific interventions—such as bicycle and pedestrian trails and bridges (Hoefsloot et al., 2016; Li and Faghri, 2014)—to changes at the network level (Beria and Rafaele, 2014; Brey et al., 2017; Gotschi, 2011). CBA is generally applied in ex-ante, while ex-post CBAs of active mobility projects are limited in the literature (one example is Chapman et al., 2018). Moreover, studies that have compared ex-ante with ex-post CBA to validate the results of previous appraisals are not present in the literature.

CBA frameworks have also been used to compare the different societal costs imposed by different transport modes (including walking and cycling) on society in order to advocate in favor of more sustainable transport but also in order to include a wider array of effects in evaluations. For instance, Gössling and Choi (2015) found that in Copenhagen the societal costs borne to society from each km traveled by car is more than six times higher than the same km traveled by bike, if all effects are included (especially health). Similarly, Gössling et al. (2019) estimated that the total passenger-kilometer driven by car in the European Union impose an external cost of more than € 500 billion per year, while cycling and walking kilometers, due to positive health effects, are worth € 24 billion and € 66 billion per year respectively.

A major point when it comes to CBA is the demand forecasting of future infrastructure projects. In the literature, multiple approaches have been proposed, ranging from simple assumptions to more complex approaches depending on the tackled research question, as well as the level of detail and data available. The approach employed by Sælensminde (2004) and Gotschi (2011) is most commonly adopted: present volumes of pedestrian and bicycle traffic are estimated using average statistical figures, sometimes supplemented by traffic counting and surveys, whereas future induced volumes are estimated using assumptions accompanied by sensitivity analyses to account for uncertainty (ibid.). More complex approaches involve the use of potential analysis scans to identify short car trips (Lovelace et al., 2017), system dynamic modeling techniques that capture positive and negative feedback loops (Macmillan et al., 2014) and traditional multi-modal traffic simulation models to better capture changes in consumers' surplus (as in the case of Beria and Rafaele, 2014; Hoefsloot et al., 2016).

3.3 Cost-Effectiveness Analysis

CEA is another common assessment method for appraising walking and cycling measures, more so in the field of health economics then transport economics (Abu-Omar et al., 2017). That is the case because the promotion of safe walking and cycling is seen by many health authorities—such as the WHO—as a prevention policy to tackle the risks associated to physical inactivity (World Health Organization, 2020). In fact, multiple studies over the years have tested the effectiveness of different programs (including the promotion of active mobility) aiming at reducing physical inactivity against their cost (some systematic reviews have been conducted by Campbell et al., 2015; Garret et al., 2011; Mueller-Riemenschneider et al., 2009).

For example, Wang et al. (2004) performed a CEA of bicycle and pedestrian trails to illustrate how cost-effectiveness changed depending on the activity levels of the population. Cobiac et al. (2009) performed a CEA to measure the health outcomes against the costs of six different physical activity interventions compared to identify the most cost-effective option (the comparison included travel smart programs that rewarded travelers for reducing car trips and choosing to walk and cycle).

In the majority of studies produced in the field of health economics, the cost-effectiveness is expressed in terms of a ratio of gained health (usually expressed as Quality-Adjusted Life Years or QALY) or averted DALYs (Disability-Adjusted Life Years) to the costs required to achieve a unit of result. In the field of transport economics, CEA considers also other traffic-related effects, namely road crashes costs, pollution, congested hours as goal criterion.

For example, Hatziandreu et al. (1995) applied CEA to three different approaches (law enforcement, community-based and school education) aiming at promoting the use of bicycle helmets among pupils. Their study used pre-post data and compared the costs of the program with the effect in terms of bicycle-related head injury and deaths. Other studies, such as Peters and Anderson (2012), Wijnen et al. (2013) and Jiao et al. (2019), applied CEA to measure the efficacy of traffic calming aiming at reducing accidents costs. Others such as Gunn et al. (2014) have focused on the effects of sidewalks to increase levels of transport walking and related health effects, while Gu et al. (2016) analyzed the cost-effectiveness of bicycle lanes as means to both improve health of the general population and reduce crashes.

CEA is also often used as an instrument to prioritize program investments. In the field of cycling, a simple example is the study conducted by the City of San Donato Milanese (Italy) (Ruffino and Jarre, 2019) in which the investment priority in cycle routes was sorted by means of a CEA using an accessibility index as effectiveness criterion. The goal of the administration was in fact to provide a transport option alternative to the car to the largest number of residents, commuters, school pupils etc., at the lowest price. The study therefore followed these steps:

1. The investment costs for each bicycle route was determined.
2. An accessibility index of each cycle route was defined that fitted the administration goals.
3. A ratio between the km-costs and the index was performed in order to determine the Cost-Effectiveness.
4. The cycle routes were sorted by least cost in order to determine the intervention with the highest effectiveness at the lower costs.

Table 5 illustrates the results.

Table 5 CEA results example.

Cycleroutes	Investment cost per km	Accessibility index	Cost-effectiveness
Cycle route number 3	€ 196	63	€ 3.1
Cycle route number 5	€ 5.772	59	€ 98.5
Cycle route number 1	€ 21.063	135	€ 156
Cycle route number 4	€ 9.707	57	€ 171.8
Cycle route number 6	€ 19.523	93	€ 209.8
Cycle route number 2	€ 20.560	87	€ 237.5
Cycle route number 8	€ 22.435	28	€ 788.3
Cycle route number 9	€ 50.879	48	€ 1.067.8
Cycle route number 7	€ 95.394	31	€ 3.094.6

Ruffino and Jarre (2019)—Reworked by authors.

This approach clearly shows, once the objective is clear, what measures should be prioritized according to the analysis.

Similar studies have been performed in other contexts using more complex methods. For instance, to determine investment priorities in bicycle highways in the Haaglanden (conurbation surrounding The Hague in the Netherlands), a transportation model was used to calculate the cost-effectiveness of bicycle highways in terms of reduced short car trips and congested hours as effectiveness criterion (Decisio, 2016).

CEA has been applied both in ex-ante and ex-post studies using different methods: ex-post studies have mainly used direct pre-post measurements and/or (interrupted) time series, sometimes complemented by surveys (self-report, etc.); on the other hand, ex-ante studies relied mostly on scenarios, using a variety of statistical techniques (ranging from simple trend analysis to regression analyses and Markov models) and applying sensitivity analysis to assess the robustness of the obtained results. For instance, Moodie et al. (2011) measured the cost-effectiveness of school programs to increase active mobility among pupils aged 10–11 by sharing of a small pilot survey and then extrapolated the results to the entire pupil population of Australia. Dallat et al. (2013) used a quasi-experimental before-and-after household survey and different scenarios to measure the cost-effectiveness of urban greenways in improving physical activity levels. Gu et al. (2016) used regression analysis to calculate the effect of marginal improvements of bicycle lanes in NYC in terms of ridership in order to assess the related health effects.

Yu et al. (2018) used stochastic Markov models to measure in ex-ante the cost-effectiveness of expanding the NYC bicycle share program to other parts of the city.

3.4 Multi-Criteria Analysis

Conventional reductionist approaches have been criticized for leading to sub-optimal decisions due to the inherent complexity of sustainability dilemmas, such as transport policies (Browne and Ryan, 2011; Gasparatos et al., 2008; Omann, 2000). In this perspective, MCA is increasingly being proposed as a viable alternative also in the field of walking and cycling appraisal (Glavic et al., 2019; Grisé and El-Geneidy, 2018) since:

- There is a need to include and deal with effects that are typically difficult to quantify and monetize yet relevant for planning walking and cycling infrastructure (such as comfort, aesthetic quality etc.) as well as addressing equity questions.
- Secondly, there is a need to incorporate opportunities and risks related to the type of infrastructure measure proposed.
- Finally, stakeholders' views and equity issues can be better represented by assigning weights.

In particular, MCA integrated with GIS (also defined as MCDM-GIS) is becoming increasingly popular to appraise walking and cycling projects (Larsen et al., 2013; Rybarczyk and Wu, 2010). For example, Larsen et al. (2013) and Rybarczyk and Wu (2010) were among the first scholars to propose MCA and GIS to identify and prioritize investments by integrating both supply- and demand-analysis criteria for cycling planning. Later, Milakis et al. (2012) and Milakis and Athanasopoulos (2014) expanded on this approach including inputs from cyclists in a participatory setting to plan Athens' metropolitan cycle network. Guerreiro et al. (2018) applied MCA, GIS and data mining techniques to plan and compare the investments in a cycling network. Canu et al. (2018) proposed spatial MCA for the assessment of walkability of intersections and the prioritization of pedestrian-oriented policies. Kent and Karner (2018) explored the application of GIS-MCA to prioritize low-stress and pleasant bicycle routes. Besides traditional infrastructures, spatial MCA has been widely applied to bicycle share systems analyses (Croci and Rossi, 2014; Kabak et al., 2018; Milakis and Athanasopoulos, 2014; Moshref Javadi et al., 2013). However, to the best of our knowledge, no study has compared competing investments in walking or cycling with investments in other modes of transport using MCA.

In most cases, MCA has been applied as an ex-ante appraisal method to either assess planned walking and cycling projects (such as Glavic et al., 2019) or to prioritize investments (Guerreiro et al., 2018; Kabak et al., 2018). Although possible, no study has been performed ex-post, hence no reported experiences of the effects and/or the usefulness of the method at a later stage are available.

There is currently no standard framework for MCA, which is tailored to address each specific case. Criteria included in walking and cycling MCA range depending on the planning scale, the method used, the available data and the study design. Usually, at a strategic level (such as in Grisé and El-geneidy, 2018; Milakis et al., 2012) network characteristics, mobility demand patterns, socio-economic features, proximity to destinations, characteristic of the landscape and built environment are observed. At a tactical-operational level (such as in Canu et al., 2018), more detailed criteria related to the specific context as well as technical aspects are included. Some studies have also explicitly included equity criteria in their own analysis (examples are Grisé and El-geneidy, 2018; Kent and Karner, 2018).

4. Strengths and weaknesses of appraisal methods for walking and cycling

In this paragraph we present and compare the main strengths, weaknesses and limitations of the four methods for appraising walking and cycling projects. Table 6 provides a summary.

4.1 Balance Sheet Calculation

The main advantage of this type of analyses is that it provides a clear summary of the direct financial effects from a specific project and the range of variation across different scenarios and assumptions. This is particularly useful for budgeting and ensuring long-term financial sustainability of a project.

However, the social effects are often neglected as they are less relevant for the research objective or too complex to be accounted. Even when positive/negative "social" impacts of the project are considered, these are either qualitative ones (e.g., "bikers will feel safer") or, when quantitative, they are expressed as non-comparable unit of measurements (e.g., "pollution will go down 10% in the area"). Based on investment costs and impacts (if any), relevant actors decide based on their own judgment, i.e., they introduce their own weighs on the importance of impacts for specific stakeholders and value them against the projected costs (Bakker et al., 2010).

Table 6 Comparison of different appraisal methods for walking and cycling.

	BS	CBA	CEA	MCA
		Specific for walking and cycling		
Application	Predominantly on infrastructure projects, bike sharing programs and some behavioral measures	Predominantly on infrastructure projects, bike sharing programs and some behavioral measures	Predominantly on policies aiming at improving physical activity levels	Predominantly infrastructure projects
When used	Ex-ante	Ex-ante	Ex-ante and some ex-post in the field of medicine	Ex-ante
Trend in use	Always performed	Increasingly used but far less than for other transportation projects	Widely used in the field of medicine, less in the field of transport	Increasingly used in combination with GIS as alternative to CBA due to lack of data
Indicator	Financial balance (mainly)	Benefit-cost ratio	Cost-effect ratio	Decision ranking
Positive impacts considered	Cash flow	Predominantly health, travel time savings and reduced car externalities	Predominantly health	Potentially all benefits could be included
Stakeholder participation	Possible but not required and not documented in the literature	Possible but not required and not documented in the literature	Possible but not required and not documented in the literature	Institutionalized in the process and in some cases performed

Impact on decision-making	Unknown	Unknown	Unknown	Increased legitimacy of the planning process
Ease of communication	May be difficult to interpret and explain	Simple	Simple	May be difficult to interpret and explain
Transparency	Transparent calculation but subjective decision criterion	Not clear, many assumptions are made behind results	Not clear, many assumptions are made behind results	Clearer but subjectivity in weights
Ease of use	Easiest as only direct financial aspects are considered	Difficult to monetize impact and forecasting walking and cycling demand presents greater challenges	Relatively easier but challenges in predicting the effectiveness if they entail behavior change	Easier to tailor to a specific need and in the case of absence of data
Others	Welfare effects not accounted	May never be able to quantify properly all impacts correctly	May never be able to quantify properly all impacts correctly	It may lead to lengthy discussions

Many walking and, especially, cycling projects are often evaluated only through a Balance Sheet Calculation; this mainly happens because such method is the quickest and cheapest of all, as it can require, at its minimum, no further analysis besides the financial and technical feasibility studies that are required by the law, and the "*appraisal*" of the project is done through pure judgment by the decision-maker(s). This allows for ample discretion on his/her side, which of course is an advantage or a disadvantage depending on one's position.

Even when impacts are considered, the weighing phase introduces a high degree of subjectivity, not only on which impacts are considered relevant but also by which stakeholder(s). In fact, these simple and straightforward tools are also the most limited in scope and objectivity: first, as effects are analyzed separately it is not possible to provide a comprehensive comparability of different options. Moreover, the subjectivity of the decision-making might accelerate the process only if interests among stakeholders are aligned, which is seldom the case in public policies and even more so for transport projects: when differences of interests emerge, and no clear power structure that can impose a decision exists, the Balance Sheet Calculation method does not contribute in reaching a shared decision, and the process can be slowed down or altogether stopped.

Hence, in a situation in which budget is limited, the costs are high, the potential number of alternatives increases and/or several stakeholders are involved, the Balance Sheet Calculation approach is usually integrated with other methods such as Cost-Benefit Analysis and/or Multi-Criteria Analysis.

4.2 Cost-Benefit Analysis

CBA applied to walking and cycling present similar methodological strengths and weaknesses already discussed by the literature on general transport CBA. Namely, CBA enables the comparison between costs and benefits of policies and programs targeting different travel modes, which can be a straightforward and convincing way to present arguments of economic efficiency as it has an allure of scientific soundness (Browne and Ryan, 2011). Currently, most of the cases in literature use CBA for this purpose, for example, in Gössling and Choi (2015) and Gössling et al. (2019).

Moreover, CBA may have potential applications to rank program priorities and projects selection for financing, especially when used at the early stages of the decision-making process (Eliasson et al., 2015; Mackie et al., 2014).

Another potential application currently not investigated is the use of CBA in policies aiming at internalizing externalities of walking and cycling (i.e., quantify the value of km reimbursement for bike-to-work schemes).

Finally, CBA may prove to be valuable to structure a debate and improve learning, communication and trust among stakeholders when used in a participatory setting (Beukers et al., 2014), although in this case too the literature lacks concrete examples for walking and cycling.

Despite the growing literature on the social and economic effects of walking and cycling, there are substantive limitations to the quantifications and valuation of these effects. Van Wee and Börjesson (2015) and Decisio (2017) have discussed these in detail.

A major weakness of CBA is that it is extremely "data hungry"; this is particularly evident when it comes to estimating current and future demand for the infrastructure. Demand forecast is a crucial first step also for other assessment methods such as CEA. How many cyclists or pedestrians will use the infrastructure once opened? How will the urban traffic change as a result of the pedestrianization of a specific street? What will be the revenues of a bicycle parking at station? These are questions that are impossible to answer without a model. Hence, the quality of a CBA highly depends on the type of model used as well as the quality of the input data. The integration of walking and cycling into traditional transport simulation models is a "*recent and complicated affair*" (see for a detailed discussion Barnes and Krizek, 2005; Buehler and Dill, 2016; Hollander, 2016; Porter et al., 1999; Turner et al., 1997).

In synthesis, current difficulties with cycling and/or walking modeling include the following.

- There are many gaps in our understanding of what factors play a role in motivating people to choose to walk and cycling instead of driving and building cycle paths alone does not necessarily explain bicycle use on their own. Therefore, a simple correlation between infrastructure quantity and cycling/walking rates is unlikely to be robust.
- Cycling is much more affected by the interaction with other traffic modes, the environment, seasonality, weather conditions and other factors than car traffic. These factors are typically difficult to include in a model.
- Bicycle use and behavioral change according to trip purpose, age groups and the level of some benefits depend on the physical activity levels of the targeted population which is often unknown in an origin-destination matrix.

- For walking in particular it is difficult to determine what counts as a walking trip and distinguish by motive.
- Another issue is related to the zoning of the model which needs to be more refined as walking and cycling trips take place usually at short distances meaning that calculations become more cumbersome and data less reliable.
- Network coding is usually a difficult and lengthy process and the quality of information is not always readily available and requires many more assumptions.
- With walking and cycling infrastructure "the devil is in the detail." Some slight design choices and infrastructure characteristics (type of pavement, etc.) may have a greater impact on route choice and behavior than on typical road infrastructure.
- Finally, it is also currently difficult to predict the added value of marginal improvements in cycling infrastructure especially in countries in which these type of infrastructure projects might be common such as in the Netherlands and Denmark.

Even though nowadays models have become far better at predicting and estimating the effects of policies and road adjustments to walking and bicycle traffic, in practice these models are not always available, and it is simply impossible to gain a satisfactory level of data coverage. Hence, several academics and practitioners recur to other means to predict induced traffic such as potential analysis tools which observe short car trips to enable the testing of modal shift scenarios (one example is the Propensity to Cycle Tool developed in the UK, see Lovelace et al., 2017). Although the uncertainty of these methods is high, the use of models is not necessarily a guarantee of improved accuracy considering that interventions happen in a non-closed system (Næss and Strand, 2012).

Another prominent issue is related to the quantification and valuation of specific effects. In particular:

- Limited research is available about specific travel time valuation (VoT) of pedestrian and cyclists. Related aspects such as the valuation of reliability, waiting time and search time (i.e., when parking a bicycle) have not been investigated either. Moreover, VOT of different target groups and travel motives (utilitarian vs recreational) could be significantly diverging. Moreover, there is limited literature and research on comfort evaluation, travel experience and perception of safety mainly because of the challenge in defining, measuring and attaching a monetary value to this concept (Van Ginkel, 2014). However, it is likely that comfort, along with perception of safety, are important factors in motivating people to travel by bicycle or on foot (Handy et al., 2014).

- Although the literature generally suggests that increasing the level of physical activity has positive health consequences (Kelly et al., 2014). Including these effects into CBAs presents several uncertainties. The extent to which people actually become "healthier" is strongly related to the individual herself and his/her lifestyles (Haskell et al., 2007; Pate, 1995): inactive people who start cycling, for example, may have greater health effects than already-active people. Moreover, it is important to assess which means of transport is substituted (car, public transport, e-bike, etc.). The extent to which health effects are internalized is also uncertain. Börjesson and Eliasson (2012) pointed out that most cyclists accounted for health effects when choosing to cycle and argued therefore that there might be a risk of overestimating the size of the external effects. However, it is also unclear to which extent cyclists and walkers are able to quantify the order of magnitude of these effects (ibid.). Another issue is related to new mode of travels such as electric bicycles, steps and pedelecs which are becoming increasingly popular among different target groups and require less effort from the user, limiting the magnitude of the health effects. However, such evidences are difficult to collect everywhere, and it is unlikely to get this specific information for a specific intervention site in which a CBA may be used as appraisal technique. In addition, it is unclear how to trade-off health effects from potentially increasing pollution intake. Finally, there is a lack of understanding on the extent to which increased cycling rates create substitution effects from other sport activities and influences self-selection. Since health benefits are usually very high in slow mode-related CBAs studies (Brown et al., 2016).
- Improving road safety is another important rationale for improving walking and cycling facilities (Pucher and Buehler, 2012). However, including the effects on road safety in CBAs on walking and cycling remains tricky as knowledge on road-type specific disaggregated risk factors is often lacking and the use of aggregated statistics may lead to underestimations of the risks effects for short car trips happening in urban areas which are usually the target of cycling policies (Stipdonk and Reurings, 2012). Moreover, there is some evidence that increasing cycling levels substantially reduce the risk of accidents due to the so called "safety-in-number," i.e., the fact that vehicle drivers become more accustomed to cycling/walking people and more capable of anticipating their

behaviors and, thus avoid accidents (Jacobsen, 2003; Wegman et al., 2012). However, it is also true that the relationship is inverse, and that when cycling/walking becomes safer (e.g., thanks to infrastructure improvement), more people start to walk/bike.

- There are other intangible effects that are discussed in the literature that can be relevant for the appraisal of cycling and walking project such as increased urban quality and attractiveness (Pucher and Buehler, 2012), increased option value (Geurs et al., 2006; Laird et al., 2009) and reducing transport poverty (Martens, 2013).

4.3 Cost-effectiveness analysis

The main advantage of CEA compared to other methodologies is that it is cheaper and effective as a tool to rank options. This allows decision-makers to easily sort between alternative options that ensure that a goal will be reached at the least possible cost. However, this is also its main limitation as transport policies may not only want to address one objective at a time. Typically, there are in fact a number of competing objectives to be balanced such as: improving health, reducing accidents, alleviate congestion and improve environmental quality (Litman, 2012). Hence, CEA may not be the most suitable method if the objective is to fully consider a wide range of effects in one decision criterion (Browne and Ryan, 2011). Secondly, the results of CEA have limited transferability due to heterogeneous study designs and the context-specific nature of its application, as well as the limited number of ex-post assessment which hinders the generalizability of results. Thirdly, some long-term benefits of cycling and walking that may not occur immediately and other synergistic effects resulting from an intervention (i.e., installing bike lanes may increase bicycle traffic improving health but also reducing car traffic alleviating congestion and pollution) may be underrepresented due to the static picture that a CEA provides.

Similarly, to CBA, there are important limitations related to forecasting which require the analyst to make strong assumption and predictions (ibid.), and uncertainties on how to quantify and value effects (such as s adverted DALY or gained QALY).

4.4 Multi-Criteria Analysis

In general, the main advantage of MCA is that it can incorporate quantitative and qualitative analysis of economic, environmental and social impacts and, therefore, the results can be more informative than quantitative analysis alone, as is the case in CEA or CBA (Browne and Ryan, 2011). Secondly, MCA can account for multiple stakeholders' opinions, leading in principle to more legitimate approaches as it allows for the inclusion of qualitative and process-related aspects which, for example, the CBA typically does not (Dean, 2020). Finally, it can be used as a policy learning tool, where the objective is process-oriented rather than result-oriented and can be modified to weight criteria with stakeholder input and explicit opinions or values (ibid.).

On the other hand, MCA may be subject to ambiguity and subjectivity in applying weights, it holds risks of double counting and it can present lack of consistency (see Beria et al., 2012; Dean, 2020). In addition, the specificity of the context makes the transferability of the results impossible to generalize and highly subjective. Despite this, most studies underlined some important lessons such as the importance of considering the perspective of multiple actors and to choose the appropriate study design. For example, MCA has been used by Moshref Javadi et al. (2013) to identify the most suitable locations for bicycle share stations. They reported that the most import criteria in determining the final location were proximity to bicycle paths, transportation and networks, demand, and use type. Milakis and Athanasopoulos (2014) included the opinions of cyclists in their study, proposing a four-step methodology for bike-share network planning using multi-criteria and GIS methodology. The methodology was considered to be suitable for cities attempting to introduce and prioritize cycling infrastructures, since it focuses on determining where cyclists would prefer to cycle. Another positive aspect of MCA is the flexibility to tailor the instrument based on the data availability which is typically low for walking and cycling. In addition, the ad hoc definition of criteria may also induce (intended or unintended) manipulations that steer the results to a specific (desired) outcome. Furthermore, certain increasingly popular concepts such as "walkability" and "bikeability" and more broader concepts of fairness find hardly a common definition.

4.5 Impact of appraisal methods on decision-making

Some scholars (Annema et al., 2015; Eliasson et al., 2015; Mouter, 2017a,b) have already investigated the use and view of appraisal methods by politicians. It is argued in this chapter, that appraisals conducted on walking and cycling might be used similarly. In particular, CBA may be one of the instruments used by policy entrepreneurs to promote different framings of walking and cycling as transport and instrumentally use CBA while harnessing political support as suggested by Weber (2014) and Aldred (2015). However, concrete evidence of the views and uses of CBA applied to walking and cycling by policymakers and other stakeholders remains underexplored. This constitutes an interesting avenue for further research, considering that most of the use of this appraisal technique on walking and cycling is to promote political debate and enhance a positive public dialog (see for instance ECF, 2016). The purpose of the development of methodological guidelines and tools such as HEAT stems from this very need to provide an instrument to justify investments into active modes from a health-economic standpoint. Weber (2014) has pointed out that there may be value in pointing the research into this direction and has proposed the use of the Multiple Streams Framework (MSF) and other policy process framework as a possible lens to study the use of CBA and other appraisal methods for walking and cycling within decision-making processes. However, multiple other theories and lenses of policy processes could be used as well (see a review by Sabatier, 2019). From the comparison of multiple lenses, a better understanding of the impact of appraisal methods on decision-making outcome on walking and cycling projects may be identified. Filling this knowledge gap may promote a better integration of CBA within the decision-making processes, promote communicative rationality in transport planning and support the creation of stronger stakeholder coalitions.

5. Conclusion

The appraisal methods that have been discussed were initially developed for traditional transport projects, by which we mean somewhat large-sized projects, mainly concerning infrastructure for motorized private vehicles and/or public transport systems. Such established methods have been adapted to active mobility projects out of reconsiderations about the traditional transport system, which has led to increased interests in active mobility forms and in the methods to evaluate their costs and benefits. At the same time, the last two decades of research are increasingly suggesting that active mobility has a positive impact on society, however, this might be framed, in most contexts. In this sense, appraisal methods have both shaped and are shaped by the increasing interest in active mobility. However, research is unsettled in most, if not all, aspects of evaluation of cycling and walking projects and programs, as the existing methods have been adapted to the new(er) active mobility field with mixed results in terms of analysis capability, applicability, reliability and communicability.

The evaluation of projects based exclusively on the costs (and revenues) of the proposal (such as the Balance Sheet), technical aspects and intuitive assessments of the merits and flaws remains the only practice that is adopted by most decision-makers across the world. On the one hand, its simplicity promises quicker and clearer decisions, as fewer input data are required, and the decision-maker oversees establishing relevant criteria. However, the BS—and in some way even CEA—considers only the feasibility of the project, which is hardly a justification for the necessity of implementing it, without touching upon the benefits of active mobility projects and thus reducing the room for discussion about the desirability of a project. Although simpler methods promise speed of adoption thanks to the few parameters to be considered and evaluated, this very feature can easily backlash and lead to ill-informed and often inconclusive debate. On the contrary, methods such as CBA or MCA, though more complex to both develop and explain, explore the full spectrum of possible impacts, thus fostering a more comprehensive and informed discussion about the role of active mobility within society.

However, the choice for simpler appraisal methods is mostly driven by considerations of costs, time and increasingly so data unavailability. In particular, cycling and walking demand modeling is probably the largest source of uncertainty and variability to the usability of economic appraisal methods, especially when plans, and not single infrastructures, are concerned. Not being able to quickly, cheaply and reliably assess the effects on cycling or walking level of a certain intervention creates a "garbage in, garbage out" type of problem, especially if forecasts are made through the introduction of a significant number of hypotheses. In that sense, the practitioner has fundamentally two opposite possibilities: (a) increase the modeling effort (combined with data collection in most cases) and provide an improved forecast or correlation linking intervention and results; (b) shift the focus from "*modeling and forecasting*" to "*what if*" scenarios, which would remain more general but would assess scenario impacts without claims of prediction.

However, improved modeling and increased data collection and availability about active mobility would anyway be necessary in most cases in which a certain degree of correlation between the proposed intervention (and relative costs) and expected benefits must be made. This is true for cycling and even more so for walking, for which very little modeling effort has been carried out in the past.

One of the most fundamental issues for economic appraisal methods stems from the necessity to monetize the relevant impacts: in particular, many effects have been identified and quantified to a (somewhat) high degree of certainty, such as the value of time, several types of environmental impacts, value of congestion etc. However, even when impacts can be determined and precisely quantified, it is the phase of their monetization that introduces the largest variabilities and uncertainties. These uncertainties stem from three main factors: (1) the consequences of the impact cannot be determined to the same level of certainty (e.g., the consequences of local air pollution on health); (2) the consequences of the impact, though determined, cannot be reflected into a direct economic measure (e.g., the loss of biodiversity from a specific eco-system); (3) the economic measure attached to the impact, though determinable in principle, is highly context-dependent and subjective (e.g., the value of time). For these reasons, the uncertainty that surrounds economic appraisal methods is significant, thus increasing the variability of the results and potentially hindering the model reliability.

Moreover, the high variability introduces an important drawback for CBA in particular: the possibility to quantify and monetize the impacts, although complicated, appears to support the case for a purported objectivity/neutrality of the method, which seemingly suggests that the decision can be demanded to the results of the CBA. On the other hand, room for discretion always exists and lies in the hands of the practitioner performing the analysis, who must ultimately choose, even if within ranges, which values to consider and which ones to discard; this is particularly relevant when considered parameters are highly variable (i.e., the value of CO_2 emissions, the value of statistical Life, etc.).

In this sense, the main difference between the CBA and the MCA is that for the latter the subjectivity is clearly visible and transparent, in that the weights are openly discussed and assigned according to personal criteria. On the other hand, the subjectivity of CBA is somewhat hidden, as the practitioner is forced to choose among possible values or evaluation methods for the considered impacts. The best practice for CBA reporting, in fact, is to fully state the introduced hypothesis and communicate median values and variability ranges of the results, as well as providing a sensibility analysis if possible. Nevertheless, CBA results are often not accepted by the audience because choices about parameters range have been made solely by the practitioner and not by a group of stakeholders. This is particularly relevant in fields of application where choices are often "emotionally loaded," such as the case for cycling infrastructure that diminishes space dedicated to motorized vehicles or policies that disincentive their use.

Officials from the City of Amsterdam and Munich within the Handshake project, for example, have argued that they prefer to adopt MCA rather than CBA because of the "perceived subjectivity" of the latter, which induces confusion and hinders the discussion. Our own experience suggests that debate about an emotionally loaded project will not be easily solved by the results of a CBA, as these would be interpreted differently by different actors in policy controversies (more on this is discussed by Rein and Schön, 1996). Quite paradoxically, a higher acceptability could characterize the results from the "highly subjective" MCA, because the weighs can be made explicit and part of a transparent participatory process. In that sense, the evaluation of effects within CBA could also be part of a participatory process, as it has been underlined by Beukers et al. (2014).

One aspect that hinders, or at least slows down, the improvement of economic appraisals is that any attempt to reduce the uncertainty and variability of impact monetization in CBA must include a high degree of cross-sectorial expertise, as the process from impact identification to its quantification and then to its monetization requires a very different set of skills. For example, the quantification of air pollution emissions form vehicles is an engineering problem, the diffusion of pollutants depending on the specific context is an environmental scientist-type of problem, whereas the health effects of pollution concentration requires epidemiological studies, whose results must then be assessed in terms of monetized impact through sociological and economic studies about the consequences of increased illness and premature deaths. This type of knowledge-chain is often specific to each identified impact and, in many cases, to each case-study when local context can significantly change conditions.

Finally, the presented methods have been considered as "alternatives," but they really should not. In fact, these methods can embrace the full spectrum of socio-economically-relevant consequences of increased cycling/walking conditions only when combined, i.e., only when more than one method is applied to the same case-study. A plurality of methods is seldom applied to a single case-study for obvious resource-scarcity reasons, which force the practitioner or the decision-maker toward the single method that can deliver the best results given the constraints (usually, time and money). Bakker et al. (2010) had already suggested to combine, for the evaluation of integrated transport policies, the strengths of MCA and CBA, specifically for projects where impacts might be harder to monetize. On the other hand, no case-study of such (or other) combinations of methods has been published so far to the best of our knowledge.

However, academics and private researchers might aim at constructing new tools that could develop the potential and overcome the weaknesses of the existing methods, which have been historically developed for quite different contexts and might therefore not be the best possible solution. In this regard, the combination of two or more of the presented tools, and even the transposition of a different appraisal method altogether, might benefit the field and increase the possibility for fast, reliable and high-quality appraisals.

References

Abu-Omar, K., Rütten, A., Schätzlein, V., Messing, S., Suhrcke, M., 2017. The cost-effectiveness of physical activity interventions: a systematic review of reviews. Prev. Med. Rep. 8 (July), 72–78. https://doi.org/10.1016/j.pmedr.2017.08.006.

Aldred, R., 2015. A matter of utility? Rationalising cycling, cycling rationalities. Mobilities 10, 1–20. https://doi.org/10.1080/17450101.2014.935149.

Aldred, R., Watson, T., Lovelace, R., Woodcock, J., 2019. Barriers to investing in cycling: stakeholder views from England. Transp. Res. A Policy Pract. 128, 149–159. https://doi.org/10.1016/j.tra.2017.11.003.

Annema, J.A., Mouter, N., Rezaei, J., 2015. Cost-benefit analysis (CBA), or multi-criteria decision-making (MCDM) or both: politicians' perspective in transport policy appraisal. Transp. Res. Rec. 10 (July), 788–797. https://doi.org/10.1016/j.trpro.2015.09.032.

Bakker, P., Koopmans, C., Nijkamp, P., 2010. Appraisal of integrated transport policies. In: Integrated Transport: From Policy to Practice, pp. 117–136. https://doi.org/10.4324/9780203850886.

Banister, C., 1990. Planning for cycling. Plan. Pract. Res. 5, 27–29. https://doi.org/10.1080/02697459008722763.

Banister, D., 2005. Unsustainable transport: city transport in the new century. In: Transport Development and Sustainability. https://doi.org/10.1016/j.jtrangeo.2006.09.002.

Barnes, G., Krizek, K., 2005. Estimating bicycling demand. Transp. Res. Rec. 1939, 45–51. https://doi.org/10.3141/1939-06.

Beale, S.J., Bending, M.W., Trueman, P., Naidoo, B., 2012. Should we invest in environmental interventions to encourage physical activity in England? An economic appraisal. Eur. J. Public Health 22 (6), 869–873. https://doi.org/10.1093/eurpub/ckr151.

Beinat, E., 2001. Multi-criteria analysis for environmental management. J. Multi-Criteria Decis. Anal. 10 (2), 51.

Beria, P., Rafaele, G., 2014. Cost benefit analysis to assess urban mobility plans. In: Consumers' surplus calculation and integration with transport models. 59590, 20. http://mpra.ub.uni-muenchen.de/59590/.

Beria, P., Maltese, I., Mariotti, I., 2012. Multicriteria versus cost benefit analysis: a comparative perspective in the assessment of sustainable mobility. Eur. Transp. Res. Rev. 4, 137–152. https://doi.org/10.1007/s12544-012-0074-9.

Bertolini, L., le Clercq, F., 2003. Urban development without more mobility by car? Lessons from Amsterdam, a multimodal urban region. Environ. Plan. A. 35 (4), 575–589. https://doi.org/10.1068/a3592.

Beukers, E., Bertolini, L., Te Brömmelstroet, M., 2014. Using cost benefit analysis as a learning process: identifying interventions for improving communication and trust. Transp. Policy 31, 61–72. https://doi.org/10.1016/j.tranpol.2013.12.002.

Bloyce, D., White, C., 2018. When transport policy becomes health policy: a documentary analysis of active travel policy in England. Transp. Policy 72 (September), 13–23. https://doi.org/10.1016/j.tranpol.2018.09.012.

Boadway, R., 2006. Principles of cost-benefit analysis. Public Policy Rev. 2 (1), 1–44.

Boadway, R.W., Bruce, N., 1984. Welfare Economics. B. Blackwell, New York.

Boardman, A.E., Pearson Education, 2014. Cost-Benefit Analysis: Concepts and Practice. Pearson Education Limited, Harlow.

Börjesson, M., Eliasson, J., 2012. The value of time and external benefits in bicycle appraisal. Transp. Res. A Policy Pract. 46, 673–683. https://doi.org/10.1016/j.tra.2012.01.006.

Braun, L.M., Rodriguez, D.A., Cole-Hunter, T., Ambros, A., Donaire-Gonzalez, D., Jerrett, M., Mendez, M.A., Nieuwenhuijsen, M.J., de Nazelle, A., 2016. Short-term planning and policy interventions to promote cycling in urban centres: findings from a commute mode choice analysis in Barcelona, Spain. Transp. Res. A Policy Pract. 89, 164–183. https://doi.org/10.1016/j.tra.2016.05.007.

Brey, R., Castillo-Manzano, J.I., Castro-Nuño, M., López-Valpuesta, L., Marchena-Gómez, M., Sánchez-Braza, A., 2017. Is the widespread use of urban land for cycling promotion policies cost effective? A Cost-Benefit Analysis of the case of Seville. Land Use Policy 63, 130–139. https://doi.org/10.1016/j.landusepol.2017.01.007.

Brown, V., Diomedi, B.Z., Moodie, M., Veerman, J.L., Carter, R., 2016. A systematic review of economic analyses of active transport interventions that include physical activity benefits. Transp. Policy 45, 190–208. https://doi.org/10.1016/j.tranpol.2015.10.003.

Browne, D., Ryan, L., 2011. Comparative analysis of evaluation techniques for transport policies. Environ. Impact Assess. Rev. 31 (3), 226–233. https://doi.org/10.1016/j.eiar.2010.11.001.

Buehler, R., Dill, J., 2016. Bikeway Networks: a review of effects on cycling. Transp. Rev. 36, 1–19. https://doi.org/10.1080/01441647.2015.1069908.

Buehler, R., Pucher, J., Gerike, R., Götschi, T., 2017. Reducing car dependence in the heart of Europe: lessons from Germany, Austria, and Switzerland. Transp. Rev. 37, 4–28. https://doi.org/10.1080/01441647.2016.1177799.

Bullock, C., Brereton, F., Bailey, S., 2017. The economic contribution of public bike-share to the sustainability and efficient functioning of cities. Sustain. Cities Soc. 28, 76–87. https://doi.org/10.1016/j.scs.2016.08.024.

Campbell, F., Holmes, M., Everson-hock, E., Davis, S., Woods, H.B., Anokye, N., Tappenden, P., Kaltenthaler, E., 2015. A systematic review and economic evaluation of exercise referral schemes in primary care: a short report. Health Technol. Assess. 19 (60), 1–s. https://doi.org/10.3310/hta19600.

Canu, D., Congiu, T., Fancello, G., 2018. A Spatial multi-criteria analysis method for the assessment of walkability to guide the design of interventions in urban crossings. In: Smart Planning: Sustainability and Mobility in the Age of Change. Springer, pp. 271–284.

Cavill, N., Kahlmeier, S., Rutter, H., Racioppi, F., Oja, P., 2008. Economic analyses of transport infrastructure and policies including health effects related to cycling and walking: a systematic review. Transp. Policy 15 (5), 291–304. https://doi.org/10.1016/j.tranpol.2008.11.001.

Centraal Utrecht 2030, 2012. Fietsparkeren Utrecht Centraal. Pilot Fietsparkeren West. Available at https://www.cu2030.nl/images/oud/CONT/R/rapportage_fietsparkeren_utrecht_centraal_pilot_west_definitief_8_maart_2012_copy1.pdf.

Chapman, R., Keall, M., Howden-Chapman, P., Grams, M., Witten, K., Randal, E., Woodward, A., 2018. A cost benefit analysis of an active travel intervention with health and carbon emission reduction benefits. Int. J. Environ. Res. Public Health 15, 962. https://doi.org/10.3390/ijerph15050962.

Cobiac, L.J., Vos, T., Barendregt, J.J., 2009. Cost-effectiveness of interventions to promote physical activity: a modelling study. PLoS Med. 6 (7). https://doi.org/10.1371/journal.pmed.1000110.

COWI & City of Copenhagen, 2008. Economic Evaluation of Cycle Projects—Methodology and Unit Prices. Available at: https://www.cycling-embassy.dk/wp-content/uploads/2010/06/COWI_Economic-evaluation-of-cycle-projects.pdf.

Croci, E., Rossi, D., 2014. Optimizing the position of bike sharing stations. In: The Milan case, CERE Working Paper 68. https://doi.org/10.2139/ssrn.2461179.

Dallat, M.A.T., Soerjomataram, I., Hunter, R.F., Tully, M.A., Cairns, K.J., Kee, F., 2013. Urban greenways have the potential to increase physical activity levels cost-effectively. Eur. J. Public Health 24, 190–195. https://doi.org/10.1093/eurpub/ckt035.

de Hartog, J.J., Boogaard, H., Nijland, H., Hoek, G., 2010. Do the health benefits of cycling outweigh the risks? Environ. Health Perspect. 118, 1109–1116. https://doi.org/10.1289/ehp.0901747.

de Sá, T.H., Tainio, M., Goodman, A., Edwards, P., Haines, A., Gouveia, N., Monteiro, C., Woodcock, J., 2017. Health impact modelling of different travel patterns on physical activity, air pollution and road injuries for São Paulo, Brazil. Environ. Int. 108, 22–31. https://doi.org/10.1016/j.envint.2017.07.009.

Dean, M., 2018. Assessing the Applicability of Participatory Multi-Criteria Analysis Methodologies to the Appraisal of Mega Transport Infrastructure. Ph.D. Dissertation, The Bartlett School of Planning, University College London, UK. https://www.academia.edu/43180035/Assessing_the_Applicability_of_Participatory_Multi-Criteria_Analysis_Methodologies_to_the_Appraisal_of_Mega_Transport_Infrastructure.

Dean, M., 2020. Multi-criteria analysis. In: Advances in Transport Policy and Planning, vol. 6. Elsevier, pp. 165–224.

Decisio, 2012. The Social Costs and Benefits of Investing in Cycling. Available at http://www.dutchcycling.nl/library/file/Decisio%20-%20Social%20costs%20and%20benefits%20of%20bicycle%20-%20Summary%20(1).pdf. Article accessed 06/07/2020.

Decisio, 2016. Themaplan Snelfietsroutes Beter Benutten Vervolg. https://denhaag.notubiz.nl/document/5206603/1/RIS296705_bijlage_Themaplan_snelfietsroutes_Beter_Benutten_vervolg.

Decisio, 2017. Waarderingskengetallen MKBA Fiets. https://www.rwseconomie.nl/binaries/rwseconomie/documenten/rapporten/2017/12/20/waarderingskengetallen-fiets/171215+Waarderingskengetallen+MKBA+Fiets_definitief.pdf.

Deenihan, G., Caulfield, B., 2014. Estimating the health economic benefits of cycling. J. Transp. Health 1, 141–149. https://doi.org/10.1016/j.jth.2014.02.001.

Eliasson, J., Börjesson, M., Odeck, J., Welde, M., 2015. Does benefit-cost efficiency influence transport investment decisions? JTEP 49, 377–396.

Elvik, R., 2000. Which are the relevant costs and benefits of road safety measures designed for pedestrians and cyclists? Accid. Anal. Prev. 32 (1), 37–45. https://doi.org/10.1016/S0001-4575(99)00046-9.

Etemadi, M., et al., 2016. A review of the importance of physical fitness to company performance and productivity. Am. J. Appl. Sci. 13, 1104–1118.

European Cyclists' Federation (ECF), 2016. Calculating the Economic Benefits of Cycling in EU-27, ECF. https://ecf.com/groups/calculating-economic-benefits-cycling-eu-27.

Fishman, E., Schepers, P., Kamphuis, C.B.M., 2015. Dutch cycling: quantifying the health and related economic benefits. Am. J. Public Health 105, e13–e15. https://doi.org/10.2105/AJPH.2015.302724.

Gärling, T., Ettema, D., Friman, M., 2014. Handbook of Sustainable Travel. Springer, Netherlands. https://doi.org/10.1007/978-94-007-7034-8.

Garrett, S., Elley, C.R., Rose, S.B., Dea, D.O., Lawton, B.A., Dowell, A.C., 2011. Are physical activity interventions in primary care and the community cost-effective? A systematic review of the evidence. March, 61, 125–133. https://doi.org/10.3399/bjgp11X561249.

Gasparatos, A., El-Haram, M., Horner, M., 2008. A critical review of reductionist approaches for assessing the progress towards sustainability. Environ. Impact Assess. Rev. 28 (4–5), 286–311.

Geurs, K., Haaijer, R., Van Wee, B., 2006. Option value of public transport: methodology for measurement and case study for regional rail links in the Netherlands. Transp. Rev. 26, 613–643. https://doi.org/10.1080/01441640600655763.

Geurs, K.T., Boon, W., Van Wee, B., 2009. Social impacts of transport: literature review and the State of the practice of transport appraisal in the Netherlands and the United Kingdom. Transp. Rev. 29, 69–90. https://doi.org/10.1080/01441640802130490.

Glavić, D., Mladenović, M.N., Milenković, M., 2019. Decision support framework for cycling investment prioritization. J. Adv. Transp. 2019, 7871426.

Gössling, S., Choi, A.S., 2015. Transport transitions in Copenhagen: comparing the cost of cars and bicycles. Ecol. Econ. 113, 106–113. https://doi.org/10.1016/j.ecolecon.2015.03.006.

Gössling, S., Choi, A., Dekker, K., Metzler, D., 2019. The social cost of automobility, cycling and walking in the European Union. Ecol. Econ. 158, 65–74. https://doi.org/10.1016/j.ecolecon.2018.12.016.

Gotschi, T., 2011. Costs and benefits of bicycling investments in Portland, Oregon. J. Phys. Act. Health 8 (Suppl. 1), S49–S58. https://doi.org/10.1123/jpah.8.s1.s49.

Götschi, T., Tainio, M., Maizlish, N., Schwanen, T., Goodman, A., Woodcock, J., 2015. Contrasts in active transport behaviour across four countries: how do they translate into public health benefits? Prev. Med. 74, 42–48. https://doi.org/10.1016/j.ypmed.2015.02.009.

Grant-Muller, S.M., MacKie, P., Nellthorp, J., Pearman, A., 2001. Economic appraisal of European transport projects: the state-of-the-art revisited. Transp. Rev. 21 (2), 237–261. https://doi.org/10.1080/01441640119423.

Grisé, E., El-Geneidy, A., 2018. If we build it, who will benefit? A multi-criteria approach for the prioritization of new bicycle lanes in Quebec City, Canada. J. Transp. Land Use 11, 217–235. https://doi.org/10.5198/jtlu.2018.1115.

Gu, J., Mohit, B., Muennig, P.A., 2016. The cost-effectiveness of bike lanes in New York City. Inj. Prev. 23, 1–5. https://doi.org/10.1136/injuryprev-2016-042057.

Guerreiro, T.D.C.M., Kirner Providelo, J., Pitombo, C.S., Antonio Rodrigues Ramos, R., Rodrigues da Silva, A.N., 2018. Data-mining, GIS and multicriteria analysis in a comprehensive method for bicycle network planning and design. Int. J. Sustain. Transp. 12 (3), 179–191.

Gunn, L.D., Lee, Y., Geelhoed, E., Shiell, A., Giles-corti, B., 2014. The cost-effectiveness of installing sidewalks to increase levels of transport-walking and health. Prev. Med. 67, 322–329. https://doi.org/10.1016/j.ypmed.2014.07.041.

Guo, J.Y., Gandavarapu, S., 2010. An economic evaluation of health-promotive built environment changes. Prev. Med. 50 (Suppl), S44–S49. https://doi.org/10.1016/j.ypmed.2009.08.019.

Handy, S., Van Wee, B., Kroesen, M., 2014. Promoting cycling for transport: research needs and challenges. Transp. Rev. 34, 37–41. https://doi.org/10.1080/01441647.2013.860204.

Haskell, W.L., Lee, I.M., Pate, R.R., Powell, K.E., Blair, S.N., Franklin, B.A., MacEra, C.A., Heath, G.W., Thompson, P.D., Bauman, A., 2007. Physical activity and public health: updated recommendation for adults from the American College of Sports Medicine and the American Heart Association. Med. Sci. Sports Exerc. 39, 1423–1434. https://doi.org/10.1249/mss.0b013e3180616b27.

Hatziandreu, E.V.I.J., Brown, R., Taylor, W.R., Rosenberg, M.L., Graham, J.D., 1995. The cost effectiveness of three programs to increase use of bicycle helmets among children. Public Health Rep. 110 (3), 251.

Hicks, J., 1939. The foundations of welfare economics. Econ. J. 49 (196), 696–712.

Hoefsloot, N., de Pater, M., van Ghent, D., de Boer, S., Steegman, S., 2016. S Maatschappelijke kosten en baten Sprong over 't IJ. In: City of Amsterdam (2017). Bijlagen bij Nota van Uitgangspunten Sprong over het IJ. Available at https://assets.amsterdam.nl/publish/pages/823469/concept_nvu_bijlage_1_6_mkba.pdf. Article accessed 06/07/2020.

Hollander, Y., 2016. Transport Modelling for a Complete Beginner. CTthink press.

Hopkinson, P., Wardman, M., 1996. Evaluating the demand for new cycle facilities. Transp. Policy 3 (4), 241–249. https://doi.org/10.1016/S0967-070X(96)00020-0.

IEA, 2020. Changes in Transport Behaviour During the Covid-19 Crisis. IEA, Paris. Available at https://www.iea.org/articles/changes-in-transport-behaviour-during-the-covid-19-crisis. Article accessed 06/07/2020.

Italian Government, 2020. Legislative Decree 20th May 2020. Available at http://www.governo.it/it/articolo/il-decreto-rilancio-gazzetta-ufficiale/14623. Article accessed 06/07/2020.

Jacobsen, P.L., 2003. Safety in numbers: more walkers and bicyclists, safer walking and bicycling. Inj. Prev. 21, 271–275. https://doi.org/10.1136/ip.9.3.205.

Jiao, B., Kim, S., Hagen, J., Muennig, P.A., 2019. Cost-effectiveness of neighbourhood slow zones in New York City. Inj. Prev. 25, 98–103. https://doi.org/10.1136/injuryprev-2017-042499.

Kabak, M., Erbas, M., Çetinkaya, C., Ozceylan, E., 2018. A GIS-based MCDM approach for the evaluation of bike-share stations. J. Clean. Prod. 201, 49–60. https://doi.org/10.1016/j.jclepro.2018.08.033.

Kahlmeier, S., Götschi, T., Cavill, N., Fernandez, A.C., Brand, C., Rueda, D.R., Woodcock, J., Kelly, P., Lieb, C., Oja, P., Foster, C., Rutter, H., Racioppi, F., 2017. Health Economic Assessment Tools (HEAT) for Walking and for Cycling: Methods and User Guide on Physical Activity, Air Pollution, Injuries and Carbon Impact Assessments. World Health Organization—European Office. https://www.euro.who.int/en/publications/abstracts/health-economic-assessment-tool-heat-for-walking-and-for-cycling.-methods-and-user-guide-on-physical-activity,-air-pollution,-injuries-and-carbon-impact-assessments-2017.

Kaldor, N., 1939. Welfare propositions of economics and interpersonal comparisons of utility. Econ. J. 49 (195), 549–552.

Kampman, B., De Bruyn, S., Den Boer, E., 2006. Cost-Effectiveness of CO_2 Mitigation in Transport. CE Delft. Available at http://www.ce.nl/art/uploads/file/06_4184_20.pdf. Article accessed 06/07/2020.

Kelly, P., Kahlmeier, S., Götschi, T., Orsini, N., Richards, J., Roberts, N., Scarborough, P., Foster, C., 2014. Systematic review and meta-analysis of reduction in all-cause mortality from walking and cycling and shape of dose response relationship. Int. J. Behav. Nutr. Phys. Act. 11 (1), 132. https://doi.org/10.1186/s12966-014-0132-x.

Kent, M., Karner, A., 2018. Prioritizing low-stress and equitable bicycle networks using neighbourhood-based accessibility measures. Int. J. Sustain. Transp. 13, 100–110. 8318. https://doi.org/10.1080/15568318.2018.1443177.

Laird, J., Geurs, K., Nash, C., 2009. Option and non-use values and rail project appraisal. Transp. Policy 16, 173–182. https://doi.org/10.1016/j.tranpol.2009.05.002.

Larsen, J., Patterson, Z., El-Geneidy, A., 2013. Build it. But where? The use of geographic information systems in identifying locations for new cycling infrastructure. Int. J. Sustain. Transp. 7 (4), 299–317.

Li, M., Faghri, A., 2014. Cost-benefit analysis of added cycling facilities. Transp. Res. Rec. 2468, 55–63. https://doi.org/10.3141/2468-07.

Litman, T., 2012. Integrating Public Health Objectives in Transportation Planning. Victoria Transport Policy Institute.

Litman, T., 2020. Quantifying the benefits of nonmotorized transportation. Victoria Policy Institute. Available at https://www.vtpi.org/nmt-tdm.pdf. Article accessed 06/07/2020.
Lovelace, R., Goodman, A., Aldred, R., Berkoff, N., Abbas, A., Woodcock, J., 2017. The propensity to cycle tool: an open source online system for sustainable transport planning. J. Transp. Land Use 10 (1), 505–528. https://doi.org/10.5198/jtlu.2016.862.
Mackie, P., Worsley, T., Eliasson, J., 2014. Transport appraisal revisited. Res. Transp. Econ. 47 (1), 3–18. https://doi.org/10.1016/j.retrec.2014.09.013.
Macmillan, A., Connor, J., Witten, K., Kearns, R., Rees, D., Woodward, A., 2014. The societal costs and benefits of commuter bicycling: simulating the effects of specific policies using system dynamics modeling. Environ. Health Perspect. 122 (4), 335–344. https://doi.org/10.1289/ehp.1307250.
Maizlish, N., Woodcock, J., Co, S., Ostro, B., Fanai, A., Fairley, D., 2013. Health cobenefits and transportation-related reductions in greenhouse gas emissions in the San Francisco Bay Area. Am. J. Public Health 103, 703–709. https://doi.org/10.2105/AJPH.2012.300939.
Martens, K., 2007. Promoting bike-and-ride: the Dutch experience. Transp. Res. A Policy Pract. 41, 326–338. https://doi.org/10.1016/j.tra.2006.09.010.
Martens, K., 2013. Role of the bicycle in the limitation of transport poverty in the Netherlands. Transp. Res. Rec. 2387 (1), 20–25. https://doi.org/10.3141/2387-03.
Milakis, D., Athanasopoulos, K., 2014. What about people in cycle network planning? Applying participative multicriteria GIS analysis in the case of the Athens metropolitan cycle network. J. Transp. Geogr. 35, 120–129. https://doi.org/10.1016/j.jtrangeo.2014.01.009.
Milakis, D., Athanasopoulos, K., Vafeiadis, E., Vasileiadis, K., Vlastos, T., 2012. Planning of the Athens metropolitan cycle network using participative multicriteria GIS analysis. Procedia. Soc. Behav. Sci. 48, 816–826. https://doi.org/10.1016/j.sbspro.2012.06.1059.
Moodie, M., Haby, M.M., Swinburn, B., Carter, R., 2011. Assessing cost-effectiveness in obesity: active transport program for primary school children—travel SMART schools curriculum program. J. Phys. Act. Health 8, 503–515.
Moshref Javadi, M.H., Ghandehari, M., Hamidi Pouyandeh, V., 2013. Locating of bicycle stations in the City of Isfahan using mathematical programming and multi-criteria decision making techniques. Int. J. Acad. Res. Account. Financ. Manag. Sci. 3, 18–26. https://doi.org/10.6007/IJARAFMS/v3-i4/271.
Mouter, N., 2017a. Dutch politicians' attitudes towards Cost-Benefit Analysis. Transp. Policy 54, 1–10. https://doi.org/10.1016/j.tranpol.2016.11.001.
Mouter, N., 2017b. Dutch politicians' use of cost–benefit analysis. Transportation 44, 1127–1145. https://doi.org/10.1007/s11116-016-9697-3.
Mueller, N., Rojas-Rueda, D., Cole-Hunter, T., de Nazelle, A., Dons, E., Gerike, R., Götschi, T., Int Panis, L., Kahlmeier, S., Nieuwenhuijsen, M., 2015. Health impact assessment of active transportation: a systematic review. Prev. Med. 76, 103–114. https://doi.org/10.1016/j.ypmed.2015.04.010.
Mueller-Riemenschneider, F., Reinhold, T., Willich, S.N., 2009. Cost-effectiveness of interventions promoting physical activity. Br. J. Sports Med. 43, 70–77. https://doi.org/10.1136/bjsm.2008.053728.
Næss, P., Strand, A., 2012. What kinds of traffic forecasts are possible? J. Crit. Realism 11, 277–295. https://doi.org/10.1558/jcr.v11i3.277.
Oldenziel, R., Albert de la Bruhèze, A., 2011. Contested spaces: bicycle lanes in urban Europe, 1900–1995. Transfers 1, 29–49. https://doi.org/10.3167/trans.2011.010203.
Omann, I., 2000. How can multi-criteria decision analysis contribute to environmental policy-making? A case-study on macro-sustainability in Germany. In: 3rd International Conference of the European Society for Ecological Economics, May 3rd–6th, Vienna, Austria.

Opus consultants, 2016. Cadboro Bay Road Bike Lane Feasibility Study. Available at https://www.oakbay.ca/sites/default/files/municipal-hall/Cadboro%20Bay%20Rd%20Cycle%20Feasibility%20FINAL%20Feasibility%20Report%2020161018.pdf. Article accessed 06/07/2020.

Pate, R.R., 1995. Physical activity and public health-reply. JAMA 274, 535. https://doi.org/10.1001/jama.1995.03530070031018.

Peters, J.L., Anderson, R., 2012. The cost-effectiveness of mandatory 20 mph zones for the prevention of injuries. 35 (1), 40–48. https://doi.org/10.1093/pubmed/fds067.

Porter, C., Suhrbier, J., Schwartz, W.L., 1999. Forecasting bicycle and pedestrian travel: state of the practice and research needs. Transp. Res. Rec. 1674, 94–101. https://doi.org/10.3141/1674-13.

Priemus, H., van Wee, B., 2013. International Handbook on Mega-Projects. https://doi.org/10.4337/9781781002308.

Pucher, J., Buehler, R., 2008. Making cycling irresistible: lessons from the Netherlands, Denmark and Germany. Transp. Rev. 28, 495–528. https://doi.org/10.1080/01441640701806612.

Pucher, J., Buehler, R., 2012. City Cycling. MIT Press. Issue November https://doi.org/10.1080/01441647.2013.782592.

Pucher, J., Dill, J., Handy, S., 2010. Infrastructure, programs, and policies to increase bicycling: an international review. Prev. Med. 50, S106–S125. https://doi.org/10.1016/j.ypmed.2009.07.028.

Ramjerdi, F., Flügel, S., Samstad, H., Killi, M., 2010. Value of Time, Safety and Environment in Passenger Transport Time. Transportøkonomiskinstitutt. Available at https://www.toi.no/getfile.php/1316059-1294645315/Publikasjoner/T%C3%98I%20rapporter/2010/1053B-2010/1053B-summary.pdf. Article accessed 06/07/2020.

Rein, M., Schön, D., 1996. Frame-critical policy analysis and frame-reflective policy practice. Knowl. Policy 9, 85–104. https://doi.org/10.1007/bf02832235.

Robinson, R., 1993. Cost-effectiveness analysis. BMJ 307 (6907), 793–795. https://doi.org/10.1136/bmj.307.6907.793.

Rodrigues, P.F., Alvim-Ferraz, M.C.M., Martins, F.G., Saldiva, P., Sá, T.H., Sousa, S.I.V., 2019. Health economic assessment of a shift to active transport. Environ. Pollut. 228, 113745. https://doi.org/10.1016/j.envpol.2019.113745.

Rossi, P., Lipsey, M., Freeman, H., 2004. Evaluation: A Systematic Approach, sixth ed. Sage.

Ruffino, P., Jarre, M., 2019. Valutazione dei Costi e dei Benefici della Mobilità Attiva. Caso di San Donato Milanese. Available at https://www.comune.sandonatomilanese.mi.it/wp-content/uploads/2020/02/Report_CBA_SdM_Final.pdf. Article accessed 06/07/2020.

Rybarczyk, G., Wu, C., 2010. Bicycle facility planning using GIS and multi-criteria decision analysis. Appl. Geogr. 30 (2), 282–293. https://doi.org/10.1016/j.apgeog.2009.08.005.

Sá, T.H., Parra, D.C., Monteiro, C.A., 2015. Impact of travel mode shift and trip distance on active and non-active transportation in the São Paulo Metropolitan Area in Brazil. Prev. Med. Rep. 2, 183–188. https://doi.org/10.1016/j.pmedr.2015.02.011.

Sabatier, P., 2019. Theories of the Policy Process. https://doi.org/10.4324/9780367274689.

Sælensminde, K., 2004. Cost-benefit analyses of walking and cycling track networks taking into account insecurity, health effects and external costs of motorized traffic. Transp. Res. A Policy Pract. 38 (8), 593–606. https://doi.org/10.1016/j.tra.2004.04.003.

Sieg, G., 2014. Costs and Benefits of Bicycle Helmet Law for Germany. Institute for Transport Economics Münster. Working paper No- 21, March.

Stipdonk, H., Reurings, M., 2012. The effect on road safety of a modal shift from car to bicycle, Traffic Inj. Prev. 13 (4), 412–421. https://doi.org/10.1080/15389588.2012.660661.

St. Luis (City Government), 2014. Bike Share Study. Available at http://www.stlbikeshare.org/uploads/7/8/3/3/7833643/bike_share_feasibility_study_final_report.pdf. Article accessed 06/07/2020.

Taylor, M., Scuffham, P., 2002. New Zealand bicycle helmet law—do the costs outweigh the benefits? Inj. Prev. 8 (4), 317–320. https://doi.org/10.1136/ip.8.4.317.

Turner, S., Hottenstein, A., Shunk, G., 1997. Bicycle and Pedestrian Travel Demand Forecasting: Literature Review, Study No. 0-1723. Texas Transportation Institute, The Texas A&M University System, College Station, TX. https://d2dtl5nnlpfr0r.cloudfront.net/tti.tamu.edu/documents/1723-1.pdf.

UK Department for Transport, 2014. TAG UNIT A5.1 Active Mode Appraisal. May https://www.gov.uk/government/uploads/system/uploads/attachment_data/file/427098/webtag-tag-unit-a5-1-active-mode-appraisal.pdf.

UK Government, 2020. 2 Billion Package to Create a New Era for Cycling and Walking. Available at https://www.gov.uk/government/news/2-billion-package-to-create-new-era-for-cycling-and-walking. Article accessed 06/07/2020.

Van Ginkel, J., 2014. The Value of Time and Comfort in Bicycle Appraisal. Utwente Master Thesis. Available at https://www.utwente.nl/en/et/tem/education/Master/finished_graduation_projects/afstudeerders_per_jaar_2/pdf/2014-jeroen-vanginkel-the-value-of-time-and-comfort-in-bicycle-appraisal.pdf. Article accessed 06/07/2020.

Van Wee, B., Börjesson, M., 2015. How to make CBA more suitable for evaluating cycling policies. Transp. Policy 44, 117–124. https://doi.org/10.1016/j.tranpol.2015.07.005.

Walker, T., et al., 2017. The longitudinal relation between self-reported physical activity and presenteeism. Prev. Med. 102, 120–126.

Wang, G., Macera, C.A., Scudder-soucie, B., Schmid, T., Pratt, M., Buchner, D., 2004. Cost effectiveness of a bicycle/pedestrian trail development in health promotion. Prev. Med. 38, 237–242. https://doi.org/10.1016/j.ypmed.2003.10.002.

Wardman, M., Tight, M., Page, M., 2007. Factors influencing the propensity to cycle to work. Transp. Res. A Policy Pract. 41, 339–350. https://doi.org/10.1016/j.tra.2006.09.011.

Wattles, M., et al., 2003. The relationship between fitness levels and employee's perceived productivity, job satisfaction, and absenteeism. J. Exerc. Physiol. 6 (1), 24–32.

Weber, J., 2014. The process of crafting bicycle and pedestrian policy: a discussion of cost-benefit analysis and the multiple streams framework. Transp. Policy 32, 132–138. https://doi.org/10.1016/j.tranpol.2014.01.008.

Wegman, F., Zhang, F., Dijkstra, A., 2012. How to make more cycling good for road safety? Accid. Anal. Prev. 44, 19–29. https://doi.org/10.1016/j.aap.2010.11.010.

Wijnen, W., Weijermars, W.A.M., Bos, Y.R., 2013. Update effectiviteit en kosten van verkeersveiligheidsmaatregelen.

World Health Organization, 2014. Health Economic Assessment Tools (HEAT) for Walking and for Cycling—Methods and User Guide, 2014 Update. In WHO Website.

World Health Organization, 2020. Regions and Cities of the WHO European Region Commit to Safe Mobility and Transport for Urban Populations. Available at https://www.euro.who.int/en/countries/sweden/news/news/2020/3/regions-and-cities-of-the-who-european-region-commit-to-safe-mobility-and-transport-for-urban-populations. Article accessed 06/07/2020.

Yu, W., Chen, C., Jiao, B., Zafari, Z., Muennig, P., 2018. The cost-effectiveness of bike share expansion to low-income communities in New York City. J. Urban Health 95, 888–898.

CHAPTER EIGHT

Appraisal of freight projects and policies

Lóránt Tavasszy[a,*] and Vasco Reis[b]
[a]Delft University of Technology, Delft, The Netherlands
[b]CERIS, Instituto Superior Técnico, Universidade de Lisboa, Lisboa, Portugal
*Corresponding author: e-mail address: l.a.tavasszy@tudelft.nl

Contents

Abstract

Freight transport systems are facing ever-growing demand and increasingly stringent requirements. Governments are pressured to develop new policies and fund new projects that drive forward the freight transport systems. We provide an overview of typical evaluation approaches used for freight transport policies and projects, from the public policy perspective.

We make a simple introduction to the freight transport system, including the most representative agents and components. We introduce a basic framework, briefly reviewing some key literature on the topic and describe the salient features of the state of freight transport appraisal practice today. We also introduce the main freight transport modeling approaches that support project appraisal. We distinguish three types of freight projects according to their geographical scope—global, national and local level—as the appraisal techniques differ. Cost-Benefit Analysis is the prevalent technique in global level projects and very common in national level projects. Multicriteria Analysis type approaches dominate at the local level. Finally, we identify research challenges related to appraisal of freight transport projects and policies.

Advances in Transport Policy and Planning, Volume 7
ISSN 2543-0009
https://doi.org/10.1016/bs.atpp.2021.01.002

Keywords: Freight transport, Project appraisal, Cost-benefit analysis, Multi-criteria analysis, Freight transport models

1. Introduction

Freight transport is the lubricant of the modern world, enabling the movement of goods—raw material, and intermediate or end products—between many distant locations. For example, the emergence and gradual spread of the globalization phenomenon was spurred by advancements in the freight transport sector. In the mid-1950s, Malcom McLean, an owner of a trucking company, was struggling with the high costs and transit times of transport services (Mayo and Nohria, 2005). Notably, the transhipment times between ships and trucks at the port was painfully long. By that time, goods were carried in bulk on ships' decks and platforms. Eventually, Malcom McLean came forward with the idea of using a box—the future maritime container—to transport the goods. The goods would be loaded into the box, which would be the only object to be handled between vehicles along the journey. On 26 April 1956, the ship Ideal X made its maiden voyage from Port Newark to Houston in the USA. It carried 58 metal container boxes (35 ft. long). McLean's fundamental insight about the container was that a transport company's mission was moving freight—rather than moving vehicles. The consequences were overwhelming: (un)loading times of ships were compressed up to 85% and handling costs at ports were reduced up to 95% (Levingson, 2006). What is really interesting with this story is that the breakthrough did not rest on the container itself. McLean established an entirely new paradigm of moving freight, which included the development of new vehicles (e.g., container ships, trucks or wagons), ports and terminals, technology (e.g., cranes) or organizational and operational improvements among the shippers. In the ensuing years, standardization bodies, such as the International Standardization Organization, worked hard to enable worldwide interoperability, so that a container could efficiently be carried regardless the owner, location or type of cargo. Currently, maritime containers account for approximately 60% of all world seaborne trade (Statista Research Department, 2020). In the abovementioned example, new equipment (e.g., containers, cranes, ships or trucks) opened the door for a new paradigm for the organization of freight transport services. This had great impact on the surrounding infrastructure for all related modes of transport.

With the wave of containerization behind us, what new reasons could motivate the need to have systematic appraisals of freight transport projects and policies? Freight systems have continued to evolve at an unprecedented pace, spurred by developments at multiple levels:

- Rapid digitalization of economies and societies is paving the way to new business models and markets, and to profound changes on how goods are traded and transported.
- Heterogeneous generational mix with fundamentally different values and beliefs. Younger generations are digital natives and avid on-line consumers (spurring e-commerce); whereas older generations remain faithful to the physical stores.
- Growing environmental awareness is leading consumers and policymakers demanding low carbon freight transport solutions.
- New materials and fuels are leading to the development of new low-emissions and ultra-energy efficient vehicles and equipment.
- Significant technological developments in the realm of computational power—e.g., Artificial Intelligence or Big Data Analytics—is enabling the development of enhanced tools and equipment.

As an effect of the above, freight transport systems are facing ever-growing demand and increasingly stringent requirements. The pressures to improve performance levels of supply chains, in terms of costs, speed, reliability or safety, are still increasing. Governments are pressured to develop new policies and fund new projects that could drive forward the freight transport systems. In an increasingly volatile and dynamic world, also the appraisal of freight projects and policies is becoming increasingly complex. We started this chapter with the example of Malcom McLean to demonstrate the profound impact that investments in freight transport systems may have on society. Appraisal, therefore, is potentially a daunting task, no less complex than evaluations of projects for mobility of people.

In this chapter, we provide an overview of typical evaluation approaches used for freight transport policies and projects, from the public policy perspective. We introduce a basic framework, briefly review some key literature on the topic and describe the salient features of the state of freight transport appraisal practice today. The chapter is built up as follows: Section 2 focuses on the framework including the main terminology used to denote parts of the system, freight-typical definitions of appraisal components and an outline of the main types of quantitative models used for appraisals. Section 3 provides an overview of the main approaches and issues behind appraisal at three different levels of spatial analysis: global, national and urban. Section 4 summarizes the main topics of freight transport appraisal and concludes the chapter.

We continue this chapter with an introduction of some commonly used terms and frameworks for freight policy evaluation.

2. Terms, frameworks and models

2.1 Freight transport system

The freight transport system is defined as a set of interconnected markets that together serve to have goods available for consumption everywhere around the world (Fig. 1).

There are many stakeholders who act inside this system, either by driving demand, carrying out services, investing in infrastructure or experiencing the system in an indirect way including:

- Producers and consumers. Note that manufacturers, wholesalers, retailers and private households are all producers and consumers and therefore also both senders and receivers of goods. The chain of manufacturers, wholesalers and retailers that results in the supply of a product on the market is called a supply chain. Supply chains are intertwined in many complex ways supply networks.
- Logistics Service Providers (LSPs) are frequently hired by shippers to organize logistics. This may be limited to transportation, but sometimes extends to warehousing, handling and other services. A classical role here is that of the forwarder, who organizes movements from A to B.

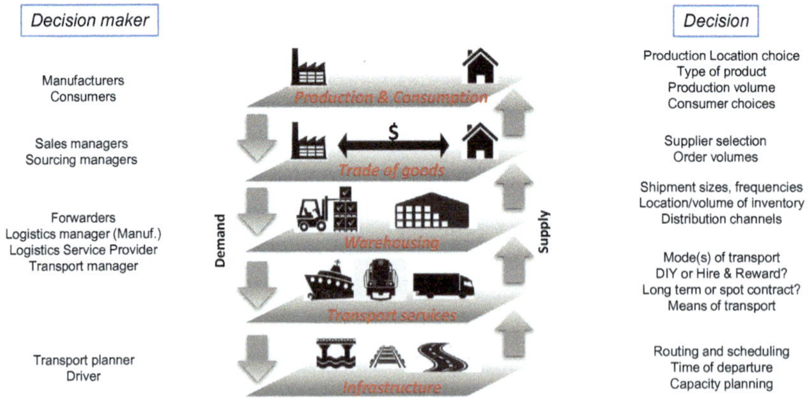

Fig. 1 The freight transport system.

– The above organizations have in common that they can contract freight transport services. In this role, they are sometimes taken together and defined as shippers.
– Carriers execute transportation services between two points or in a roundtrip. The carrier can be part of the shipper's organization (own account carrier), or of an LSP, or an independent, hire-and-reward carrier.
– Government authorities typically invest in collective goods like shared infrastructures, and regulate markets through norms and standards, access control and financial instruments.
– Indirectly, the system affects many other people via external effects (especially of social and environmental nature) of activities or via indirect economic effects.

2.2 Freight transport networks

Freight transport systems are typically operated via infrastructure networks. Over the network a wide paraphernalia of transport equipment is used to ensure the physical movement of the goods. A network is made of links within a set of nodes. A link connects two nodes. The link is a route and it is materialized in terms of a mode of transport, such as roadways, railways, airways, waterways or pipelines. Nodes can be either origins or destinations of the freight. Additionally, they may be intermediary locations in a network where the freight is handled and temporarily stored. Often, they serve as transfer points between modes of transport—i.e., links. Examples of nodes include ports, airports, terminals or warehouses. Specific equipment ensures the physical movement of the freight over the network (links and nodes) from origin until destination. On the links, each mode of transport requires specific vehicles, such as trucks, trains, aircrafts or ships. At the nodes, there is a wide diversity of devices, including cranes, forklifts, reach stackers, tractors, or platforms.

Commonly, links are owned by the government, due to their interest to the social and economic development of the regions and country, and because of sovereignty reasons. There are other reasons that justify public ownership such as the fact of some transport infrastructure, such as railways, being natural monopolies; or, when the economic rationale is dubious (e.g., very long payback terms, or uncertain demand). Large nodes, such as ports, airports or railways terminals are also typically publicly owned; although in some geographies these could be privately financed (Burns, 2015; Graham, 2018). Smaller nodes are often privately owned.

In what concerns the management of the transport network, it can be done by either public or private companies. The latter situation involves specific schemes of very long-term concessions.

In some cases, public and private entities can work together in the development (e.g., design, construction, maintenance, etc.) of a specific link or node. Such kind of cooperation is designated as Public-Private Partnership (PPP) (OECD, 2012). PPP gained widespread popularity in some regions, notably Europe, in recent decades (Roumboutsos, 2016). By way of example, at the European Union level, the majority of the PPP have been implemented in the field of transport. A PPP is defined as long-term contractual arrangements between the government and a private partner whereby the latter delivers and funds public services using a capital asset, sharing the associated risk (European Court of Auditors, 2018). PPPs become popular among policy makers and private companies. On the one hand, they allow the public sector to benefit from private sector capacities and resources, leading to increased quality of transport infrastructure development and management, for lower prices, and with faster delivery times. On the other hand, private companies de-risk their position in the project, which increases their financial and economic return, and sign a long-term and stable contract with a reliable customer.

Transport equipment is commonly owned and managed by private stakeholders. Some stakeholders are transport companies—i.e., link operators—(e.g., air transport companies, rail transport companies), while others are terminal operators—i.e., node operators—(e.g., airport handling companies or port handling operators). Other stakeholders can operate both links and nodes, such as logistic companies or freight forwarders. These stakeholders are responsible for organizing and managing the freight transport services between nodes, on behalf of the shippers or receivers. Some transport services involve one mode of transport; whereas others combine two or more modes of transport. The utilization of one mode of transport is prevalent in continental distances. Road transport is the primary mode of transport. To illustrate, at the EU level, road transport is responsible for transport of more than 80% of all goods (European Commission, 2019). The combination of modes of transport is commonly used in intercontinental transport services. In these services, sea and air transport is used to bridge the continents, while road (and, to some extent, rail) connect the port or airport with the origin or end node. Different designations can be employed to name transport services that use two or more modes of transport, namely: multimodal transport, intermodal transport, combined transport, co-modal transport or synchro-modal transport. The specific designation depends on several factors,[b] such as: organization level, types of modes of transport, or intensity of utilization. Out of the five, synchro-modal transport is arguably regarded as a most advanced concept. Synchro-modal transport is defined as the coordination of logistics chains, transport chains and infrastructure, in such a way that, given aggregated transport demand, the right mode is used at every point in time (TNO, 2011).

2.3 Impact assessment for freight projects

Here, we introduce terms that apply especially for freight transport projects. Roughly assessment follows the same line of thinking as assessments for passenger transport. The common terms for assessment are very similar. For example, direct benefits of transport policies and projects include those that can be measured at the level of transport system users. The usual approach is to measure changes in consumer surplus based on changes in (monetized) utility and on transport flows. The monetary effect of a policy is usually assessed using the price changes and transport time changes monetized using a value of transport time[c] (VOT). Indirect welfare effects, that are additional to the direct effects, could occur if there are market imperfections that prohibit impacts from being fed back to transport system users. The freight system has its peculiarities, which make the approach different in details from passenger transport appraisals. In line with the definition of the freight transport system, the appraisal includes the following interesting elements[d]:

- The value drivers of societal benefits from freight transport investments are manifold. The first, direct beneficiary in the supply chain from an improved freight transport system is the carrier, as he will experience lower costs to fulfill the contracted service.
- The carrier will consider how to use this benefit. Reduced costs may lead to increased profits. However, with very (close to perfectly) competitive carrier markets, if his competitors also profit from the improvement, the benefit will be passed on quickly to the shipper, by means of decreased transport prices. The same reasoning holds for benefits associated with increased speed of transport—the carrier may decide to use this to work more efficiently, or to provide better services.

---

[b] The definition of each concept lies outside the scope of this text. The interested reader is referred to Reis (2015).

[c] Further detail about the value of travel time and travel time reliability can be found in De Jong and Kouwenhoven (2020).

[d] We refer the interested reader to Blauwens et al. (2006) and Lakshmanan (2011).

- Note that travel time is not always a key requirement, but rather fulfillment of window delivery times. Often, the shipper defines specific window times for delivery. In such cases, early arrivals (i.e., shorter transit times) are not highly valued.
- Beyond the shipper lies the wider supply chain. Upstream we find the shipper's suppliers who may be impacted by a change in demand for goods and services. Downstream lies the client of the shipper, ultimately the consumer. If all these markets are perfectly competitive, the gains from transport improvement will propagate on, without any new benefits being generated.
- This propagation is not linear and has multiple branches as logistics decisions may result in a shift between routes, modes of transportation, a shift away from transportation into warehousing, a shift in demand for products, and so on.
- The benefits will not remain in the transport sector but will be transferred to transport using sectors. Besides the markets for products and services, there are important links with other markets related to, e.g., fleet investments, real estate and the capital market, which may all be affected by changes in transport prices.
- In the freight market, several imperfections can be found, which will lead to additional impacts being generated, including external effects, regulated markets for services, products or production factors, scale effects and oligopolistic market situations.
- Finally, there are intricate linkages to passenger transport systems. Consumers will undertake shopping trips, which is one of the motives of transport. The labor market will be affected by freight prices, which determines commuting patterns. Business trips are tied to production and storage locations, which may change as an effect of freight projects.

Guidelines for transport appraisal rarely include chapters specifically for freight transport. As a result, many of the above questions have received very little, or no attention in the literature.

2.4 Freight transport models

To measure the welfare effects of freight policies and projects, we need to know how these effects are built up through the markets of the transport system. This implies a comprehensive, quantifiable understanding of the different markets, the supply and demand functions in these markets and how these interact. The complexity of the many possible responses of firms to freight policies is daunting, however—a condensed summary of supply chain decisions would lead to at least 48 decisions. Therefore, practical, empirical models of the freight system focus on only a handful of these decisions (Tavasszy et al., 2019). It concerns those decisions that are immediately affected by freight policies and infrastructure projects, and include route choice, vehicle type and mode choice, use of inventories, trade and production.

Remarkably, these come from very different economic disciplines. Economic geography has produced a range of models that, in an integrative fashion, describe production, consumption and trade. The Nobel Prize winning work of Krugman (1991) provided the scientific backbone for the current range of Spatial Computable General Equilibrium (SCGE) models. The SCGE family of models uses production functions that predict demand, supply and trade of goods and services, measured in monetary terms. The Input-Output (I/O) models and regional production function models can be derived as a reduced model (Tavasszy et al., 2011). Equally rooted in neoclassical economics, but empirically developed in the research area of transportation are the discrete choice models (also developed via Nobel Prize winning work of McFadden (1981) and operationalized in Ben-Akiva and Lerman (1985)). Discrete choice models are formulated from a demand perspective, predict choice probabilities and can be applied to any fitting choice problem (Marikawa et al., 2002). The well-known gravity model lies between these two areas, as an aggregate, pragmatic empirical model of trade activities, that can be derived from both approaches.[e] We can also find mixed approaches such as the LUTI (Land Use Transport Interaction) and MRIO (Multi-Regional Input/Output) models that apply discrete choice models to predicts changes in production and consumption.

In practical freight appraisals, several combinations of these models can be used, resulting in a variation of architectures for freight transport models (Tavasszy and De Jong, 2014). We briefly introduce the dominant combinations below (Fig. 2).

Freight generation models are based on I/O models or economic aggregates (direct freight generation) and will typically not allow a prediction of the impacts of changes in the transport system on the demand or supply of goods. Advanced consumption models can be added that represent consumer or retailer behavior as a response to changes in product prices. Focusing on the geography of trade, gravity models will allow to assess

[e] Some further detail about transport models can be found in Van Nes and De Jong (2020).

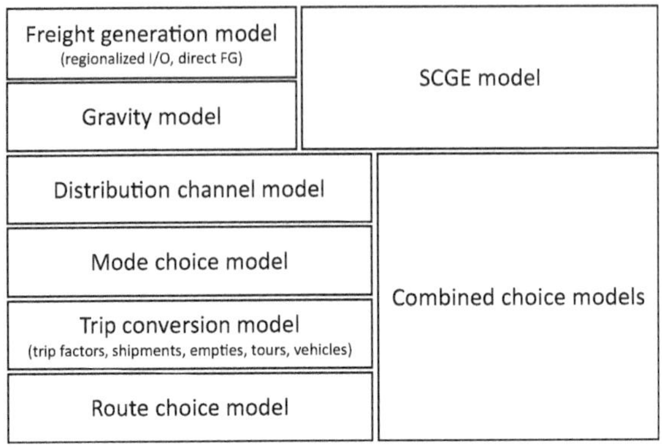

Fig. 2 Main options for composition of freight transport system models.

the impacts of policies on volumes of freight between regions, where the total volume of trade is assumed to remain stable. If one wishes to predict changes in demand and supply, SCGE models are the only viable (theoretically supported) option. Where we see different choice models applied to deal with transportation choices, these can also be combined in various forms.[f] Most freight models in the literature concern the choice of mode. Route choice models in practice are usually simplified and operate together with passenger transport models. Distribution channel choice models predict changes in the use of distribution centers and thus in total transport distances. They are relatively new but have been shown to add significantly to the price elasticity of freight transport demand. The function of trip conversion models is to convert freight flows expressed in tonnes (per year, usually) to flows expressed in vehicles. Originally, these models were using factors which were not sensitive to changes in transport prices or times, but recently, new models have emerged. These explain the choice of shipment size, tour formation (including empty trips) and the use of different vehicle types.

A full-fledged freight transport system model that takes transport price and time (generalized cost) changes as inputs may be able to predict the total welfare effect: direct effects and indirect effects will together propagate into the economy. The resulting changes in trade could also be fed back to the transport system, which would allow to assess direct effects according to the classical CBA definitions, as used in most countries.

[f] The interested reader is referred to Reiche (2017), Stinson et al. (2017), or Rich et al. (2009).

3. State-of-practice in appraisal

3.1 Relevance of geographical levels

There is a hierarchy in the spatial organization of the freight transport networks at the local, regional and global levels. The spatial dynamics of freight transport vary considerably with distance, and so does the type of projects.

- *Global networks* support the trade of all kinds of goods, including raw materials, energy products or manufactured products, among countries worldwide. Global networks connect nodes located in different continents, typically by sea and air transport or pipeline (of oil or gas). In recent years, rail services have gained increased relevance in these global networks. An example is the Eurasian Land Bridge, a flagship project of China's Belt and Road Initiative (BRI) (Box 1). In particular, global structures have been put in place to ensure projects and freight transport market evolves according to globally agreed strategic objectives. At the global level, the World Trade Organization (WTO) is the most relevant intergovernmental organization. The WTO established a framework for trade policies, supported in five principles, being: non-discrimination, reciprocity, binding and enforceable commitments, predictability and transparency, more benefits for less developed countries, and environmental protection. Supporting project funding structures include the World Bank and the regional development banks that work along the

BOX 1 The Chinese Belt and Road Initiative.
By way of example, at the global level, the Chinese Belt and Road Initiative[a] (BRI), launched in 2013 by President Xi Jinping, entails an overland Silk Road Economic Belt and the Maritime Silk Road. The plan includes creating a network of railways, energy pipelines, ports and highways. From a geographic dimension, the BRI stretches both westward—through the mountainous former Soviet republics—and southward, to Pakistan, India, and the rest of Southeast Asia. Overall, the BRI cover +65 countries, including 65% of the world's population and 40% of the global gross domestic product as of 2017 (Campbell, 2017; Chatzky and McBride, 2020). The most common estimates for the current proposed total budget for BRI are $1 trillion and $1.3 trillion (Rolland, 2019).

[a] Formerly known as One Belt One Road.

same principles. Some projects of global significance, like the BRI, are co-funded by multiple organizations.

- *National level networks* ensure primarily the movement of intermediary products and commodities within the regions, often originating from (or with destination to) nodes of global networks. The intermediary products are commonly moving along larger supply chains (e.g., spare parts for cars). Examples of commodities include food (e.g., beef or certain common juices), fuels or metals. National networks link together to stretch out across continents. These networks tend to make extensive utilization of land-based links, notably road transport. In the United States, the National Highway System is a network of strategic highways, including the interstate highway system and other roads (e.g., strategic highway network, or intermodal connectors) serving major airports, ports, rail or truck terminals, railway stations, pipeline terminals and other strategic transport facilities. National networks may be internationally coordinated, based on a joint vision or strategy, as is the case in Europe for the Trans-European Networks for Transport (TEN-T).
- *Local level networks* refer to those networks that serve urban regions and surrounding areas. These networks are very dense. They make use of the land base links, notably road and rail (including metropolitans, trams and others). The nodes include a myriad of locations including retail activities (e.g., supermarkets or shops), service activities (e.g., activities, hotels, restaurants or coffee shops), warehouses, or households. Cities are densely populated areas and important business districts. People acquire consumer products and service companies also tend to import and export final products. Cities are not only consumption locations, but also relevant producers of waste and other products (e.g., recycling material). At local level, a wide diversity of projects, notably within the realm of urban logistics, are being funded by public and private entities. These include urban consolidation centers, urban rail freight services, electric fleets of freight vehicles, just to mention a few.

As mentioned above, policies at national and supra-national level are strongly linked, where linkages depend on the geographical scope. Governments may establish joint "regional[g]" trade policies. Currently, there are several regional blocks worldwide, such as:

[g] This term is also often used to denote a region of the world, as opposed to the regional geographical scale in between national and local scale

- The European Union (EU) is arguably the most developed and ambitious political and economic intergovernmental union. In 2020, it has 27 member states. The EU has developed the world's largest single market area. Free trade among its members was one of the EU's founding principles. EU policies aim to ensure the free movement of people, goods, services and capital within the internal market. The EU has a Common Transport Policy, aimed at opening-up of transport markets and creating of the Trans-European Transport Network (Box 2) (European Parliament, 2020a).
- The North America Free Trade Agreement (NAFTA) is an agreement signed, in 1994, by Canada, Mexico, and the United States, creating a trilateral trade bloc in North America. One of the founding objectives of NAFTA was to eliminate barriers to trade in, and facilitate the cross-border movement of, goods and services between three members. NAFTA led to the progressive elimination of tariffs and all duties and quantitative restrictions, with a few exceptions, by 2008.
- Association of Southeast Asian Nations (ASEAN) Free Trade Area (AFTA) is a trade bloc agreement, signed in 1992, signed by the ASEAN. The ASEAN has 10 members. The AFTA aims at supporting local trade and manufacturing in all ASEAN countries, and facilitating economic integration with regional and international allies. Duty tariffs for goods originating within AFTA are being progressively eliminated.
- South American trade bloc (MERCOSUR) is an agreement signed in 1991 and 1994 between Argentina, Brazil, Paraguay and Uruguay,

BOX 2 The transport netwok that connects European Member States.

The Trans-European Transport (TEN-T) Network, an EU flagship program, aims at implementing and developing an EU-wide network of railway lines, roads, inland waterways, maritime shipping routes, ports, airports and railroad terminals connecting all member states. The TEN-T Network comprises two network layers: (i) the Core Network includes the most important connections, linking the most important nodes, and (ii) the Comprehensive Network connects all European regions to the Core Network. The backbone of the TEN-T Core Network is the rail transport. A total of nine Core Network corridors crossing the EU member states are planned. The TEN-T proposed budget for the 2021–2027 period amounts to EUR 42.4 billion (European Parliament, 2020b). Individual projects generally have budgets that run into billions of Euro.

subsequently joined by Venezuela. Seven other South American countries are associate members. MERCOSUR purpose is to promote free trade and the fluid movement of goods, people, and currency. MERCOSUR includes a customs union, in which there is free intra-zone trade and a common trade policy between member countries.

Methodological preferences differ at different scales. The spatial dimension of the freight network—global, regional or local—will define the country or countries of interest, the political context of decision making, the laws and regulations governing appraisal projects, the supporting quantitative models and data available, among other actors. This results in different approaches at different levels:

- At the global level, changes in trade policies, new tax regimes and mega-projects like the BRI require availability of global models for trade and transport, and assessment is found in various forms, focusing on general principles of simplified cost-benefit analysis.
- At the national level, cost-benefit analysis (CBA) approaches are practised most clearly, because of the link to national accounts and state level politics, and come with detailed guidelines (though varying by state) that sometimes prescribe sophisticated tooling or approaches.[h]
- At the local level, the approaches used become more diffused and scientifically less narrow, with MCA type approaches dominating at the city level.

We explore the usual practices at these three spatial levels in more detail in the next section.

3.2 Global level practices

Funding institutions also require appraisals before agreeing on financing a given project. At the global level, the *World Bank* is a key source of financial and technical assistance to developing countries worldwide. The World Bank does not have specific guidelines or practices regarding freight transport projects.

In order to fund a project, the World Bank institutions require a full appraisal, which covers independently economic, financial, institutional, environmental and social aspects. The purpose is to give stakeholders an opportunity to review the project design in detail and resolve any pending

[h] For comparisons of current practices within and outside Europe, we refer the reader to reports of the IASON and HEATCO projects of the EU Transport Research Program, both aimed at developing appraisal guidelines.

questions. The national governments and the World Bank review the work done and confirm the expected project outcomes, intended beneficiaries and evaluation tools for monitoring progress. The approval of a lend by the World Bank depends on the expectation of net benefits from the project. If both agree, then an agreement is reached on the viability of the project and on the post implementation monitoring program. The World Bank appraisal requires answering to the following 10 questions (Gwilliam, 2000):

1. What is the objective of the project?
2. What will happen if it is implemented, and what if it is not?
3. Is the project the best alternative?
4. Are there any separable components, and how good are they separately?
5. Who are the winners and losers?
6. Is the project financially sustainable?
7. What is the project's fiscal impact?
8. What is the project's environmental impact?
9. Is the project worthwhile?
10. Is this a risky project?

Additionally, the appraisal should follow these set of principles (Omega Centre, 2010):

1. Benefits and costs should be measured against the situation without the project.
2. All projects should be compared against alternatives, including the alternative of doing nothing.
3. If a project is expected to generate benefits in non-monetary terms the analysis has to show that the project represents the cheapest way of attaining the stated objectives.
4. Long-term economic and environmental sustainability must be assessed, taking into account the chances of survival of the project based on stakeholder incentives.
5. Analysis should consider the courses, magnitude and effects of the risks associated with a project by taking into account the possible range in the values for basic variables and assessing the robustness of the project outcomes with respect to changes in these values.
6. The economic analysis should examine the consistency with the Bank's poverty reduction strategy.
7. The economic evaluation of Bank-financed projects should take into account any domestic or cross-border externalities.

In what concerns the economic evaluation, the key aim is to measure the magnitude of the economic impact resulting from the investment.

The World Bank adopts a CBA for transport projects (The World Bank, 2005). The key issues to be included the CBA are (i) impacts, (ii) modes of transport, and (iii) study area. The World Bank adopts the following formula (The World Bank, 2005):

$$\text{Overall Economic Impact} = \text{Change in transport user benefits} + \text{Change in system operating costs and revenues} + \text{Change in costs of externalities} - \text{Investment costs}$$

The estimation of the *overall economic impact* entails the consideration of the following aspects:

- The scope of the appraisal in terms of mode, study area and range of impacts;
- The calculation of transport user benefits (consumer surplus);
- The calculation of impacts on transport providers and the government (includes producer surplus and investment costs);
- Monetary valuation of time and safety;
- The treatment of environmental impacts and other externalities;
- The mechanics of the process including inputs, project life, discounting, aggregation of benefits and costs, unit of account.

3.3 National level projects and their linkages

The standard economic appraisal technique of the European Commission is the CBA (European Commission, 2014). The EC has been promoting CBA for the appraisal of major infrastructure projects above €50 million. The basic rules of conducting CBAs were included, for the first time ever in the secondary legislation and are binding for all beneficiaries in the 2014–2020 program period. CBA is explicitly required, among other elements, as a basis for decision making on the co-financing of major projects included in operational programs of the European Regional Development Fund and the Cohesion Fund. A major project is defined as a project which comprises of an economically indivisible series of works fulfilling a precise technical function having clearly identified aims and whose total cost taken into account in determining the contribution of the funds exceeds 50 million euro or 75 million euro in the case of a transport project. The approval of the Commission is required at the individual project level (European Court of Auditors, 2018). The standard CBA adopted by the European Commission is structured in seven steps, as follows: (i) Description of the context, (ii) Definition of objectives, (iii) Identification of the project, (iv) Technical feasibility and Environmental sustainability, (v) Financial analysis, (vi) Economic analysis, and (vii) Risk assessment. Apart some minor differences, the CBA techniques adopted by the EIB and the EC[i]are similar.

The time horizon or reference period is a key decision in a CBA, as it affects the appraisal results. The EC proposed the reference periods listed in Table 1.

Key methodological topics specific of freight transport projects at the national level are the freight value of time, road vehicle operating costs. These form key inputs to the calculation of benefits of transport projects as they are the multipliers for the key economic drivers of project feasibility: speed (due to improved road quality, upgrading of roads and reduced congestion) and distance (shorter routes). We discuss these below.

Value of time: reduction in travel times accruing from the transport project will benefit freight traffic in terms of (1) reduced driver (and any other persons necessarily traveling with the load) wage costs per trip; (2) reduced vehicle operating costs per trip; and (3) improved reliability, i.e., timely delivery of transported goods. EIB acknowledges that the value of time is the outcome of a consumer decision process. In many situations, consumers have to trade between time and money. These situations can be described by models. Common models are mode choice models, route choice models or alternative choice models within the same mode and route, but with different travel time and costs. Data used in model estimation can be classified as revealed preference (RP) data (actual choice data) or stated preference (SP) data (choices as stated by shippers in interviews).

The European Commission indicates that the methodology for the estimation of time value for freight should be based on the capital lock-up approach. This approach considers that the value of time related to the movement of goods includes the interest costs on the capital invested in

Table 1 European Commission's reference periods by sector.

Sector	Reference period (years)
Railways	30
Roads	25–30
Ports and airports	25

[i] Comparing with the traditional CBA, see Koopmans and Mouter (2020) and Mouter (2021), the EIB and EC CBA techniques exhibit some conceptual differences, such as a clearer assessment of the technical and environmental sustainability.

the goods during the time that the transport takes (important for high-value goods), and a reduction in the value of perishable goods during transit. Additionally, it considers that the production process can disrupted by missing inputs or that customers cannot be supplied due to lack of stock. The valuation of the freight's value of time requires therefore an in-depth analysis of the member state's transport and logistic and supply sectors.

There is a rich literature dedicated to estimating the freight value of time.[j] Table 2 presents a selected list of reference compiled by Feo-Valero et al. (2011). The main evidence is the wide diversity of situations and findings, which raises difficulties in the moment of choosing a value for international projects.

Road vehicle operating costs: a key impact of road projects, after time savings in most developed countries, is the reduction of Vehicle Operating Costs (VOCs). Operating cost relationships for road vehicles are relatively generic and transferable within countries. The main components of VOCs and their relative contributions used by EIB are listed below (Table 3).

These numbers are the subject of national guidelines and their application is typically obligatory, as in the case of passenger transport.

Table 2 Selected value of time for freight transport.

Country	Mode	Geographical domain	Freight value of time (2005, €per hour and tonne)
United States	Road, Rail, Air	National, International	• Regular shipments: 0.012€ per day per dollar of value; • Emergency shipments: 0.49€ per day per dollar of value
France	Road, Rail	National, International	• Shipment in batches: 3.1 • Isolated shipment: 4.83 • Shipment in containers: 3.28 • Shipment in pallets: 9.84 • Shipment origin—warehouse: 4.14 • Shipment origin—factory: 4.83 • Shipment origin—distribution centre: 3.28

[j] Further detail about the value of travel time and travel time reliability can be found in De Jong and Kouwenhoven) of this book.

Table 2 Selected value of time for freight transport.—cont'd

Country	Mode	Geographical domain	Freight value of time (2005, €per hour and tonne)
Italy	Road, Maritime	National, International	• (0.14–1.63) average 0.65
Italy	Road, Maritime	International	• (3.31–7.4) average 3.71
Spain	Road, Maritime	International	• Full-loaded shipments 1.85
Norway	Road	National	• Edible refrigerated goods: (0.41–340.73) with an average of 14.72
Sweden	Road		• Company owns its lorries: 2.45 • Company hires lorries: 0.35 • Short-distance shipment: 5.18 • Long-distance shipment: 0.38
United Kingdom	Road	National	• Own transport: 1.1 • Transport subcontracted: 1.75 • Specialized in complete shipments: 1.56 • Specialized in consolidated shipments: 1.41
Netherlands	Road	National	• Low-value raw materials and semi-processed goods: 2.55 • High-value raw materials and semi-processed goods: 2.81 • Final consumer perishables: 2.35 • Final consumer non-perishables: 2.15
Finland	Road	National	• Willingness to pay, one-hour reduction in transit time: 0.98 • Willingness to accept one-hour increase in transit time: 2.24 • Forestry industry: 0.28 • Metal industry: 2.03 • Electronics industry: 3.22 • Consumer goods: 1.44 • • Technical goods: 0.93
Belgium	Road	International	2.88

Source: Feo-Valero et al., 2011.

Table 3 Components of VOCs and their relative contributions

Component	**Percentage contribution (trucks)**
Fuel	10–30
Lubricating oil	<2
Spare parts	10–30
Maintenance (labor)	<8
Tyres	5–15
Depreciation	10–40
Crew costs	5–50
Other costs and overheads	5–20

3.4 City level appraisals

Urban logistics is "the means over which freight distribution can take place in urban areas as well as the strategies that can improve its overall efficiency while mitigating externalities such as congestion and emissions. It includes the provision of services contributing to efficiently managing the movements of goods in cities and providing innovative responses to customer demands" (Rodrigue and Dablanc, 2020). Urban logistics is a very complex system on its own. The concentration of three aspects on a relatively small area makes this system very complex:

- the issues generated specifically by freight transport, including congestion, the degradation of infrastructure and local emissions.
- the ecosystem of stakeholders like producers, logistics and freight transport operators, retailers, citizens or public authorities.
- the diversity of logistics sub-networks, in terms of the type of goods (e.g., food vs non-food delivery), location (e.g., office vs home deliveries), nature (e.g., express services).

Most of the urban freight logistic distribution is made by road vehicles (two-wheelers, cars, vans and small trucks). These vehicles compete against private and public transport vehicles for the scarce road transport infrastructure. Add to this, freight vehicles, notably trucks, are slower and occupy more space than cars. The outcome is the worsening of traffic conditions—that is congestion (e.g., a double parked truck creates a bottleneck in the traffic capacity of the road), growing conflicts with other users, notable pedestrians (in case of parking on side walk), increase in fuel consumption, increased unreliability, etc. The impacts of congestion on the efficiency of transport operations are well documented (Figliozzi, 2010). Every year €100 billion, or 1% of the EU GDP, are lost to the European economy as a result of delays and pollution related to urban traffic (ALICE and ERTRAC Urban Mobility WG, 2015). In parallel with congestion, annoyance and unsafety due to loading and unloading operations are another relevant challenge of urban freight logistics operations, with significant impacts on the safety of road users and pedestrians (Fig. 3). Often, parking occurs outside designated parking bays in illegal conditions (e.g., second lane, bus lanes, on the sidewalks or on illegal parking places). Such practices reduce the road or sidewalks capacity, leading to congestion or forcing pedestrians to divert, eventually onto the street. On the other hand, the very movement of goods in between the vehicle and the shops is prone to accidents and conflicts with users. The roots are diverse, but include the lack of suitable parking places (indeed, parking places for freight vehicles are scarce, often located in secondary roads away from shops, and when available can be occupied by private vehicles). Also, many deliveries are done in a very short period of time (<3 min). In these cases, there is a higher propensity to commit illegal actions (for example, park the vehicle in double lane). The time of the illegal act is short and the probability to be caught by public authorities is low.

Degradation of local environment is another relevant impact of urban freight logistics. A recent study concluded that if we compare a city with a fleet including only euro 6 vehicles in 2030, to the same city in 2010 composed by an average EURO 4 fleet, the reduction in emissions from the vehicles, all things being equal, could be of 80% for PM and 90% for NOx (ALICE and ERTRAC Urban Mobility WG, 2015). The impact on quality of life, notably health-related problems cannot be neglected. An additional impact concerns the noise of urban freight logistics operations,

Fig. 3 Unlawful (un)loading of beverages on the sidewalk in Lisbon downtown. *Source: V. Reis.*

this refers not only to the very movement of freight vehicles (including engine), but mainly to the loading and unloading operations (e.g., opening and closing doors, moving carts back and forth, loading and unloading the vehicle). A recurrent challenge relating to urban freight logistics refers to the enforcement of legislation and regulations. Indeed, an adequate enforcement is the key to ensure that law and regulations are complied with.

Another relevant challenge stems directly from the eminently private nature of urban freight logistics, which is the stakeholders' general low interest for cooperation. Policymaking in such a context requires well-designed consultation and participation processes due to the complexity of issues involved and diverse interests of various stakeholders. This allows the full narrative about impacts to be known beforehand, which is necessary to understand critical factors and helps to avoid sub-optimization.

Solutions suggested to support urban freight transport and mitigate its impacts are manifold, and there is an extensive literature that discusses pros and cons of alternative policies (Heitz and Dablanc, 2019; Taniguchi et al., 2016; Ville et al., 2010). Policies that can be implemented at the local level roughly fall into three categories:

- Infrastructure measures, e.g., street lay-out and consolidation centers for public use,
- Traffic management measures, e.g., access regulation and route guidance,
- Pricing measures, e.g., congestion charging or environmental access charges.

Despite the strong involvement of academia and consultants in local policy initiatives, systematic evaluations, and comparisons of evaluation results across cities, are rare (Gonzalez-Feliu, 2018). Many times, evaluations are limited to the single company level and it remains unclear to what extent citizens will benefit of new schemes. Methods followed for the actual assessment exercises will depend on the type of initiative and may involve CBA, life cycle cost analysis, MCA, etc.

Arguably, the first appraisal methods of urban logistics initiatives[k] were discussed in the first international conference for urban logistics and published in the respective proceedings (Mizutani, 1999; Ooishi and Taniguchi, 1999; Takahashi and Hyodo, 1999). The proposed methodologies were essentially simulation and scenario analyses. Since then, several other authors have contributed with either refinements of these methodologies or the proposal of new ones. The initial simulation methodologies focused more on

[k] More info at https://citylogistics.org/ (accessed on the 15th May 2020),

the modeling aspects of urban logistics dynamics. By way of example, Regan and Garrido (2000) used a classical four-step model to estimate freight flows, operating costs and environmental footprint. Meanwhile Gentile and Vigo (2013) argue that the classical four step model is unsuitable for modeling the demand for urban logistics). Another approach was the appraisal of urban initiatives, notably environmental impacts, using available (or producing) data, including logistics (e.g., French Urban Goods Transport surveys), socio-economic (e.g., location of commerce, retail and other business activities, waste management) or demographic data (e.g., household trip surveys). Segalou et al. (2004) proposed an estimate on the environmental impacts of urban logistics based on the transport flows taken from several databases, including the French Urban Goods Transport survey. Recently, with the emergence of e-commerce, other authors conducted surveys and measurement to appraise e-commerce delivery systems. The key indicators (or decision variables) were mainly logistical (e.g., vehicle routing, total distance traveled, number and location of stops) and environmental (e.g., total emissions of greenhouse gases, which could be derived from the previous types of indicators). These approaches were mainly motivated by the analysis and discussion of the results; and not so much by the use of the impacts in decision-making processes.

One of the first systematic and comprehensive CBAs was proposed by van Duin et al. (2008) using a vehicle routing optimization model, the authors estimated the monetary costs in accordance with the CBA of several medium-term development scenarios of urban consolidation centers. Other works using CBA analysis have been published by Holmgren (2018) or Gonzalez-Feliu (2014).

Notwithstanding, the literature on urban freight policy assessment has shown to favor MCAs, for very practical reasons (Gonzalez-Feliu et al., 2013; Huang et al., 2020; Jamshidi et al., 2019; Wątróbski, 2016; Wątróbski et al., 2017):

- No need for specialized training in economics,
- Simple to understand and communicate to stakeholders, including politicians and the public,
- Transparent and stable in evaluation criteria and their weights,
- Possible to record situational preferences of stakeholders at very low costs,
- Easy presentation of the decision problem in simple tables and charts.

An increasingly known method, that acknowledges the diversity of agents and respective strategies and ambitions, is the Multi-Actor Multi-Criteria Analysis (MAMCA), as originally published by Macharis (2000, 2007).

Table 4 Selected authors and criteria.

Authors	**Categories and criteria**
Morana and Gonzalez-Feliu (2015)	Around 5–10 indicators, chosen from a pool of around 80 indicators
Melo and Costa (2011)	Around 50 indicators, manly economic and operational
Patier and Browne (2010)	Around 65 indicators from 6 categories (economy, social, environmental, equity, feasibility, plausibility)
Patier et al. (2008)	More than 30 indicators from 5 categories: (economic, environmental, societal, ergonomic and regulatory)

Unlike a conventional multicriteria analysis where alternatives are evaluated on several criteria, the MAMCA methodology explicitly includes the points of view of the different stakeholders. Over the years an increasing number of indicators and criteria have been proposed for these evaluations. Table 4 presents a selected list of authors and respective amount and types of criteria.

These growing lists of criteria are symptomatic for the increasing use of appraisal in fast-paced incremental innovation processes, where the steps made are smaller and the potential impact of decisions is therefore lighter. This allows for the necessary attention to the embedding of decisions in local stakeholder circles, with refined and continuous measurements of impacts. These so-called "living labs" form a new governance context for appraisals, which differ vastly from the "big bang" innovation context that city logistics projects and policies have suffered from (Quak et al., 2016).

4. Conclusions and research agenda

Appraisals of projects and policies in the area of freight transport have many common traits with passenger transport projects, but there are also interesting differences. As appraisal practice has mostly depended on passenger transport projects, it is interesting to understand these better with an aim to improve appraisal guidelines and practices. We summarize the policy relevant traits of freight system appraisal below and include some recommendations for research in the discussion.

Generally, in an appraisal process, the narrative about the foreseen impact pathway of a project is a very important starting point for quantitative assessment. The freight transport system can play a major role in these stories, even if projects are not directly or not only intended for freight transport. As the freight side of the study is often neglected, it is worthwhile to try to increase our understanding of all the mechanisms of the system and how these are intertwined with passenger transport processes, and economic activity in general. Freight transport serves market for products and services worldwide, through global supply chains, reaching firms and consumers everywhere. With that, the potential scope and breadth of a freight transport project appraisal is daunting. The users of the freight transport system are companies who supply a service to other companies or to consumers—the chain from infrastructure projects and policies to consumer benefits is many times indirect, and influenced by many different decisions of these actors. Freight transport also has important linkages with passenger transportation through transport motives like shopping, commuting and business. These motives interact at the level of economic activities (through firms and individuals buying, producing and selling goods) and at the level of traffic (through congestion). Guidelines for integrative appraisals are rare. Also, integrative models that link freight and passenger transport processes, as described in this chapter, are lacking in practice and are therefore not applied in policy appraisal. Research can help to map freight and passenger transport interactions, develop consistent system models and support the development of integrative guidelines for appraisal.

Freight transport appraisal has its own specific analysis problems, which deserve continuous research. These include the propagation of costs and benefits through supply chains (carriers transferring cost increases to their clients, shippers absorbing cost increases through logistic trade-offs), the complex question of additionality of quantified impacts (ensuring in the appraisal that impacts are collectively exhaustive and mutually exclusive) and the wide reach of indirect effects (supply chains quickly lead to effects of an international or even global nature, to a point where these effects become intractable for most studies). These issues all require research, to allow us to conceptualize and quantify impacts in a consistent way, with broad agreement from stakeholders.

There is a major imbalance in processes and methods of appraisal between countries around the world and between geographical layers (local, national, international). This is a problem when projects are multi-jurisdictional, when there is no clear joint decision power and where some degree of consensus or consistency needs to be reached. Projects with overlapping or connected jurisdictions can be many: a city project may desire co-financing from the national level, or countries may want to invest together in shared infrastructure. The dominant practice at the national level and above is cost-benefit analysis (CBA), with methods and techniques being slightly less rigorously prescribed at the higher spatial level. Internationally, the distribution of benefits does not seem to play a role in the appraisals and decisions about major infrastructure projects. At the urban level, appraisals have mostly relied on multi-criteria analysis (MCA), hindering the connection with national level cost-benefit analysis. How to move from this system of geographically inconsistent and disconnected appraisal approaches is unclear. Research could inform policy makers about new directions for appraisal to repair this caveat.

References

ALICE, & ERTRAC Urban Mobility WG, 2015. Urban Freight Research Roadmap. Retrieved from http://www.ertrac.org/uploads/documentsearch/id36/ERTRAC_Alice_Urban_Freight.pdf.

Ben-Akiva, M.E., Lerman, S.R., 1985. Discrete Choice Analysis: Theory and Application to Travel Demand. Massachusetts Institute of Technology Press, Boston, MA, United States. Retrieved from http://books.google.pt/books/about/Discrete_Choice_Analysis.html?id=oLC6ZYPs9UoC&pgis=1.

Blauwens, G., De Baere, P., Voorde, E., 2006. Transport Economics. Duculot, Belgium. Retrieved from http://books.google.com/books?id=_na0YamsAgwC&pgis=1.

Burns, M., 2015. Port Management and Operations. CRC Press, Boca Raton, FL.

Campbell, C., 2017. China Says It's Building the New Silk Road. Here Are Five Things to Know Ahead of a Key Summit. Time. Retrieved from https://time.com/4776845/china-xi-jinping-belt-road-initiative-obor/.

Chatzky, A., McBride, J., 2020. China's Massive Belt and Road Initiative. Retrieved May 15, 2020, from https://www.cfr.org/backgrounder/chinas-massive-belt-and-road-initiative.

De Jong, G., Kouwenhoven, M., 2020. Value of travel time and travel time reliability. Chapter 2. In: Mouter, N. (Ed.), Standard Appraisal Methods. Advances in Transport Policy and Planning, vol. 6. Elsevier, Amsterdam.

European Commission, 2014. Guide to Cost-Benefit Analysis of Investment Projects. https://doi.org/10.2776/97516.

European Commission, 2019. Statistical Pocketbook 2019: EU Transport in Figures. Luxembourg: European Union. https://doi.org/10.2832/729667.

European Court of Auditors, 2018. Public Private Partnerships in the EU: Widespread Shortcomings and Limited Benefits. Retrieved from https://www.eca.europa.eu/Lists/ECADocuments/SR18_09/SR_PPP_EN.pdf.

European Parliament, 2020a. Common Transport Policy: Overview. Retrieved May 15, 2020, from https://www.europarl.europa.eu/factsheets/en/sheet/123/common-transport-policy-overview.

European Parliament, 2020b. Financing the Trans-European Networks. Retrieved May 15, 2020, from https://www.europarl.europa.eu/factsheets/en/sheet/136/financing-the-trans-european-networks.

Feo-Valero, M., García-Menéndez, L., Garrido-Hidalgo, R., 2011. Valuing freight transport time using transport demand modelling: a bibliographical review. Transplant. Rev. 31 (5), 625–651. https://doi.org/10.1080/01441647.2011.564330.

Figliozzi, M.A., 2010. The impacts of congestion on commercial vehicle tour characteristics and costs. Transport Res. E-Log. 46 (4), 496–506. https://doi.org/10.1016/j.tre.2009.04.005.

Gentile, G., Vigo, D., 2013. Movement generation and trip distribution for freight demand modelling applied to city logistics. Eur. Trans.\Transporti Europei 54, 1–6.

Gonzalez-Feliu, J., 2014. Costs and Benefits of Railway Urban Logistics: A Prospective Social Cost Benefit Analysis. (No. halshs-01056135). Lyon, France. Retrieved from https://halshs.archives-ouvertes.fr/halshs-01056135/file/Costs_and_benefits_of_railway_urban_logistics.pdf.

Gonzalez-Feliu, J., 2018. Sustainable Urban Logistics: Planning and Evaluation. Wiley.

Gonzalez-Feliu, J., Grau, J.M.S., Morana, J., Mitsakis, E., 2013. Urban logistics pooling viability analysis via a multicriteria multiactor method. In: Petit-Lavall, V., Martinez-Sanz, F., Recalde-Castells, A., Puetz, A. (Eds.), La nueva ordenación del mercado del transporte. Marcial Pons, Madrid, pp. 867–882.

Graham, A., 2018. Managing Airports: An International Perspective. Routledge.

Gwilliam, K., 2000. Transport Project Appraisal at The World Bank. Retrieved from https://ppiaf.org/sites/ppiaf.org/files/documents/toolkits/highwaystoolkit/6/bibliography/pdf/transport_project_appraisal_at_the_world_bank.pdf.

Heitz, A., Dablanc, L., 2019. Freight in urban planning and local policies: results from a new survey in twenty French cities. In: International Conference City Logistics. Croatia.

Holmgren, J., 2018. Using cost-benefit analysis to evaluate city logistics initiatives: an application to freight consolidation in small- and mid-sized urban areas. In: City Logistics 2. John Wiley & Sons, Inc., Hoboken, NJ, USA, pp. 271–290. https://doi.org/10.1002/9781119425526.ch17.

Huang, H., Lebeau, P., Macharis, C., 2020. The Multi-Actor Multi-Criteria Analysis (MAMCA): New Software and New Visualizations. pp. 43–56. https://doi.org/10.1007/978-3-030-46224-6_4.

Jamshidi, A., Jamshidi, F., Ait-Kadi, D., Ramudhin, A., 2019. A review of priority criteria and decision-making methods applied in selection of sustainable city logistics initiatives and collaboration partners. Int. J. Prod. Res. 57 (15–16), 5175–5193. https://doi.org/10.1080/00207543.2018.1540892.

Koopmans, C.C., Mouter, N., 2020. Cost-benefit analysis. Chapter 1. In: Mouter, N. (Ed.), Standard Appraisal Methods. Advances in Transport Policy and Planning, vol. 6. Elsevier, Amsterdam.

Krugman, P., 1991. Geography and Trade. MIT Press and Leuven University Press, London.

Lakshmanan, T.R., 2011. The broader economic consequences of transport infrastructure investments. J. Transp. Geogr. 19 (1), 1–12. https://doi.org/10.1016/j.jtrangeo.2010.01.001.

Levingson, M., 2006. The Box: How the Shipping Container Made the World Smaller and the World Economy Bigger. Princeton University Press, Princeton, New Jersey.

Macharis, C., 2000. Strategische modellering voor intermodale terminals. Socio economische evaluatie van de locatie van binnenvaart/weg terminals in Vlaanderen. Vrije Universiteit Brussel, Brussels.

Macharis, C., 2007. Multi-criteria analysis as a tool to include stakeholders in project evaluation: the MAMCA method. In: Haezendonck, E. (Ed.), Transport Project Evaluation. Extending the Social Cost-Benefit Approach. Edward Elgar Publishing, Cheltenham, pp. 115–131.

Marikawa, T., Ben-Akiva, M., McFadden, D., 2002. Discrete choice models incorporating revealed preferences and psychometric data. In: Franses, P., Montgomery, A. (Eds.), Econometric Models in Marketing. Elsevier Science Ltd, pp. 29–55.

Mayo, A.J., Nohria, N., 2005. The Truck Driver Who Reinvented Shipping. Retrieved May 15, 2020, from https://hbswk.hbs.edu/item/the-truck-driver-who-reinvented-shipping.

McFadden, D., 1981. Econometric models of probabilistic choice. In: Manski, C. (Ed.), Structural Analysis of Discrete Data with Econometric Applications. MIT Press, Boston, pp. 199–272.

Melo, S., Costa, A., 2011. Definition of a set of indicators to evaluate the performance of urban goods distribution initiatives. In: Macharis, C., Melo, S. (Eds.), City Distribution and Urban Freight Transport2. Edward Elgar Publishing, Cheltenham.

Mizutani, T., 1999. Measures to enhance the efficiency of urban freight transport in Hiroshima city. In: Taniguchi, E., Thompson, R.G. (Eds.), City Logistics1. Institue of Systems Science Research, Kyoto, pp. 289–301.

Morana, J., Gonzalez-Feliu, J., 2015. A sustainable urban logistics dashboard from the perspective of a group of operational managers. Manag. Res. Rev. 38 (10), 1068–1085. https://doi.org/10.1108/MRR-11-2014-0260.
Mouter, N., 2021. Standard transport appraisal methods. Chapter 1. In: Mouter, N. (Ed.), New Methods, Reflections and Application Domains in Transport Appraisal. Advances in Transport Policy and Planning, vol. 7. Elsevier, Amsterdam, pp. 1–7.
OECD, 2012. Recommendation of the Council on Principles for Public Governance of Public-Private Partnerships. Retrieved from https://www.oecd.org/governance/budgeting/PPP-Recommendation.pdf.
Omega Centre, 2010. International Appraisal Systems for Transport and Other Projects. Retrieved from http://www.omegacentre.bartlett.ucl.ac.uk/open/OMEGA-3-RAMP-Study-International-appraisal-systems-for-transport-and-other-projects.pdf.
Ooishi, R., Taniguchi, E., 1999. Effect and profitability of constructing the new underground freight transport system. In: Taniguchi, E., Thompson, R.G. (Eds.), City Logistics1. Institute of Systems Science Research, Kyoto, pp. 303–3016.
Patier, D., Browne, M., 2010. A methodology for the evaluation of urban logistics innovations. Procedia. Soc. Behav. Sci. 2 (3), 6229–6241. https://doi.org/10.1016/j.sbspro.2010.04.033.
Patier, D., Henriot, F., Gerardin, B., Bossin, P., 2008. Méthodologie d'évaluation des innovations en matière de logistique urbaine. Laboratoire Aménagement Économie Transports, Lyon.
Quak, H., Lindholm, M., Tavasszy, L., Browne, M., 2016. From freight partnerships to city logistics living labs—giving meaning to the elusive concept of living labs. Transp. Res. Proc. 12, 461–473. https://doi.org/10.1016/j.trpro.2016.02.080.
Regan, A.C., Garrido, R.A., 2000. Modeling freight demand and shipper behaviour: state of the art, future directions. In: 9th International Association for Travel Behaviour Research Conference. Queensland, Australia.
Reiche, S., 2017. A Disaggregate Freight Transport Model for Germany. Springer, Berlin.
Reis, V., 2015. Should we keep on renaming a +35-year-old baby? J. Transp. Geogr. 46, 173–179. https://doi.org/10.1016/j.jtrangeo.2015.06.019.
Rich, J., Holmblad, P.M., Hansen, C.O., 2009. A weighted logit freight mode-choice model. Transport Res. E-Log. 45 (6), 1006–1019. https://doi.org/10.1016/j.tre.2009.02.001.
Rodrigue, J.-P., Dablanc, L., 2020. What is City Logistics? Retrieved May 15, 2020, from https://globalcitylogistics.org/?page_id=92.
Rolland, N., 2019. A Concise Guide to the Belt and Road Initiative. Retrieved May 15, 2020, from https://www.nbr.org/publication/a-guide-to-the-belt-and-road-initiative/.
Roumboutsos, A., 2016. Public Private Partnerships in Transport: Trends and Theory. Routledge.
Segalou, E., Ambrosini, C., Routhier, J.-L., 2004. The environmental assessment of urban goods movement. In: Tanuguchi, E., Thompson, R. (Eds.), Logistics Systems for Sustainable Cities. Emerald Group publishing limited, pp. 207–220. https://doi.org/10.1108/9780080473222-015.
Statista Research Department, 2020. Container Shipping—Statistics & Facts. Retrieved May 15, 2020, from https://www.statista.com/topics/1367/container-shipping/.
Stinson, M., Pourabdollahi, Z., Livshits, V., Jeon, K., Nippani, S., Zhu, H., 2017. A joint model of mode and shipment size choice using the first generation of commodity flow survey public use microdata. Int. J. Transp. Sci. Technol. 6 (4), 330–343. https://doi.org/10.1016/j.ijtst.2017.08.002.
Takahashi, Y., Hyodo, T., 1999. A simulation study on the effect of physical distribution in the Tokyo metropolitan region. In: Taniguchi, E., Thompson, R.G. (Eds.), City Logistics. Institute of Systems Science Research, Kyoto, p. 163.

Taniguchi, E., Thompson, R.G., Yamada, T., 2016. New opportunities and challenges for city logistics. Transp. Res. Proc. 12, 5–13. https://doi.org/10.1016/j.trpro.2016.02.004.
Tavasszy, L.A., De Jong, G., 2014. Modelling Freight Transport. Elsevier, Amsterdam.
Tavasszy, L.A., Thissen, M.J.P.M., Oosterhaven, J., 2011. Challenges in the application of spatial computable general equilibrium models for transport appraisal. Res. Transp. Econ. 31 (1), 12–18. https://doi.org/10.1016/j.retrec.2010.11.003.
Tavasszy, L., de Bok, M., Alimoradi, Z., Rezaei, J., 2019. Logistics decisions in descriptive freight transportation models: a review. J. Supply Chain Manag. 13, 74–86. https://doi.org/10.18757/jscms.2019.1992.
The World Bank, 2005. A Framework for the Economic Evaluation of Transport Projects. Retrieved from http://documents.worldbank.org/curated/en/360501468327922938/pdf/339260rev.pdf.
TNO, 2011. Final Report Implementation Roadmap Synchromodal Transport System. Delft, The Netherlands.
van Duin, R., Quak, H., Munuzuri, J., 2008. Revival of the cost benefit analysis for evaluating the city distribution concept? In: Taniguchi, E., Thompson, R.G. (Eds.), Innovations in City Logistics. Nova Science Publishers, New York, pp. 97–114.
Van Nes, R., De Jong, G., 2020. Transport models. Chapter 4. In: Mouter, N. (Ed.), Standard Appraisal Methods. Advances in Transport Policy and Planning, vol. 6. Elsevier, Amsterdam.
Ville, S., Gonzalez-Feliu, J., Dablanc, L., 2010. The limits of public policy intervention in urban logistics: the case of Vicenza (Italy) and lessons for other European cities. July 2010, In: 12th World Conference on Transport Research, p. 13. Lisbon.
Wątróbski, J., 2016. Outline of multicriteria decision-making in green logistics. Transp. Res. Proc. 16, 537–552. https://doi.org/10.1016/j.trpro.2016.11.051.
Wątróbski, J., Małecki, K., Kijewska, K., Iwan, S., Karczmarczyk, A., Thompson, R., 2017. Multi-criteria analysis of electric vans for city logistics. Sustainability 9 (8), 1453. https://doi.org/10.3390/su9081453.

CHAPTER NINE

Cost-benefit analysis in developing countries

Euston Quah[a,b], Tsiat Siong Tan[c], and Zach J.L. Lee[a,b,*]
[a]Nanyang Technological University, Singapore, Singapore
[b]TUMCREATE, Singapore, Singapore
[c]Singapore University of Social Sciences, Singapore, Singapore
*Corresponding author: e-mail address: tstan@suss.edu.sg; zachlee@ntu.edu.sg

Contents

Abstract

There are compelling reasons for governments in developing countries to evaluate public projects and policies using cost-benefit analysis to ensure that a socially optimal choice is undertaken. However, the conduct of cost-benefit analysis in developing countries is often fraught with complexities and may require a different treatment from standard textbook cost-benefit analysis. The chapter discusses the differing labor, goods, and financial markets in developing countries, and their implications for cost-benefit methodologies. Examples from transportation and other sectors are weaved in to provide context for such issues. The relevance of behavioral economics affecting cost-benefit analysis is also discussed, leading to an overview of the challenges in valuation techniques and an introduction to an alternative method of valuation involving paired-wise comparison. The chapter concludes with a discussion on the key criticisms of cost-benefit analysis as an effective project and policy planning tool.

Advances in Transport Policy and Planning, Volume 7
ISSN 2543-0009
https://doi.org/10.1016/bs.atpp.2021.02.002

Keywords: Cost-benefit analysis (benefit-cost analysis), Developing countries, Project appraisal, Market difference, Valuation techniques, Limitations of CBA, Behavior and CBA, Transport infrastructure

1. Introduction

Nobel laureate and economist Simon Kuznets put forth the concept of Gross Domestic Product (GDP) in response to the need for good data in public policy planning in the 1930s. Since then, policymakers have increasingly relied upon GDP and other national income indicators. If only one macro indicator is available in any given country, chances are the indicator is the country's GDP. This demonstrates the extent to which national income has become the most important macroeconomic indicator. However, as Kuznets himself and other critics of GDP have repeatedly pointed out, national income statistics are not ideal measures of welfare (Kuznets, 1934). Of the many criticisms, two of the more prominent are the lack of consideration of equity and the fact that these statistics only measure economic activity and do not account for the non-economic costs of growth (Kuznets, 1962).

The good news is that equity considerations are increasingly being accounted for by augmenting national accounts with measures of inequity (e.g., Gini coefficient) as discussed in the chapter on equity (van Wee and Mouter, 2021). Unfortunately, no indicator for measuring the non-economic costs of growth has been as successful as GDP in gaining wide acceptance. As a result, national income statistics continue to present only one side of the picture. The need for more data is clear—optimal policy formulation requires information on the trade-offs between choices.

The costs of economic growth are often non-market in nature, such as environmental harm or loss to psychological well-being. The list of non-market items is long. To properly account for the full costs of growth, all such items should be quantified, and any changes in their levels should be meticulously recorded. Additionally, to utilize the data to analyze trade-offs, it is necessary to assign monetary values to them. While this form of accounting may seem difficult to carry out, some semblance of it already exists in the form of what is popularly termed "green accounting" (Magablih, 2017).

Notwithstanding the obvious merits of green accounting, maintaining a complete record of changes in the levels of all non-market goods is more of a grand vision than an achievable goal. The costs involved in such an endeavor are too high especially for most developing countries. Often, developing nations account for these costs by relying more heavily on analysis at a micro level when considering public projects, differing from their developed counterparts in this respect. The apparent suitability of Cost-Benefit Analysis (CBA) for developing countries, primarily because of its financial feasibility relative to large-scale green accounting, still requires further modifications in its application. There is a need to approach CBA in developing nations differently to account for the inherent behavioral and executional differences.

2. The need for CBA in developing countries

The pursuit of economic growth is often coupled with widening wealth and income gap, and brings about environment and health threats, especially in developing countries. Economic theory stipulates that efficiency requires CBA. For developing countries, there are five broad reasons why the need for CBA is especially pressing.

Firstly, to catch up to developed economies, developing economies need to grow fast. The shorter the time frame for convergence, the faster developing countries need to grow. Based on the average growth rate over the past decade, it would take the least developed countries[a] approximately 190 years to catch up to the countries in the Organization for Economic Cooperation and Development (OECD). Sixty years could be shaved off the catch-up process if the least developed countries instead grow at a rate of 1% faster,[b] and choosing efficient policies is critical for faster growth. Achieving efficient policies goes beyond simply minimizing costs, and CBA has the capability to attain the former, while various other policy evaluation tools such as Cost-Effectiveness Analysis only reconciles the latter objective.

Secondly, most of the world's natural resources are concentrated in developing countries. The world's tropical forests are primarily located in developing nations (FAO, 1997), and the Amazon—the largest unbroken rainforest in the world—is largely located across Brazil and Peru. There is growing international pressure on developing economies to take on greater responsibility for sustainable development, and for these nations to bear the

[a] As defined by the United Nations Statistics division. The list of all 49 countries may be obtained from http://unstats.un.org/unsd/methods/m49/m49regin.htm#least.

[b] The data involved in the calculation were obtained from the World Bank World Development Indicators Database.

future responsibility for reducing carbon emissions. CBA allows developing countries to account for these natural capital which are otherwise unpriced.

Thirdly, governments of developing countries face significantly greater budgetary constraints than their developed counterparts. Taken together the heightened urgency for development, the strong international pressure for environmental conservation, and the relative lack of financial resources at the governments' disposal, developing countries have to be extremely prudent about their choices of projects. Since developing nations face the greatest need for optimal decision-making, CBA becomes an important tool to ascertain the net benefits of proposed projects. Compared to policy impact analyses such as Environmental Impact Analysis and Difference-in-Differences regressions, CBA provides a more straightforward answer to weighing policy options.

Fourthly, CBA improves transparency and consistency in decision-making. While there are valid critiques about the process and policy transparency in CBA (Cecot and Hahn, 2020), such as because of data not being made publicly available, the alternative is worse. Especially for developing countries, CBA, at minimum, still improves the public's understanding of complex policies and informs decision-making through a systematic and rigorous framework, without which policy choices are often susceptible to ambiguity.

Lastly, there is a greater role for public projects in developing countries in the provision of merit and/or public goods such as public transport. As discussed in Chapter 6 (van Oort and Yap, 2021), public transport projects provides an illustration through the 5E model: effective mobility, efficient city, economy, environment and health, and equity.

Table 1 provides some examples of straightforward and conventional CBA in developing countries that were conducted for transport projects. The proposed cost and benefits in these analysis are notably cost-revenue based. However, in developing countries, public transport projects are not only aimed at reducing congestion, saving journey time, increasing travel options, or meeting peak demand. Rather, it serves the pressing objectives of basic accessibility and social inclusion. Public transport projects also rely heavily on public funding due to high fixed costs and low profits, often because of cost-based pricing. The incurred costs and generated benefits are largely beyond cost-revenue analysis. For example, the introduction of a single bus service affects not only the new users of the bus, but also existing users of other modes of transports (private car owners and pedestrians), other transport operators, the environment (air, noise and heat pollution),

Table 1 Examples of CBAs conducted for transport infrastructure projects in developing countries.

Case study of CBA in developing countries	Reasons for project implementation	Proposed benefits	Proposed costs	Outcome and evaluation
Paving a gravel road	Road is only 24 feet wide Dust in the summer occasionally forces vehicles to keep a substantial distance apart and passing is then difficult	Reduced vehicle operating costs Elimination of maintenance costs of a gravel road Time savings for vehicles (including truck and bus drivers) but not for passengers and freight Increase in the comfort of the trip for drivers and passengers by providing a smoother ride, eliminating dust in dry seasons, facilitating passing etc.	Capital costs of paved road Maintenance costs of paved road	*Reasonably justified:* Net present value (NPV) of Rs 6.7 million at a discount rate of 12% Cost-benefit ratio (BCR) is 1:1.15 Internal rate of return (IRR) < 14% Conclusion of the analysis is not particularly sensitive to the assumption about generated traffic and to assumptions about maintenance costs, only exception being capital costs
Widening the pavement of a road	In many developing countries, a considerable part of the intercity road network has pavement less than 18 feet wide and much of it may be only 12 feet wide	Reduced vehicle operating costs Reduced road maintenance costs	Paving costs	*Badly justified:* NPV of Rs 829,000 a mile when discounted at 12% IRR of 12% at a traffic level of 380–390 vehicles a day in the base year Conclusion of the analysis is affected by the discount rate used, composition of

Continued

Table 1 Examples of CBAs conducted for transport infrastructure projects in developing countries.—cont'd

Case study of CBA in developing countries	Reasons for project implementation	Proposed benefits	Proposed costs	Outcome and evaluation
				traffic and the projected growth of traffic
				No allowance made for nonmotorized traffic, which in many developing countries tends to be significant
				Reality is that the quality of earth roads can vary widely, depending on weather, the condition of the soil etc. is not considered
				No allowance made for the value of time for passengers and freight
				Neglects the impact of a wider pavement on accident reduction, which might be significant in some situations
				No allowance made for the greater comfort and convenience of travel on a wider pavement, especially at higher traffic levels

Table 1 Examples of CBAs conducted for transport infrastructure projects in developing countries.—cont'd

Case study of CBA in developing countries	Reasons for project implementation	Proposed benefits	Proposed costs	Outcome and evaluation
Construction of a major highway	A road in a port city has a 12 foot-wide, single-lane pavement which is in poor condition, and there are frequent pavement failures Maintenance is expensive because the road was not designed for the existing traffic level and because some of the embankment is waterlogged	Reduced vehicle operating costs on the new highway for traffic diverted from the old road, generated traffic, and traffic diverted from the railway Reduced vehicle operating costs for the traffic remaining on the old road Time savings for passengers and freight	Capital costs Maintenance costs	*Well justified:* NPV of about Rs 263 million when discounted at 12% BCR is 1:1.7 IRR > 17% Conclusion is generally robust to assumptions

Source: Adler, H.A., 1987. Economic appraisal of transport projects: a manual with case studies (English). World Bank Institute (WBI) development study. EDI series in economic development. World Bank Group, Washington, DC. Available from: http://documents.worldbank.org/curated/en/383421468767365929/Economic-appraisal-of-transport-projects-a-manual-with-case-studies

congestion in general, and also the economy at large from greater accessibility and inclusion. CBA serves to capture these widespread effects of public projects which are not accounted for in financial analysis.

3. A brief review of CBA principles

Given the differences in the circumstances faced by developed vis-à-vis developing economies, should carrying out CBA in developing countries differ? Answering this question requires a review of some fundamental principles of CBA (Mishan and Quah, 2020). First, CBA must account for all benefits and costs of direct and indirect effects, including externalities. In addition, valuations must be as accurate as possible, reflecting the true social costs and benefits. This requires measuring use and non-use values, distortions in prices due to taxes or subsidies, and opportunity costs. Future benefits and costs must be discounted to allow a fair comparison in current dollar term, double-counting must be avoided, transfer payments should be ignored, and uncertainty and equity must be accounted for through sensitivity analysis.

A sensitivity analysis serves to provide a distribution for the various cost and benefits under consideration due to changes in measures, assumptions, and the possible range of inputs. As discussed in Chapter 5 (van Wee and Mouter, 2021) various equity types and metrics can be considered and sensitivity analysis can be applied to compare the outcomes across them. Even if only one measure such as the Willingness to Pay for Fairness (WTPFF) is selected, the response distribution will have to be included in a sensitivity analysis if different socio-economic groups (with different weightages in the equity considerations) are surveyed. Shi and Zhou (2012) provide a more sophisticated sensitivity analysis where an accruement of benefit by one social group, among many, results in a relative decrease for others, and how this varies across social groups.

The circumstances under which developed and developing economies operate may be different but they have no bearing on the fundamental principles underlying CBA. However, in applying these principles, certain valuation techniques and other procedures commonly used in developed countries are not appropriate for developing countries. To shed light on this, this chapter examines how labor, goods, and financial markets differ between developing and developed economies, and how these differences may result in erroneous CBA if certain valuation techniques are used. The chapter then discusses behavioral aspects, and the relative advantages and disadvantages of employing various valuation techniques in conducting CBA in developing countries. Finally, the chapter looks at whether the limitations of CBA are more severe for developing nations.

4. Differences in markets and the implications on CBA

4.1 Labor markets

There are three differences between developed and developing economies' labor markets that could significantly influence the results of CBA. The first is the higher level of disguised unemployment in developed economies, the second is the higher level of household production, and the third is the incompleteness of labor markets in developing nations.

Unlike in developed nations, the majority of the workforce in developing nations is employed in agriculture. The International Labour Organization estimates that 59% of the labor force in low income countries is employed in the agricultural sector compared to a world average of 26.5% (ILO, 2020). This in itself will not necessarily distort a CBA. However, a significant portion of these agricultural workers are actually only employed in name and paid a token wage despite making no marginal contribution to the production process. This practice is not uncommon in developing nations, where farm owners routinely hire family members and pay them a token wage, even when there are clearly no additional gains to be made from their employment apart from familial goodwill.

This phenomenon has serious implications for CBA, which requires that items be valued at their opportunity cost. The opportunity cost to reallocate a disguised unemployed laborer to a new position is zero. However, conventional CBA values the cost of labor using the wage rate. If a government project resulted in a laborer moving from disguised unemployment to a new, productive position, that forgone wage would count as a cost for a project. But in reality, there is no opportunity cost associated with that laborer's prior position—the prior employer loses no productivity when the worker leaves, and just saves the wage. In this instance, the benefit of creating employment is understated.

The challenge posed by disguised unemployment is illustrated in the following scenario. Imagine a communal farm that currently produces $9000 worth of output every year. The farm is co-owned by the whole village that has a population of 30 people. All the villagers who work on the farm received an equal share of the total output's value, i.e., $300 per year. Ten of the workers do not actually contribute to the total farm output.

That is, even if they stopped working, the farm output would remain exactly the same. Therefore, the marginal output of the last 10 farmhands working in the village is zero.

Now, imagine that the government proposed to start a project in this particular village that would generate $1000 in benefits. To carry out this project, the government will have to hire 10 local workers, at a total cost of $3000, which is the exact amount those 10 villagers would have earned working at the farm for the year. A typical practice in CBA is to enter the prior wages of the workers who switch jobs as a cost item, because it is assumed that their prior wages represent their productivity at their past jobs. Since the project reallocates their labor, the opportunity cost is the work they would have otherwise been doing.

Using this calculus, the hypothetical project yields net costs, because the wages of $3000 are greater than the benefits of $1000. However, in truth, the opportunity cost for the 10 farmhands giving up their previous employment should be zero, since their marginal productivity was zero. When they quit working at the farm, it continues to generate $9000 worth of output. The average output per farmhand increased from $300 to $450, because 10 of the original workers no longer draw income from the farm. Those 10 workers, in their new positions, together generate $1000 worth of value. Adding together the farm and the new government project, the total productivity for the village is now $10,000. Indeed, the government could pay for the project by taxing the 20 villages that remained as farmhands, and everyone could be made better off by the new project's additional benefits.

There is a caveat. Although hiring the disguised unemployed or the unemployed is said to carry zero opportunity cost based on productivity, this does not account for the value of forgone leisure or household production, including unpaid childcare and household work and maintenance. Such items may be significant if leisure is highly valued by individuals, or if a large portion of the disguised employed are indeed actually employed in valuable household production.

This leads us to our next point—there is a higher level of household production in developing nations than in developed nations. Household production is defined as the production of goods and services by members of a household for their own consumption, using their own capital and their own unpaid labor.[c] This value is difficult to measure, but not zero. Valuation methods generally fall into two categories: the opportunity cost

[c] For a more detailed definition, see Ironmonger (2001).

method, where household production is valued at the forgone wage rate, and the replacement cost method, where the value is the cost of employing other people to do the work (Quah, 1993).

In developed economies, household production can be priced because labor markets are generally efficient and provides a measure of opportunity costs, and because demand and the market for hired help exists. The same cannot be said for developing economies, where labor markets are largely incomplete, and households undertake most of their own household production. The households do not pay themselves for their household production, and therefore, such production cannot be easily priced. The same problem can be seen in the production that occurs in the underground economy, where illicit transactions of goods and services are not captured. This problem is presumably more prevalent in developing nations as well, due to a weaker enforcement and monitoring system.

The valuation problem is twofold. First, there is the methodological issue that techniques relying on market behaviors to measure preferences will be inadequate because markets for hired help either do not exist or are significantly incomplete in developing countries. Second, the higher levels of production undertaken by households mean that CBA, which cannot easily incorporate this production in developing countries, is biased and inaccurate. While developed nations may sometimes face similar problems in conducting CBA, the scale of the impact is much smaller. Accordingly, the accuracy of CBA is much higher because of the existence and relative efficiency of the market for hired help, and much lower levels of household production.

The third difference between labor markets in developed and developing economies is their relative incompleteness and hence, inefficiency of the latter when compared to the former. This arises for a variety of reasons, including the extent of information failure and the ability of employers in developing countries to exercise monopsonistic power in the labor market.

The implication of the above differences is that wages in developing countries rarely reflect an individual's valuation of job attributes. In an efficient labor market, by contrast, undesirable job attributes are compensated with wage premiums, which may then be used to place a value on the job attributes. The wage premiums represent individuals' Willingness-to-accept (WTA) for the disutility arising from the undesirable job attribute. The implication for CBA in developing countries is that intangible job characteristics, such as status and location, cannot be valued using hedonic pricing.

A specific implication is the potential error in estimating the Value of Statistical Life (VoSL). One method to estimate VoSL is to directly survey respondents and elicit their Willingness-to-Pay (WTP) for a reduced health risk, or WTA for the opposite, subject to their budget constraints in reality (Mishan and Quah, 2020). A WTA elicited through such surveys will not reflect the VoSL accurately. Moreover, given the time and cost of such surveys, a common practice is use a benefit transfer approach to transfer such values, obtained in developed countries, to developing ones, with adjustments for income differentials across countries. Again, the distortion in wage premiums will affect such an adjustment.

Using wage premiums that do not accurately reflect the compensation required for the differing levels of risk results in an erroneous VoSL. This has far-reaching implications for all other CBAs that are used to evaluate projects that impact health and safety, since the values of many costs and benefits are a derivative of VoSL.

A thorough treatment on the use of value of time (VoT) in transport projects is given by Jong and Kouwenhovent (2020). The lack of precision in valuing one's labor or productivity also leads to inaccurate estimates of the VoT. For example, in transport infrastructure construction projects or road improvement schemes, a key benefit component is the value of journey time savings, usually in opportunity cost or marginal product (or wage). It is necessary to attach a monetary value on time savings for comparison with other components in CBA, including construction costs, road accidents, private vehicle operating cost savings and others. There is usually also a distinction drawn between work time and non-work (or leisure) time, but this distinction is even much less defined for developing countries.

4.2 Goods markets

Another major difference between developing and developed economies is that the goods markets in developing economies are likely to be less efficient than those of developed economies because of information asymmetry. The disparity is even more apparent since the advent of the Internet, which has, by and large, been more accessible to and more effectively utilized by the developed world. This point is best illustrated by the growth of online shopping and financial technology (FinTech), which has driven down prices in the developed world but have not had the same impact in the developing world.

Additionally, unlike in developed economies, the goods markets of developing countries are more likely to be distorted by or uncorrected with taxes, subsidies, or other forms of governmental interventions (Dinwiddy and Teal, 1996). The inefficiencies and distortions of the goods markets mean that prices may not reflect the true values of goods. Therefore, using prices to value input items, as is usually done in developed countries, would likely result in an inaccurate CBA in a developing country.

An imperfect goods market has greater confounding effects on goods and services with a derived demand, such as transport. As discussed in Nes and Jong (2020), standard transport models used in transport planning, and hence CBA of related policies and projects, need to take into account the demand and travel behavior of commuters.

Demand for public transport is usually derived from its associated functions: to reach the workplace, for haulage of goods, to access certain goods or services etc. Transport is demanded not for its own characteristics, other than the case where it has a "journey value" in which commuters derive utility from the trip itself because of comfort or safety among other reasons. An example of this "true" demand is a luxury cruise, where one pays for the experience and journey. One would expect that this "non-derived" demand is more pronounced in developed countries. Being almost entirely a derived demand in developing countries, demand is a function only of related products and services. Across the various goods markets, the price distortions compounds, and estimating transport in developing countries becomes a messy task.

On the other hand, one could also argue that because of a less vibrant market, forecasting demand is more straightforward. Transport alternatives do not differ much in attributes such as standard of service and convenience, or that the basket of related goods is less varied, or that transport fee structures and concessionary fares are less complex to account for. Price elasticity of demand, at least for public transport, is also therefore less dynamic and arguably more inelastic if price is low. To add on, evaluating transport projects in developed countries requires careful consideration of network effects. A bus subsidy diverting commuters toward certain bus services cannot be assessed in isolation since it affects all other transport modes within the same network. Eventually, different groups of commuters and operators may face either benefits or disbenefits. Incidence groups are closely correlated, and so are their costs and benefits, and the consequent distributional impacts can be challenging to determined as briefly covered earlier in Section 3.

While existing transport networks in developed countries are generally less convoluted, travel forecasts and the benefits derived from it should be adjusted for near-term and long-term induced demand, in the form of latent and generated demand. Cervero (2011) uses the example of gridlocked traffic in highly congested and poorly planned developing country cities that creates a pent-up demand for mobility. This is likely to induce many newly generated trips following a transport network upgrade. A static value of travel time savings will not accurately capture such dynamics.

An indirect issue that arises from the inefficiencies and distortions of the goods markets is the valuation of intangibles and externalities. In developed economies, where the goods markets are considered efficient, intangibles and externalities can be valued in relation to consumption through a revealed preference approach. For example, in estimating the value of national parks and related recreation in the United States, the travel cost approach is commonly used. This approach obtains a demand curve by examining the price of recreation in a national park, which is the cost visitors are willing to pay to travel to visit the park (Beal, 1995; Fix and Loomis, 1997). However, the credibility of such revealed preferences breaks down when the market does not produce prices that reflect the true value of a good. In the example of the national park, if fuel were distributed through a rationing system, then the private cost of traveling would be very hard to determine, and the demand curve obtained through typical techniques would be inaccurate. Rations and other forms of price distortions are prevalent in many countries in the developing world. The consensus is that where there are market distortions, shadow prices—the estimated prices of a good or service for which no accurate market price exists—should be used.[d]

The calculation of shadow prices is also subject to complications and much debate. Tradable goods in developing economies are an example of a class of goods for which it is difficult to obtain shadow prices. The problem arises due to the fact that exchange rates are required in the calculation of shadow prices for tradable goods. Unlike developed economies, the exchange rates of developing economies may fluctuate wildly and may not be reflective of the appropriate exchange rates and purchasing power. This exacerbates the issue of accuracy when using CBA, especially the technique of shadow price calculation.

[d] This issue is not a new one, and there is an abundance of literature dealing with the matter. Boardman et al. (2006) provide a good summary of the literature and methods.

The use of stated preference (SP) data have been growing since the 1980s (Johnston et al., 2016). The same issues from the earlier discussion on VoSL applies when trying to conduct SP surveys in developing countries or use benefit transfer from developed countries' SP data.

4.3 Financial markets

Like the labor and goods markets, the financial markets in developing economies are also weaker than those in developed economies. Private banks in developing countries usually wield considerable monopolistic power, which they may exploit by charging interest rates above what a free market would otherwise produce (Yildirim and Philippatos, 2007). This bears on the issue of discounting in CBA. A descriptive or opportunity cost of capital approach to discounting will entail choosing a discount rate that is grounded in actual behavior and equivalency of public and private investments, while a prescriptive approach incorporates societal, intergenerational, and ethical considerations (Mouter, 2018).

In developed economies, the opportunity cost of capital is usually estimated by the market interest rate. This is reasonable because financial markets in developed economies are generally mature enough to generate sufficient competition to drive down the market interest rate so that it truly reflects the opportunity cost of capital. Thus, it is less contentious to use the market interest rate to represent the opportunity cost of capital in calculating the social discount rate in developed economies. Unfortunately, the same cannot be said for developing economies.

Interest rates in developing economies are likely to be higher than the true opportunity cost of capital, because of profiteering by private banks. If the social discount rate for developing economies is calculated using the market interest rate as the opportunity cost of capital, the result is a higher social discount rate than is appropriate for measurement. Consequently, both future benefits and costs are more heavily discounted, and CBA is biased in favor of projects that yield short-term benefits and long-term costs. Thus, the opportunity cost rate in most cost-benefit studies need adjustment downwards.

Besides the opportunity cost of capital, the social time preference rate also requires additional considerations, as developing and developed societies are influenced by different social and economic circumstances.

Populations in developing economies have shorter lifespans and lower incomes. Thus, these populations often have a higher preference for current, rather than future, consumption when compared to the preferences of populations in developed countries. Developing societies are likely to have shorter time preferences, and ceteris paribus, their social discount rate will therefore be higher. This difference in preference further raises social discount rates, albeit not as a result of some inefficiency in the market, but more reflective of genuine differences in individual preferences.

Overall, the nature of the labor, goods, and financial markets in developing economies clearly differs from those in developed economies. These differences can significantly affect the result and accuracy of a CBA if certain valuation or discounting techniques are used. These distinctions between developed and developing economies should be kept in mind by analysts seeking to develop accurate measures of the costs and benefits of social policies in developing countries. A list of possible ways to overcome the challenges described in this section is provided in Table 2.

Table 2 Examples of recommendations that analysts can use to overcome the challenges of measuring cost and benefits in developing countries.

Markets	Recommendations
Labor	• Face-to-face interview in the event of low literacy rates • Time-use surveys (i.e., diaries) in low resource settings • Instead of valuing all changes in consumption, weight the changes according to a consistent distributional index • A central finance or planning ministry should provide guidelines on the use of common shadow prices which are uniformly applied to all projects
Goods	• When show prices differ from market prices, there should be an adequate return to the project owners and producers besides the national economy • Labor (physical units of output foregone) should be valued at world rather than domestic prices • Where benefit estimates are illustrative rather than definitive, cost-minimization criteria may have to replace standard cost-benefit comparisons • Use dynamic assignment models to account for traffic congestion more accurately
Financial	• Adjust the opportunity cost of capital rate downward in developing countries • Use real sovereign borrowing rates as the social discount rates for evaluating public projects

5. Behavioral economics and CBA

In addition to fundamental differences between developed and developing countries with regards to discount rates, differences in behaviors also affect valuation survey design and results. This difference in behavior detracts from traditional CBA, suggesting that both gains and losses have to account for physical as well as psychological attributes.

5.1 Loss aversion

In practice, the study of loss aversion is the most common example which alters measurement values in CBA. Abstracting from significant income effects, gains and losses should be identical in nature and hold the same valuation when it comes to measurement. In the case of gains, it is the maximum amount that a person is willing to pay (WTP) while losses account for the maximum payment that a person is willing to accept (WTA) for the loss. Results of cost-benefit analysis should then be a summation of the respective valuations of gains and losses, with the end results being similar (Henderson, 1941; Mishan and Quah, 2020).

Yet, there is a significant disparity with measured values that accounted for a person's WTA being far larger than his WTP (Knetsch and Sinden, 1984; Putler, 1992). Knowing that differences do arise when considering people's valuations of losses and gains, failing to account for this will create inefficient and often biased decision-making. This is especially the case when analyzing developing countries where the majority of the population is often low income, making them more risk averse since their margin for error is lower as compared to individuals in developed countries, and therefore the higher degree of loss aversion.

This also presents a danger in policymaking in developing countries as policies that aim to counter actions that have negative externalities, such as pollution, are likely to yield an under-weighted WTP, and there may be an undue encouragement of activities that have negative consequences. This explains lax environmental standards especially since the benefits of economic growth are quantitatively apparent while the costs are subject to measurement bias.

5.2 The choice of measure

Following the previous argument, framing stated preference survey questions as a loss or gain must be carefully considered. The choice of measure should depend on the current assignment of property rights, which in itself could be less well-defined and defendable in developing countries. Say, if the victims of pollution supposedly have the right from pollution, the researcher should be asking the affected general public or local residents their WTA as compensation for a lower environmental quality as a result of the proposed policy change. If instead the polluters have the right to pollute at status quo, which is most often the case in least developed nations, questions should ask for the victims' WTP to avoid a worsened environmental state due to the same policy change. Yet, the public is expected to be more familiar with and accepting of the concept of the polluter-pay principle (compensation for environmental losses) rather than the victim-pay principle (payment to avoid environmental losses), and here lies the difficulty in eliciting preferences.

Furthering the discussion, negative changes can also occur in the domain of gains and, therefore, should not be treated as a loss but as a reduction in gains. The choice of WTP and WTA thus becomes even trickier. For a detailed discussion on welfare measures concerning gain and loss domains, see Knetsch et al. (2012) and Knetsch (2013).

5.3 Sunk costs

Another behavioral oddity is that of sunk costs. Behavioral economics have found many people mistakenly considering such costs. This has serious implications for the evaluation of infrastructure expansion. For example, an old ferry's fixed cost is $1 million. In considering a new ferry which will yield a net benefit of $0.5 million, this is in itself a desirable undertaking. However, if one were to mistakenly consider the $1 million which has been previously invested in the old ferry and is now "wasted," the wrong conclusion of not purchasing the new ferry would be reached as the net benefit would be -$0.5 million. In developed economies, this may not pose a major problem with a larger budget, but in poorer developing countries, it makes a big difference as to whether the old ferry is kept or scrapped. The correct decision based on CBA and neoclassical economics disregards sunk costs. The decision to invest in the new ferry only considers the net benefits from the project, and the choice to keep or scrap an old ferry only depends on whether the ferry can cover its costs conditional on whether the new ferry is purchased.

6. Challenges of valuation techniques in developing countries

To reiterate, valuation techniques in CBA may be broadly classified into two categories: revealed preference approaches and stated preference approaches. Revealed preference approaches are indirect methods that attempt to discern the values of items by observing how people behave. To find out the value people attach to a particular view from a house (for example, with a sea view, or staying right by the highway and experiencing noise pollution), hedonic pricing—a revealed preference approach—may be employed. This involves comparing the prices of two houses that are similar in every aspect apart from the view. The price differential is then taken to be the value people attach to the view. Stated preference approaches are methods based on directly eliciting the individuals' preferences. Going back to the example of valuing a view, a stated preference approach—the contingent valuation method—could be used. It would entail a survey requiring people to state how much they would be willing to pay for a particular view (e.g., Quah and Tan, 1999). Hedonic pricing and the contingent valuation method are the prototypical examples of each approach.

Neither method is perfect. Most revealed preference approaches, including hedonic pricing and the travel cost method, require strong assumptions of rationality, perfect information, and perfect mobility to be valid (Quah and Ong, 2009), while stated preference approaches, including the contingent valuation method, are susceptible to a large number of behavioral effects as discussed in Section 5 (Carson et al., 2001; Kahneman and Knetsch, 1992) and methodological biases. While some of these issues have been gradually ironed out as discussed by Koopmans and Mouter (2020), in the context of a developing nation, such flaws may be magnified. We look at each approach in turn.

As illustrated previously, incomplete accounting in the labor, goods, and financial markets in developing economies make the assumptions required by revealed preference approaches untenable. Stated preference approaches may not be entirely suitable for developing economies either. The behavioral effects may be even more pronounced in developing economies because of the relative rarity of people's experiences in survey participation. List (2003) shows that behavioral effects are, at least in part, brought about by a lack of experience with the hypothetical decision-making circumstances. Therefore, the magnitude of behavioral biases in stated preference approaches is likely to be much more significant in developing nations. Methodological biases in stated preference approaches also tend to be larger in developing nations because of the lack of trained interviewers (Hanley and Barbier, 2009). One common problem is the inability of both interviewers and interviewees to differentiate between willingness to pay and ability to pay. Such misunderstandings are further exacerbated by illiteracy, cultural and linguistic differences. Access to individuals, households and industries may be limited due to informality or incomplete land and business registries. Additionally, surveys typically carry significant costs that cash-strapped governments will be hard-pressed to cover. Thus, particularly for developing nations, these two valuation techniques have obvious pitfalls which may render results dubious.

A third valuation technique, the paired comparison approach, may prove to be the best solution, as it avoids the obvious flaws of the other two methodological classes (Quah et al., 2006). The paired comparison approach uses a survey to elicit individual preferences for public and other non-market goods such as the environment. Sets of elements are presented in pairs as discrete binary choices in a survey. The set may include gains, losses, activities, environmental resources, or anything else being scaled. Respondents choose the item that they feel is more important, in that sense that larger compensation should be paid for it than for the other (Rutherford et al., 1998). The variance stable rank method is then used to derive the ranking. This method takes the total number of times an element is selected by all respondents and divides it by the maximum number of times it could have been selected. Ordinal rankings are derived based on the results, with some degree of discretion allowed since some elements may have the same ranking. A brief comparison of the paired comparison approach and the more common discrete choice experience is given in Table 3.

Since a paired comparison uses surveys, like stated preference methods, it avoids the need for the strong assumptions required by revealed preference methods. It also overcomes the key behavioral effect that plagues contingent valuation methods, which is known as loss aversion or the endowment effect. Loss aversion, as described earlier, is a result of differences in referencing WTP from a buyer's point of view with WTA from a seller's perspective. These

Table 3 Comparison of paired comparison approach and discrete choice experiments.

Discrete choice experiments (DCEs)	Constant-sum paired comparisons (CSPCs)
Ask respondents to choose a single preferred option from two or more alternatives	Ask respondents to allocate a fixed budget between two alternatives
Over a series of choice tasks can elicit preferences for the different attribute levels that define each alternative	In contrast to the "pick one" nature of a DCE, respondents can choose to allocate the entire budget to alternative A, to alternative B, or to some combination of the two, including an equal split

different reference points results in different valuations (Knetsch and Sinden, 1984). Paired comparison offers a third reference point—that of the selector. As no real or perceived loss occurs in this case, behavioral effects like loss aversion, which can impact the results of a WTP or WTA survey, are avoided (Kahneman et al., 1999).

Detractors claim that the paired comparison method has the severe drawback of not providing a measure of the monetary net benefits derived from a project. While the method may indicate a society's priorities and may prove useful to policymakers in deciding which projects should take precedence over others, this method does not provide policymakers with information on how to get the maximum mileage out of their dollars. However, this concern can be addressed by including monetary items in the paired comparison choice set. Ranking of all items, both monetary and non-market, can then provide estimates of the upper and lower bounds of the monetary values of the non-market items.

While neither revealed nor stated preference approaches are entirely suitable for developing nations, a paired comparison approach may prove to be a valid and useful option. Nonetheless, in conducting CBA, governments of developing economies will have to exercise caution in choosing the most appropriate valuation method for their purposes in order to avoid distortions.

7. Severity of limitations

A serious criticism of CBA is that it may result in forgoing equity in the pursuit of efficiency. The underlying basis of CBA is meeting the Kaldor-Hicks criterion, also known as the potential Pareto criterion. In a typical CBA, the value of a dollar does not reflect who receives the benefits of a project, or who pays its costs. The primary objective is to maximize social welfare in aggregate terms. Hence, it is conceivable that CBA could increase inequity by approving projects that yield net benefits even when most of the benefits accrue to the rich and most of the costs are borne by the poor. In a developed nation, this is not a major problem, as there are usually governmental channels, such as progressive taxation and estate taxes, to redistribute wealth and prevent the income gap from widening too much or too quickly. Such redistributions realizes the "potential" of the Pareto improvement. Developing nations, however, tend to lack such channels. In fact, prevalent corruption, a chronic problem for most developing nations, specifically prevents the formation of such channels, because it is often in politicians' interests to line the pockets of their business-sector donors. Additionally, income inequality is generally a larger problem for developing nations than for developed nations. When ranked by their Gini coefficient, most countries with the highest income inequalities are developing nations and vice versa (World Bank, 2020).

CBA need not completely ignore equity. One commonly proposed strategy is to apply weights to costs and benefits, to reflect the relative importance of monetary values to different socioeconomic stratas. For example, benefits or costs accruing to low-income groups may be multiplied so that the costs and benefits to them are magnified, and projects in their favor will have better chances of being approved. While this principle is basically sound, the application of this weighting is highly problematic. First, there is the technical issue of determining what weights should be employed to adequately address inequity. While it is clear that the greater the importance attached to inequity issues the larger the weights should be, the appropriate number is still difficult to calculate or ascertain. One possible solution in developed countries is to infer the implicit weights attached to different social groups by examining existing policies. However, this solution is less applicable for some developing countries with existing biases and weights that may be completely unjustified in the first place.

A second concern is the possibility of abuse. With equity weighting, CBA could be manipulated to produce any result desired simply by adjusting the weights attached to a particular group's welfare. In developing countries, the possibility of abuse is higher because of the relative lack of checks and balances on ruling powers. This further renders the usage of weights to address the inequity issue unsuitable for developing economies and consequently, reduces the ability of CBA to take into account inequity issues in these economies.

Lastly, one criticism of CBA is also that of the sequential investment problem, or the Scitovsky paradox. That is, the Kaldor-Hicks criterion on which CBA is based on can produce contradictory welfare results. This is illustrated in Fig. 1. Kaldor's criterion is met when the gainers from the policy measures can compensate the losers and still be in a better position, i.e., going from X to Y, Y to X or Y to Z, but not when going from Z to Y. However, Hicks' criterion is only met when the new state is socially preferable to old state if the losers from the policy change from old to new state can't profitably bribe the gainers into not making the change from old to new state, i.e., only when going from Y to Z, but not from X to Y or Y to X due to the new higher utility actually being lower at another

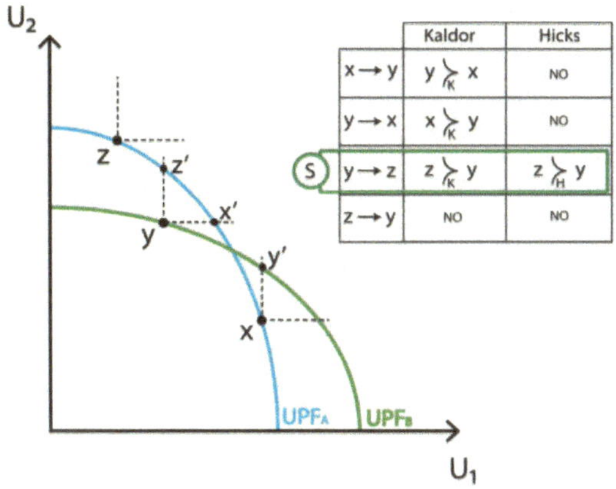

Fig. 1 Scitovsky paradox.

point on the indifference curve (UPF_B). Therefore, when comparing state Y to Z, winners can compensate the loss of the losers, but losers cannot compensate the other part in order to avoid the change. This is the only case in our example where the Scitovsky criterion is met, making Z preferred to Y.

A series of different projects that could seemingly improve social welfare in their individual implementation could eventually lead to a decrease in welfare in the long run. Hypothetical Pareto principle judgments are not guaranteed to be transitive. To illustrate, using CBA, we might rightly conclude that project B is Kaldor-Hicks superior to project A, and subsequently project C improves on B. However, the state of social welfare with project C could be that worse off than that in A, the initial project. The risk of this non-transitivity is logically higher where many small projects are analyzed in isolation, wherein lies the risk of applying CBA in developing countries.

8. Conclusions

There are both similarities and differences between CBA conducted in developed and in developing countries. While the fundamental principles underlying CBA remain unchanged, the methodologies that are most appropriate in each context may differ. In fact, it is precisely in abiding by those principles that certain valuation techniques may become unsuitable. For example, it is specifically through the desire to achieve accurate valuation—a cardinal principle of CBA—that the incompleteness of the labor, goods, and financial markets in developing economies may render revealed preference approaches unsuitable and inferior to stated preference and paired comparison approaches. The continued improvement of such techniques rank high in the research agenda.

In addition, the overall merits and limitations of CBA shift depending on the state of economic advancement. The need for CBA is indeed more pressing for developing economies, since they must contend with a number of conflicting and yet critically important goals, such as increasing economic growth while nonetheless, conserving natural resources. However, CBA has severe limitations regarding equity concerns, which poses a pronounced challenge for developing economies utilizing the technique. This is an area where one would expect more research would lead to improvements in eliciting such preferences.

The question then follows: should governments of developing economies employ CBA as a decision-making tool? This evaluation has argued that CBA can and should be used by the developing world. CBA remains a very useful tool for policymakers. Conducting the analysis requires asking important questions, including what costs and benefits should be measured and how to measure them; what communities and stakeholders will receive the benefits and pay the costs; how uncertainties and equity issues will be addressed; what the appropriate investment decision criteria are; and whether there are constraints on the results. Systematic decision-making that uses consistent and transparent methodologies is valuable in formulating public policy in both developed and developing countries. At the same time, CBA can only fulfill its potential if three important issues are taken into account. First, CBA is only meant to be a guide and should not be the final or only arbiter of project proposals. Second, in conducting CBA, the appropriate valuation techniques must be selected. Finally, potential equity issues must be independently considered and treated as an imperative complement to a robust CBA.

Acknowledgments

This work is supported by the Singapore National Research Foundation under its Campus for Research Excellence and Technological Enterprise (CREATE) program. The authors would like to thank Clement Tan Jun Wen, Joshua Lake and Tan Jun Rui for their able research assistantship.

References

Beal, D.J., 1995. A travel cost analysis of the value of Carnarvon Gorge National Park for recreational use. Rev. Mark. Agric. Econ. 63 (2), 292–303.

Boardman, A., Greenberg, D., Vining, A., Weimer, D., 2006. Cost Benefit Analysis: Concepts and Practice, third ed. Prentice Hall, Upper Saddle River, NJ.

Carson, R.T., Flores, N.E., Meade, N.F., 2001. Contingent valuation controversies and evidence. Environ. Resource Econ. 19, 173–210.
Cecot, C., Hahn, R.W., 2020. Transparency in agency cost-benefit analysis. In: Administrative Law Review. Available from https://papers.ssrn.com/sol3/papers.cfm?abstract_id=3531224.
Cervero, R., 2011. Going Beyond Travel-Time Savings: An Expanded Framework for Evaluating Urban Transport Projects (Report). World Bank, Washington, DC. (published 27 June 2012) Report Number 70206. Available from http://documents.worldbank.org/curated/en/466801468178764085/pdf/702060ESW0P1200s0in0Urban0Transport.pdf.
Dinwiddy, C.L., Teal, F.J., 1996. Principles of Cost-Benefit Analysis for Developing Countries. Cambridge University Press, Cambridge.
Fix, P., Loomis, J., 1997. The economic benefits of mountain biking at one of its meccas: an application of the travel cost method to mountain biking in Moab, Utah. J. Leis. Res. 29 (3), 342–352.
Food and Agriculture Organization of the United Nations (FAO), 1997. State of the World's Forests. FAO, Rome.
Hanley, N., Barbier, E.B., 2009. Pricing Nature: Cost-Benefit Analysis and Environmental Policy. Edward Elgar, Northampton, Mass.
Henderson, A.M., 1941. Consumer's surplus and the compensation variation. Rev. Econ. Stud. 8 (2), 117–121.
International Labour Organization, 2020. ILOSTAT Database [Database]. Available from https://ilostat.ilo.org/data/.
Ironmonger, D.S., 2001. Household production. In: Smelser, N.J., Baltes, P.B. (Eds.), International Encyclopedia of the Social and Behavioral Sciences. vol. 20. Pergamon, Oxford, pp. 6934–6939.
Johnston, R.J., Kevin, B.J., Adamowicz, W., Bennet, J., Brouwer, R., Cameron, T.A., Ryan, M., 2016. Contemporary guidance for stated preference studies. J. Assoc. Environ. Resour. Econ. 4 (2), 320–405.
Jong, G., Kouwenhovent, M., 2020. Value of travel time and travel time reliability. In: Mouter, N. (Ed.), Advances in Transport Policy and Planning: Standard Transport Appraisal Methods. vol. 2. Academic Press, Elsevier, pp. 44–70.
Kahneman, D., Knetsch, J., 1992. Valuing public goods: the purchase of moral satisfaction. J. Environ. Econ. Manag. 22 (1), 57–70.
Kahneman, D., Ritov, I., Schkade, D.A., 1999. Economic preferences or attitude expressions?: an analysis of dollar responses to public issues. J. Risk Uncertain. 19 (1–3), 230–235.
Knetsch, J.L., 2013. Behavioural effects and cost-benefit analysis: lessons from behavioural economics. In: Quah, E., Toh, R. (Eds.), Cost-Benefit 14 Analysis: Cases and Materials. Routledge, Taylor & Francis Group, pp. 84–98.
Knetsch, J.L., Sinden, J.A., 1984. Willingness to pay and compensation demanded: experimental evidence of an unexpected disparity in measures of value. Q. J. Econ. 99 (3), 507–521.
Knetsch, J., Riyanto, Y., Zong, J., 2012. Gain and loss domains and the choice of welfare measure of positive and negative changes. J. Benefit Cost Anal. 3 (4), 1–18.
Koopmans, C., Mouter, N., 2020. Cost-benefit analysis. In: Mouter, N. (Ed.), Advances in Transport Policy and Planning: Standard Transport Appraisal Methods. vol. 1. Academic Press, Elsevier, pp. 1–36.
Kuznets, S., 1934. National income, 1929-1932. Natl. Bur. Econ. Res. Bull. 49, 1–12.
Kuznets, S., 1962. How to Judge Quality. New Republic. October 20.
List, J.A., 2003. Does market experience eliminate market anomalies. Q. J. Econ. 118 (1), 41–71.

Magablih, A.M., 2017. The impact of green accounting for reducing the environmental cost in production companies. J. Mod. Account. Audit. 13 (6), 249–265.
Mishan, E.J., Quah, E., 2020. Cost-Benefit Analysis. Routledge, New York.
Mouter, N., 2018. A critical assessment of discounting policies for transport cost-benefit analysis in five European practices. Eur. J. Transp. Infrastruct. Res. 18 (4), 389–412.
Nes, R., Jong, G., 2020. Transport models. In: Mouter, N. (Ed.), Advances in Transport Policy and Planning: Standard Transport Appraisal Methods. vol. 4. Academic Press, Elsevier, pp. 101–126.
Putler, D.S., 1992. Incorporating reference Price effects into a theory of consumer choice. Mar. Sci. 11 (3), 287–309.
Quah, E., 1993. Economics and Home Production. Ashgate, Singapore.
Quah, E., Ong, Q., 2009. Cities and happiness in environmental goods. In: Ooi, G.L., Yuen, B. (Eds.), World Cities: Achieving Liveability and Vibrancy. World Scientific, Singapore, pp. 277–298.
Quah, E., Tan, K.C., 1999. Pricing a scenic view: the case of Singapore's east coast park. Impact Assess. Proj. Apprais. 17 (4), 295–303.
Quah, E., Choi, E., Tan, K.C., 2006. Use of damage schedules in environmental valuation: the case of urban Singapore. Appl. Econ. 38, 1501–1512.
Rutherford, M.B., Knetsch, J.L., Brown, T.C., 1998. Assessing environmental losses: judgements of importance and damage schedules. Harv. Environ. Law Rev. 22 (1), 51–101. United Nations Development Programme (UNDP). (2016). Human Development Report 2016. New York: UNDP.
Shi, J., Zhou, N., 2012. A quantitative transportation project investment evaluation approach with both equity and efficiency aspects. Res. Transp. Econ. 36 (1), 93–100.
van Oort, N., Yap, M., 2021. Innovations in the appraisal of public transport projects. Chapter 6. In: Mouter, N. (Ed.), New Methods, Reflections and Application Domains in Transport Appraisal. Series: Advances in Transport Policy and Planning, vol. 7. Elsevier, Amsterdam, pp. 127–164.
van Wee, B., Mouter, N., 2021. Evaluating transport equity. Chapter 5. In: Mouter, N. (Ed.), New Methods, Reflections and Application Domains in Transport Appraisal. Series: Advances in Transport Policy and Planning, vol. 7. Elsevier, Amsterdam, pp. 103–126.
World Bank, 2020. Gini index (World Bank Estimate). Available from https://data.worldbank.org/indicator/SI.POV.GINI.
Yildirim, H.S., Philippatos, G., 2007. Efficiency of banks: recent evidence from the transition economies of Europe 1993–2000. Eur. J. Financ. 13 (2), 123–143.

CHAPTER TEN

Research priorities in appraisal methodology

John Stanley*
Institute of Transport and Logistics Studies, The University of Sydney Business School, Sydney, NSW, Australia
*Corresponding author: e-mail address: John.Stanley@sydney.edu.au

Contents

Abstract

Appraisal is an important part of the policy cycle. This chapter looks at research priorities for transport appraisal through the lens of the policy cycle, with an emphasis on the initial stages of that cycle: identifying societal goals and associated needs for improving goal achievement, through transport initiatives. This is initially done by exploring some of the key value assumptions that underlie transport appraisal, particularly associated with individual preferences and including application in cost benefit analysis and multi-criteria analysis appraisal. Some challenges for appraisal in the environmental and social goal areas are then highlighted, with important research implications. The chapter also looks at transport and economic performance and notes some significant gaps in understanding of wider economic benefits.

Keywords: Appraisal, Climate change, Cost-benefit analysis, Multi-criteria analysis, Social inclusion, Value judgments, Wider economic benefits

Advances in Transport Policy and Planning, Volume 7
ISSN 2543-0009
https://doi.org/10.1016/bs.atpp.2021.01.003

1. Introduction

Appraisal in the transport sector has a history extending back around 60 years, in terms of application at scale, with antecedents going back to at least the French economist and engineer, Jules Dupuit, over a century earlier. The magnitude of most countries' transport spending, both public and private, together with the pervasive influence of transport on life opportunities and scale of transport external benefits and costs, provides continuing impetus to the development of the art and science of transport appraisal.

Appraisal is typically (not always) government driven. Accordingly, development and refinement of appraisal methodologies is commonly spurred by government expectations about the justification required to support allocation of scarce public funds. This is particularly so in jurisdictions where the national government controls most of the purse strings and distributes largesse to lower levels of government (often a reflection of vertical fiscal imbalance) and/or to other stakeholders (e.g., businesses). The Unites States, United Kingdom, Sweden, the Netherlands and Australia, for example, all have long histories in this area, particularly associated with expectations around appraisals to support federal/national government own-project requirements and also around requirements required to support funding flows from the national/federal government for initiatives sponsored by lower levels of government or other stakeholders.

In turn, governmental appraisal requirements are often supported by production of appraisal guidelines, which describe government expectations and ways of meeting those expectations. The UK Treasury Greenbook (HM Treasury, 2018a) and associated transport webtag materials[a] is a well-respected example. The existence of guidelines, in turn, has helped to stimulate the extensive back-end research evidence base needed by quality appraisal methodologies and to support the practical front-end applications of those methodologies that give credence to the value of both the guidelines and of appraisal as a process.

This *appraisal ecosystem* forms an integral part of the wider governmental policy development and implementation process (Fig. 1). The strategic goal setting and need identification stages in this cycle are critical but are typically underweight in terms of the focus they receive, as compared to the fine detail of the appraisal stage. This runs the risk of relatively too much effort being

[a] https://www.gov.uk/guidance/transport-analysis-guidance-webtag

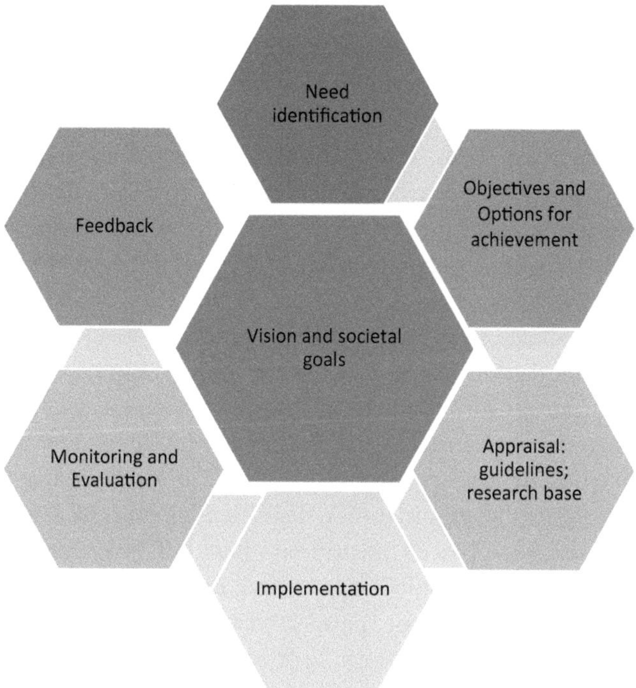

Fig. 1 The policy cycle. *Source: adapted from Stopher, P. and Stanley, J. (2014). Introduction to Transport Policy: A Public Policy View, Cheltenham: Edward Elgar Publishing.*

spent on *doing things right* rather than on *doing the right things*. The goal setting/need identification stages of the cycle are the key focus of this chapter, in terms of shaping expectations of appraisal more around doing the right things.

Given its usual context as part of a policy cycle, appraisal is influenced by an evolving mix of societal values, political priorities, theoretical foundations and practical applications, with significant research opportunities present in all these areas. 60 or so years ago transport appraisals were most common for road projects, where the scope of included benefits and costs was narrow and research priorities focused on exploring a few benefit/cost items in some depth, particularly travel time savings and the way road maintenance costs varied with (for example) pavement type, road condition, traffic volume and mix. External costs were not the issue then that they are today, although congestion and congestion pricing has been of research/appraisal interest for around 50 years.

As understanding of the linkages between transport and other elements of wellbeing has broadened, and transport external benefits and costs become more important community concerns, so the scope of appraisal has necessarily been extended and the supportive research base on which it draws has widened. Thus, a range of environmental outcomes, wider economic benefits and, to a lesser extent, recognition of the role transport can play in promoting social inclusion have become more important priorities for policy, appraisal and related research. However, this broadening of interest has often been more about adding to the appraisal toolkit rather than using the knowledge so gained to help generate better ideas at the front-end of the policy cycle: more about better impact assessment than better needs identification. This capacity to absorb a growing range of outcomes of value to society and decision-makers has been important for the continuing relevance of appraisal and will remain critical for on-going relevance. The chapter argues that this, in turn, is dependent on successful development and implementation of need identification within integrated policy and planning frameworks, of which appraisal is a core part.

An illustration of the broader perspective that is increasingly common in transport is provided by the new Scottish National Transport Strategy (Transport Scotland, 2019). The strategy's vision is (Transport Scotland, 2019, p. 5):

"We will have a sustainable, inclusive, safe and accessible transport system, helping deliver a healthier, fairer and more prosperous Scotland for communities, businesses and visitors."

Elaborating on this vision, in terms of what are essentially societal sustainability goals, key intended outcomes are about

- reducing inequality
- taking climate action
- helping deliver inclusive economic growth and
- improving health and wellbeing.[b]

The goals of the Scottish Strategy are typical of those set out in integrated urban land use transport plans. This should be no surprise, given that the demand for transport is mainly a derived demand, valued for what it enables rather than for itself. As leading land use transport planning expert Professor Rob Cervero has reminded us, major transport projects have such large city-shaping potential that you need to first be clear about the kind of city

[b] A detailed implementation plan now needs to accompany that progressive new Strategy, to show how goal achievement will be accomplished.

(or region) you want and then plan your transport networks to help achieve that city (or region) (Cervero, 2014).

In terms of relative priorities, the Scottish Strategy suggests that all outcome areas are equally important, as is common of strategic plans. However, it emphasizes that action in the transport arena to reduce climate change and reduce inequality has climbed the priority ladder (Transport Scotland, 2019). A key role that good appraisal can play is to inform the decision-making process about the best ways to contribute to achievement of identified high-level goals and to illuminate associated trade-offs that will need to be confronted along the pathway to achievement.

Most of the focus of the literature has been on detailed examination of elements of an appraisal toolkit, such as measurement of the value of time (De Jong and Kouwenhoven, 2020) and wider economic benefits (Pogonyi, 2020), transport modeling (Van Nes and De Jong, 2020) and on different appraisal methodologies such as Cost-Benefit Analysis (Koopmans and Mouter, 2020) and Multi-Criteria Analysis (Dean, 2020). There are important research priorities for appraisal in all such areas and the literature has highlighted some relevant examples. In contrast, the research priorities that are expressed in the current chapter unapologetically reflect a personal bias toward achieving closer alignment, within integrated strategic policy and planning frameworks, between societal goal setting/need identification and supportive transport appraisal methodologies. This then requires a solid evidence-based understanding of connections between transport and such societal outcomes, which helps to shape appraisal methodologies. In taking this approach, the chapter also seeks to retain a focus on the value basis of appraisal techniques, a research area that is touched on in several chapters in this book but typically neglected, It is very important in terms of shaping the why and how of appraisal.

The chapter illustrates research priorities throughout the policy cycle that are important for appraisal methodology development. It is encouraging, in terms of content, to see similar strategic and institutional issues raised by authors such as Worsley and Mackie (2015) and Marsden and Docherty (2019). Urban land transport examples are often used in the chapter to illustrate points being explored, recognizing that this is where over half the world's people spend most of their time, and more so in developed economies.

Section 2 of the chapter explores some of the value judgments that underpin appraisal. Much of the discussion is about individual preferences and the role these should play in appraisal (recognizing that this involves personal value judgments from the author, which are hopefully exposed!). The section includes brief consideration of cost-benefit analysis (CBA) and multi-criteria appraisal techniques. Section 3 contrasts appraisal that is essentially impact assessment with appraisal that is grounded in need identification. Section 4 looks in more detail at appraisal research priorities for mobility-related social inclusion, wider economic benefits and greenhouse gas emissions, three key societal outcomes. Section 5 summarizes the chapter's conclusions.

2. Some issues of preferences

2.1 Judging if society is better off

In market economies, most resource allocation is the outcome of decisions made by large numbers of consumers and producers, based on their needs and preferences. Adam Smith, for example, talked about the efficiency of the "invisible hand" of the market (Smith, 1776). While markets might be efficient ways to allocate resources in large numbers of situations, there are well recognized situations where markets fail. Stopher and Stanley (2014) identify the following sources of market failure: public goods; merit goods; externalities; natural monopoly; limited extent of markets; lack of information; and distributional considerations. In the transport sector, all these issues are relevant, with externalities (e.g., agglomeration economies, congestion, air pollution, greenhouse gas emissions) and distributional considerations (e.g., mobility related social exclusion) perhaps the most common concerns.

Market failures such as these are the main reasons why governments become involved in transport policy, the (usually implicit) presumption being that some form of intervention to rectify identified market failure will deliver better outcomes for society than a failing market. This presumption raises a fundamental, question for research in transport appraisal: How can we know that some course of action will make society better off, when it will typically involve

- a range of potential consequences or impacts (benefits/costs)
- on different groups of people and nature (other species)
- over time?

All these areas involve value judgments and practical challenges in measurement. Nash et al. (1975a,b) argue that thought is required about what value judgments should underpin choice of an appraisal methodology. This is an area where there are ultimately no right answers, albeit that alternative value judgments can be proposed, debated and their underlying moral notions and associated appraisal implications discussed.

Arrow's famous Impossibility Theorem (Arrow, 1963) showed that there is no way to add together individual ranked preferences to identify one unique social preference ranking that meets five reasonable conditions that a democratic decision rule should possess. However, if measures of strength of preference can be used then it might be possible to conclude that situation A is better for society than situation B. Appraisal is essentially about seeking measures of strength of preference, to help identify whether some course of action is likely to make a "society" better off. As Nash et al. (1975a,b) point out, this requires consideration of matters such as:

- What it to be valued?
- How is it to be valued?
- How are trade-offs to be made between valued items?
- How should different (groups of) people be treated?

The most widely used method of transport project appraisal that seeks to handle such complexities is CBA, which is comprehensively discussed in Koopmans and Mouter (2020).[c] CBAs seek to quantify in money terms the expected benefits and costs of a course of action (e.g., policy, program or project) under consideration, using *willingness to pay* as its indicator for measurement of a benefit (or *willingness to accept* compensation for a cost). In broad terms, following the Hicks (1939)—Kaldor (1939) test, a course of action is generally regarded as worthwhile (an improvement for society as a whole) provided that its benefits, to whomsoever they accrue, exceed its costs. Nash et al. (1975a), p. 122) point out that this approach contains two implicit value judgments:

1. The decision criterion shall reflect individuals' preferences.
2. These preferences shall be weighted by market power.

In terms of the key societal outcomes that are increasingly being sought from transport, these value judgments raise many challenges, some of which are illustrated below.

2.1.1 Equity

As indicated by the second value judgment, the standard CBA decision rule includes both *efficiency* and *equity* elements. This cannot be avoided, since use of market prices implicitly accepts the existing distribution of income and wealth, from which those prices derive, as being of normative significance for societal resource allocation questions (Nash et al., 1975a,b).

[c] Cost effectiveness analysis is also common, where the focus is essentially on appraising alternative ways of achieving a given outcome. CBA involves multiple valued outcomes.

For analysts/stakeholders/decision-makers concerned about the market power implications of the existing distribution of income and wealth, benefit/cost weighting techniques have been developed to support different ways of aggregating monetary measures of benefits and costs across different income groups. This is important since, after all, it is the expected value (or utility) arising from a course of action that is ultimately being assessed, to form a view on whether or not society will be better off, rather than money per se. Money is simply a measuring rod with which to estimate expected value or utility gains and it is widely acknowledged that a dollar or euro is not of equal value to all. The UK Treasury Greenbook outlines the logic behind distributional weights based on expected diminishing marginal utility of income as income levels increase (HM Treasury, 2018a). Sources of disadvantage or social inequity other than income are also often important and need consideration in appraisal. Chapter 5 of this book (van Wee, 2021) includes extensive discussion on equity in transport appraisal.

Further developing appraisal techniques that reflect both efficiency and equity perspectives is important, extending progress that has been made with income-based equity weighting. A starting point is disaggregated assessment of benefits and costs by stakeholder groups, which is discussed further in Section 2.3. The issue of equity/disadvantage is further explored in Sections 2.3, 3 and 4.2 below.

2.1.2 The environment

An important point about the first value judgment (individual preferences) is that it is anthropocentric: it says that things only have value when they are valued by individuals (people), which brings in questions like the rights of species other than our own. Biodiversity loss and species extinction is happening at an increasing rate, compounded by climate change, notwithstanding the establishment of international conventions and national/state legislative and policy frameworks intended to protect the natural world (e.g., Biodiversity Protection legislation and associated lists of rare and threatened species). For example, the current extinction rate is up to 1000 times faster than the natural or background loss rate, and increasing, with threshold levels for survival little understood (Berger, 2004). As well as loss of species, the abundance of species is down by 60% since 1970 (World Economic Forum, 2019). Due to climate change alone, about one third of species will be lost by mid-century, if extinctions continue at the same pace (IPCC, 2007). To put these numbers in some context, very little is known about an estimated 8.7 million species (Sweetlove, 2011). The risk is that species are being lost before they are even really known!

How to handle this matter in CBA has been an area of discussion for decades. Pearce and Turner (1990) point out that environmental literature identifies three types of value relationships underlying the policy and ethics adopted in society:

- values expressed through individual preferences—what the individual preferences value judgment in CBA is concerned with
- public preference value which finds expression via social norms—e.g., which underlie matters such as public provision of health care and education (what economists sometimes call merit goods) and is also relevant to the discussion in Chapter 4 about collective willingness to pay (Mouter, 2021). Developing Public Private Partnerships is partly about aligning public preferences (through government) with the private preferences of potential commercial partners (Beck and Hensher, 2015)
- functional physical ecosystem value—where the intrinsic, non-preference related, value of ecosystems is recognized.

The distinction between the three is not necessarily clear-cut, since people may include intrinsic values within their individual preferences, sometimes known as existence values. To illustrate this in an Australian context, when asked, people oppose extinction (Garnett, 2012): 75% of surveyed people said they would become upset if a bird became extinct (only 7% disagreed) and 74% said there was a moral obligation to protect threatened birds (5% disagreed).

Environmental economists like Pearce and Turner (1990) use the idea of protecting the stock of natural capital as one way of approaching biodiversity loss, which focuses on the third type of values, through ecosystem protection. This, in effect, imposes an environmental system constraint against which CBA takes place. Implementation requires tightening of relevant international and national/state legislative and regulatory frameworks, and allied compliance and enforcement measures, to deliver more effective biodiversity conservation (protecting natural capital). Sectoral strategic planning processes then need to ensure that a multiplicity of individual project appraisals do not push the sector in the wrong direction. Sections 2.2 and 4.3 include further consideration of possible environmental constraints and appraisal.

2.1.3 Implications

Questions of preferences related to equity and the environment, as illustrated, are core challenges for appraisal. How do you ensure that your appraisal tool is not (unintentionally) reinforcing social disadvantage and/or compounding biodiversity loss? The author proposes that strategic solutions are required at the goal setting/need identification stages in the policy cycle to deal with such high-level concerns, rather than dealing with them as incidental outcomes of initiatives that have their origins in some other purpose.

2.2 Which preferences?

Saying that the appraisal tool to assess initiative desirability should generally reflect individual preferences poses many questions for analysts, decision-makers and those interested in the appraisal process and/or its findings (Nash et al., 1975a,b), some examples of which follow.

Whose preferences should count—in line with the individual preferences value judgment, prima facie the preferences of anyone whose wellbeing is affected by, or has an interest in, a project/initiative that is to be the subject of appraisal should be included within the scope of the appraisal, even if that effect is indirect. A difficult question is how appraisal should deal with preferences of future generations? Building on the argument in Section 2.1, the view of Pearce et al. (1989) is that future generations interests should be protected by ensuring that they have access to a stock of natural capital no less than the current stock and have the opportunity to make decisions about the use of that stock to enhance their welfare in their own time.

Are there any groups whose preferences should not be included, for moral reasons—which need to be spelt out? For example, children's preferences are rarely included within appraisals. Why not? The Scottish National Transport Strategy (Transport Scotland, 2019), for example, is notable for its emphasis on tackling child poverty, through appropriate transport initiatives. How should children be involved in need identification and assessment of alternatives? Stanley et al. (2020), for example, include a chapter on what makes a good city for children.

When should individual preferences not count—some people argue that a lack of knowledge about the potential benefits/costs of a course of action justifies ignoring the preferences of the "uninformed." In other words, leave it to the experts and/or those who understand these things! The present author's view is that it is better to provide people with good information and then let them express a preference. However, as noted in Section 2.1, there may be some issues, such as existential issues relating to biodiversity loss/climate change, that warrant governmental policy or legislation being used to set thresholds, which effectively form binding target conditions that constrain potential courses of action in sectors such as transport, over-riding the individual preferences that have contributed to the crisis. Identification of such matters should be argued by the government(s) in question, especially given the low and declining levels of trust in many governments (Edelman, 2020), and thresholds set in a context of stakeholder engagement.

Section 4.3 considers the issue of thresholds in relation of climate change and Section 4.2 includes discussion about mobility-related social exclusion, arguing that this is another outcome area where over-riding individual preferences is defensible.

2.3 What about the non-monetary bits—How should preferences be aggregated?

The holy grail for many analysts undertaking appraisal is the production of a single number as an indicator of the merit of a course of action, such as a benefit/cost ratio (or variant, such as Net Present Value). National level appraisals usually tend to focus at this level. Deriving such a measure requires aggregation across different types of impacts (including on nature), different stakeholders and time, where measurement of any impact might be in either money terms, physical impact units, intangible or some combination thereof. Any useful project appraisal methodology needs to be able to span these complexities.

Difficulties of valuing all initiative benefits and costs in monetary terms, so that (for example) they can be added up and traded-off, often leads analysts to use a tool such as some form of Multi-Criteria Analysis (MCA) (Department for Communities and Local Government, 2009), often using this to extend CBA. Dean (2020) provides a comprehensive treatment of this topic. This form of analysis extends back to work such as Hill's Goals Achievement Matrix (Hill, 1968). MCA essentially uses a rating mechanism of some form to aggregate monetary, physical and intangible impacts into a single measure of project or initiative merit.[d] A resulting challenge, for those who are believers in the individual preferences value judgment, is that rating across the various types of impact is often performed by an expert or group of experts, which is fundamentally at odds with this value judgment. However, groups of affected/interested stakeholders can be asked to rate the consequences of initiatives across monetary, physical and intangible effects, to

[d] A serious concern with much MCA is that weighting of the relative importance of individual impacts, by type, is often undertaken *before* detailed assessment of potential project impacts have been identified. Nash et al. (1975b) point out that, for resulting assessments to be meaningful in terms of relative option performance, this requires highly restrictive assumptions about the nature of preference trade-offs. Weighting of types of impacts should emerge during an appraisal process, rather than be an input to that process.

form a view of overall initiative value from their perspectives, as they can in an extended CBA. Chapters 3 (Shortall, 2021) and 4 (Mouter, 2021) include discussion of ways in which such engagement might occur.

If a single measure of initiative/project merit is being sought through an appraisal, some key issues for the present author are: (1) the extent to which the resulting appraisal reflects preferences of affected/interested stakeholders for particular impacts, expressed in a setting of knowledge and understanding, rather than reflecting opinions/values of 'experts'—where informed individual preferences is preferred by the author; (2) whether weighting of different valued outcome areas is evolved during the appraisal by affected/interested stakeholders, or imposed on it as an input (e.g., from experts)—development by stakeholders during the appraisal is preferred; and (3) how resulting stakeholder assessments are combined to form an overall view of initiative merit. The ultimate decision-maker(s) will, implicitly at least, eventually specify their relative weights for different valued outcome types and the importance to be attached to the preferences of particular stakeholders groups but that is not inconsistent with the appraisal process informing the decision-maker on how affected/interested stakeholders see such weighting.

Multi-Actor-Multi-Criteria-Analysis (MAMCA) as a means to elucidate the preferences of different groups of stakeholders across monetary, physical and intangible effects, assessed in terms of particular economic, environmental and social outcomes that a project is intended to achieve or might impact, shows promise (Keseru et al., 2016). It is consistent with the individual preferences value judgment and can be used to develop criteria weights for different stakeholder groups as part of an evolving appraisal process. It is easy to be critical of the way impact areas (or types of valued outcomes) are specified in such an approach but the same challenge confronts all appraisal tools that look to derive overall measures of initiative value across a range of outcome areas.

Given the complexities involved, it is arguable that the loss of important decision-making information in the production of a single indicator of initiative merit will lead to a loss of transparency and accountability of the appraisal process. It may also mean a loss of relevance of appraisal. For example, city decision-makers are commonly interested in specific desired project/initiative outcomes, such as what it might mean for job growth, productivity, road safety outcomes, the public transport mode share, air pollution levels, social inclusion (of particular groups, for example) or such like. The national level origin, and economic efficiency focus, of most appraisal methodology development is often blind to the color and movement that arises in the places where people live and carry out their daily lives. For appraisals to be of most value to decision-makers, the outputs from the appraisal need to (among other things) inform key concerns that confront those decision-makers, introduce them to other concerns and to new opportunities (Worsley and Mackie, 2015).

The significance of this point has been well demonstrated by several papers on the use of CBA in Swedish public transport. For example, Vigren and Ljungberg (2020) have found that most regional public transport authorities do not rely on CBA to inform key resource allocation decisions, since CBA outputs are not what matters to those decision-makers. Swedish national transport policy has economic efficiency as its primary goal and uses CBA to inform national project ranking but this does not carry through to regional PT service planning. These two authors, and Johansson et al. (2020), found that regional PT planners' two main objectives are increasing the market share of PT, relative to car, and providing a social service. In Stockholm, Johansson et al. (2020) suggest that making Stockholm Europe's most attractive metropolitan area is also a key purpose of PT. More broadly, Johansson et al. suggest that PT is increasingly being judged in terms of environmental issues, land use, and labour market effects. These are the purposes which integrated strategic land use transport plans are increasingly targeting.

Reporting appraisal outputs primarily in terms of benefit-cost ratios, net present values or other comparable measures is not information-rich and does not provide much enlightenment to the decision-maker concerned about multiple outcomes. The UK Treasury Greenbook (HM Treasury, 2018a) uses an Appraisal Summary Table to bring together disparate initiative impacts, with supporting tables providing further detail. Non-monetized benefits and costs are to be recorded, presented as part of the appraisal and, where possible, 'assessed in another way, providing an understanding of their magnitude' (HM Treasury, 2018a p. 74). Multi-Criteria Decision Analysis (MCDA), using swing weighting (essentially a way of identifying how significant an impact needs to be to change the ranking of alternatives) is noted as one way of approaching such challenges. This seems a transparent and accountable way of managing the complexity involved in appraisal.

3. Needs identification or impact assessment?

Too often project or initiative appraisal is separated from the process that led to project need identification in the first place. For example, someone higher up in an agency asks its evaluation team to undertake a CBA on a project whose inception has not involved that evaluation team. In this case, project appraisal is essentially a form of impact assessment. The preferred approach is for appraisal to be firmly rooted in a policy cycle process, with societal objectives and need identification as the starting point and option appraisal a stage in the process, informed by the starting points of goals and needs. Thus, for example, a focus on equity as a priority at the goal setting stage, as in the Scottish Transport Plan (Transport for Scotland 2020), should lead to efforts to define just what this means in terms of desired outcomes (not easy, as Section 4.2 below and Chapter 5 of this book show), use of suitable metrics to identify needs (i.e., existing and/or emerging inequities) in terms of the resulting interpretation of equity.

The increasing use of a 'business case' discipline, within which appraisal is located, should serve to strengthen a goals/needs focus. For example, the UK Treasury Business Case guidelines indicate a requirement for 5 reports (HM Treasury, 2018b): the strategic case; the economic case; the commercial case; the financial case; and the management case. The strategic case should provide solid evidence of need, to ground subsequent appraisal. Evidence of relevant societal values that are defining the key needs to be tackled should figure strongly in shaping in the Strategic Case and in subsequent detailed appraisal.

For urban/regional land transport appraisal, integrated strategic land use transport policy and planning processes should be the starting point, founded on societal values and reflected in vision and goal/outcome statements and associated need identification. This process needs to be driven at city/region level. Cities such as Vancouver (Canada) and Freiburg im Breisgau (Germany) are leaders here, with community consultation programs providing the glue for stable long-term integrated strategies.

Stanley et al. (2020) point out that strategic land use transport plans are becoming increasingly broad, since they impinge on so many outcomes that are valued by citizens. For example, shaping a city or region to benefit from emerging structural economic changes, requires supportive land use and transport initiatives. Similarly, affordable housing is increasingly seen as an integral part of land use transport planning, including planning of Transit Oriented Development (where gentrification is often a concern, implying a need to include affordable housing in the development). Transport appraisal must be alert to the need to take this increasingly broader perspective.

Goals and relative priorities can be expected to differ across layers of government to some extent. Vertical fiscal imbalance will inevitably mean that the goals/needs identified at urban (regional) level, and resulting transport priorities, will need some negotiation with higher government as part of a planning and funding cycle, if funding assistance is being sought from higher government. Local government will also need to be engaged if it exists at sub-city/sub-region level. Worsley and Mackie (2015), noting the relative weakness of the strategic focus in UK national appraisal, suggest that this funding context will lead to what they call a two-fence approach to project generation and appraisal, where projects seeking financial support from higher government will need to meet appraisal expectations at that level as well as locally. Initiatives such as City Deals and Sub-national Transport Bodies (STBs) may help to bridge the gaps in the UK between vertical layers. In an Australian setting, Stanley et al. (2020) have argued for federal government involvement in urban land use transport strategy formulation at the goal setting/need identification stage, where this is a state government responsibility, to smooth the processes of such inter-governmental negotiations, and for the major cities to have a city-level entity that speaks for the city, like the Mayor of London The next few years should demonstrate whether emerging institutional arrangements in the UK are improving policy line-of-sight and supporting more integrated pursuit of outcomes across governmental layers.

4. Some specific appraisal priorities

4.1 Purpose

The intent of this section is to illustrate some more specific research priorities for the development of an appraisal process that is more closely attuned to integrated thinking about how transport can further high-level societal goals.

4.2 Social inclusion

The specification of social goals in integrated strategic land use transport planning is not nearly as well developed as it is for economic or environmental goals. For example, Stanley et al. (2020) identify almost twenty different ways of elaborating social goals identified among various urban plans, suggesting that the goal area is still at a relatively undeveloped state. In similar vein, Chapter 5 of this book identifies multiple possible interpretations of transport equity (van Wee, 2021). Such lack of clarity often leads to transport plans focussing narrowly on some aspect of spatial disadvantage, such as relative accessibility to jobs between different parts of a city or region, with little appreciation of the knowledge base for improving social outcomes for the target clientele.

Following the innovative work of the UK Social Exclusion Unit (SEU 2003), the present author favors a focus on social inclusion as a useful way to shape thinking about the social goal in land use transport plans. Importantly, the author and colleagues have demonstrated a direct positive association between increased social inclusion and higher levels of wellbeing (and a number of other positive psychological outcomes), which the author believes is ultimately what matters for those at risk of mobility-related exclusion (Stanley et al., 2011a,b). Transport is an important input into accessing friends, goods and various activities, with poor transport opportunities often a source of social exclusion—defined as lacking the capacity to participate in mainstream society. In the SEU work, links were drawn between the exclusion of people who do not have access to a car, and their needs for education, employment, access to health and other services and to food shops, as well as to sporting, leisure and cultural activities. Findings from the SEU's transport study were organized into five groups of barriers that need to be addressed in order to improve transport-based accessibility to key services considered by the SEU authors to be central to social inclusion. Subsequent European and Australian work has broadened the research base to examine connections between transport, social capital, community connectedness and well-being (see, for example, Currie, 2011; Mollenkopf et al., 2005; Stanley et al., 2011a,b).

Most people in an industrialized society have the capabilities and access to resources to facilitate their inclusion. However, some groups remain at risk of social exclusion, such as those with limited education and on a low income, those in poor health and/or with a disability, people who are geographically isolated, some disadvantaged youth, some older people and single parent households. Social exclusion tends to become self-reinforcing when the only affordable living locations are those with the poorest infrastructure, services and job opportunities. Thus, social exclusion is in large part an issue of public policy and planning for the availability of the means for people to be included, through the provision of relevant infrastructure and services, including the transport/mobility required to access opportunities.

UK webtag tools provide useful ways to identify many groups likely to be at risk of mobility-related social exclusion and identify some of their accessibility challenges (Department for Transport, 2019). Such data could provide a basis for the political process to debate provision of reasonable accessibility levels to nominated activities for all, as an issue of social justice (or merit good[e]). This would involve spelling out the kinds of activities to which people ought to have access (e.g., schools, shops, medical care, recreation opportunities, nature, etc) and then ensuring that the means of providing such access are available, whether by provision of suitable mobility opportunities (e.g., local bus services) and/or by improving the location of those activities.

A concern with this approach, however, is that Stanley et al. (2011a,b; 2019) suggest that, when provided with improved mobility opportunities, those at risk of mobility-related social exclusion tend to first increase travel that builds their social capital (e.g., visiting friends, recreation). Stanley et al. (2011a, 2019) show that building social capital has a high value to these people and provides them with a pathway to access other resources (e.g., jobs). That research concluded that it is better, therefore, to not specify those activities to which excluded people should have access but to provide them with the means to access opportunities that improve their wellbeing *as they see it* (a non-paternalistic approach, as compared to identifying those types of opportunities that people should have access to). This implies less focus on accessibility to specific activities and more emphasis on wide availability of part-publicly funded public transport/active travel opportunities, again together with well-located services.

CBAs typically seek monetary measures of benefit/cost. If social inclusion is seen as a matter of social justice, then perhaps such monetary values are not required: politically determined (public preferences) service levels as of right, for example, might suffice. However, given the pressure on funding of local public transport services in many jurisdictions, and the role such services play in supporting mobility-related social inclusion, the case for supporting public transport (and active travel) to promote inclusion may benefit from evidence of monetization. There is only one body of research of which the author is aware that pursues such monetization in terms of reducing risks of mobility-related social exclusion.

Building on UK research (Burchardt et al., 2002), Stanley et al. (2011a, b) measured social exclusion risk using five dimensions (income, employment status, political activity, social support and participation) and then sought to identify associations between exclusion risk, personal wellbeing (self-assessed) and a number of explanatory variables, including trip making, personality,

[e] Stopher and Stanley (2014, p 24) describe a merit good as: '... one which society, through its political processes, has decided should be provided on the basis of considerations of need rather than ability and willingness to pay. The good is provided in the private market place, but there is a social decision to ensure some base level is available, irrespective of individual preferences or circumstances.'

psychological wellbeing, social capital, age and household income. The research estimated the value of an additional trip by a person at risk of mobility-related exclusion in both Melbourne and regional Victoria (Australia), finding it to be of high value and of increasing value as household income reduces. Stanley and Hensher (2011) conclude that the resulting social inclusion benefits are the largest single benefit from Melbourne's urban route bus services, being considerably larger than the cost of service provision. They suggest that a boarding rate of 10–11 per hour is enough for a Melbourne urban route bus service to break-even in terms of social inclusion benefits plus congestion cost savings. Stanley et al. (2019) undertake similar analyses for regional Victorian urban route bus services, finding that a boarding rate of 6–7 persons/h would suffice for the service to break-even on social inclusion benefits alone. Such an approach is thus one way to go about need identification from a social goal perspective (if the focus on social inclusion and wellbeing is accepted as a useful way to approach social equity/justice in transport).

A focus on enhancing mobility-related social inclusion underlines the importance of the goal setting and need identification stages in the policy cycle coming to grips with concepts such as transport equity, transport disadvantage and mobility-related risk of social exclusion, building awareness of key causalities (e.g., social capital, community connectedness, personality, trip making, household incomes, etc), and understanding how transport opportunities, and improvements therein, might affect such outcomes and the associated wellbeing of at-risk people. These should be research priorities for improved appraisal, as should exploring the social justice case for provision of core public and active travel opportunities being supported through the public purse, together with further studies on the monetary value of improved mobility for those at risk of mobility-related social exclusion.

The research on the social inclusion benefits of improved mobility opportunities summarized above is mainly about benefits to the at-risk person. This research needs to be extended to incorporate potential external benefits flowing from reduced social exclusion. Thus, for example, exclusion is expected to be associated with higher unemployment, increased crime and poorer health. Reducing exclusion should imply associated benefits flowing in such areas. The present author is not aware of studies that have systematically measured such flow-on benefits in a way that would permit their application in transport cost benefit analysis. However, research on the benefits of bus services undertaken for the UK's Urban Transport Group recognizes the probability of such flow-on benefits and elaborates specific examples of public agencies (e.g., health, education) whose activities and budgets can be expected to benefit from well targeted bus services (see, for example, Fuller, 2019; Abrantes et al., 2013). The investigation of such externalities should be a priority for improved transport appraisal. They are likely to strengthen the public policy case for government(s) supporting local public and active travel opportunities.

4.3 Wider economic benefits

An extensive body of research has emerged on transport and economic development, much of it with a focus on cities and productivity growth, parts looking at the transport influence therein. Research on agglomeration economies, arising from economic density has been central. The origins of such productivity gains have been understood for some time, summarized by Puga (2010) as sharing, matching and learning.

In urban settings, productivity increases (agglomeration externalities) of 3–8% from doubling city size (Rosenthal and Strange, 2004) and 4.5–6% from doubling employment density in a city (Ciccone, 2002; Ciccone and Hall, 1996) are widely cited. The meta-analysis by Melo et al. (2009) suggests a mean elasticity value of 3% across all its reviewed studies, with considerable variation between studies. Graham and Gibbons (2019), in a more recent study, find an unweighted elasticity value across 47 international studies of 4.6%. More recent research has tended to strengthen support for the lower end of the elasticity range, as issues such as firm selection and sorting have been recognized (see, for example, Behrens et al., 2014). Relative output increases in service industries, particularly knowledge-intensive industries, many of which tend to concentrate in CBDs and other urban hubs, are typically at the high end of the elasticity range. Melo et al. (2009) for example, report an elasticity of urban agglomeration for service industries of about 8%.

Evidence of the existence of agglomeration economies is then suggestive of opportunities for external benefits from transport initiatives that can enhance the effective economic density on which such agglomeration economies depend, such as by extending catchment scale, with resulting benefits being additional to direct transport user benefits (subject to measurement approach). Significant contributions to incorporating agglomeration benefits in transport appraisal have been made by authors such as (for example): Venables (2007), who developed a graphical demonstration of the opportunity for, and additionality of, agglomeration benefits; Graham (2007) for early estimates of relevant elasticities in the UK; Venables et al. (2014), who reviewed the subject area and highlighted strengths and gaps; Graham and Gibbons (2019), who have presented a forensic assessment of the identification and measurement of agglomeration and associated benefits; and Department for Transport (2018) for its guidelines on concepts and estimation.

Estimation of potential agglomeration benefits in transport appraisal requires three steps, as outlined by Graham and Gibbons (2019):

1. calculate a connectivity metric to represent agglomeration (or effective density)
2. estimate elasticities of productivity with respect to agglomeration
3. quantify the agglomeration impacts arising from transport schemes using the values derived from steps 1 and 2.

Graham and Gibbons outline research priorities through these three steps, to which the interested reader is referred. They include, for example, testing for the additionality of agglomeration benefits and using alternative specifications for economic mass and for the decay function in the economic density equation. However, in terms of the subject matter of this chapter, with its particular interest in land use transport integration, the present author highlights two key research questions requiring attention.

First, given the widespread interest in poly-centric urban and regional land use development patterns, a key question is how far the concept of agglomeration economies might extend to poly-centric cities or regions. This subject seems to have a relatively small research base. An important question, for example, is whether individual cities within a polycentric region might 'borrow' from each other's sizes to capture some scale benefits, sometimes described as network economies or network externalities (Boix and Trullén, 2007). Agglomeration economies are generally thought to decay with distance whereas network externalities are thought to be dependent on the strength of functional relationships and less distance dependent. Meijers and Burger (2010) examined this question in a US setting and found that, other things being equal, polycentricity seems to be beneficial for productivity, particularly in smaller metropolitan areas, but a collection of cities does not provide a substitute for the urbanization externalities of a single large city, even though the size of the population in both may be similar. A stronger knowledge base in this area would be extremely helpful for jurisdictions seeking to spread the benefits of productivity gains more broadly across a city or region through transport improvements (e.g., Melbourne and Sydney in Australia; Skåne in Sweden, extending across to Copenhagen).

The second priority area is estimation of mode-specific agglomeration effects. The scarcity of such estimates is a major concern in terms of quantifying agglomeration benefits, since it is usually major rail initiatives that are added to support a stronger mono-centric city. Graham and Gibbons (2019) suggest that mode-specific estimation is fraught with econometric difficulties and recommend against deriving such estimates. This does little to remove unease about using modally agnostic agglomeration benefit estimates, since transport initiatives are inherently mode specific. Further research on how to resolve the relevant estimation problems is encouraged, so that the results are a better reflection for decision-makers and planners of the expected outcomes of the actual transport interventions that are the subject of appraisal, rather than of something more generic.

In terms of appraisal methodology more broadly, there are many important research questions concerning the transport-economic development connection. These include the following, many of which are inter-related and go to the heart of the need for integrated land use transport thinking and planning, especially in an urban/regional setting.

- In what circumstances does transport appraisal need to go beyond traditional user benefit measures to reflect total economic benefits (and costs)?
- How does transport, and transport improvement, impact the location decisions of people and businesses (Hensher et al., 2021; Ho et al., 2020) and on what evidence base can we rely for answers to such questions? For example, will travel time savings from transport improvements get taken out as longer travel times, a common occurrence in sprawling Australian cities and, if so, how should the economic effects of the relevant transport changes that lead to such behavior changes be assessed, particularly given the external costs of sprawl? Agglomeration measurement is usually static, assuming away such relocation effects. In what circumstances might this produce misleading conclusions for appraisal?
- To what extent is the economic change (e.g., jobs, productivity, value added) flowing from transport improvement a net improvement (sometimes called additionality), as compared to redistribution between areas/people? It should be noted that both possible outcomes are relevant in appraisal if costs and benefits to *whomsoever they accrue* is used as the criterion for benefit/cost inclusion, as the present author believes is appropriate.

- How can transport improvements be used to help drive beneficial structural economic change? Melbourne and London are examples of good practice here, in different spatial settings (Stanley et al., 2020).
- What can land value tell us about the impact of transport on economic performance? To what extent would including land value gain in project benefits constitute double counting of user benefits? If used as benefit indicators, should land valued be amended to recognize differences between market and social discount rates?
- How can/should local and regional outcomes be identified and reconciled with national outcomes? This goes to the argument in Section 3 about retaining disaggregated appraisal results through the appraisal process. Spatial Computable General Equilibrium models are being used for this purpose in some settings. What is best practice here?

Answers to research questions such as these will help to ensure that transport appraisal can continue to provide well-founded evidence-based advice to the decision-making process and, in a broader sense, help shape more sustainable cities, regions and countries.

4.4 The environment: Greenhouse gas emissions

Section 2.2 raised the issue of whether governments should over-ride individual preferences in some situations, using biodiversity loss as an example. Climate change caused by increasing greenhouse gas emissions is a contributory factor in biodiversity loss but also of concern for other reasons (e.g., temperature rise and its impact on liveability, increasing incidence of extreme weather events/wildfire and their costs in terms of lives lost, property destroyed, economic activity, infrastructure condition, etc. Current emissions trajectories and policy settings are inconsistent with achievement of the Intergovernmental Panel on Climate Change target of temperatures rising no more than 1.5 degrees Celsius above pre-industrial levels. Transport sector emissions are a significant part of the problem. The Scottish National Transport Strategy, for example, sees this area as a high priority for action in Scotland, transport sector emissions accounting for 37% of Scottish GHG emissions in 2020 (Transport Scotland, 2019).

Transport project appraisals often claim an environmental benefit for a project because it is forecast that it will marginally reduce greenhouse gas emissions. Project appraisal guidelines reinforce this when they suggest a shadow price for carbon, such values converting marginal CO2 emissions reductions into a project benefit. For example, UK webtag advisory material indicates transport appraisal should use a central carbon price of £60.3/tCO2e in 2020, with a range from £30.6 (low) to £92.6 (high).[f] However, if a country is well off track for meeting its emissions targets, this apparent 'benefit' is a seriously misleading indicator of performance.

Because of the global consequences of climate change and the transport sector contribution thereto, national greenhouse gas emission targets should play a crucial role in transport policy and program/project development, starting at the goal setting/need identification stages, with national targets sourced from relevant IPCC agreements and national stakeholder collaborations relating thereto (which provide an opportunity for public preferences to be discussed). Some countries have chosen to establish a national commission, or similar body, to lead the process of national target setting and monitor/report on achievement, akin to the role played by central banks in monetary policy. Hopkinson and Sloman (2019) argue, in a UK context, that linked sectoral targets (carbon budgets) should be set for major emissions sectors, including the transport sector, since this is both a large emitting sector in most jurisdictions and regularly underperforming in terms of emissions reductions.

The current author agrees that global warming has reached the climate emergency stage and binding transport sector emission targets are now appropriate within a country, consistent with that country's overall carbon budget and targets (his national government would not agree!). Such an approach imposes a carbon constraint within the sector's goal setting process, which should condition subsequent policy, program and project development. Stanley et al. (2011c, 2019), have shown what a carbon budget for Australian road transport might look like and explored the behavioral and technological requirements likely to be needed for target achievement.

Sector planning and governance arrangements then need to ensure that initiatives/projects that are the subject of appraisal are consistent with the sector's carbon threshold, which becomes a constraint on the bundles of initiatives that are assembled. A major area for research is thus management of the way GHG emissions are handled through appraisal. The review of transport governance arrangements in the UK by Marsden and Docherty (2019) demonstrates the complexity of current arrangements, which suggests that establishing and implementing workable sectoral carbon budgets will provide the subject-matter for multiple PhDs.

[f] https://www.gov.uk/government/publications/tag-environmental-impacts-worksheets.

5. Conclusions

While recognizing that appraisal is not only used in a policy cycle, this paper has purposefully looked at appraisal as an integral part of a well-functioning policy cycle. Moving through the steps in the policy cycle, the author proposes that transparent and accountable transport appraisal should

- begin with, and be clear about, needs identification, grounded in vision/societal values and shaped through integrated strategic planning processes (strategic focus). Both at a spatial level (e.g., a city or region), and nationally, this requires open community/stakeholder engagement from the start, initially around vision/societal goals, key strategic issues (opportunities and challenges) and need identification. This stage is where any threshold issues/constraints should be flagged, such as setting GHG emission thresholds/carbon budgets or targets for minimum public transport service standards and active travel opportunities for social inclusion, since this will have a critical influence on how such matters are managed in appraisal. It is also where the research base on wider economic benefits should be used to help shape strategic land use development directions to enhance productivity performance. In the current author's view, the strategic goal setting/need identification stages are the most important, but least developed, in the policy cycle
- recognize that the strategic focus in transport will usually need to span multiple layers of government. Vertical integration should be approached with the intent to achieve policy line-of-sight on critical matters through the participating governmental layers, with the driving energy coming from the responsible layer of government. A sub-text here is the growing importance attached to localism, and the need for better access to own-source revenues at lower levels of government. Appraisals need to be relevant across the layers involved
- clearly identify value judgments implied in choice of appraisal technique and test appraisal results for sensitivity to value judgments (values focus)
- identify and assess alternative possible ways of meeting identified needs (option identification), again in an open and transparent way, with on-going stakeholder engagement. Rapid appraisal techniques, such as the UK Early Assessment Sifting Tool[g] and the MetroScan model

[g] https://assets.publishing.service.gov.uk/government/uploads/system/uploads/attachment_data/file/4475/east-guidance.pdf

(Hensher et al., 2021) can be helpful in sorting outliers from options that are worthy of more detailed examination

- measure impacts of alternative courses of action at the highest level possible, without stretching the credibility of the quantification involved, either across types of impact or stakeholders (technical assessment)
- engage different stakeholder groups in undertaking initial values/goals and needs identification, subsequent development of possible options and assessment of what such options might mean for them. This includes deriving preference indicators for impact scales and relevant importance weights across various valued outcome categories that reflect the values and preferences of different stakeholder groups. Establishing linkages between such analysis and potential funding models might then provide an opportunity for considering how initiative funding might be structured
- ensure open discussion about, and retain full information on, the range of impacts and trade-offs involved, and stakeholder views thereon, to support the decision-making process (transparency and accountability), rather than placing undue reliance on a single indicator of initiative performance.

Improving the performance of each of these steps should be research priorities for enhancing appraisal methodologies, with identifying key strategic threshold constraints (particularly social and environmental) and engaging affected stakeholders as personal priorities, including enabling/supporting them to engage fully throughout the process. Major initiatives, and programs of smaller initiatives, should emerge from this strategic integrated process, rather than being imposed on it one-by-one in response to apparent planning/transport problems (such as traffic congestion).

References

Abrantes, P., Fuller, S., Bray, J., 2013. The Case for the Urban Bus: The Economic and Social Value of Bus Services in The Metropolitan Areas. Public Transport Executive Group, Leeds. http://www.urbantransportgroup.org/resources/types/reports/case-urban-bus-economic-and-social-benefits-investing-urban-bus. Viewed 29 January 2020.

Arrow, K., 1963. Social Choice and Individual Values. John Wiley, New York.

Beck, M., Hensher, D., 2015. Finding long-term solutions to financing 21st century infrastructure—a think piece. Road Transp. Res. 24 (3), 57–61.

Behrens, K., Duranton, G., Robert-Nicoud, F., 2014. Productive cities: sorting, selection, and agglomeration. J. Polit. Econ. 122 (3), 507–553.

Berger, S., 2004. Species dying 1000 times faster. Age 18, 12.

Boix, R., Trullén, J., 2007. Knowledge, networks of cities and growth in regional urban systems. Pap. Reg. Sci. 86 (4), 551–574.

Burchardt, T., LeGrand, J., Piachaud, D, 2002. Degrees of exclusion: developing a dynamic, multidimensional measure. In: Hills, J., Le Grand, J., Piachaud, D. (Eds.), Understanding social exclusion. Oxford University Press, Oxford, pp. 30–43.

Cervero, R., 2014. Land use transport integration: implications for infrastructure in North American and Australian cities. In: Stanley, J., Roux, A. (Eds.), Infrastructure for 21st Century Australian Cities: Papers from the ADC Forum National Infrastructure and Cities Summit, March. ADC Forum, Melbourne.

Ciccone, A., 2002. Agglomeration effects in Europe. Eur. Econ. Rev. 46, 213–227.

Ciccone, A., Hall, R.E., 1996. Productivity and the density of economic activity. Am. Econ. Rev. 86, 54–70.

Currie, G. (Ed.), 2011. New Perspectives And Methods In Transport And Social Exclusion Research. Emerald Group Publishing Limited, Bingley.

De Jong, G., Kouwenhoven, M., 2020. Value of travel time and travel time reliability. Chapter 2. In: Mouter, N. (Ed.), Standard Appraisal Methods. Advances in Transport Policy and Planning. vol. 6. Elsevier, Amsterdam, pp. 43–74.

Dean, M., 2020. Multicriteria analysis. Chapter 6. In: Mouter, N. (Ed.), Standard Appraisal Methods. Advances in Transport Policy and Planning. vol. 6. Elsevier, Amsterdam, pp. 165–224.

Department for Communities and Local Government, 2009. Multi-Criteria Analysis: A Manual. Author, London.

Department for Transport, 2018. TAG Unit A2.1. Wider Economic Impacts Appraisal. Author, London. https://www.gov.uk/government/publications/tag-unit-a2-1-wider-economic-impacts. Viewed 19 February 2020.

Department for Transport, 2019. TAG Unit A4.1. Social impact appraisal. Author, London. https://www.gov.uk/government/publications/tag-unit-a4-1-social-impact-appraisal. Viewed 20 February 2020.

Edelman, 2020. Edelman Trust Barometer 2020. https://cdn2.hubspot.net/hubfs/440941/Trust%20Barometer%202020/2020%20Edelman%20Trust%20Barometer%20Global%20Report.pdf?utm_campaign=Global:%20Trust%20Barometer%202020&utm_source=Website. Viewed 26 February 2020.

Fuller, R., 2019. The Cross-Sector Benefits of Backing the Bus. Urban Transport Group, Leeds. hpttp://www.urbantransportgroup.org/resources/types/reports/cross-sector-benefits-backing-bus. Viewed 29 January 2020.

Garnett, S., 2012. Saving Australian endangered species—a policy gap and political opportunity. In: The Conversation. 26 November https://theconversation.com/saving-australian-endangered-species-a-policy-gap-and-political-opportunity-10914. Viewed 26 February 2020.

Graham, G., 2007. Agglomeration, productivity and transport investment. JTEP 41 (3), 320–343.

Hensher, D., Ho, C., Teye, C., Liu, W., Wei, E., 2021. Integrating business location choices into transport and land use planning tools. JTEP 54 (2), 121–150.

Graham, D.J., Gibbons, S., 2019. Quantifying wider economic impacts of agglomeration for transport appraisal: existing evidence and future directions. Econ. Transp. 19. https://doi.org/10.1016/j.ecotra.2019.100121.

Hicks, J., 1939. The foundations of welfare economics. Econ. J. 49 (196), 696–712.

Hill, M., 1968. A goals achievement matrix for evaluating alternative plans. J. Am. Inst. Plann. 34 (1), 19–29.

Ho, Q., Hensher, D., Ellison, R., 2020. Endogenous treatment of residential location choices in transport and land use models: introducing the MetroScan framework. J. Transp. Geogr. 64, 120–131.

Hopkinson, L., Sloman, L., 2019. Getting the Department of Transport on the Right Track. Friends of the Earth and Transport for Quality of Life. https://policy.friendsoftheearth.uk/print/pdf/node/108. Viewed 26 February 2020.

IPCC (Intergovernmental Panel on Climate Change), 2007. Summary for policymakers. In: Climate Change 2007: Impacts, Adaptation And Vulnerability. Cambridge University Press, Cambridge UK. Contribution of Working Group 11 to the Fourth Assessment Report of the Intergovernmental Panel on Climate Change.

Johansson, E., Hiselius, L., Koglin, T., Wretstrand, A., 2020. Evaluation of public transport: regional policies and planning practices in Sweden. Urban Plann. Transp. Res. 5 (1), 59–77.

Kaldor, N., 1939. Welfare comparisons of economics and interpersonal comparisons of utility. Econ. J. 49 (195), 549–555.

Keseru, I., Bulckaen, J., Macharis, C., De Kruijf, J., 2016. Sustainable consensus: the NISTO evaluation framework to appraise sustainability and stakeholder preferences for mobility projects. Transp. Res. Proc. 14, 906–915.

Koopmans, C.C., Mouter, N., 2020. Cost-benefit analysis. Chapter 1. In: Mouter, N. (Ed.), Standard Appraisal Methods. Advances in Transport Policy and Planning. vol. 6. Elsevier, Amsterdam, pp. 1–42.

Marsden, G., Docherty, I., 2019. Governance of UK Transport Infrastructures. Foresight, Government Office for Science, UK. https://assets.publishing.service.gov.uk/government/uploads/system/uploads/attachment_data/file/780871/governance.pdf. Viewed 20 February 2020.

Meijers, E.J., Burger, M.J., 2010. Spatial structure and productivity in US metropolitan areas. Environ. Plan. A 42, 1383–1402.

Melo, P.C., Graham, D., Noland, R.B., 2009. A meta-analysis of estimates of urban agglomeration economies. Reg. Sci. Urban Econ. 39 (3), 332–342.

Mollenkopf, H., Marcellini, F., Ruoppila, I., Szeman, Z., Tacken, M. (Eds.), 2005. Enhancing Mobility in Later Life: Personal Coping, Environmental Resources and Technical Support. The Out-of-Home Mobility of Older Adults in Urban and Rural Regions of Five European Countries. IOS Press, Amsterdam.

Mouter, N., 2021. Willingness to allocate public budget and Participatory value Evaluation. Chapter 4. In: Mouter, N. (Ed.), New Methods, Reflections and Application Domains in Transport Appraisal. Series: Advances in Transport Policy and Planning, vol. 7. Elsevier, Amsterdam, pp. 83–102.

Nash, C., Pearce, D., Stanley, J., 1975a. An evaluation of cost-benefit analysis criteria. Scott. J. Political Econ. 22 (2), 121–133.

Nash, C., Pearce, D., Stanley, J., 1975b. Criteria for evaluating project evaluation techniques. J. Am. Inst. Plann. 41 (2), 83–89.

Pearce, D., Turner, V., 1990. Economics of Natural Resources and the Environment. Harvester Wheatsheaf, Hemel Hempstead.

Pearce, D., Markandya, A., Barbier, E., 1989. Blueprint for a Green Economy. Earthscan, London.

Pogonyi, C.G., 2020. Wider economic benefits of transportation. Chapter 5. In: Mouter, N. (Ed.), Standard Appraisal Methods. Advances in Transport Policy and Planning. vol. 6. Elsevier, Amsterdam, pp. 129–164.

Puga, D., 2010. The magnitude and causes of agglomeration economies. J. Reg. Sci. 50 (1), 203–219.

Rosenthal, S.S., Strange, W.C., 2004. Evidence on the nature and sources of agglomeration economies. In: Henderson, J.V., Thisse, J.-F. (Eds.), Handbook of Regional Science and Urban Economics, Volume 4, Cities and Geography. Elsevier, Amsterdam, pp. 2119–2171.

Shortall, R., 2021. Deliberative appraisal methods. Chapter 3. In: Mouter, N. (Ed.), New Methods, Reflections and Application Domains in Transport Appraisal. Series: Advances in Transport Policy and Planning, vol. 7. Elsevier, Amsterdam, pp. 51–82.

Smith, A., 1776. An Inquiry into the Nature and Causes of the Wealth of Nations. W. Strahan and T. Cadell, London.

Stanley, J., Hensher, D., 2011. Economic modelling. In: Currie, G. (Ed.), New Perspectives and Methods in Transport and Social Exclusion Research. Emerald Group Publishing, United Kingdom, pp. 201–219.

Stanley, J., Hensher, D., Stanley, J., Vella-Brodrick, D., 2011a. Mobility, social exclusion and well-being: exploring the links. Transp. Res. A 45 (8), 789–801.

Stanley, J., Hensher, D., Stanley, J., Currie, G., Greene, W., Vella-Brodrick, D., 2011b. Social exclusion and the value of mobility. JTEP 45 (2), 197–222.

Stanley, J., Hensher, D., Loader, C., 2011c. Road transport and climate change: stepping off the greenhouse gas. Transp. Res. A 45 (10), 1020–1030.

Stanley, J., Stanley, J., Balbontin, C., Hensher, D., 2019. Social exclusion: the roles of mobility and bridging social capital in regional Australia. Transp. Res. A 125, 223–233.

Stanley, J., Stanley, J., Hansen, R., 2020. How Great Cities Happen: Integrating People, Land Use and Transport. Edward Elgar Publishing, Cheltenham.

Stopher, P., Stanley, J., 2014. Introduction to Transport Policy: A Public Policy View. Edward Elgar Publishing, Cheltenham.

Sweetlove, L., 2011. Number of species on earth tagged at 8.7 million. In: Nature. 23 August https://www.nature.com/news/2011/110823/full/news.2011.498.html. Viewed 26 February 2020.

Transport Scotland, 2019. National Transport Strategy: Protecting Our Climate and Improving Our Lives. Author, Glasgow. https://www.transport.gov.scot/media/47052/national-transport-strategy.pdf. Viewed 16 February 2020.

HM Treasury, 2018a. The Green Book: Central Government Guidance on Evaluation and Appraisal. Author, London. https://assets.publishing.service.gov.uk/government/uploads/system/uploads/attachment_data/file/685903/The_Green_Book.pdf. Viewed 5 February 2020.

HM Treasury, 2018b. Guide to Developing the Program Business Case. Better Business Cases: For Better Outcomes. Author, London. https://assets.publishing.service.gov.uk/government/uploads/system/uploads/attachment_data/file/749085/Programme_Business_Case_2018.pdf. Viewed 5 February 2020.

Van Nes, R., De Jong, G., 2020. Transport models. Chapter 4. In: Mouter, N. (Ed.), Standard Appraisal Methods. Advances in Transport Policy and Planning. vol. 6. Elsevier, Amsterdam, pp. 101–128.

van Wee, B., 2021. Evaluating transport equity. Chapter 5. In: Mouter, N. (Ed.), New Methods, Reflections and Application Domains in Transport Appraisal. Advances in Transport Policy and Planning, vol. 7. Elsevier, Amsterdam, pp. 103–126.

Venables, A., 2007. Evaluating urban transport improvements: cost-benefit analysis in the presence of agglomeration and income taxation. JTEP 41 (2), 173–188.

Venables, A., Laird, J., Overman, H., 2014. Transport Investment and Economic Performance: Implications for Project Appraisal. Department for Transport, London.

Vigren, A., Ljungberg, A., 2020. Public transport authorities use of cost-benefit analysis in practice. In: CTS Working Paper 2020:8. Centre for Transport Studies, Stockholm.

World Economic Forum, 2019. The global risks report 2019, fourteenth ed. World Economic Forum, Davos.

Worsley, T., Mackie, P., 2015. Transport Policy, Appraisal and Decision-Making. RAC Foundation, London.

Further reading

Meijers, E.J., Burger, M.J., Hoogerbrugge, M.M., 2016. Borrowing size in networks of cities: city size, network connectivity and metropolitan functions in Europe. Pap. Reg. Sci. 95 (1), 181–198.

Stanley, J., Ellison, R., Loader, C., Hensher, D., 2018. Reducing Australian motor vehicle greenhouse gas emissions. Transp. Res. A 109, 76–88.

FSC
www.fsc.org
MIX
Papier | Fördert gute Waldnutzung
FSC® C083411

Kolibri 360 GmbH
Ferdinand-Jühlke-Straße 7
99095 Erfurt, Deutschland
produktsicherheit@kolibri360.de